STEVE SILVA

JUDICIAL WEB

Steve Silva

JUDICIAL WEB

*Copyright © 2025 by Steve Silva "All rights reserved,"
including the right to reproduce this book, or any
portions thereof, in any format whatsoever.*

*Book cover artwork, design, cover concept,
layout, and text, by Steve Silva.
Third printing 06/20/25*

STEVE SILVA

"TRUTH IS LIKE THE SUN. YOU CAN SHUT IT OUT
FOR A TIME, BUT IT AIN'T GOIN' AWAY."
-Elvis Aaron Presley

"NO LIE CAN LIVE FOREVER."
-Dr. Martin Luther King Jr.

"TRUTH CRUSHED TO EARTH SHALL RISE AGAIN."
-William Cullen Bryant

"THERE AIN'T NO LAWS, THERE AIN'T NO JUSTICE,
THERE'S JUST US, AND WE AIN'T THEM."

-Author Unknown

JUDICIAL WEB

A fictionalized memoir inspired, in part, by true events of government corruption, treachery, cover-up, and intrigue!

Steve Silva © 2025 (All Rights Reserved)

STEVE SILVA

BOOK DESCRIPTION

"*JUDICIAL WEB*" is a Fictionalized Memoir inspired, in part, by true events of government corruption, treachery, betrayal, cover-up, and intrigue. It's taken me 28-plus years to complete the following personal memoir of my criminal plight. How, against all odds, I rose like the Phoenix, and was able to reverse the injustice I was wrongfully served, and how, after spending nearly eight painstaking years in federal prison, while serving a 35-year sentence, without parole, I won my freedom having successfully overturned my drug kingpin felony conviction. Without sounding biased, my story is a captivating read, a page turner, jam-packed with adventure, humor, and lots of courtroom drama. I hope you enjoy the read.

JUDICIAL WEB

PREFACE

FINALLY, I can share my story with anyone wishing to read it. It's taken me 28 years to piece it all together and share these events, which took place during the darkest period of my life. I needed to share this story to rid myself of the pain and guilt I've locked inside all these years, and reveal the harsh realities of our criminal justice system, which continues to run rampant over our precious constitutional liberties. My story depicts wrongdoings, cover-up, negligence, betrayal, gross government misconduct, and numerous miscarriages of justice perpetrated against me by our '*JUST US*' judicial system, featuring government officials looking only to feed their alter egos in order to secure another illicit conviction while abusing their powerful government positions by obstructing justice, suborning perjury, and so much more.

As the author of this fictionalized memoir, I've chosen to remain anonymous for well-founded reasons. Upon reading my story, I hope you'll come away with a completely different outlook about how easy it is, in one fell swoop, for one to lose everything he/she has ever worked for in their life and how unjust our judicial system remains to this very day. As for me, I wish to remain anonymous. I prefer not to ruffle any feathers or rock any boats. Why open a Pandora's Box when all I wish to accomplish is share my story and protect my family from any and all future unwanted intrusions. I'd much prefer to live in good health, peace, harmony, and happiness for the remaining years of my life. I hope you enjoy the read.

STEVE SILVA

TABLE OF CONTENTS

DEDICATION 1
SPECIAL ACKNOWLEDGMENT 2
AUTHOR'S NOTE 3
PROLOGUE 6
FORWARD 8
MAIN CHARACTERS 13
MY SENTENCING HEARING 19
SOME PERSONAL BACKGROUND HISTORY 34
IT'S PARTY TIME 40
THINGS BEGIN TO GO SOUR 45
THE MADNESS CONTINUES 57
IT'S PAYBACK TIME 72
PRE-ARREST EVENTS 88
DAY OF ARREST 91
POST ARREST EVENTS 97
MIAMI BAIL HEARING 106
LIFE AT THE BALTIMORE CITY JAIL 126
LIFE CONTINUES AT THE CITY JAIL 139
MEETING SUGAR BEAR AND FOOTBALL 147
SECOND BAIL REVIEW HEARING 153
ARRAIGNMENT DAY 172
LIFE AT THE VOA 190

CI#4	198
WHAT A DIFFERENCE A DAY MAKES	205
LIFE AT THE VOA CONTINUES	220
MY BIG SURPRISE VISIT	234
A STROKE OF GOOD LUCK	249
THE MARYLAND TRIAL	266
SENTENCING DAY	276
LIFE AT THE FMC	283
POST CONVICTION RELIEF ERA	291
DOING TIME GOING OUT OF MY MIND	299
DIESEL THERAPY	317
FCI FORT DIX	326
MY EVIDENTIARY HEARING	336
BACK TO THE FOURTH CIRCUIT	353
POST RELEASE YEARS	368
EPILOGUE	383
AFTERWORD	386
EXHIBIT LIST	395
EXHIBITS 1-9	396
GLOSSARY TERMS & ACRONYMS	405

DEDICATION

I dedicate this book to my family, friends, and legal advisors who stood by me throughout my arduous ordeal and subsequent fight for my freedom.

From the bottom of my heart, with deepest appreciation and gratitude for all your support, efforts, and prayers, in my quest for justice to prevail, I sincerely thank all of you!

Most of all, I especially dedicate this book in fond memory of my younger brother, Gary, who lost his battle to survive from a rare blood disorder he fought to stave off, which eventually, on May 29, 2008, took his life at the young age of fifty-eight.

SPECIAL ACKNOWLEDGMENT

This Special Acknowledgment is made in memory of my beloved parents, Michael and Muriel, the two most wonderful parents in the whole world.

How very lucky I truly was to have been blessed with such loving, caring, and most of all, understanding parents throughout the years. Especially, for their loyal support and confidence, that in the end things would one day turn out right for me.

Perhaps, even more significantly for their unyielding efforts in seeing justice prevail in the uphill battle of my life.

As I write this Special Acknowledgment, I can't help thinking about what I would have done without my mom and dad (may they both rest in eternal peace), always at my side, throughout all my struggles and ultimate achievements in gaining my freedom.

With the greatest of love, affection, and deepest admiration, I also dedicate this book to both of you.

AUTHOR'S NOTE

Perhaps the most thrilling moment for any author is to learn that through his writing, he can make a small difference. However, once in a blue moon, there comes a time when an opportunity arises, enabling him to make a big difference.

I'd like to share with you a remarkable story involving a travesty of justice, one that caused me great suffering, and how I was able to change the course of events surrounding the dark cloud that had otherwise overshadowed my life and that of my family for many years.

This story will take you on a journey from the Medellín Drug Cartel's cocaine processing laboratories, in the deepest jungles of South America, to the Oval Office's doorsteps, between 1985-1995.

It's a story where obstruction of justice within the United States Department of Justice and unethical conduct is routinely practiced in many federal courtrooms across the country. Where government informants, agents, prosecutors, and other law enforcement officials were turning the power of the United States Government against the American people and immigrants alike, who were being falsely accused, denied justice, and made to serve draconian sentences without the benefit of parole.

Our courtrooms were being turned into battlegrounds, where anything and everything was permissible, as long as the end result netted another conviction, even if it meant trampling over one's precious Bill of Rights in order to do so.

Testimonies were being solicited, handsomely paid for with taxpayers' money, and rewarded in secret subversive fashion. One person's uncorroborated testimony, without a solid shred of substantial evidence, perhaps from an event that occurred many years earlier, could and more often than not, wind up putting an accused behind bars for many years, sometimes for even life without the benefit of parole.

Government agencies, special agents, and informants (also referred to as rats or snitches) were profiteering from confiscated assets, money, and real estate, valued in the hundreds of millions of dollars. An inside confidential informant, working for a percentage of confiscated goods and assets, could convict almost anyone he or she was commissioned to target.

The plea-bargaining process had run afoul. It was constantly being abused to scare, sometimes even torment, innocent victims into releasing some, if not all, of their worldly possessions so that their wife and other family members wouldn't be threatened with prosecution and a draconian prison sentence upon one's eventual conviction.

This country's federal conspiracy laws are devastating, and enough to scare even the best of mankind. Read them! Title 18 U.S.C., Sections 371, 372, and 373. Also, Title 21 U.S.C., Section 846. To this very day, the chances of winning an acquittal in any U.S. Federal Courtroom still remain at less than five percent.

Many government agents and federal prosecutors believe they are on some divine and righteous mission while stripping an individual's basic inalienable rights, which have been with us as a Nation for (248) years, as of this writing.

The American public is alarmingly unaware that their basic Constitutional rights have been, and in many respects continue to be, slowly stripped and cast aside one by one.

Drug hysteria, the ongoing 'War on Drugs,' and the entire drug issue have turned our country toward a police state.

We've now grown accustomed to allowing almost anyone with a badge to exert their power and trample over its citizens' Constitutional Rights to life, liberty, and the pursuit of happiness.

Case in point: *UNITED STATES OF AMERICA VS. STEVE SILVA, ET AL.,* Baltimore, MD, in and for the United States Courthouse for the District of Maryland, 1986.

The actual names, dates, and places of the individuals mentioned in this book have been, at my discretion, changed to fully protect their identities and to otherwise avoid bringing up past legal issues, which could possibly cause them embarrassment, or call any undue attention to them, their families, and their ongoing endeavors since the conclusion of my criminal and civil matters.

Additionally, I fully respect their privacy and choose not to mention them here by their true and/or individual identity. I've taken extraordinary precautions in telling my story so as not to create any unnecessary potential wrath, or perhaps legal jeopardy, while still maintaining the integrity of my story in all aspects as told, with both *fiction* and *non-fiction* events.

PROLOGUE

JUDICIAL, as defined in Webster's New World Dictionary published edition, 2018, is defined as: *"Pertaining to courts of law, or to judges. Sanctioned or enforced by a court of competent jurisdiction. Proper to the character of a judge."*

(and)

WEB, is defined as: *"A fabric formed by weaving. A thin, silken material spun by spiders and some other insects. Any complicated pattern or network. A carefully woven trap. To ensnarl or entrap."*

(together)

The words *JUDICIAL WEB*, this author suggests, would logically mean: *"A network of carefully woven traps, whereby one is thwarted and unable to effectuate justice."*

Imagine being an insect, say an ordinary household fly. Then one day, without any warning, you suddenly find yourself helplessly ensnarled in a spider's web. A web so finely woven, so amazingly invisible it caught and consumed you in mid-air, leaving you motionless, powerless, and without any means of self-defense.

On Tuesday, April 22, 1986, at approximately 8:15 a.m., while in the prime of my life, I found myself paralyzed in what I've now coined, a... *JUDICIAL WEB*.

Any American citizen or permanent resident who believes they were born with certain inalienable rights, such as life, liberty, and the pursuit of happiness is gravely mistaken.

Upon reading my memoir, you'll come away with a totally different perspective towards life.

The events you are about to read are real, and while at times may tend to seem overly exaggerated, they are sure to shock even the most curious and unconvincing minds.

It's now been thirty-eight plus years since that most horrific day of my life. Since then, I've had plenty of time to reflect on the events of that eventful day, which nearly put me behind bars for the rest of my adult life.

I've decided to write this book after carefully analyzing all the pain, suffering, agony, horror, and injustice I, along with my family, have endured during the years of my incarceration and the grave injustice I was wrongfully served by our judicial system, so that many of you in the so-called free world will come to learn, understand, and truly respect the harsh and hidden limits of your freedom. While I've been most fortunate to have acquired financial wealth, personal growth, knowledge, wisdom, and self-satisfaction during the years following my incarceration, nevertheless, I'm still searching for *peace of mind,* something I may never enjoy once again in my life.

JUDICIAL WEB

FORWARD

This is an emotional and extraordinary series of events, which occurred in early Spring, 1986. It's about an individual approaching the prime of his life, and while climbing the ladder of success, he finds himself caught up in a network of lust, greed, money, and power, all of which ultimately consumes him and leads to the near total destruction of his life.

On Tuesday, April 22, 1986, at approximately 8:15 a.m., the United States Government exercised its police power and proceeded to take away what had otherwise taken me a lifetime to legally acquire.

The early morning dawn gave rise to what would become a beautiful, bright, and sunny day. As it did, an army of SWAT team personnel, Metro Dade County Police Department officers, Drug Enforcement Agents, and a host of specially invited media personnel from the major TV networks, had all gathered for a final briefing just prior to storming my home with a court-ordered search warrant. A warrant that should never have been granted, as I learned years later while fighting to uncover the injustice and the many wrongdoings surrounding my criminal ordeal.

As everyone proceeded to get positioned for the big circus showdown and storm my home, tearing it apart, finding not a single shred of evidence, none whatsoever, no illegal weapons, no drugs, or money, nothing of any incriminating nature or consequence, I was embarrassed like never before in my life, especially by the unprofessional manner in which my arrest was conducted.

Let me digress for a moment and share with you just how horrific it was. It was probably around 8:00 a.m., just after my daughter had left to catch the school bus down the street from where we lived, a routine she would do every weekday morning during the school year. Aside from some parked cars in the street, which were undercover vehicles, unnoticeable to my daughter at the time, everything else looked like a pretty normal day.

The sun was steadily rising, and everything seemed peaceful. The neighbors surrounding my townhouse property were hustling out of their homes and going off to work while I was also showering and preparing to get on with my day.

I heard, what appeared to be some knocking noises, and as moments passed, they seemed to be getting louder and louder, and the tiled shower floor below my feet began to vibrate violently. At first, I thought nothing of it, as we often had construction going on all around our complex, so I really paid no attention to any of it until I began hearing loud noises and rumbling sounds. The chaos seemed very much out of the ordinary, and after washing the soap from my eyes, my mind began to wonder if it could have been an earthquake. Rationally, that didn't seem possible because Florida, to the best of my knowledge, had never experienced an earthquake before. And just then, as I began to open my eyes, the shower door swung open, and a pair of female hands grabbed me from the shower and began yelling uncontrollably to get down on the ground, ordering me to put my hands behind my back and began to handcuff me while reading me my Miranda Rights: "You have the right to remain silent. You have the right to consult an attorney. Anything you say may be held against you," and blah, blah, blah! My mind went blank.

I thought I was in some sort of a bad dream, movie, or perhaps time warp set. I refused to believe this was happening. I was stark naked and laying on my bathroom floor; my hands were cuffed, and a female swat team officer had her booted foot smashing into my face, pressing it to the floor, with what appeared to be, as best as I could view, an AK-47 pointed at my head. Then came a swoon of DEA and metro police officers, who began yelling at me, "Where're the drugs, Silva? Where's the money? Where is it, Silva? We know you have a stash here, and we want it NOW," came the words of the head DEA case agent assigned to my criminal case. The government exercised its search and seizure arrest warrants against me, and shortly thereafter six others were also indicted on that eventful day. A day I will never forget for the rest of my life!

The room was spinning as the minutes ticked on, my mind was rushing for clarity, and I was trying desperately to gain my composure. It became clear to me that this must have had something to do with Marshall, Doc, Bennie, and who knows who else. I'd predicted several years earlier that something involving them would one day catch up with all of us, including me. However, mind you, I had severed my relationships with these people for over a year by now and hadn't seen or heard from any of them in a very long time. All of this was very confusing to me. I thought it must have been an act of mistaken identity, but that was quickly laid to rest when one of the arresting officials, who would later go on to prosecute me, bent down and whispered in my ear, if I didn't give him what he wanted I wouldn't be seeing my children and my family for a long time, and I'd be spending a considerable amount of years behind bars. That's when it became clear to me that this was no joke or a mistaken identity issue.

After being dressed by several of the agents who were all laughing at their catch of the day, while seeing me naked and snickering at each other, I felt so ashamed while all kinds of thoughts were running rampant through my mind. I was a total wreck!

I was escorted outside, only to see a slew of my neighbors in total shock. The TV cameras were in my face. It was a media circus with me making headline news that evening. I could barely shout to my next-door neighbor, who was on his way to work, to make sure to let my daughter know what happened and for her to call my sister for updates.

I feared now, more than anything else, how my daughter was going to react to all this drama at the young and innocent age of 17, with no mother in her life, only me as her support team, having raised her as a single parent since she was nine years old, and the tears began running uncontrollably down my face.

The front door to our home was smashed in; the house was ransacked and left in shambles. Both my daughter's and my personal property were violated and, in many instances, destroyed by overzealous government agents. When they didn't find a shred of incriminating evidence, they became angry and very destructive. The entire scene was so devastating and horrific that I just wanted to wake up from the dream and get on with my day. However, that wasn't going to be the case, as the rest of the day's events got even uglier as the day wore on.

In one fell swoop, I was taken away from my family, loved ones, and closest friends. All my assets and worldly possessions were seized. Everything I'd ever worked for in my life was gone.

I soon learned that the worst tragedy of all was yet to come. One of the government's witnesses, who later turned out to be its '*star witness*,' *Jon Gerritt, a/k/a Doc* (by his closest friends), was granted full immunity from prosecution. Doc was a close friend of mine throughout the years.

It was Doc's crushing testimony, replete with perjury, which caused me to be convicted and sent to federal prison for thirty-five years without the benefit of parole. Mind you, this was perjured testimony, which was later proven the federal prosecutors 'knew' or 'should' have known all about at the time their 'star witness' took the witness stand during my criminal proceedings.

JUDICIAL WEB

For the next nearly eight years of my life, I found myself ensnarled in a network of carefully woven traps, lies, and deceit, riddled with gross government misconduct, corruption, treachery, cover up, and intrigue. It was like being totally consumed in a web, with no way out, a *JUDICIAL WEB*.

MAIN CHARACTERS

Steve Silva: After having been stripped of all his assets and worldly possessions, Silva was convicted and subsequently sentenced to 35 years, without parole, in federal prison. During the nearly eight years of incarceration, Silva studied law and became a certified paralegal while serving his time at multiple federal prisons and penitentiaries across the USA. While conducting research into his own criminal case, which took him nearly seven years to uncover, Silva eventually learned his entire prosecution team, coupled with the government's 'star witness' in his criminal investigation and eventual prosecution, conspired to obstruct justice, the root of which stemmed from all of them 'knowingly' allowing perjury to be committed during Silva's criminal proceedings.

Gary Silva: Brother of Steve Silva was also convicted and sentenced to serve a 15-year sentence in federal custody. Gary was initially fully exonerated of any criminal conduct in an offshoot case held in Virginia, but the double jeopardy clause of the U.S. Constitution was not upheld when he was again tried in Maryland for the same exact crimes, for which he was acquitted of in Virginia.

Jon Gerritt: A former South Florida police officer, and the government's '*star witness*' in Silva's criminal investigation and prosecution. Gerritt was granted full immunity for all his illegal acts and drug dealing activities until it was uncovered several years later by the same government prosecution team that prosecuted Steve Silva, Gary Silva, and other members named in his criminal indictment, that Gerritt had committed substantial perjury during many phases of his testimony, especially during both his initial proffer sessions with government personnel, also during his lengthy grand jury testimony, and most significantly, during his trial testimony in Steve Silva's fourteen-week criminal trial.

Raul Rafael: A Colombian National with direct ties to the Medellín Drug Cartel and its *'founding fathers,'* Pablo Escobar, Carlos Leder, and Jose Rodriquez Gacha. All totaled, it was reported that Rafael successfully imported 6,000 kilos of the cartel's cocaine for distribution into the United States. Rafael was eventually caught red-handed, with nearly a ton of cocaine, at Orlando's International Airport in the late summer of 1986. He quickly turned into a witting government witness shortly thereafter since he was facing a life sentence, without parole, at the time of his arrest. Word on the street was that through Rafael's extensive cooperation with DEA personnel at the highest levels, Gacha, a/k/a El Mexican, along with his young son, were both killed during a drug raid that Colombian Drug Task Force agents conducted at Gacha's clandestine ranch in late December of 1986. Rafael, for all his cooperation and efforts, coupled with information leading to the whereabouts of one of the highest profile drug cartel members on the planet, was set free and returned to his homeland in Colombia. However, fate has a way of dealing with people, and Rafael was no exception. It was later learned, during my criminal trial, that Raul Rafael had died of a brain aneurysm soon after he returned home.

Sandy Jones: Head DEA Agent in Silva's criminal investigation. According to the public records, Agent Jones was responsible for successfully prosecuting over 52 convictions stemming from Silva's criminal case. Special Agent Jones was a 20-year veteran of the DEA, and one of the Agency's top special drug task force agents at the time of Silva's criminal case. Special Agent Jones was also personally responsible for the arrests of Silva's brother and others indicted in Silva's criminal investigation and subsequent prosecution. Agent Jones also became the key player in the travesty of justice perpetrated against Steve Silva and others, as it was later uncovered several years after Silva's prosecution. Court records showed that Agent Jones '*knew*' or '*should*' have known all along his '*star witness,*' Jon Gerritt, had unclean hands, as they say in legal circles, and committed perjury at the time of his testimony during Silva's criminal proceedings. Having done so, Agent Jones suborned perjury and obstructed justice.

Greg Wells: Was the lead prosecutor in Silva's criminal proceedings. He, along with Assistant U.S. Attorney Andy Nolan, prosecuted the Silva brothers and all the others indicted in Silva's criminal case back in 1986-87. Like Nolan, court records later proved, beyond a reasonable doubt, that both U.S. Attorneys also '*knew*' or '*should*' have known that their '*star witness,*' Jon Gerritt, was committing perjury when he took the witness stand in Silva's criminal trial, yet he, too, neglected to do anything to expose this to either the trial court or Silva's defense counsel, as required by federal law. Mr. Wells, likewise, was guilty of suborning perjury and obstruction of justice.

Andy Nolan: Was the government's lead prosecutor in Jon Gerritt's prosecution and subsequent trial, along with fifty-two other convictions stemming from Silva's criminal investigation and trial. Nolan was also the co-counsel for the government's prosecution team during Silva's criminal proceedings and trial. Mr. Nolan was a Delaware State prosecutor prior to becoming an Assistant U.S. Attorney (AUSA) for the District of Maryland. AUSA Nolan sensed that the Silva criminal case would be a rise to his personal notoriety, promotion, and aspirations of one-day sitting on the federal bench. Also, as unethical as it was, AUSA Nolan and his co-counsel partner, AUSA Wells, actively participated in Silva's actual apprehension, arrest, and execution of search and seizure warrants on the eventful day of Silva's arrest. He also '*knew*' or '*should*' have known that Gerritt was committing perjury during his testimony before the grand jury, as well as other proffer sessions, which eventually earned Gerritt complete immunity from prosecution. AUSA Nolan was equally guilty of suborning perjury and obstruction of justice due to his willful failure to report the same to his superiors and take proper action to undo the grave injustice perpetrated against Steve Silva.

Judge Moore: A sitting Senior Judge, for the District of Maryland. One of the oldest federal judges back in the 1980's. As it turned out, Judge Moore became the presiding judge in Silva's criminal proceedings, as well as several other offshoot trials, stemming from Silva's criminal investigation. As such, Judge Moore also turned a blind eye to Gerritt's perjury issues. He too denied Silva, at every turn, his '*quest for justice.*' Judge Moore was in his early 80's when he presided over Silva's criminal trial. After Silva's trial, Judge Moore was politely asked to resign from the bench, but he refused to do so. Rumors spread that he was getting on in years, and he was beginning to make irrational decisions from the bench that the Fourth Circuit Court of Appeals later remanded in several high-profile cases. Silva's criminal case became one of those high-profile cases in which Judge Moore, now in his early 90s, was reprimanded for committing erroneous rulings during Silva's post-conviction and controversial resentencing phases. Judge Moore, shortly thereafter, stepped down from the federal bench and died peacefully not long after doing so.

David Irving: Silva's defense counsel, initially started out on the other side of the defense table. He chose the legal career path of being a federal prosecutor until he woke up one day, and smelled the roses, realizing that he could earn much more money defending alleged criminals rather than prosecuting them. The only problem was that David was still a prosecutor at heart, which proved detrimental to his ability to defend Silva properly. To make matters even worse, Silva later learned that his criminal matter was the first case David took on as a defense attorney against the same attorneys he worked alongside while he was an Assistant U.S. Attorney just a few months earlier. There was no way they would allow David to beat them in federal court under any circumstances. This was going to be payback time for switching sides and no longer prosecuting the bad guys but rather now defending them. At least, that was the opinion Silva formulated after he eventually learned more about David's legal mind and background, but it was too late to do anything about it. David did the best he could under the circumstances and with what he had to deal with, which was a government prosecution team who did everything they could to thwart justice, and see that Silva was found guilty, at all costs no matter what, and sent away to federal prison for the rest of his adult life. The odds were heavily stacked against Silva. The prosecution team, some of whom had worked directly under Mr. Irving, when he was an Assistant U.S. Attorney, wound up making a mockery of him, prior to, during, and well after Silva's criminal trial and Direct Appeal process.

Vincent Flannigan: A long-time childhood friend of Silva's. Back in the day, during their formative high school wrestling years, they grappled with one another on adversarial high school wrestling teams and thus began their close friendship. Even though Silva, who maintained a perfect 13-0 high school, undefeated wrestling record, beat Vincent on both their grappling meetings, Vincent proved to be a very worthy opponent that Silva came to respect and continues to admire. Vincent was the first individual Silva had contacted when he was arrested and sought his legal advice, which proved invaluable as the ensuing criminal case against Silva continued to unfold. Vincent was the one who first broke the news to Silva about the government's 'star witness' against him, as he was about to be indicted for perjury, among other criminal acts committed during Silva's criminal trial and subsequent appeal process, which eventually lead to Silva's release from federal prison, his 35-year, without parole, sentence, and his CCE Drug Kingpin conviction overturned and vacated.

Gerry Rutledge: Silva's post-conviction relief attorney and the true champion for his continued '*quest for justice*' to prevail. Gerry had a small but very successful law practice located in Baltimore, Maryland. He remains to this day a solo practitioner with a loyal secretary by the name of Dinah, who without her help Gerry would not have been able to manage the workload necessary to handle Silva's voluminous documents and record-keeping needs. Silva would often drive them both crazy with phone calls and scores of letters from prison, making certain that they dotted their i's and crossed their t's, at every step of Silva's post-conviction relief process and court filings. Gerry also handled Silva's Rule 33 Motion for a new trial, and when that went nowhere, which he knew up front would most likely be the case, Silva chose Gerry to stay on board and file his last bite of the '*apple of justice*' to write and eventually file his Rule 2255 Motion to vacate, set aside, or correct his sentence. Silva had a good feeling that Gerry was the perfect attorney he needed to finally right the wrongs the entire U.S. Attorney's Office had unfairly dealt him for the District of Maryland. Gerry was a stand-up lawyer whose moral fiber Silva felt wouldn't let him down. He'd make certain that no stone was left unturned. Most of all, Gerry wasn't afraid of going up against the '*Just Us*' judicial system, which failed Silva miserably in the past. Reflecting, after all these years having passed, without any hesitation, whatsoever, without Gerry's assistance, compassion, and his understanding of Silva's criminal plight, coupled with his willingness to fight until the very end, seeing that justice finally prevailed in Silva's criminal case, Silva, most likely would still be serving his thirty-five-year non-probable sentence.

MY SENTENCING HEARING

I was in the prime of my life and found myself obsessed with the fascination of sex, greed, and rock n' roll. It was this insatiable quest for fame, fortune, and power that nearly cost me to spend the rest of my adult life in federal prison.

It was Tuesday, April 22, 1986, a typical warm sunny April morning, with a slight overcast and a forty-percent chance of rain later in the day. For me, it was just another normal, fun, and productive workday. I usually slept until around 9:00 a.m. or so and did the usual shit, shower, and shave routine. However, on this particular day, it would be anything but routine. For me, it turned out to be the most horrific day of my life.

Here I was, turning 40 in just a couple of months, and who would've ever believed that I'd be spending my '*Big Day*' in the '*Big House*,' the Federal Bureau of Prison (a/k/a the BOP), as it's often referred to. This is my story and yes, it's sad but true.

Fast forward to Monday, April 27, 1987, almost a year to the day of my arrest. The sun was shining, but some clouds had formed over the Federal Courthouse in Baltimore, Maryland. I'd just entered the building and headed toward Courtroom 'C', where my sentencing hearing was about to commence. I was found guilty by a jury of my peers on all counts as charged, and today was the day Judge Moore was to sentence me.

It was 9:00 a.m. sharp when the bailiff entered and announced, "*All rise, the Honorable Judge Moore presiding in criminal case number MM-041986, United States vs. Silva.*" I'll never forget that moment for the rest of my life. Judge Moore, pushing 83 years old, a rather small-framed, frail man with a full head of hair as white as snow, his face withered from his many years of chain-smoking, entered the courtroom from his chambers through a hidden door just behind his podium. Our eyes met, and his cold stare alerted me as to what was coming. His essence and taunting demeanor sent a chill throughout my body, and my heart began racing. I turned and glanced at my parents, both with heavy hearts, and hard as it was for them they both managed to crack a smile. My daughter was also seated in the visitor's gallery. I noticed a hanky in her hands as she proceeded to wipe away her tears as the judge uttered, "*Be seated*," in his weak and frail-sounding voice.

My lawyer, David Irving, and the government's prosecuting attorney, Andy Nolan, both addressed the Court.

David pleaded with Judge Moore for leniency on my behalf. He requested that the Court impose only the required minimum sentence of 10 years for my conviction under Title 21 U.S.C., Section 848, otherwise known as the Continuing Criminal Enterprise '*Drug Kingpin*' statute. Mind you, this was the harshest criminal offense in the government's arsenal of federal criminal statutes, with a maximum sentence of life without parole, worse than had I killed the President of the United States, for which one could conceivably be granted parole. However, the AUSA Andy Nolan, on behalf of the U.S. Government, had a much harsher sentence request in mind. He suggested to the Court, due to the nature of my '*alleged*' and now convicted crimes, all of which I'd been found guilty by a jury of my peers, that Judge Moore should impose a sentence of sixty years, without the benefit of parole. I didn't believe what I was hearing. I heard my daughter cry hysterically, and my mother and father were both in shock. The judge pounded his gavel and demanded order in the court. My father immediately escorted my mother and daughter out of the Courtroom for fear that their actions would further hamper the judge's final sentencing decision, which turned out to be of no consequence.

Finally, after an hour and a half of back-and-forth deliberations and arguments on both sides, it was now my turn to speak and muster as much courage as I could in delivering my constitutionally afforded right to an allocution, that being the right to personally address the sentencing judge in the mitigation of my sentence, for which he was about to impose.

Moments earlier, Judge Moore had heard from Mr. Nolan, who requested, on behalf of the U.S. Government, to impose a sentence of sixty years without parole. David, my counsel, on the other hand, had pleaded with the court for leniency on my behalf and requested Judge Moore to impose the required ten-year minimum mandatory sentence for my Title 21-U.S.C., Section 848 '*Drug Kingpin*' felony conviction.

It was now my turn to try and convince the sentencing judge that I was indeed worthy of my lawyer's earnest sentencing request. The following excerpts have been extracted directly from the Sentencing Court's hearing transcripts.

I stood and addressed the Court as follows:

THE COURT: *Mr. Silva, do you want to be heard?*

THE DEFENDANT: *Yes, I do. Should I stand here, or come closer Your Honor?*

MR. IRVING: *Stand here will be fine.*

THE COURT: *Okay.*

THE DEFENDANT: *First, let me try to gain my composure. I have had a lot of time to think about what I am about to talk to you about. So, forgive me if I have some thoughts that I want to try to recapitulate in my mind. To begin with, I would like to ask Your Honor a question if I may. Last night on national television there was an ABC Special news program called: 'Drugs Across America.' Was Your Honor aware of this program?*

THE COURT: Yes, I was.

THE DEFENDANT: I assume that your Honor watched this program.

THE COURT: I don't know that that is an appropriate question, but, in any event, I will answer it by saying I saw about twenty minutes of it.

THE DEFENDANT: Okay. I must say, I was devastated having watched this program from my jail cell, and I can only assume that Your Honor must have been equally, if not more, devastated.

THE COURT: I will say for the record, whatever sentence the Court shall impose here today is totally without reference to the program many had watched last evening.

THE DEFENDANT: Fine.

THE COURT: Is that clear?

THE DEFENDANT: Yes, Your Honor.

THE COURT: The Court is not unaware of the world we live in.

THE DEFENDANT: Okay, Your Honor. On that basis, I shall proceed. I stand before you today, a broken-hearted man. I have a lot of built-up anger. A lot of bitterness lives within me, yet I feel a lot of remorse for all the loved ones I've hurt.

I believe, Your Honor, the biggest mistake I've made in this trial was not taking the witness stand. I've had nine weeks to think about all this. I don't profess to make any excuses for the crimes against society of which I was found guilty in this Court. However, I do believe in my heart that there was a grave injustice foisted upon me. I say this with conviction because of the prejudicial material contained in my pre-sentencing report, with specific reference to the Government's Memorandum Order submitted to this Court, which the prosecution team knew many of its assertions to be totally untrue, without any merit, nor substantiated facts in support of the same.

I know I am not standing before you on trial today. However, as one sometimes takes the roller coaster ride of life, they sometimes make some poor judgments along the way. I think, more than anything else, I was guilty of poor judgment, and for that, I do have a great deal of remorse.

I took the time this morning, Your Honor, for about an hour to read over the government's memorandum concerning the allegations they made about me. Just some of the smaller things that were mentioned, the fact that, as Mr. Irving reported to you, that my Pre-sentence Investigation Report (PSI) incorrectly calculated and severely exaggerated my total net worth to be $467,000.00. I went over these figures very carefully in my mind. If we had the time, which I know we don't, it would be proven that those assets do not exist in the manner in which the government maintained they did. One example was a $20,000 racing boat. Your Honor, I acquired that boat for $500.00 from the marina, where it was ready to be disposed of to a local scrap dealer.

I only bring this to your attention because it would stand to reason if the Government is making these allegations regarding how big of an international drug smuggler I have been, with the multi-thousands of kilos of cocaine that I was supposed to have dealt in. I would like to know for myself where all of my money is that I supposedly earned. I mean it just doesn't exist. I've never made millions of dollars, as the Government has alleged. I worked very hard to obtain the monies that I have made, and whatever bit of success I have reaped.

Like Mr. Irving has stated on my behalf, I'm forty years old, I haven't had a prior record. I have done a lot of good things in my life. At a very young age, I became a member of the Masonic Order

JUDICIAL WEB

of free and accepted masons, which is a rather unique and elite prestigious worldwide organization. I am an educated man and I have raised a daughter since the tender age of nine, as a single parent I might add, and I do believe I've done a fine job of doing so.

This morning, the government, one small example, took a pass concerning the passport issue they alleged was found in my home. At the time of trial, that seemed like a big deal because it was going to prove that I had control over my brother's comings and goings, in and out of the country. Then today, because of the tremendous weight of all the other evidence, it suddenly becomes a small and insignificant part of my having controlled my brother.

I have searched my mind as to how the Government concluded that my brother's passport was found and seized from my home on the day of my arrest. So, I asked Mr. Irving to go and check out the inventory record control sheets to find out if in fact, my brother's passport was confiscated and listed as part of the seizure items taken from my home on the day of my arrest. And the truth of the matter is, Your Honor, the passport was found in my brother's living room where the arresting officers confiscated it on the day of his arrest and not mine. All I know is that my brother's passport was never listed on my inventory control sheets. Why the Government prosecutors said otherwise was deceitful and an outright lie.

Also, Your Honor, I'm not going to stand here and try and vindicate myself to you because I did plead guilty in Maryland.

THE COURT: *You mean Virginia?*

THE DEFENDANT: *I'm sorry, Your Honor, in Virginia to the crime of.*

THE COURT: *You pleaded guilty in Maryland to a crime you committed in Virginia.*

THE DEFENDANT: Yes, Your Honor. and I would also like to state for the record, if I may, that before I exercised my constitutional right to go to trial in order to prove that I was not guilty of being an 848 felon, and in my heart, I will always believe that no matter what Your Honor sentences me here today, I would like the Court to know that the Government called me into their offices to ask me if I was willing to, or maybe it might have been my attorney who arranged for a meeting with the Government to call me into their offices to.

MR. NOLAN: Your Honor, I am going to object to that. I think reference to that would be prohibited by Rule 11, Your Honor.

THE DEFENDANT: The point of reference, Your Honor, I am trying to make.

THE COURT: What are you seeking to establish?

THE DEFENDANT: I am going to seek to establish the fact that originally my possible sentence if I would have gone to...

MR. NOLAN: Objection.

THE COURT: Just a moment. Let me...what is the basis of your objection? I don't quite understand.

MR. NOLAN: Your Honor, I do believe that Mr. Silva is about to embark on references to some discussions, which may have been part of plea negotiations.

THE COURT: Are you talking about the Virginia case?

THE DEFENDANT: No, Your Honor, I am talking about the Maryland case in which I felt in my heart that by not accepting the Government's original offer or negotiating an offer that we would all agree to, and instead opting to go to trial to exercise my constitutional right to a trial by jury, is why I now believe that a much harsher sentence is being requested by the government here today.

JUDICIAL WEB

THE COURT: You may proceed.

THE DEFENDANT: Thank you, Your Honor. I am basing my conversation on when I went to have an informal dialogue with the Government's counsel, and during these informal dialogues, I was asked to discuss my case. I told the Government what I believed to be true about our case as it pertained solely to my involvement in the case, and the degree of culpability I believed I shared.

However, when I left the interview office of the U.S. Attorney, I was later informed by my lawyer that the Government didn't accept any of my story, and yet their offer, at the time was 12-15 years' maximum. They said with a good time and extra credits, I could be home after serving only 1/3 of the agreed-upon sentence. But they said they didn't believe I was telling them the truth.

(Just to break the dialogue for a moment, as it later turned out, some nearly eight years later, I was able to prove the Government knew all along that I was telling the truth, which subsequently earned me a new trial and my ultimate freedom from my otherwise draconian 35-year sentence, without the possibility of parole).

So, at that point, the Government agents informed me that the Title 21-848 criminal offense I was charged with couldn't be dismissed from my Maryland Indictment. In other words, it wasn't negotiable.

The Government agents went on to further stipulate that if I didn't accept the terms of their plea bargain, which was to plead guilty to the 848 offence as charged and hence fully cooperate, there was no further deal on the table. That is exactly what the dialogue was.

At that point, I was prepared to plead guilty in Maryland to the crimes of conspiracy and certain other overt acts that I had pleaded guilty to in my Virginia Indictment.

Under no circumstances did I authorize my attorney to inform the Government that I would remotely consider pleading guilty to the criminal offense of being an 848 CCE offender.

All along, I felt deeply that I was never guilty of being a CCE drug kingpin offender, the harshest of all drug felony statutes in the Government's arsenal of criminal offenses.

Your Honor, I was very aware of what this crime consisted of, and as such, I knew that I did not fit this profile.

Then I wind up going to trial, and my attorney made the decision that I should not take the witness stand. However, at the last minute, having listened to the entire testimony rendered during my criminal proceedings in my most unusual lengthy criminal trial, and how a total disregard for the integrity of our judicial system ensued as the trial against me began to unravel, I started having second thoughts about not doing so.

Your Honor, the lies, deceit, misstatements of material facts, and false and inaccurate allegations severely prejudiced me during my criminal trial. I had the yearning to take the stand on my own behalf and, once and for all, set the record straight in many regards that were at the time distorting the truth while denying me my due process of the law. However, it was collectively decided that it would be best for all parties concerned that I did not take the witness stand, which I believe was a grave mistake on the part of my counsel.

My counsel strongly advised me against taking the witness stand. He said that due to my brother and another co-defendant still being on trial, anything I divulged to the Court during my testimony could have major repercussions by the end of my trial. It was therefore collectively decided I would not take the witness stand. Hence, I waived my constitutional right to do so, which ultimately, I believe, paved the way for an almost certain guilty verdict by the jury.

JUDICIAL WEB

THE COURT: *I want to interject and indicate I presided over your entire trial, which lasted for over three months.*

THE DEFENDANT: *Yes, Your Honor.*

THE COURT: *I will say to you, Mr. Silva, that you were represented by truly outstanding attorneys.*

THE DEFENDANT: *Absolutely.*

THE COURT: *I want the record to reflect that.*

THE DEFENDANT: *Thank you very much, Your Honor. So, upon my counsel's advice and my discussions with him and other family members, I decided to abide by his legal reasoning and waived my right to testify. Perhaps, this was not such a good decision after all.*

I stand before you today listening to the Government making recommendations for you to give me a sixty-year sentence (without parole) for things I believe in my heart, Your Honor, that they 'knew' I did not do, nor was I guilty of. I truly believe this to be the case.

The only chance I am going to have to prove this, God willing, is if I get a chance on Direct Appeal for something that might have been done wrong in this trial, which would warrant a reversal of my conviction, and then come back before this very Court, this next time around, and tell my story that I was not a drug kingpin, or the kingpin, as this Court has chosen to label me. Period!

For the things that I was guilty of and that I did wrong, I am fully prepared to serve my punishment but not the things I was clearly not guilty of, despite having been found guilty of them by a jury of my peers.

I hope Your Honor did, in fact, read my personalized letter, which I addressed to the Court.

THE COURT: Yes, I did read it.

THE DEFENDANT: Thank you, Your Honor. I spent a good part of my life trying to make a better way for myself and my family. And, yes, I am guilty of being greedy. I am officially guilty of that in this case. There is no doubt about that. I cannot get around that. I berate myself every day for having been guilty of being too greedy in my life.

I think I basically have given you a feeling of who I am. You have seen firsthand who I am from the many videos presented during my trial.

In conclusion, I only ask the Court to take into consideration all the evidence. The good, bad, and indifferent. I know you took a lot of time to take notes during my fourteen-week trial. I am hoping that the years of experience you've had on the bench and within our judicial system as an outstanding Senior Judge will lead you to see through certain major flaws of my trial and grant me a fair and just sentence.

Certainly, as Mr. Irving said, it would be nice if we came in here today based upon what the Government really knew I was guilty of, and my lawyer could have convinced them to have done the right thing with their sentencing recommendations to the Court. Sadly, Your Honor, I'm afraid it appears that that is not how the system works. The scales of justice, Your Honor, have been severely tampered with and equally unbalanced here. The truth is, you are the only person who can right this wrong, here and now today.

I have a two-year-old son who will grow up without his father being around for him during the most important years of his youth. And yes, that's my fault because I did some things wrong that I must now pay the price for. And I also have a young teenage daughter sitting behind me that's crying because she doesn't have a mother she can turn to and now no longer a father as well. I have *two ailing parents that need me around for them, too. I know none of this shall play a part in the sentence you will hand down today, but I wanted to make you aware of the heavy heart I now have to carry while I'm away.*

I am amazed that I can still stand here and speak to you this way without breaking down. However, I promised my father I would be strong for our family, and that's why I am going to leave this Courtroom today, strong and praying that justice shall prevail when all is said and done.

All I ask of you, Your Honor, is to be lenient as you can with me based upon the circumstances I've tried my very best to lay out to you here today during my allocution to the Court. I would like another chance in life. Thank you! I have nothing further to say, Your Honor.

This concluded my portion of the sentencing hearing. While reflecting and reading over my allocution wording, I noticed many things I would have said differently. I would have cut out a lot of repetitive words and made my speech much shorter. It seemed like the Judge was just letting my words go in one ear and out the other.

After hearing all that I'd just stated, and taking into consideration all the facts you've just read, Judge Moore, having heard the same during the long weeks of my trial, which began in mid-December 1986, and concluded in late March 1987 (not including several weeks of pre-trial hearing conferences) it was now Judge Moore, who would solely determine my fate.

Judge Moore now possessed the sole power to grant me either a sentence of ten years without parole (the minimum mandatory sentence under Title 21, Section 848), or he could impose a sentence of up to life without parole.

Everyone in the Courtroom was on pins and needles. Reporters lined the visitor's section, taking notes and writing as fast as possible. This was the highest-profile case this Court had seen in decades. At least, that's how the media and press portrayed it.

My family and close friends were seated directly behind me, waiting with bated breath for the Judge to render his final words before passing his sentence upon me.

My heart was racing, and I began to break into a cold sweat. I knew, unlike anyone else in the courtroom that day, what was coming. I was going to be made an example of. I was about to get hammered by this feisty, old-school, draconian sentencing Judge. An extremely conservative Judge, whom everyone knew was a stiff sentence giver, all of which sent chills up and down my spine.

Judge Moore rambled on for at least thirty-minutes as to how he believed the government's version of my criminal involvement, and how he wholeheartedly felt the government, indeed, proved its case beyond a reasonable doubt.

Judge Moore even went so far as to state on the record that as far as he was concerned, the evidence against me during my trial and the testimony offered by the government's '*star witness*,' Jon Gerritt, was so overwhelmingly convincing, which clearly proved I was a classic example of being a drug kingpin, and stated the following on the record:

"You were truly a classic example of a drug kingpin, and as far as I'm concerned, they should have named the statute after you. With the power vested in me, I will sentence you, Steve Silva, to thirty-five years in federal prison, without the benefit of parole."

And after those words were uttered and finally sunk into my brain, I was devastated, speechless, and motionless. The Courtroom turned into a frenzy. Reporters zoomed out of the Courthouse, rushing to their desks to get the big lead story for their local papers the next morning, and boy did they have a field day doing so. It was horrific for my family to witness, and as I was taken away, in handcuffs, by the U.S. Marshals, I yelled as loud as I could so everyone in that Courtroom heard me utter these departing words...

"*I'll be back, as truth crushed to earth shall rise again, and no lie can live forever!*"

I couldn't help but notice several reporters still lingered around jotting down those exact words, and years later, they came back to haunt everyone in that Courtroom, from that eventful day, back in April 1987.

Fast forward nearly seven years later, since that draconian sentence was passed upon me, I've tried to muster all the energy, knowledge, willpower, self-discipline, and courage necessary to prove to the world I wasn't guilty of the harshest felony offense in the Government's arsenal of criminal statutes, which a jury of my peers had found me guilty of.

Now, as many of you may recall, Paul Harvey would often say during his weekly national radio broadcasts: "***AND NOW FOR THE REST OF THE STORY!***"

Against all odds, remember less than 5% of those federally indicted and who choose to go to trial, ever prevail with a not-guilty verdict during their criminal trial. The percentage of those prevailing on post-conviction relief filings is even much less than that, some say in the 1% to 2% range. Those were devastating odds for me to overcome. But if there's one thing I've learned, while being locked up for all those years, '*It's not over until the fat lady sings*,' and she had not yet begun to sing. She would sing and sing very loud, but not before I was able to effectuate justice with my post-conviction relief efforts.

A wrongful and tainted conviction from a jury of my peers had served me a grave injustice. A jury who was misled by way of false and perjured testimony, as was clearly proven years later, which the Government's prosecution team '*knew*' or '*should*' have known about at the time of my criminal proceedings and eventual trial. Not to mention a conspiratorial group of overly ambitious and zealous prosecutors, and a seemingly senile Judge, who together failed our judicial system, which they swore to uphold and keep sacred, but who also failed me and society as a whole when they prevented me from having a fair and just trial, and a proper sentence for my involvement in the overall drug conspiracy, which I was clearly guilty of according to the way our federal conspiracy statutes are coded and written. There was no way of getting around that. But a drug kingpin, I was not! So, that was what I now set out to prove, and upon my doing so I would look to eventually have my draconian 35-year, no-parole sentence, which I was now wrongfully made to serve, overturned and removed from my criminal record.

The ***Judicial Web*** I was now ensnarled in would eventually lead me to learn of the government's gross misconduct, corruption, treachery, and cover-up (all of which was of a criminal nature), surrounding my criminal investigation, indictment, prosecution, and subsequent conviction as a Title 21, Section 848 CCE (managing a continuing criminal enterprise) Drug Kingpin.

SOME PERSONAL BACKGROUND HISTORY

Because I believe it is important, I would now like to share with you a little bit of my personal background and growing up years.

I was born in 1948, on a cold and rainy day, in early December, so my parents told me years later. Elizabeth, New Jersey, was my official birthplace.

Basically, from day one, I was a good baby, healthy, the first-born son of a middle working-class family and loved by all.

I was an inquisitive child, always yearning to know life's how, what, where, why, and when. Sometimes this insatiable thirst of curiosity caused some mischievous behavior on my part, but nothing more than the usual growing-up boyhood syndrome.

I always liked being a leader rather than a follower, and all in all, I must say I had a very enjoyable childhood.

After graduating from High School in 1965 and having achieved the status of a *'Varsity star wrestler'* with an undefeated 13-0 senior year season, a record which still stands to this very day, over 55 years later, I chose to attend a local New Jersey college, now a University, on a full wrestling scholarship. However, surgery was required due to an unfortunate knee injury I sustained during my freshman year. My knee was never the same, nor was my college wrestling career. I was forced to leave the team, and my scholarship was rescinded.

Nevertheless, I continued my college career and became very active in other activities while studying business administration and business law, but mostly enjoyed playing my drums on the weekends with a rock band I'd put together to help support my way through college.

Upon graduating college in 1969 with a Bachelor of Science Degree, I continued with my graduate studies at a nearby New York college during the evenings. Eventually, in 1972, I received my Master's degree in International Business with a minor in Hospital Administration.

After graduating with my MBA degree, I enrolled in the LaSalle Law School University correspondence curriculum. However, due to financial pressures and a lack of adequate study time, I reluctantly dropped out of the curriculum.

My first career position, upon graduating college, was with a local Hospital in the quaint town of Elizabeth, New Jersey. After several tedious and scrutinizing interviews, I was appointed the Hospital's Professional Nurse Recruitment Director. That was my official title. I also continued earning extra income from my music career on the weekends and truly enjoyed my life. I stayed employed at this local Hospital until the latter part of 1972.

Wishing to better myself, I soon became employed with Johnson & Johnson (the baby products' company) as their South Jersey sales representative. My official job responsibilities were to demonstrate the company's exclusive line of surgical instruments to surgeons, operating room nurses, and hospital administrative staff members up and down the South Jersey coast. I scrubbed with some of the finest surgeons from around the country and watched pretty much every kind of surgical procedure you could think of, from the birth of a newborn baby to the removal of a bullet from a young victim's brain.

Surgeons would often invite me, in their respective fields, to demonstrate our unique line of surgical instruments, and inquire with me about designing specific ones to suit their individual needs, which the company would often authorize. This seemed to make for great advertising and publicity for both the company and surgeons alike. Those were spectacular years for me to have experienced and been a part of.

My position with Johnson & Johnson was intriguing and very challenging, however, I was getting tired of New Jersey and the brutal winters. The cold weather didn't sit very well with me. I was married at the time and the proud father of our daughter, Stacy. She was truly the love of my life. A *'daddy's girl'* at heart, and a very special child she was. Stacy was the first grandchild to be born in our family, and she was named after my mom's mother, Grandma Stacie.

Both Stacy and my wife at the time, Rosette, were often ill with colds and the flu. It seemed they spent more time indoors than out. Hence, we decided to make the big move to the Sunshine State. I felt the warmer climate would reap less illness for the family, and so off we went to seek our fame and fortune in sunny Miami, Florida. It was now the fall of 1975.

We moved to a cozy apartment in South Miami, a recently built, young-adult community complex with lots of children our daughter's age, and we quickly settled in. Shortly thereafter I interviewed with a competitor of my previous employer, by the name of Air Shields. They were a medical equipment company located in Charlotte, North Carolina. Having been impressed with my educational background, business acumen, and medical sales experience, they immediately hired me as their Florida East Coast sales representative. I received a huge increase in salary, bonus and commission incentives, a brand new company car, plus a lucrative business expense account. Life was great, and I was on a roll once more.

While at Air Shields, I was responsible for servicing over 135 of their distributors up and down the East Coast of Florida. However, as fate would have it, the company was poorly run, and it didn't take long to realize the company was insolvent and near bankruptcy. The company folded within twelve months of my being hired, costing me thousands of dollars in lost and unpaid commissions, which I was never compensated for.

In late fall of 1976, I searched for new employment and applied for a position as an Assistant Hospital Administrator at a world renowned hospital, in Miami, Florida. Unfortunately, at the time of my scheduled interview with the Hospital Administrator's Office, and other executive staff members, there was a big shakedown in the Administration's financial Department, at its highest levels. The Hospital Administrator and several of his assistants were the center of the shakedown and the ongoing investigation. They were all being charged with fraud and misappropriation of hospital funds.

The story made the headlines, and thereafter I became totally disenchanted with hospital work and corporate America. I was now unemployed and once again back to square one.

I kept supporting my family by performing in a local band, and doing music gigs to earn enough to cover the basic household bills. I also tried my luck in the real estate business, and after acquiring my Florida Real Estate License, I had a brief stay with Century 21.

Being a professional musician since the age of thirteen, I decided it was time for me to try my luck at something I truly enjoyed doing and was very good at, which was a career as a full-time, professional entertainer, playing the drums and singing in my own professional music group.

I was tired of working for other people and other companies while having to rely on whether they were going to be able to pay my salary each week, or if I'd be told I was fired and let go for one reason or another. I had enough of that roller coaster ride.

Sometime in early 1977, I put together my very first show band and called it the '*Golden Touch Trio.*' The group soon worked its way into becoming one of the top show bands in South Florida. We performed in all of Miami's finest night clubs, high end restaurants, hotels, you name it. We performed on a host of luxury cruise liners all over the Caribbean and the Bahamas, too. We even recorded our own records and sold them while on our cruise ship adventures. It was the greatest time of my life. I was earning a very comfortable living and traveling with my family to places I otherwise, in a million years, would never have experienced if it wasn't for my music career.

Due to a heavy demand for our group's appearances, I started my own talent agency and called it, you guessed it, '*Golden Touch Talent Consultants.*'

I soon began booking local talent all over South Florida. I even cloned some of the groups to look and sound like my successful 'Golden Touch Trio,' and created a demand that was hungry for our sound, and things just exploded from there. My company grew so big so fast, that I eventually became interested in the artist development, management, and recording aspects of the music business, which seemed to be a logical progression for me to follow.

It was now the spring of 1979. With the success and the money I'd saved, I opened a small 8-track recording studio in Hollywood, Florida. I began recording local bands and produced children's records, commercials, jingles, you name it, all under the company name of '*Golden Touch Enterprises.*'

I was still performing with my show band, but only at select, high-paying performance venues, while also running my talent agency and newly built recording studio. It was a very busy time, and life was truly blissful.

Then came a big break for me, at least at the time it seemed like a big break. I had just signed my group to a twelve-week engagement at the Miami Marriott Airport Hotel in Miami, Florida. At the time, this venue was the hottest nightclub spot in South Florida, and we were the headliner act. It was the signing of this contract which ironically led to the eventual downfall and the ultimate near ruination of my life.

IT'S PARTY TIME

Things begin to get a bit hairy! During our successful twelve week engagement at the Marriott Celebrity Roof Top Lounge, as it was called back in the day, we're talking summer of 1979, my keyboard player at the time, Bennie Rojas, who would later become a key player in the international drug conspiracy I eventually found myself ensnarled in, had befriended a local Miami Police Officer by the name of Gary Homer.

One of Homer's routine stops was that of the Miami Marriott Roof Top lounge and other hot spots around South Miami. It was during this era that Gary and Bennie would cement their friendship. Little did I know, this relationship would soon develop into a multi-million-dollar drug smuggling network. You see, Gary and Bennie had shared a very special interest. They both loved to fly airplanes. Bennie had already acquired his private-pilot's license and was multi-engine rated and jet certified by the time they met one another. Bennie agreed to teach Gary all he knew about flying, and before long Bennie was able to save some money and purchase his first twin-engine aircraft, a Queen Air, which he and Gary would use to go flying after we finished playing at 1:00 a.m. in the morning.

Miami is simply breath-taking after dark, especially on a clear summer evening with the moon as bright as ever, surrounded by an endless array of stars shining all over the Miami skyline. Bennie would often describe the experience as being one of total serenity.

Being minutes away from the Miami International Airport had made it so convenient for Bennie and Gary to just whisk away, almost every evening, after we finished performing.

The next thing I remember happening was Bennie was introduced to Jon Gerritt, by Gary, who turned out to be Gary's part-time riding partner on the so-called beat. With the increase in crime throughout South Florida, especially in Miami and the surrounding areas, due primarily to the influx of drug smuggling in South Florida, it became necessary for each law-enforcement officer to have a backup officer accompany them, especially during their night shift duty.

Holmes and Gerritt would often frequent the Roof Top Celebrity Lounge on their nights off, have a few drinks, and enjoy the scenery, the beautiful ladies of the evening, and all the attention the band members would give them, especially Bennie, who was always looking to show off, buying them drinks, and introducing them to his lady fan club members to socialize with.

The three of them struck a common bond and soon became inseparable. It turned out that Gerritt was also into flying and had been for years. He was also a licensed pilot and had logged a substantial number of flight hours to his credit. I also believe Gerritt owned or was leasing two single engine Cessna 182's, which he used to teach students how to fly in his spare time. It was later uncovered that it was during this time frame that the makings of their soon to be drug smuggling empire was born. Since Bennie, Gary, and Jon all had flying in common, they would often fly together several nights a week. It was truly a match made in heaven; no pun intended!

Soon Bennie got tired and perhaps disenchanted with the music scene. He wanted to wean himself away from it all. He was already flying part-time for a recently opened small charter company, out of the Fort Lauderdale International Airport, and making a few extra dollars doing what he truly enjoyed most in life. Flying!

Somehow, if my memory serves me correctly, Bennie and Jon had hooked up and became partners in a similar aviation venture and opened their own air-charter service. This would have been around the early 1980s time frame.

Eventually, Bennie left the band to seek his fame and fortune as a full-time air charter pilot. However, I discovered years later, during the intense legal research I did from the prison law library, the real reason why Bennie left the group. After all, if I was paying him a measly $500.00 per week for working a total of twenty-four hours, and he was able to earn $250,000.00 or more, for less than half that amount of time, on any given weekend, why should he continue to play music? Ludicrous you would think!

I lost contact with Bennie upon his departure from the band. I fully understood his ambitions, and who was I to interfere or attempt to discourage him from doing so. I learned through the grapevine Bennie had finally opened his own air and yacht charter service company. I guess he must have had either a falling out with Jon or a mutual parting of the ways. Either way, Bennie was now on his own, once and for all, and no longer had to answer to anyone but himself.

Funny how the circle of life works. As fate would have it, Bennie wound up hiring both Gary and Jon to fly for his charter service company, first as part-time pilots, and shortly thereafter they were both flying full-time for Bennie's booming entity.

However, court records and documents from my criminal case uncovered both Jon and Gary having resigned, without rhyme or reason, from their respective law enforcement careers. Gary from the Miami Police Department, and Jon from the Fort Lauderdale Sheriff's Department. They decided to go where the real money and action was booming, back in the day.

Jon was going through some very hard times during this era. His mom, who he was very close with, had suddenly died from a slip and fall in his built-in, family swimming pool. This was a horrific tragedy for Jon to have endured. He never forgave himself for not being home the day this tragic accident happened. Mrs. Gerritt was a kind woman, and they loved each other dearly. I witnessed their affection, as mother and son, whenever I'd visit Jon at his home, and she'd always be praising her son to me. I believe this loss really tipped the scales, causing Jon severe emotional pain. His ability to rationalize and make proper decisions with his life was significantly thwarted after he'd lost his mom.

Through court documents and debriefing records, Bennie, Gary, and Jon began flying drugs into the United States, from the Bahamas, through two contacts that Bennie had befriended. One of these contacts supposedly controlled the entire Island of Eleuthera, an off-shoot island in the Bahamas, lying 50 miles east of Nassau. Through these two contacts, both Bennie and Jon had amassed a small fortune. Jon, during one of his many proffer sessions with the U.S. Attorney's Office in Virginia, claimed to have made a total of three coca-paste runs during 1979 and 1980. Supposedly, Jon was paid a sum of $250,000.00, in 'Ben Franklin' U.S. dollars, however, years later it was proven to have been much more than that.

By the time 1980 rolled around, both Bennie, Gary, and Jon were rolling in it. Bennie made so much money from the drug netherworld that he retired at the young age of 27. Bennie, unlike both Jon and Gary, was smart enough to get out of the drug flying business before the heat began to brew all around South Florida by the DEA, which it did shortly after Bennie retired.

Upon retiring, Bennie offered the business to Gary and Jon. They both jumped at the opportunity and the monkey business continued. Supposedly, Bennie got a piece of every load that Gary and Jon brought into South Florida, allowing him to continue to roll in the money, without any further risk of getting caught.

This high rolling era went on for some time, and eventually Bennie heard through the grapevine that my music company was doing well, and that I was affiliated with a brand-new state of the art recording studio, located in South Miami that was turning out hit records one after the other.

We were the talk of the town, recording some of the top music talent in the country at the time. From the famous rock groups of *Bad Finger, Yes, and Foxy*, to solo performers like *Bobby Caldwell, and Wayne Cochran*, and a host of other top selling Spanish recording artists, like *Miami Latin Boys (later called The Miami Sound Machine), Willie Chirino, Lisette, and Jorge Castro*, to name a few.

Bennie was getting itchy, and looking for a change in his life. He was yearning to do something with his voice and music talent once again. Bennie was, oddly enough, a talented musician and vocalist. He could really sing, had a style like *Boz Scaggs*, and could also play a mean keyboard. I should know, as I hired Bennie to join my '*Golden Touch Trio*,' and together we created the top showband in South Florida, back in the mid to late 70's.

Bennie had it all, but he wanted more, and money was not an issue. He wanted to get back into the limelight, but this time not as a local nightclub performer, but rather as a legitimate, professional, recording artist, singing, making hit records, and performing at large venues across the U.S.A. That was Bennie's new goal in life when he decided, out of the blue, to reach out to me. He had the looks, the talent, the voice, and all the money in the world to make it happen once and for all. All he now needed was a vehicle to make his latest dreams come true. Little did I suspect, at the time, this vehicle would turn out to be me.

THINGS BEGIN TO GO SOUR

When Bennie learned that I was affiliated with a state-of-the-art recording studio, he quickly put the word out he wanted to meet with me.

I, on the other hand, had another motive in looking to meet with Bennie. It was during this time, 1981, that I was promoting an all R&B group, called '*The Platinum Boys*,' which I helped form. We were now about to sign a major worldwide recording contract with Capitol Records, through SRI, Inc., a Capitol Records subsidiary label.

I was looking for some venture capital to assist me in putting together a professional break-out promotional package to better market the group both domestically and abroad.

When I eventually spoke with Bennie, the conversation was geared around '*The Platinum Boys*' and my need for venture capital to take them to the next level. Bennie agreed to drop by the recording studio to give a listen to the group's demo, which was used to promote them to Capitol Records. Upon doing so, Bennie was very excited about their potential, and agreed to make an initial investment of $5,000.00 for a percentage of the group's debut LP.

I quickly prepared the necessary agreement between us, and the next thing I remember was Bennie coming to my home and handing me a paper bag with $5,000.00 in cash, all neatly wrapped in $100.00 bills. He told me if I did the right thing by him there would be plenty more where that came from. He also informed me not to ask him any questions about where the money came from, as it was

JUDICIAL WEB

none of my business, but he assured me the funds were 100% legitimate, and smiled as he handed me the cash.

We talked for a while as Bennie began to brag about how successful his air and yacht charter enterprise had become, and that he was looking forward to getting back into the music business, wondering if I could still do something with his voice and music talent. I found that request to be somewhat odd from someone who seemingly had it all, and was doing as well as he had purported to be. I mean, he could have gone to a much higher end studio. Why was he coming to me? This turned out to be a pivotal day in the overall scheme of things!

I told Bennie I'd be in touch with him in a few weeks, and we would discuss his music aspirations at that time, but for now my priority was to get 'The Platinum Boys' off and rolling. I was in the midst of putting together a concert tour, and it was a very hectic time for me.

As Bennie left my home, he asked me if the $5,000.00 was enough, at which time I told him it was for now, and I laughed as he hopped into his brand new BMW and took off.

As things later turned out I received another $4,000.00, in cash, and Bennie in turn received an updated contract, which yielded him a 9% vested interest in *The Platinum Boys*' debut LP.

When Bennie went back and boasted to Jon that he was now partners with me in a potentially successful music venture, and that he'd made a modest investment in '*The Platinum Boys*,' Jon inquired if he thought I'd be receptive in making him a similar offer.

You see, Jon never liked to have Bennie be one up on him on anything, and the thought of Bennie having his name on a successful record, and being affiliated with a potentially successful recording group, and not have the same opportunity didn't bode well with Jon, as I'd come to learn years later.

Supposedly, Bennie told Jon he'd see what he could do. A few months later he introduced me to Jon for the purpose of making him the same offer I'd made Bennie several months earlier.

Eventually, Jon wound up investing the same $9,000.00 as Bennie had, and likewise received a 9% vested interest in *The Platinum Boys'* debut LP.

We eventually landed the recording contract with SRI, Inc., which was the distribution arm of Capitol Records. My group went on to have a Top 10 hit song called '*Chance*,' on the Billboard music charts, followed by another smash hit called '*Just One More Dance*.' However, once again, as often is the case with music groups, the success had all gone to their heads, egos flared, and due to some irreconcilable differences between group members, along with the fact that their individual music tastes differed, the group eventually broke up, and everyone went their separate ways. So much for my dreams of being a music mogul, like Clive Davis, or Quincy Jones, and one day rubbing elbows with the big boys in New York City and LA, the two music capitals of the world.

When Jon gave me the $9,000.00 in cash, he informed me that there was a lot more where that came from. I didn't let him know that Bennie had, likewise, made me the same offer.

It was now the summer of 1982. I was hot and heavy into the music business, despite my recent losses with the breakup of '*The Platinum Boys*.' I had no idea what Bennie and Jon were into, and I could not have cared less. As Bennie had once told me, it was none of my business, and I let it go at that. I knew they both were in the air and yacht charter business, and also knew it to be a business dealing with high rollers, and people of influence who paid lots of money for private chartering services. End of story!

Reflecting on things, sure I had my suspicions, but who was I to pass judgment. If Bennie and Jon had money to invest, even cash money, which I was willing to have them invest in my legal music enterprises, so be it. I thought, no big deal! Nothing was illegal in my doing so, back in the time frame of 1981-1986. This was long before any money laundering statutes were enacted into law, which if my memory serves me correctly was around October of 1987 or thereabouts.

Out of pure curiosity, I remember one day in the fall of 1982, I decided to pay Bennie an unexpected visit. I wanted to take a firsthand look at Bennie's charter operation and see once and for all what was really going on. On that day I personally witnessed the phones ringing off the wall, a number of twin-engine airplanes were in the hanger area, and several were being serviced by mechanics. It all seemed legitimate and very much on the up and up to me. So, for the time being my nerves were calm and relaxed, knowing that I wasn't doing anything wrong by investing their hard earned money into my music enterprises.

It was now Spring, 1983, and Bennie decided he really wanted to jump back into the music business, but at a much more lucrative and professional level. He really wanted to try his luck at becoming a legitimate recording artist. All Bennie needed now was to shed a few pounds and have some hit songs written for him. At this time, I was the A&R Director of a popular state-of-the-art recording studio in Miami, FL. Many well-known recording artists frequented our studio and recorded hit records there. The studio was looking for a benefactor to invest money for our much-needed renovations. We needed to bring the studio up to par with the competition that was heating up South Florida's music boom.

We also needed funding to hire some heavyweight recording engineers, record producers, and to promote the record label we'd soon be launching. Bennie came to the rescue and invested a substantial amount of his own personal money, with the caveat that we'd help him realize his dream, and make him a successful recording artist. He realized there were no guarantees we could pull this off. He only asked for a fair shot from all of us in order to be able to do so.

As a result of Bennie's $100,000.00 investment, I was promoted to be the company's Executive Director. In addition, I was granted a 15% ownership interest in the studio, and our soon to be launched record label, for my efforts in arranging the deal. Bennie was also offered a piece of the company plus additional perks, which included having me as his personal manager, his record producer, the full reign of the recording studio to produce his debut LP, and a chance to realize his dream of becoming a legitimate recording artist. I was on a roll and loving every minute of it!

The songs being produced for Bennie's debut LP, were written by famous songwriters, who had in the past composed several #1 hits to their credit, one in particular, Bobby Caldwell's smash hit, *'What You Won't Do For Love.'*

To add a little spice to it all, I managed to miraculously fulfill Bennie's wildest dreams by having *Billy Joel's* rhythm section, his favorite music group of all time, along with *Billy Joel's* bass player and backup vocalist, Doug Stegmeyer, and his brother Al Stegmeyer, who was our #1 recording engineer, to record Bennie's debut LP. It doesn't get any better than that!

When the demo tracks were finally completed, if I do say so myself, they were superb and a well-respected piece of work by top industry standards.

However, as fate would have it, Bennie, to everyone's surprise, especially mine, got cold feet, although Bennie would never admit it, and decided to scrap the entire project. Being a true family man at heart, Bennie and his wife were expecting their first child in a few months. Simultaneously, Bennie was scheduled to begin promoting his first single off the LP we'd just completed, and he had second thoughts about going on the road and leaving his wife and newborn child, and it all got to the best of him.

Being on the road, promoting his single, doing tedious concert dates, radio appearances, interviews, in-store promotions, and just plain being away from home and family, just didn't sit well with Bennie and his wife.

To add insult to injury, I'd warned Bennie about these kinds of issues, long before we started working on making this dream of his come to fruition. This was a big bombshell for everyone involved with Bennie's production, as well as the studio, to deal with.

Bennie wound up nixing the entire project. His doing so cost me dearly, as I'd now wasted a lot of precious studio time, my effort, money, and industry favors. Not to mention, it cost me professional embarrassment among the pros in the music industry.

I became very irate with Bennie over his decision to totally scrap the project. As far as I was concerned, my debt to him was now paid in full. However, as I later came to learn, Bennie didn't quite see it that way at all. The net result of Bennie's actions was that the finished masters (recordings of the finished LP) were shelved, as they say in the music industry, and were never to be seen or heard from again.

Jon had been snooping around and watching the extraordinary excitement surrounding the evolving project. When Bennie decided to abandon his music career, Jon couldn't resist the temptation to become more involved with me and the lifestyle I was enjoying in the music business.

As time would tell, Jon had ulterior motives. Meeting all the beautiful women who liked to hang out at the studio, and after hour's clubs we'd often frequent when exploring other potential recording acts to sign to my production company. It all seemed very enticing and intriguing to Jon's ego. I must say Jon was mostly a talker, he never cheated on his wife, to the best of my knowledge while we were out recruiting new talent, and I tip my hat to him for that. He loved his wife, and was just enjoying being surrounded by a new breed of people he was not accustomed to being around. Jon sure knew how to flirt, and had a unique gift to gab, too.

Interested as Jon seemed to be, he asked if he could invest in my other flourishing music entities, and if so, what would I offer him in return for doing so. Jon told me he made a lot of money in the air charter business, flying with Bennie, and was getting tired of being away from home so much, and wanted a more stable lifestyle. Something he could eventually wind up sinking his teeth into and grow with. Years later I found out what his true motives were, he needed someone to help legitimize all his illegal money. He needed a business other than flying drugs into this country and distributing them.

I was successfully operating my Golden Touch Talent Agency, while also running my recording studio, and things were running rather smoothly at the time. I also had, among my other music entities, a children's record and production company, an artist development and management company, plus my music rehearsal studio. I also maintained vested interests in a host of potentially successful local recording artists, who were all under contract with my modeling and talent agency.

I put together a very lucrative proposal, which would allow Jon a golden opportunity to become involved with all these legitimate music business entities. The price tag was a very reasonable one. It also included, I might add, a decent starting salary for Jon, during his first year as an A&R executive for my company. A&R, just in case you may not know, stands for Artist and Repertoire. The main responsibilities of an A&R executive are to ensure the company is always supplied with new talent, and maintains a steady flow of new material from which the artists can record. In other words, to always maintain a quality source of musicians, songwriters, and vocalists.

The salary I agreed to pay Jon was meant to show good faith, trust, and confidence, which he'd placed in me, and reciprocate for the money he was about to invest in all my music business entities.

There were several months of back and forth negotiations between Jon and his wife, Sherry, who seemed very reluctant to have her husband become involved in any way with the music business, and the jet-setting lifestyle it portrayed. However, Sherry finally came around and agreed with the terms of the agreement between my talent agency and her husband, Jon.

I didn't learn until after my criminal indictment was unsealed, and sensitive documents were made available, just how much Sherry really wanted to see Jon quit flying for Bennie, and for him to become involved with something much more legitimate and substantial, other than the monkey business he and Bennie were closely and deeply involved in. Perhaps, something not so dangerous and risky as drug smuggling, which Sherry had to have known all about from day one. After all, how could she not have known, when she was driving around town sporting a brand new 280 SEL two-door red Mercedes Benz, wearing beautiful diamond bracelets, rings, expensive watches and earrings, too.

Jon lived with his wife and their two children in a luxurious Boca Raton, FL, half-million-dollar, dome-styled home, fully equipped with a professional clay tennis court, a beautifully constructed, in the ground, swimming pool, a jacuzzi and sauna, a fully equipped workout gym, a sound system and entertainment center that could wake up the entire neighborhood when cranking, and many more extras that Jon eventually would wind up forfeiting, once his bid for immunity from prosecution was lost.

I believe Sherry had known all along just how deep her husband Jon was wrapped up in the drug netherworld, and she wanted him out and done with that lifestyle, as soon as possible. After all, they had two young children they were raising.

The problem was, despite Sherry's deep inner wishes, she loved the frills and fringe benefits she reaped from her husband's illegal exploits, and seemed, for the time being, rather content to turn the other cheek. That is until the pressure began to mount against them. As fate would have it, this all turned out to my distinct benefit. You may be asking yourself, why? The answer is plain and simple, Sherry was beginning to get scared and feared if something was to happen, and she wound up losing her husband, or worse yet, he got arrested and sent to jail for a very long time, then what would she do by herself, with two young children to raise all on her own. So, she had a sudden change of heart, and encouraged Jon to finally make the music business commitment with me. We wound up consummating a lucrative business deal, to our mutual benefit, and we were off to the races. Little did I know, shortly thereafter, I'd be off to spending the rest of my adult life in federal prison, as a direct result of making this deal.

Unfortunately, for me, it didn't take very long for Jon to become disenchanted with the failures that accompanied the music business. There were no sure-fire guarantees. Investing in music entities was no exception to this rule. As such, things didn't pan out at all for Jon and Sherry's six-figure investment in my music projects. As a matter of fact, they turned out to be a disaster. Believe me, no one worked harder, devoted more time, effort, and energy, trying to make things work to our mutual benefit and financial success, than me. It seemed that every time we were close to making that next big hit, another obstacle would raise its ugly head and stand in our way, and we'd find ourselves right smack back in the middle of nowhere land, all over again.

Like Bennie, Jon eventually got fed up, and back to flying they both went, trying to quickly replace their huge losses. Losses they would eventually blame and hold me fully accountable for.

At first, they didn't seem to pressure me to make good on their sour investments, which were through no fault of mine, but they eventually needed a scapegoat. It wasn't enough for them to learn, firsthand, that the music industry had taken a plummet in the mid-1980s, but I continued to do what I had to in order to survive the crunch. I went back to my roots and began performing once again in night clubs all around town, while continuing to develop and promote my talent agency, recording studio, along with my artist development and management companies. Unlike Bennie and Jon, I wasn't about to throw in the towel just yet. I had too much of my personal time, effort, and money invested in my music entities. I wanted to prove them both wrong and kept at it, non-stop.

In the meantime, Bennie and Jon had a couple of major setbacks. The next thing I knew, I was once again on the hot seat. Bennie contacted me and informed me that I needed to attend a meeting with him and Jon. I remember it was a gloomy, rainy afternoon, in late Fall 1983. Bennie and Jon fetched me from my home in Bennie's new, red-colored BMW. Boy was she a beauty! I hopped into the back seat, commenting how fresh Bennie's new ride was, with that sweet, new car smell, and how things must have been pretty good for him since the last time we met, about a year earlier. However, I made the grave mistake of commenting on how well he must be doing with the new ride he was sporting, and that I had hoped to do the same one day myself. I also opened my big mouth and said: "Must be nice, you got tired of the black BMW and traded it in for a brand new red one."

I could sense my humor didn't get me very far that day. Instead, I noticed as I looked in Bennie's direction, he uttered in a loud voice, over the glaring music coming from his cassette player, so that I would hear him loud and clear, "Steve wasn't much for joke telling, was he!" Jon just nodded in agreement. Then Bennie chose to get really brave and proceeded to inform me that if I didn't somehow, someway, make good on both their previous investments, I wouldn't have to worry about raising my daughter by myself anymore. He said somebody else would be doing the honors for me.

Being a smart-ass back then, I quickly responded by asking, "What's that supposed to mean? Is that some sort of a threat you expect me to take seriously?" And just as I'd uttered those words, the car stopped, the door opened, and I was told to get out of Bennie's car, in the pouring rain, and was informed as they pulled away from the curb, "Remember what we just warned you about, and if I was you, I would certainly take it 100% seriously." Those words tended to wreak havoc in my life from that day forward. They said they'd be back in touch with me real soon, and for me to gather as much money for them as possible before their next visit.

Perhaps reflecting on that eventful day, I should have used my common sense, something I've been cursed with most of my life for not being astute at practicing, and gone directly to the authorities. Had I done so, maybe the subsequent misfortune I suffered in my life might never have transpired. However, I wasn't raised to be a rat, snitch, informant, whistle blower, call it what you wish. I wasn't made from that cloth. I was big enough to handle my dirty laundry, and my own problems, without the intervention of others. At least, I thought as much at the time.

After I exited Bennie's car, I was fortunate to have been able to hitch a ride back to my home and immediately fetched my car. I went directly to check on my daughter at her school. I found out she was just fine. Next, I decided to pay my brother a visit to his apartment. After I arrived at Gary's place, I explained to him exactly what had just happened between me, Bennie, and Jon, and asked for his advice on how best to handle this alarming situation.

If you recall, I mentioned earlier that if for nothing else, Gary always had an abundance of impeccable common sense. He informed me to make an appointment with Bennie and Jon, ASAP, to see what could be amicably worked out to the best of everyone's mutual interest and benefit. However, all the money they'd invested in my music related projects was already spoken for and depleted. I had invested all of it in legitimate music business ventures, but I just couldn't catch a lucky break. That is the true nature of the music business. After all, I never made Bennie or Jon any promises; they knew this to be the case from day one. I had invested plenty of my own money and sweat equity to try and make this a successful venture for the three of us.

I heeded Gary's advice, and arranged to meet with Bennie and Jon the following day. After several hours of back and forth bickering and pointing fingers, as to who was to blame for the substantial losses both Bennie and Jon had sustained, they proceeded to inform me about the facts of life. I could not believe what they shared with me. Jon's story was the most bizarre of all. Up until that moment, I really had no idea what either of them were into. I certainly had my suspicions, but I had no real concrete evidence or information to support my curiosity. I had no clue what money they were worth or the adventures and risks they both experienced, or the severe troubles they were now facing. As naïve as I was back then, I was truly in awe. In many ways, I felt sorry for both of them. Especially for their families! I informed Bennie and Jon that I would try my absolute best to help in any way I could.

Apparently, after they confessed to me the true nature of how they accumulated their wealth and the funds they had provided me for investment purposes into my music related projects, they proceeded to also inform me that they'd had a major setback with a recent delivery that went sour; they'd lost a lot of money that they were now on the hook for. I didn't delve into the specifics of their loss, and I didn't wish to know or learn anything more about it. I got the gist of their current plight and that was all I needed to know in order to fully grasp the gravity of their situation, and the reason why they'd reacted the way they did with me.

Unbeknown to Bennie or Jon, I'd already been cultivating another lucrative business relationship in the pop music genre. However, little did I know at the time, this business relationship would turn sour, and one day prove to be another significant misjudgment of character I'd foolishly made, and would wind up costing me dearly.

THE MADNESS CONTINUES

It was winter's end, 1983, and I was reflecting on my life's turmoil. I'd gone through a bitter divorce and was looking for someone to rent my home, as I wasn't ready to sell it just yet. I was living in Sunrise, Florida, raising my young, pre-teen daughter as a single dad, and having recently lost a stillborn son with my ex-wife, I was very down on life, and my self-confidence was at an all-time low. I felt I needed a change of scenery.

I placed an ad in the local newspaper to try and find a suitable tenant to rent my home. It took some time, but I finally found a young couple by the name of Alan and Teresa Coachman. They represented themselves as being married at the time they came by to view the property. Only later did I come to learn, after the fact, they were not married, but rather just boyfriend and girlfriend.

When looking back, this is where all my future legal problems first began to brew. Alan Green, alias Alan Coachman, turned out to be a fugitive from justice and was wanted in the state of California for a large-scale furniture scam, as I later learned.

Once I made up my mind I was going to relocate to another part of South Florida, I desperately needed the rental income to cover my current monthly mortgage payment.

Alan had come to learn, through conversations we had, that I was very much involved in the music business. I recall on one of my visits to collect the rent, which would have been sometime in early Spring 1984, he invited me in for a drink. Since I don't drink, I politely declined and requested a glass of ice water. Alan then proceeded to inform me about a good friend of his, Marshall Smith, and his two brothers who lived in Maryland. They'd formed a rock band and were looking to record a demo of their original music and find a manager to guide their dreams of becoming rock stars. This was music to my ears, and I was eager to learn more. Alan asked me if I'd be interested in meeting them to see what I could do to further their music careers.

At some point after my first meeting with Alan, I learned that Marshall and his two brothers came from a rather wealthy family background. Apparently, their father was a prominent eye surgeon from the Baltimore, Maryland area. Their grandmother, Mary, was independently wealthy from her land ownership, which was once a Civil War battleground area filled with precious artifacts and relics, which the U.S. Government had supposedly paid handsomely for; some of which wound up in the Smithsonian Institute. At least that's what I was led to believe when I finally met with Marshall and his two brothers.

I was told there was nothing their grandmother wouldn't do for her three grandchildren, especially if it kept them out of trouble and would afford them the opportunity of becoming rock stars one day. She knew this was their first true love and passion.

After I'd learned all this, a lightbulb went off in my head. Within a few weeks, a meeting was arranged between me, Alan, Marshall, and his two brothers, Frank and Nat.

I eventually struck a deal with Marshall, and was soon to come into a substantial sum of money once again. This time I'd fulfill my lifelong ambition, and long awaited dream of being a part-owner of a state-of-the-art recording studio. My days of being an employee, would soon be a thing of the past. Before long, I'd no longer just be a peon, or an ordinary record company executive, as I'd been at Global Sound Studios. I'd soon be the President and 50% owner of Integra Recording Studios, Inc., with our very own two-story complex and fully equipped, modern recording studio, located in South Beach, FL, valued at nearly $250,000.00, when all was said and done.

Believing that Marshall's family was very wealthy, which I was able to eventually verify. I recall, on one occasion, I was handed a large check for $175,000.00 from Marshall's grandmother, which was used to purchase a condo I'd owned, and was available for sale. Besides being a very lucrative investment property, Mary wanted her three grandchildren to have a place to live while working on their music careers.

I had absolutely no reason to suspect that anything was not 'kosher' at the time. However, as events began to unfold, I 'd soon learn that I'd been duped, conned, call it what you wish, but by now, it was too late to turn back. Marshall knew all this. He'd made sure of it and calculated his every move in doing so. He was a lot smarter than anyone had given him credit for, including me.

The studio was about to officially open for business. It was only a few months away from completion. I was making final preparations for our grand opening celebration and ribbon-cutting ceremony. The guest list included some of the most well-known music industry celebrities of South Florida, along with several prominent politicians, including the Mayor of South Beach, at the time.

Marshall invited me for dinner one evening. We're talking late summer 1984. He began by telling me that he'd not been 100% truthful with me, something I'd suspected all along. However, when Marshall informed me, he was going off to prison for a few years, he literally shocked me. At first, I thought he was joking, but I could tell from the look on his face and the tone in his voice, he was dead serious.

Marshall proceeded to inform me he'd been a victim of an undercover 'sting' operation, which involved the unlawful sale of seven-hundred pounds of marijuana to several DEA Agents, along with his partner, Alan Green. Supposedly, according to Marshall, they had plea-bargained and were given a three-year sentence. This was back in the mid-1980s when pot smuggling penalties were much more lenient, with defendants getting only a slap on the wrist with minor sentences.

I was in total shock beyond words. I remained speechless and dumbfounded. My head was spinning with all kinds of scenarios. I felt very betrayed and angry. I had everything to do to keep my composure and refrain myself from lashing out at Marshall in the restaurant we were dining at. After all, I'd never been exposed to any of this at the young age of thirty-seven. I had my suspicions of both Bennie and Doc, which had only been somewhat exposed to me by this time. I guess you could say I had lived a sheltered lifestyle, despite my music background, and contrary to what many people would have otherwise believed, being a musician and all. I never did any drugs, and as a matter of fact, I never smoked any pot until I met Marshall, and cocaine wasn't even in my vocabulary. To add insult to injury, Marshall informed me that he'd run out of money and that his grandmother had cut him off when she learned he'd soon be going off to jail. That news sent me into orbit. Evidently, Marshall had hoodwinked his grandmother as well. At least that's what I was led to believe at the time, only to learn otherwise years later.

As things now stood, we needed at least another twenty-five thousand dollars to put the studio in tip-top shape, ensure full state-of-the-art production capabilities, and be able to compete with other professional Miami-based recording studios.

Marshall informed me if I needed any more funds to complete our studio project, I'd have to collect his outstanding debts. He claimed this was money he loaned to his friends, which was still outstanding and needed to be collected.

Being the astute businessman I professed to be, I left receipts for the monies I was successful in collecting after Marshall went off to serve his time in state prison. The money collections, and the trail of receipts I'd left behind would one day, unbeknownst to me at the time, prove to be some of the most incriminating evidence that was used against me to gain the eventual wrongful and unjust conviction, for which I'd ultimately be sentenced to a draconian thirty-five-year sentence, without any benefit of parole.

It was one of those receipts I'd signed, after collecting money owed to Marshall, which subsequently opened a can of worms, and eventually lead to my criminal indictment, subsequent conspiracy, and drug-kingpin charges and ultimate convictions.

Around this same time frame, I'm thinking Fall of 1984, Ben and Doc had gotten word that I was back on top again; that I'd left my previous position as the studio manager of Global Sound Studios, and was now operating my own recording facility.

Sometime in late December 1984, just after the studio had finally officially opened for business, I was paid an unexpected visit from Bennie and Doc. They wanted to learn what was going on, and when I planned on making good the money they still claimed I owed them. I asked Bennie and Doc if they were both high on drugs and proceeded to inform them that they had better read over the contracts they signed with me. I never promised either of them any guaranteed return on their purely speculative investments. I only promised them my devoted efforts, time, and energy, coupled with my knowledge and contacts in the music business, and to strive for success in what all three of us had shared as a common goal, to succeed in securing for Bennie a recording contract, produce a hit record for him, and try to expand his music career from there, all of which he'd ultimately, on his own terms, decided to completely abandon.

However, the result from this heated conversation was that Bennie and Doc didn't want to hear any further excuses from me, and they demanded some form of a payment schedule to be established.

JUDICIAL WEB

At first, I reluctantly agreed to meet their demands, thinking I could wheel and deal, sort of play the *'Rob Peter to Pay Paul'* principle. I foolishly thought I could have Marshall help me out. However, as it turned out, he wasn't in any position to help himself out, never mind helping me, due to his current incarceration state. There was absolutely no way I could maintain the costs of running the studio I was now a 50% owner of, pay myself even a minimum salary, and still have funds left over to pay even a token amount of the money they claimed I still owed them.

I tried to make a go of it for a while, but it just wasn't working out. The result was that the studio began to suffer due to the pressure I was placed under, all of which was slowly beginning to tear me apart. Emotionally, I was a wreck and didn't know where to turn next.

Another visit soon ensued. Bennie and Doc once again showed up unexpectedly. By now, the pressure was really mounting. I finally agreed to buy back both of their 25% vested interests in my Golden Touch Talent Agency's common stock, which they were gladly willing to part with. The company has not generated any revenue or profit ever since I took over our new recording studio, which caused the talent agency to begin falling apart.

In the back of my mind, I began planting the seeds with Marshall's brothers, hoping they in turn would inform Marshall, who was soon to be released on parole, about my potential business opportunity in owning a portion of my talent agency. I was hoping to convince Marshall to invest in the talent agency and together try and make it solvent once again. This would give Marshall an additional revenue stream to profit from and further legitimize himself by doing so.

I thought if I convinced Marshall to invest in fifty percent of my *Golden Touch Talent Agency*, which was generating a six figure income at one time, this would be a win-win for the two of us. If

Marshall agreed to jump in, I'd assure him a weekly salary upon his eventual release on parole, in addition to whatever dividends he would receive from the recording studio investment.

Marshall jumped at the opportunity, just as I had hoped, and once again I was able to placate the wolves (Bennie and Doc), at least for the time being. However, I knew there'd come a time when they'd be back again, and my nerves were beginning to get fried. I wasn't myself anymore, and the company began to rapidly feel the effects of the pressure I was under. I needed to do something swiftly to straighten all this out. But what? I began to ponder my dilemma and decided to try and put Bennie, Doc, and Marshall together for mutual *'monkey business'* interests and money-making opportunities.

The motive for my madness was getting the monkey off my back once and for all, which had been eating at me for several years now. This would have been around January 1985.

Marshall had just been released from state prison. He served a minimum sentence, and with good behavior, he was released in no time.

I introduced Marshall to Bennie and Doc, shortly after Marshall had been released from prison. They subsequently teamed up and decided to do a drug deal together. I was foolishly hoping that if the deal they were contemplating came to fruition, that a fair portion of their score would eventually be applied toward the debt they claimed I still owed them. That was my grandiose and foolish wish at the time.

The continued pressure from Bennie and Doc was tearing my life apart. I was counting on something positive happening swiftly from the introduction I'd made. I was hoping that Bennie and Doc would make enough money from whatever ventures they would finalize with Marshall, and I'd no longer have to worry about looking over my shoulders, and thinking anymore about crazy threats against me and my family. I just wanted to get back to my music enterprises and recording studio endeavors. However, little did I know then, that this introduction would turn out to be one of the biggest mistakes of my life, which eventually turned sour several years later, and would wind up costing me dearly!

Bennie, Doc, and Marshall continued working together. There were some arrangements made between them, which turned out to be mutually profitable, while others proved to be disastrous. However, after all was said and done, things turned out to be a big negative.

What eventually transpired was Bennie and Doc had royally screwed Marshall, and Marshall wound up blaming me for the occurrence. Now I had to contend with not only Bennie and Doc's discontent, but Marshall's, too.

By this time, we'd already purchased the studio building, and began the extensive renovations that were necessary after our Grand Opening took place. Originally, we were unable to afford a twenty-four-track recording studio facility, and we had to settle on offering only sixteen-track services. To remain competitive, I insisted we upgrade our facility to offer 24-track recording studio capabilities. We'd recently placed deposits for new equipment upgrades, and everything was in motion.

Marshall lost a lot of money due to being screwed by Bennie and Doc, so he informed me that he was no longer able to fund the studio project, and that I needed to do whatever I felt was best, even if it meant shutting it all down. I was beside myself. I couldn't believe this was happening.

After Marshall was released from prison, there were many outstanding funds still owed to him, which needed to be collected. However, I made it clear to Marshall that I wasn't interested in doing this kind of work for him any longer. I needed to concentrate my efforts on getting the studio and music related companies off the ground.

Initially, Marshall agreed with my reasoning, but he soon realized that he was unable to trust anyone else to complete this task but me. Since Marshall was unable to leave the state of Florida, due to his parole restrictions, he informed me that if I had any hope of keeping the studio alive and funded, I'd have to collect the rest of the outstanding money due and owed to him. He suggested I get with his brothers, and together work out an arrangement to collect the balance of the monies still owed to him.

Naive as I was at first, I reluctantly agreed to own up to the task at hand. I guess you could say I was blinded by my overzealous ambitions, and my aspirations of wanting to get ahead in life. I was overcome by the '*greed factor*' while hoping to make my dreams come true by leaving my mark on the world as a music mogul. As such, I wound up collecting the outstanding debts from several sources around the country.

My involvement was now engraved in stone as a co-conspirator, in one of the largest drug conspiracies ever prosecuted in the United States District Court for the District of Maryland. A drug conspiracy, with alleged ties to the Medellín Drug Cartel, and its original infamous drug lords: *Pablo Escobar, Carlos Lehder*, and *Jose Rodriguez Gacha.*

Marshall settled back into his old ways, staying high as a kite from morning to night. His brothers pretty much did the same, while I was left with the unbearable task of keeping the record companies, the recording studio, and the talent agency all running smoothly, and at the same time collecting all of Marshall's debts, and paying all the company bills. My plate was now much more than full, in fact, it was overflowing, and my head was spinning out of control.

Day and night, seven days a week, I slaved, sometimes 18 to 20 hours a day, often without any sleep, trying to keep it all together.

JUDICIAL WEB

The competition in Miami's music recording studio business was fierce and ruthless. Everyone was relentlessly competing for any and all available business, especially in lieu of the 1985 music business crisis, and its eventual downfall as that year had ended.

Many obstacles besieged me, and it seemed every time I got closer to producing a hit record for our company, something else managed to go wrong and derail my efforts to do so. It was one failure after another. However, despite it all, I was still determined to prevail and kept plugging away. During the ensuing months, I hadn't heard anything from Bennie or Doc. I felt this was a good sign that they were finally going to leave me alone.

I heard through the grapevine that Bennie's air charter service was doing really well once again and that Doc was flying full-time for his company. Word on the street was they were both rolling in the money once more. I was happy for both of them and hoped I was finally off the hook, once and for all. You know the saying, '*Out of Sight! Out of Mind*!'

It was late March 1985 when, out of the blue, I received a telephone call from Doc's wife, Sherry. She was in hysterics and crying uncontrollably. Something to do with Doc being in a Jamaican jail, and he'd requested I go down there and help him get out of the mess he was in. Mind you, this was the same person who threatened my life a little less than a year earlier.

Sherry informed me that she called all of Doc's friends, including his partner, Bennie, but as fate would have it, none of them offered or cared to get involved. Luckily, for Doc and Sherry, I established significant and legitimate contacts in the Jamaican music business over the years. Thinking ahead, I thought perhaps my contacts there could assist me, or if for nothing else, guide me in the right direction to assist Sherry on behalf of her husband's current plight.

I told Sherry I was in no position to drop everything and run down to Jamaica. I had my daughter, who I was raising by myself, and I was very apprehensive about getting involved in something that really didn't concern me. After all, what was I looking to get myself into?

Little did I know at the time, my decision to go against all my principles, drop everything I was doing, and as things turned out, risk my life to save Doc's, would soon come back to haunt me in a very negative manner.

Like the good-natured fool that I was, I went to Doc's beck and call. I hadn't seen or spoken to him in a very long time. But I figured to myself, foolishly perhaps, that by showing Doc a sign of good faith, in his time of distress and troubles, especially when all of his other so-called friends had seemingly deserted him, including his best friend and partner, Bennie. I felt by doing so, maybe, just maybe, this kind act of courage and renewed friendship would put the past between us to rest, once and for all.

Doc claimed that I still owed him big time, and the thought of the slate being wiped clean as a possible result of my rescuing him lured me into making a very foolish decision. And foolish beyond words it turned out to be, as I nearly lost my life doing so.

When I finally arrived in Jamaica, I learned Doc was involved in a smuggling operation with his partner, Gary Holmes. Apparently, they were coming from Colombia, South America with a load of one-million Quaalude tablets they'd agreed to transport for a group of Colombian drug lords. Quaaludes were a prescription drug that was very popular among nightclub goers in the mid-70s to late 80s. It produced a melancholy high, and induced a pleasant euphoric feeling, giving rise to an unusually heightened sex drive and otherwise looseness, which attracted a large female clientele. These pills were illegally distributed in vast quantities at a 200% to 300% profit margin across many major cities throughout the United States.

JUDICIAL WEB

As fate would have it, Doc and Gary's plane had been running on fumes over Cuba, and with no place to refuel, they were forced to make an emergency landing in a tiny remote airport in Boscobel, Jamaica. Just prior to landing their distressed airplane, they threw out over the ocean, on their approach to Boscobel, a million tablets they were illegally transporting on board their aircraft.

Many natives, including the Jamaican authorities, spotted the dumping of the illegal contraband as the aircraft was making its final approach and made a successful emergency landing.

Once the plane landed, Doc and his accomplice, Gary, were immediately met by an entourage of police and C.I.D. officials, the Jamaican equivalent of our D.E.A. drug task force. Doc and Gary were placed under arrest, and subsequently charged with illegally entering and landing their aircraft, on the Island of Jamaica, without proper permission and documentation. This wound up being just the beginning of their problems.

Upon searching the aircraft, the police found an arsenal of ammunition, along with several handguns, which were strictly prohibited on the Island. Also, other incriminating evidence of their drug smuggling activities was found and confiscated.

Then came the news that the authorities had rounded up most of the Quaalude tablets from all over the Island, and by now, the heat was really brewing against Doc and Gary, big time. Their problems were further compounded by the fact that Doc never arrived where he was supposed to in Miami to deliver his payload of contraband to his anxiously awaiting Colombian partners, who had fully financed the operation. They wanted their merchandise, and it was nowhere to be found. The Colombians were getting very impatient and wanted to learn the whereabouts of Doc and Gary, and their several million dollars' worth of illegal contraband.

Word finally got out as to what had transpired, and the Colombians immediately headed for Jamaica to verify the story for themselves.

In the meantime, I found out that Doc and Gary were both facing a minimum of 10 years, of hard labor, in a Jamaican rat-infested prison for the severe criminal charges they were now facing.

A lawyer by the name of Victor Habbee was retained by Doc's wife, Sherry. Contrary to Doc's later trial testimony in my criminal proceedings, Sherry had paid for her husband's and Gary's Jamaican defense counsel, which cost $40,000.00, and that was just for starters.

Victor informed Sherry that things didn't look good at all for Doc and Gary. He informed her that the only way out of their entire mess was to pay off a few officials and smuggle Doc and Gary out of the country ASAP. The expensive King Air, which was the aircraft used for the smuggling operation, was to be forfeited to the Jamaican Air Force as part of the deal. It had a current market value of over $250,000.00. Oddly enough, Doc and Bennie miraculously retrieved the plane several months later when they had the balls to steal it from the Jamaican International Airport, where it was being stored, by paying off an official who ran the airport security. Talk about a set of brass balls.

Anyway, the deal was that on the day Doc and Gary were to be officially arraigned, by a Jamaican Judge, everything would be fixed by the lawyer and the corrupt officials, including the judge, who was also in on the payoff. We took a big risk in believing Victor had the clout to pull this off. Doc, Gary, and I all left Jamaica without ever showing up at the courthouse. We were given a two-hour head start before they would claim that Doc and Gary had escaped and were now fugitives from justice.

At first, we thought it was all a big setup. No sooner had we gotten fifteen minutes away from the courthouse when we were stopped at a roadblock. Our hearts were pumping heavily, and we thought we were busted. However, as fate had it choreographed, the police were looking for some native Jamaican youths who had just robbed

JUDICIAL WEB

a local liquor store, and off we went. Bennie was waiting at Kingston International Airport, with one of his private planes, to take all of us safely back home.

Can you imagine years later, during my grand jury and subsequent trial, Doc had the balls to testify, under sworn oath, that it was my drug deal in Jamaica, and all that happened to him there was my fault? He even had the nerve to tell the prosecutors that I ripped him off for the attorney's fees and expenses; that I was the one who retained Victor Habbee and caused all his problems in Jamaica. How's that for chutzpah!

Worse yet, when the Colombians arrived in Jamaica to learn where their merchandise was, Doc had gotten them word, claiming that I was to blame for their losses, and they put a contract out on my life. I didn't learn any of this until we were going to the Kingston airport to meet Bennie and get out of dodge. It was Victor who told me about this news on the QT, as he knew the truth about everything that happened there, and it was he who eventually convinced the Colombians who the real culprits were.

I don't know what my fate would have been had Victor not taken the initiative and shared the truth with the Colombians, who wound up approaching him after we had already departed for home on that eventful day.

At some later point in time, when I asked Doc if he knew anything about the deceitfulness just described, he told me that I was crazy for even thinking of such a thing, and I just let it go at that. Little did I know, until years later, that Victor had been telling me the truth all along.

To add to this amazing episode, and the luck that Doc and Gary had already experienced, the Colombians never pursued them again. It seems they were able to verify the story, as told by Victor, and chose to absorb their losses. Most likely, they were able to make a ton of other similar trips using other pilots to do their dirty work and continue making their multimillion-dollar drug runs.

After we arrived back home, safe and sound, Doc led me to believe that for my efforts and saving the day for him and Gary, we were really tight now and that I didn't have to worry anymore about the debt he and Bennie felt I still owed them. So, all in all, I felt I'd made the right decision after all. I'd now be able to tend to my ailing business affairs once again, especially the running of my recording studio and record companies.

During all this time, Marshall laid back and drowned himself in drugs. It became obvious to me that he had absolutely no further interest in changing his ways or making any effort to assist me with the everyday affairs of running our music related endeavors.

IT'S PAYBACK TIME

It was now early summer of 1985. Apparently, Doc hadn't learned his lesson from his close call in Jamaica several months earlier. This time he wound up being arrested and caught red-handed in Charlotte, North Carolina, with a shit load of high-grade Colombian cocaine. Mysteriously, Doc was acquitted on all his felony counts as charged. However, the civil forfeiture proceedings, which followed Doc's criminal case, resulted in a much different outcome. Doc had wound up forfeiting $500,000.00 in seized assets, including his expensive aircraft, which was confiscated as a direct result of his criminal acts.

For those non-legal buffs, under U.S. Federal laws, even if someone is fully exonerated and/or acquitted of a criminal act as charged, the possibility still exists of being sued in civil court, losing assets, and paying large fines regardless of a guilty or non-guilty verdict (e.g. OJ Simpson's civil trial and the multimillion-dollar jury rendered award to the Goldman family, on behalf of their son, Ron Goldman's wrongful death lawsuit by the Goldman estate, namely his parents, in lieu of OJ Simpson's full acquittal in his criminal proceedings). For Doc, the attorney fees were much steeper than they had been in the Jamaican ordeal. This time it cost him a whopping $350,000.00 in cash, not including the losses he sustained in his civil trial, plus whatever other amenities he wound up paying to his high-priced legal team, who once again managed to keep Doc out of jail.

The $350,000.00, as Doc had later told me, went to two very prominent and well-connected Charlotte, North Carolina attorneys, Robert Richards and Tom Delaney. Imagine, as fate would soon have it, these were the same two attorneys that eventually got Doc the deal of a lifetime, with a *'total immunity'* plea bargain agreement in my criminal case.

One evening over dinner, Doc related to me the scenario of his North Carolina acquittal. He bragged about once again beating the system, and how he had his high-priced lawyers take care of things, only this time the price tag was enormous, much more than he cared to elaborate. He said he had to take care of two F.B.I. agent friends of his who assisted him with his alibi and eventual acquittal. He clammed up when I tried to pry further about the details of his F.B.I. friends. He said that information was confidential and off limits to discuss any further.

In the meantime, Doc's liquid cash nest egg had dwindled greatly, and he desperately needed to do something ASAP to replenish it.

Against his better judgment, Doc approached Marshall, who was once again anxious to make a deal. Like Doc, Marshall was also low on liquid cash. The recording studio investment drained his pockets, and collections weren't coming in as he had anticipated. It seemed that a lot of Marshall's prior clients refused to deal with me. They only wanted to see Marshall and pay him directly. This presented a huge problem for the two of us.

As things turned out, Doc and Marshall tried putting together several successive drug deals, some of which went sour, and others paid off handsomely. However, the losses far exceeded the profits Marshall had reaped, and the pressure mounted considerably against him once again.

Apparently, neither of them learned their lesson, having worked together in the past. Marshall complained about how he believed Doc had ripped him off all over again. However, this time it cost Marshall dearly. The studio was now in serious trouble, and I was caught smack in the middle of it all. It was one nightmare after another.

It was pushing late summer 1985. Having my belly full, I decided it was long overdue for me to sever my relationship with Marshall once and for all. I felt not doing so would surely wreak havoc in my life. I let Doc know I was fed up with his shenanigans, too, and if he felt like retaliating against me, he should go right ahead and do so, otherwise I told him to leave me the hell alone. I had it, and no longer wished to be involved with his deceitful and greedy filled lifestyle anymore. It served me no further purpose to continue on this roller coaster ride with him and his two brothers. I felt, deep inside, doing otherwise could possibly result in devastating consequences.

Fast forward to summer's end 1985, where several events also led to the severing of my relationship with Doc, once and for all.

There was an investment that turned sour between Doc and I, involving a small independent commuter airline operating out of the Fort Lauderdale International Airport. Doc persuaded me, along with several others, to invest in this business opportunity. It seemed like a totally legitimate investment, which was made according to the books and heavily scrutinized by corporate counsel.

This airline, called Saturn Airlines, was looking to expand its operations and begin offering many more non-stop flights to the Bahamas and the Caribbean Islands. They needed a bigger hanger area to operate out of with several more planes. They also required a chunk of venture capital. Doc was friends with the company's founders, and came to their rescue, along with a group of his close associates, who were willing to invest in what was promised to be a very lucrative and rewarding return over the next few years.

Doc was flying for Saturn Airlines during the day, while also flying for Bennie's Coastal Airways in the evenings. Shortly after everyone jumped on board, looking to secure a windfall for their investments, it turned out that the executives of the company had a major falling out between themselves, and the company eventually folded. Initially, I never learned what the blow-up was all about. However, I had my suspicions, and years later they turned out to be quite accurate. It didn't take a rocket scientist to figure out what direction Doc was looking to take the company, and I gathered he was met with much opposition in his efforts to do so. Hence, the company never did get off the ground and soon folded. Unfortunately, everyone lost their money including me.

Doc, wanting to make good on the bad investment he got me involved in, came up with another wild business venture, which I reluctantly allowed him to pitch to me. This time it was something completely beyond my area of interest and/or expertise. The only reason I even gave Doc the time of day to try and sell me on this crazy business concept, was that I didn't have to pay a single penny of my money to jump in. It was all Doc's money, and all I had to do to earn my share of the profit would be to oversee the operation and find someone to manage the business for us. I guess you're wondering what sort of business. It was a hair cutting franchise like Super Cuts, by the name of Fabulous Sam's. This would be the straw that broke the camel's back, as the saying goes.

In late fall of 1985, Doc and I parted company on very bad terms, never to speak to each other again, at least that's what I'd hoped would be the case. The breakup was brutal and long overdue. Reflecting on things many years later, I should have bailed long before then, but unfortunately, fate prevented this from happening, as it had other plans in store for me.

If you're wondering what caused this breakup, it's an otherwise long and involved story. The long and short of it was Doc conned me into thinking that I wouldn't have to invest a single penny into the franchise, when all along he used my name, my credit, and my credentials to purchase the business in the first place. When things began to go sour, because the location Doc chose was a poor one, he bailed, took all of the expensive salon equipment, which I went on the limb for with my credit, and he left me with all the business debts, and all the headaches associated with the closing down of a now defunct business. The shit hit the fan with the landlord and creditors. Talk about another nightmare, it was the end of the line for me. To this day, I don't know how I managed to get myself out of that mess, but I did.

After I miraculously unraveled myself from the *Fabulous Sam's* debacle, I'd become totally fed up with all the scamming, deceit, conning, greed, you name it, and I just felt like I needed to get away from it all. I had my daughter, who would soon be graduating from high school, and a newborn son I wanted to raise into manhood. I knew in my heart that if I continued my association with Doc and Marshall, nothing good would come of it, and my dreams would all vanish into thin air. I wasn't about to let that happen. I'd made up my mind that I'd walk away, and I did just that.

Now, backtracking for a moment, in late 1984, I decided to close the recording studio and walk away from my dream. This was one of the hardest things I ever had to do in my life. As agreed, Marshall kept the studio building, and I would keep the recording studio equipment, which I felt I more than earned, and well deserved by working literally day and night since our grand opening, several years earlier.

After some time had passed, Doc reached out to me. He wanted a sit-down meeting to try and iron things out between us. He apologized for what he'd done to me, but said he had no other choice. He proceeded to inform me that he was forced into closing the franchise by the corporate office, which had eventually filed for bankruptcy several months later. How ironic was that! Maybe karma had something to do with it.

Anyway, I reluctantly agreed to meet with Doc, and after listening to his story and feeling somewhat sentimental, I accepted his apology and we made up, shook hands; and Doc led me to believe that everything between us was now cool, and for me to no longer worry about owing him anything more for all the trouble he'd caused me. This time we parted company on friendly terms. I told Doc to stay in touch, and we let things go at that.

Fast forward from the studio's closing to late winter of 1985, I once again used poor judgment and proceeded to introduce Doc to a gentleman by the name of Anthony, a long-time friend of my Dad. At around this time, Anthony was selling vacation timeshares on an island resort in Aruba. Aruba is a beautiful island and tourist attraction in the Dutch Antilles.

Let me digress for a moment. I was a guest on a cruise ship that one of my recording artists had been performing on at the time. Ironically, one of the cruise ship's stops was in Aruba. I decided on this trip to pay Anthony a surprise visit. After the ship had docked, I cleared customs and had a local taxi bring me to the address my dad had shared with me to meet up with Anthony. I had hours to kill before the ship's departure. I planned on doing some sightseeing and souvenir shopping at the same time.

I finally tracked Anthony down through his sales office staff. Boy, was he ever surprised to see me. My dad never mentioned to Anthony that I might be stopping by to see him, so the surprise was a big one. We enjoyed a lovely lunch together, and talked about Anthony's experiences while working in Aruba with his timeshare opportunity, where he was now the property sales manager. I inquired how he liked Aruba and the people, but much to my dismay, he opened up and had many negative things to share with me on that eventful day. One thing led to another, and after making some small talk, I got down to discussing some business inquiries with Anthony. I wanted to learn if he had any music contacts in Aruba or anywhere else in the surrounding Islands. I was interested in getting a few of my Latin music groups, Caribbean Island exposure. Anthony proceeded to inform me that he didn't know of any offhand. However, he'd keep his eyes and ears open as he frequently traveled to such places as Costa Rica, Colombia, Panama, Venezuela, and other countries in South America for the time-sharing company.

Anthony informed me that he was tired of Aruba. He suspected foul-play within the company because he wasn't getting paid his commissions promptly, and he was planning to seek employment opportunities elsewhere if things didn't turn around swiftly for him. Anthony further inquired if I knew of any potential employment opportunities for selling timeshares in South Florida. I informed him that I didn't know of any off hand, but if he needed a place to stay, he could certainly count on me to put him up for a while.

Within several weeks after I'd arrived back home, who do you think arrived at my doorstep? You guessed it, none other than Anthony, with a suitcase in hand. He said he'd quit the timeshare company due to fraudulent activities he uncovered and for non-payment of commissions owed to him. He said he was considering suing the host company to try and get the commissions they stiffed him for. I proceeded to inform Anthony that it would be a complete waste of his time, money, and effort, doing so, but he didn't seem to accept my advice.

Before leaving Aruba, while making his way to my South Florida residence, Anthony met a middle-aged gentleman by the name of Raul. He was involved in the export/import business. Anthony claimed Raul also bragged about having lucrative contacts in the music industry throughout South America, and he'd be delighted to meet Anthony and I for mutual money-making ventures. I informed Anthony that I was only interested in learning what legitimate music business contacts Raul had. I wanted to promote some exciting music concerts sporting some of the country's most popular recording artists and pop-rock bands. I needed to verify how bona fide Raul's contacts really were. I informed Anthony if he could secure the right venues through Raul's contacts, we'd make a fortune in the music concert and promotion business.

My plan was to acquire name-acts who hadn't had a hit record in a while. They wouldn't cost as much as the more popular acts, and since I had solid music connections in New York, I thought this was a no-brainer for us. I planned on having my recording artists, who were already signed to my record labels, open the shows for these named acts, thus providing my groups with maximum exposure and racking in the money for everyone.

It all sounded too good to be true, but with my thirst for success still driving me, coupled with the studio closing, and my yearning to do something big in the music business, I was all ears.

Anthony arranged for us to meet Raul in his native country of Colombia. Apparently, Raul didn't possess the required documents to travel to the United States on such short notice, at least that's what I was led to believe at the time. I don't recall the exact dates or time of year we flew to Colombia, but I was excited about making the trip and meeting Raul.

Raul met Anthony and I at the Bogotá International Airport. We then traveled directly to Medellín by way of a connecting short-excursion flight, and then settled in for the evening at the luxurious, Intercontinental Hotel.

This was my second trip to Medellín, Colombia. I visited there back in early 1983, when I hosted a rock concert with a heavy metal band I was managing at the time, to a sellout crowd of fifteen thousand ticket holders. The one thing that stood out from my last visit was the gorgeous women I met. I must admit, they were some of the most beautiful women I'd ever seen during my world travels.

Having traveled quite extensively in my life, I observed many Colombians that were poor, malnourished, and homeless, especially in the city of Medellín. At least that was the impression I had during both my visits there.

On the other hand, Bogotá, the country's prestigious capital and industrial hub of Colombia, was quite different. According to Raul, most of the country's big business deals were often conducted there.

All in all, the trip to Colombia was very enjoyable. Raul was a fine host, showing us all around the country's hot spots.

However, as things turned out, Raul never had any music contacts as he had boasted about, and I'm sorry to say nothing ever became of any music business. Instead, Raul had merely led me astray under an ulterior motive, which quickly became apparent.

It turned out, Raul's only business was illicit drug dealing. He seemingly had extensive ties to some of the world's biggest drug lords, with close ties to the Medellín Drug Cartel, as we'd soon learned. I wondered, to myself, if Anthony new this all along. Being desperate to make some quick money, Anthony pursued the opportunities firsthand. He'd often heard me speak about a friend, whose name was Doc, who made a ton of money as a pilot and drug smuggler.

Reluctantly, I arranged for Anthony to meet Doc, which later proved to be another grave mistake on my part. As things soon turned out, Anthony and Doc, along with Raul, and his top Columbian drug cartel contacts, had eventually formed their own international drug smuggling network.

During the next two years, from late 1984, just after closing the recording studio, to April of 1986, Marshall and his clan continued selling drugs up and down the East Coast.

Many of Marshall's distributors were eventually busted and they became government confidential informants, a/k/a snitches, or rats in the drug netherworld. They swiftly implicated Marshall as their main source of cocaine and marijuana, and in the same vein, they elected to name me as Marshall's main money launderer and business partner. In other words, they claimed that I was the brains behind the entire organization.

Then, through a twist of fate, as they say, Doc got caught up in the scandal via a one chance in a million happening. He was being investigated by the IRS for improprieties surrounding his Fabulous Sam's defunct haircutting salons, and their franchise operation, which went belly up due to a barrage of complaints stemming from documented discriminatory practices made by several disgruntled employees.

The IRS Agent who was conducting the extensive, and wide ranging undercover investigation, was also investigating, by mere coincidence, Marshall's top drug smuggling mule, who eventually became a witting, cooperating, government informant, as we later learned. Then, by a stroke of bad luck, the two scenarios were eventually meshed together, and the shit finally hit the fan.

Doc was quick to see it all coming down. Realizing he, too, would soon be in the hot seat, he immediately employed the expertise, once again, of none other than his two hot shot Tennessee lawyers. Remember them? To this very day, I have never figured out how they were able to acquire a plea-bargain, granting Doc complete and full immunity from any criminal prosecution, in exchange for his full cooperation, and the new informant role he'd soon play.

Imagine, total immunity from prosecution for all his previously committed drug felonies, and they were plentiful by the time he was finally caught, as well as his involvement in one of the biggest international drug-smuggling and distribution networks in the USA at the time. Now for the double 'twist of fate' in this bizarre story.

Doc makes the deal of a lifetime with the government. He offers to go to the grand jury and testify, under sworn oath, against me.

He lies to save his own neck, and places me at the apex of the entire drug-smuggling organization, naming me as his boss. He does all this, despite his immunity agreement, and his promise to tell the complete truth concerning all his illegal drug-smuggling activities and criminal involvement. Instead, Doc chooses to minimize his true involvement, all to my severe and prejudicial detriment.

Doc elected to place me at the top of the entire organization. He made me out to be the boss of all bosses, while implicating me at the hierarchy of what was to be known as the largest drug-smuggling operation on the East Coast of the United States. However, the reality all along was Doc was the real drug kingpin, and not me.

What became even more egregious was the mere fact that the government prosecutors knew or should have known all along about Doc's dishonesty, deceitfulness, his obstruction of justice, coupled with the government's subornation of perjury during my criminal proceedings. It took nearly eight-years of my life to prove all this, and to eventually undue the egregious acts of 'gross' prosecutorial misconduct, all of which eventually set the foundation for my post-conviction relief process, and the eventual reversal of my drug kingpin conviction, which finally set me free.

To recap things, Gary, Little George, Big George, Felix, Marshall, Frank, Nat, and me, along with many other co-conspirators, were rounded up and arrested on April 22, 1986, by the U.S. Marshals, DEA Agents, and local law enforcement officials, from around the country.

By the time we went to trial and halfway through the nightmare of all nightmares, there would only be three of us left in our criminal case, myself, my brother, and our only co-defendant, Little George. All the rest chose to plead guilty, cooperate with federal authorities, and agreed to forfeit all their ill-gotten gains. However, there were two exceptions. One was a Chilean by the name of Felix

Nova, and the other was Eduardo Torquet, a/k/a Big George, who was the alleged Colombian cocaine source for Marshall and his entire distribution network.

Big George went to trial separately from my other co-defendants and me, and was subsequently convicted on all counts as charged and sentenced under the drug kingpin, Title 21, Section 848 statute, to twenty-five years without benefit of parole. Nova's last known status was a fugitive from justice. He stuck his family and friends for his bond, which was $150,000.00 USD, and fled the country several days prior to going to trial. He was lucky to have been granted bail and was on house arrest. His whereabouts are still a mystery and unknown to this very day. Lucky Felix, wherever you are!

Unbeknown to Doc and the United States Attorney's Office for the District of Maryland, Raul Rafael, in the spring of 1987, along with his partner-in-crime, Victor Santes, were busted with 750 kilos of pure, Colombian cocaine, while traveling by private air charter from Colombia, South America, into Orlando International Airport. It turned out Raul's co-pilot wasn't who he professed to be, but rather an undercover DEA agent, who had successfully infiltrated the highest ranks of the infamous drug lord *'Gacha'*, and his multi-billion-dollar Colombian drug cartel. As a direct result of this major drug bust, both Raul and Victor were facing life sentences without the benefit of parole. So, as an offer of leniency, Raul and Victor decided to immediately cooperate with the U.S. Attorney's Office for the Middle District of Florida.

As the plot began to thicken, it was later discovered that Victor Santes was already cooperating with the authorities, and had set-up his partner, Raul, by vouching for the undercover D.E.A. pilot's credibility, when Victor knew otherwise to be the case. It was later learned that Victor was busted prior to making the run with Raul, and was facing serious charges at the time. Victor had no choice, and agreed to set up Raul with a big load of cocaine. His reason for doing so was the D.E.A. knew that Raul had close ties to high ranking cartel members who were supplying nearly eighty percent of the cocaine making its way into the United States during the late 1980's. The D.E.A. wanted Raul very badly, and made Victor their patsy to do their dirty work and nail him. The plan was to bust Raul, and have him become a government informant; then have him give the D.E.A. the big fish they'd been patiently waiting to reel in for many years.

Raul's initial debriefings took place during my criminal trial, and continued well into my appellate process. My criminal trial began in late December 1986 and concluded in mid-April 1987, some 14-weeks later. My Direct Appeal and Oral Argument, after I was found guilty of all counts as charged, was heard before a three-judge appellate panel before the Fourth Circuit Court of Appeals, in Richmond, Virginia, in early October 1987, six long and agonizing months later.

In early June 1988, eight months later, after waiting patiently for a miracle to happen, the Fourth Circuit Court of Appeals rendered its unanimous (per-curiam) 'Unpublished Opinion.' The Appeals Court AFFIRMED the lower court's jury verdict, and down the drain went any hope of me getting a new trial, or any relief from my thirty-five year, without parole, sentence. In other words, it appeared that all hope was now lost, and I was going to have to accept the reality that I'd be spending the rest of my adult-life in federal prison.

Raul, during all this time, was meeting with the United States Attorneys for the Middle District of Florida as well as the District of Maryland. He provided them with all sorts of contradictory information about their 'star witness,' in my criminal proceedings, as well as nineteen other similarly situated criminal trials during his cooperation. Of course, I'm talking about the infamous, Jon '*Doc*' Gerritt.

Apparently, Raul was under the impression Doc was the one who had set them up at the Orlando International Airport, when Raul and Victor were caught red handed with 750 kilos of pure Colombian cocaine.

During Raul's voluminous debriefings with top government officials, including high-level F.B.I., D.E.A. operatives, as well as Interpol agents, he inculpated not only Doc, but also many others, who he'd claimed were involved with him in the drug netherworld, at the highest levels of his international, drug-smuggling operation.

However, as fate would have it, while sharing his story, which the government felt was overwhelmingly credible and extraordinarily compelling, they would eventually be forced to name Doc as an unindicted co-conspirator in what was later known as the Anthony Dean, criminal indictment, which was unsealed, also out of the District of Maryland, in December 1988. However, for some strange, unknown, and logic defying reasons, Doc remained free as a bird, and was still yet to be indicted or arrested.

As a direct result of both Victor and Raul's cooperation, and their testimonies during Anthony's investigation, conducted by none other than Special Agent Jones, Anthony, his son, Richard, and several others were indicted in June 1989, and subsequently prosecuted out of the United States District Court for the Eastern District of Maryland. The Assistant U.S. Attorney who handled that case, was none other than Andy Nolan, the same prosecutor who prosecuted me several years earlier.

All the accused were subsequently convicted upon the conclusion of their criminal trial, with some pleading guilty, and sentences ranging from probation to ten-years in federal prison without parole.

As fate would have it, Anthony received the harshest sentence of all those prosecuted in his criminal case. The court sentenced him to ten-years, without parole, despite pleading guilty to a Title 21-Section 848, drug kingpin offense.

The Government came to Anthony with a lucrative plea bargain agreement, which wound up sparing him from a possible draconian sentence, such as mine, at the age of 65. Anthony chose this one-time offer, which, ironically, years later turned out to be the meal ticket to my eventual release, and long-awaited freedom from federal prison.

It should be duly noted that Raul was the government's '*star witness*' during Anthony's criminal trial, along with Victor Santes. Anthony's reasoning for eventually pleading out, a few weeks into his trial, was because he knew Raul's testimony would be so precise and accurate; he didn't want to chance being found guilty, which would have, no doubt, resulted in him receiving a much harsher punishment, than his otherwise generous, ten-year sentence the Government offered him.

Raul's testimony, during Anthony's trial, which continued after he'd pleaded out, had unequivocally exculpated me of being a drug-kingpin. Truth be told, it was Raul's otherwise convincing testimony, which was completely contradicting, and exculpatory as to what Doc had falsely testified to during my criminal investigation, grand jury testimony, and follow-up trial proceedings, back in 1986.

The horror of it all was the government had known all along that Doc was lying, and Raul's testimony was the true version of the events surrounding my criminal investigation and subsequent indictment, for which I was wrongfully and prejudicially convicted of, under the harshest criminal statute in the government's arsenal of criminal offenses, a Title 21 U.S.C. Section 848, Continuing Criminal Enterprise Statute, a/k/a as the Drug Kingpin statute.

Furthermore, to add insult to injury, Raul had exculpatory information about my alleged criminal activities, for which Doc had been lying, under oath, while testifying and committing perjury throughout my entire criminal investigation, and subsequent criminal proceedings, especially during my trial.

This highly exculpatory information was readily available to the prosecution team in my criminal proceedings, including Special Agent Jones, both Assistant U.S. Attorneys, the U.S. Attorney, and the F.B.I. agents involved in my criminal proceedings, all of which had been intentionally withheld prior to, during, and long after my criminal trial, appeal process, and post-conviction relief proceedings, which were, without question, to my severe and prejudicial detriment.

Had this pertinent and exculpatory evidence been made available to my attorney in a timely fashion, according to the federal discovery laws, under the Brady Discovery Act, I strongly maintain that the outcome of my criminal trial would have produced a much more favorable verdict and sentencing outcome.

Equally important, had this information been properly presented to the grand jury as well as during my criminal trial, I maintain that I never would've been found guilty of being a drug kingpin. In all likelihood, I would never have been indicted or made to serve a single day in federal prison in the first place.

Instead, in prejudicial fashion, the government's prosecution team saw it more convenient to subvert justice, and conveniently bury their heads in the sand. You could say they were hoping it would all go away totally undetected. Boy, were they soon to be in for a rude awakening!

Remember the opening pages of my book where the quotes read, *'Truth Crushed To Earth Shall Rise Again,'* and *'No Lie Can Live Forever.'* As my story continues to unfold, these quotes will soon come to life, and play a significant part of my adventurous story.

PRE-ARREST EVENTS

It was now the winter of 1986, mid-February to be precise, and unbeknown to me at the time, nearly one-thousand miles away, in a city known primarily for its heavy smog and pollution, Baltimore, Maryland, at the United States Courthouse, located at 101 West Lombard Street, a Federal Grand Jury had convened to seek a true bill, otherwise known as a criminal indictment against me, and seven other co-conspirators as named. The government's '*star witness,*' as you must have already surmised by now, was the infamous Jon 'Doc' Gerritt.

Even as far back as February 1986, as it will later be made clear to you, the Government '*knew*' or '*should*' have known that Doc had committed perjury when he testified before the grand jury in my criminal case.

I'd like to now share with you a chronology of events leading up to my eventual arrest and conviction under the harshest federal offense in the government's arsenal of criminal statutes. An offense, if you can fathom this for a moment, was worse than had I attempted to assassinate the President of the United States. When Hinckley attempted to kill President Reagan, his sentence upon conviction, unlike mine, came with parole possibilities.

As I later learned, nearly seven years later, Doc's grand jury testimony was replete with perjury. Perjury, so antithetical to my right to due process, had the Government treated me fairly, in all likelihood I would never have been indicted under the Continuing Criminal Enterprise, Title 21-Section 848 Drug Kingpin statute. I wouldn't have been given a 35-year, non-parolable sentence or lost all my worldly possessions, including my home. I wouldn't have been taken away from my daughter I'd been raising as a single parent, and my son, who recently turned a year old, and needed me around to help raise him. Furthermore, I wouldn't have lost nearly eight precious years of my life, while wasting away in numerous federal prisons around the country like I did.

Reflecting on the winter of 1986, I was tired of Miami's hustle and bustle lifestyle that surrounded me at the time. I'd been involved in several unsuccessful legitimate business ventures, and financially I was barely getting by. During this time frame, the only thing keeping me afloat was the mild success my brother and I achieved from our thoroughbred horse racing entity.

I guess you could say we experienced beginner's luck. Our first claimer, 'Shadow Boy,' won five consecutive races before he was claimed for a whopping $70,000.00. Less than a year earlier, we claimed 'Shadow Boy' for only $7,500.00. All totaled, we grossed $250,000.00 during our first year of racing. However, training expenses, high vet bills, coupled with the unexpected losses of two of our prized stallions, due to viral infections, caused us to nearly lose our horse-racing enterprise.

My plans were to immediately liquidate the few assets I had left, sell my townhouse, and relocate to the West Coast of Florida. Once there, I planned to open another recording studio, and my brother and I were anxious to continue developing our horse racing business. The only obstacle from executing this well-thought-out plan was that my daughter would be graduating from high school in the spring. I knew I couldn't make any sudden moves until then.

Back in Baltimore, Maryland, the grand jury voted to indict and seal criminal case number, MM-041986, and my fate was soon etched in stone.

My criminal indictment was eventually unsealed by the Eastern District Court in Baltimore, Maryland, and arrest, search and seizure warrants were subsequently executed on April 22, 1986.

JUDICIAL WEB

The defendants named in the indictment, as they appeared in the original document, were listed as follows:

Marshall Smith, a/k/a 'Mo'

Eduardo Torquet, a/k/a 'Big George'

Steve Silva, a/k/a 'Steve'

Nat Smith, a/k/a 'Nat the Cat'

Frank Smith, a/k/a 'Frankie'

Jorge Christo, a/k/a 'Little George'

Felix Nova, a/k/a 'Felix the Cat'

Gary Silva, a/k/a 'Gary'

It was now approaching the early spring of 1986, and the weather was beginning to get warmer, with the annual '*Spring Weekend*' just around the corner.

It was a wonderful time of the year for me. I was in the prime of my life, looking very much forward to my daughter's high school graduation, and our plans to relocate were looking brighter by the day.

I enjoyed raising my one-year old son, Joshua, along with his mom. Our racing stable was on the verge of recuperating from a streak of bad luck, and life was good. I couldn't have been happier at this time in my life. However, soon all this would dramatically change from a most unexpected, life-changing event, which would take me on a whirlwind ride, with trials and tribulations, and nearly had me spending the rest of my adult life in federal prison.

DAY OF ARREST

I've already explained the circumstances that led to my eventual arrest. However, in this chapter I wish to elaborate in much greater detail on this most horrific day of my life. It was Tuesday morning, April 22, 1986. I'll never forget this day for as long as I live.

I don't know why, but I experienced a very restless night. I didn't get to sleep until after 1:00 a.m. The next day was supposed to be an exciting one for me and Gary. That afternoon one of our horses was finally going to make his racing debut. I needed to get to the paddock area by noon to speak with our trainer and to make certain all systems were a go for the race.

The weather forecast called for a forty-percent chance of rain that day. We had an inclination our thoroughbred would race well on the slow and muddy track if it rained long and hard enough prior to post-time. Our trainer felt confident our horse would be in the money and earn us a decent winning purse, coupled with the parlay bets we had all planned to make.

My daughter awoke to her usual 6:00 a.m. bedside alarm, hopped into the shower, dressed, grabbed a bite to eat, and was out the door by 7:15 a.m. The school bus picked everyone up on the corner by 7:30 a.m., and Stacy would arrive for her first class by 8:00 a.m. that morning.

At a nearby shopping plaza called *Honeybees*, a stone's throw from my home, a slew of DEA and FBI special agents, along with other local law enforcement personnel, were conducting a tactical and logistical pre-raid briefing in the adjacent parking lot.

JUDICIAL WEB

They orchestrated their game plan for executing arrests and search and seizure warrants for Gary and me, along with Marshall, Frank, and Nat.

Across from my residence, in the nearby visitor's parking lot, unbeknown to me at the time, were several federal marshals who had been monitoring the activities at my front door since early morning.

As my daughter left for school and passed the agents, who were conveniently camouflaged, they radioed to everyone at the shopping plaza that the coast was clear, that my daughter had left for school, and all systems were now a go to catch their '*big fish*' of the day.

Taken directly from the DEA, Form-6 document, this is exactly what the report read concerning my arrest on that eventful day (with actual names and dates changed).

Details:

1). On April 22, 1986, at about 6:30 a.m., Special Agents Sandy Jones, Lawrence Foley, and Jay Robins, of the Washington, D.C. District Office (DEA), accompanied by (IRS-CID) Special Agents Bob Baits, Ron Trent, from Baltimore, Stanley Lambert, and Lenny Bleski, from Fort Lauderdale, AUSA Greg Wells, and AUSA Andy Nolan, Baltimore, U.S. Attorney's Office, all of whom met with Miami Group 5 Agents, at the Miami District Office (MDO), for a pre-raid briefing conducted by G/S Patrick Shell, and S/A Betsy Culliham.

2). At about 7:30 a.m., raid teams for both Smith's and Silva's residence met with uniformed North Miami Beach Police Officers, near Sunny Isles Blvd and Northeast 45th Avenue, in North Miami Beach. A final brief gathering was conducted before the arrests and execution of search warrants were enforced at Smith's and Silva's residence.

3). Shortly before 8:00 a.m., S/A Lawrence Foley, accompanied by S/A Jay Robins and MDO S/A's Danacheski, Williamsport, (IRS-CID), S/A's Bleski, Trent, and AUSA Greg Wells knocked several times on Silva's front door without a response. A next-door neighbor advised S/A Foley that Silva was not at home. The decision was immediately made to forcibly enter Silva's residence to execute the search warrant. Shortly thereafter, the front door of Silva's family residence was forcibly opened, and Silva was located by Special Agent (S/A) Williamsport in the second-floor master bedroom shower, where he was subdued and arrested. S/A Foley advised Silva of his constitutional Miranda rights. Silva declined to make any statements and asked to speak with his attorney. S/A Foley advised Silva that he'd be allowed to speak to an attorney after he arrived at the MDO for processing.

4). Silva was transported by S/A's Foley and Trent to the MDO for processing once Silva's residence was secured after the execution of the search warrant. After Silva was processed at the MDO, he was turned over to the U.S. Marshals Service in Miami for incarceration, pending a bond hearing before the Honorable U.S. Magistrate Holyfield, on April 28, 1986, Monday morning at 9 a.m.

The above-captioned notes were transcribed verbatim from my D.E.A. Form-6 files dated April 29, 1986, and signed off by Senior Head D.E.A. Special Agent Sandy Jones (only the names and dates have been changed to protect individual identities and their personal interests).

On this bleakest day of my life, a combination of more than twenty U.S. Marshals, DEA and FBI special agents, as well as local law enforcement personnel swarmed down on my residence at exactly 8:00 a.m. I remember the time vividly, as the alarm in my master bedroom sounded at precisely 8:00, and by the time I arose and shut it off and jumped into the shower, I heard the pounding sounds, which I didn't pay any attention to at the time. It sounded like the noise was coming from the next-door neighbor's residence.

JUDICIAL WEB

The next thing I remember was being dragged out of my shower, stark naked, handcuffed, and thrown to the floor. I was then told that I was under arrest, that I had the right to remain silent, that anything I said could and would be held against me in a court of law, and that I had the right to an attorney.

Then, an entourage of DEA agents came rampaging through my home from every nook and corner. They came with enough firepower to wipe out the entire neighborhood. I guess you could say I was literally scared to death. I didn't know what to think or say as I lay frozen on my bathroom floor, trying desperately to make sense of the entire situation. I had to muster every bit of strength in my mind and body to refrain myself from going into shock, that's how bad it was. I couldn't move a single muscle in my entire body as one of the agents, a female I might add, had placed her grime-laced, fatigue boot smack in the center of my right cheekbone and pressed hard on my face so that I would remain still. Talk about barbaric conduct, but that's exactly how it all went down.

By now the local news reporters, and neighborhood curiosity seekers, were all over my property. TV crews from every local network were parked outside my front door, awaiting a glimpse of the government's '*big fish*' of the day. However, as fate would have it, years later they'd all learn just how wrong they all got it. The Government's prejudicial conduct was egregious against me. I was merely a '*guppy*' in a big ocean. As events continued to unfold, the really '*big fish,*' perhaps one of the biggest fish of the decade, came awfully close to getting away scot-free.

My home was trashed as if a herd of wild stallions had just run rampantly through it, leaving it in total shambles. I could only imagine how my daughter would react when she returned from school later that afternoon and saw our home totally ransacked.

By now all the neighbors had gathered around my broken and smashed in front door and shattered glass picture window, all in total shock. They must have all watched in awe, as government agents turned my home inside out while executing the Court ordered search and seizure warrant. I'm sure it was a day they'd never forget.

As I began slowly coming to my senses, I remember telling the arresting officers that there must have been a major mistake. I even recall saying '*April Fool's Day*' has come and gone. With that comment floating in the air, one of the DEA Special Agents remarked: "*We have a comedian among us, fellows.*" Just then I heard, "*Silva, you're going to be going away for a long, long time. Make no mistake about that!*" It was one of the agent's voices coming from my crowded bedroom.

Then the head case agent, Sandy Jones, spoke to me sternly, "*We know all about your drug smuggling operation. You can talk to us now and tell us everything you know, and we'll see to it that you wind up getting the minimum mandatory 10-year sentence (without parole) or you can choose to play hard-ball with us, and in that case we'll see to it that you'll get a life sentence without the benefit of parole. Do you copy that?*"

I thought I was having a very bad nightmare, and soon it would all be over. Not so! On the contrary, this experience was to be the greatest living nightmare of my entire life.

The weirdest thing of all was the chain of events that took place shortly after my arrest. It hit me hard as nails to discover the friends I once thought I had, were all gone in one small puff. The one very close friend of mine, at least I thought this was the case, turned out to be the one most responsible for my current predicament. His name, you already know, is Jon 'Doc' Gerritt. And to think this was the same person whose life I'd saved on more than one occasion, seemed so unfair and hurtful to me.

I'm ashamed to say it, but I literally cried uncontrollably when I first learned that it was Doc who went to the grand jury back in

JUDICIAL WEB

January of 1986, and through his shear lies, deceitfulness, conniving and cunning ways, he was able to convince the grand jury to indict me, along with seven other co-conspirators who were also named in the unsealed criminal indictment.

Doc was so good that he convinced the U.S. Government, and their entire prosecution team, that I was the drug kingpin and not him. After all, who wouldn't believe someone like Doc, with an extensive and impressive law enforcement background, decorated for valor, a ten-plus year veteran of the Fort Lauderdale Sheriff's Department, who claimed to be an undercover agent for the FBI, DEA, and U.S. Customs Services, all at the same time. Who would believe Doc could be involved in the drug-smuggling netherworld, never mind being very involved. The problem now for me was how would I prove all this to be otherwise.

Obviously, the government thoroughly believed Doc's side of the story, having granted him full immunity from prosecution if he agreed to cooperate and testify truthfully. The only problem was Doc lied! He did such a great job of doing so, that he convinced the grand jury to indict me, and then my trial jury to convict me of crimes that he alone was guilty of.

At my sentencing hearing, referencing Doc's compelling trial testimony, which was riddled with lies and deceitful statements, and sworn under the penalty of perjury, the Government insisted I receive a sixty-year sentence without the benefit of parole.

For the record, I was a first-time offender with no prior criminal record whatsoever. I had no prior run-ins with the law, and the evidence at trial was wholly circumstantial at best, which was based solely on the Government's snitches and their deceitful hearsay testimonies.

POST ARREST EVENTS

After my arrest, I was escorted by U.S. Marshals to their Miami District Office (MDO) for further processing. Marshall, Frank, and Nat were accompanying me in the Marshals' van. They'd been arrested moments earlier. Together we stared at one another, trying to assess the seriousness of the situation. I began to quickly put together the pieces of the puzzle in my mind. I hadn't seen the Smith brothers for many months prior to the day of our arrests.

When I first laid eyes on Marshall and Nat, I felt truly sorry for both of them. They were '*three sheets to the wind.*' In other words, stoned and drugged out of their minds. As I later learned, they'd been smoking crack cocaine for days and didn't know who they were, where they were going, or what was in store for them. They seemed totally oblivious to their surroundings, and the fact they'd just been busted and immediately arrested by Federal Drug Enforcement Agents had yet to sink in or startle them.

Marshall broke down and cried like a baby, and Nat did the same. I was sitting between both of them, numb as could be, and thinking about one thing and one thing only, what a shock this was going to be for my daughter, who was about to graduate from high school in a few weeks. The thought of not being there for her sent chills up and down my spine.

Stacy was due home from school in a few hours, and when she arrived, she'd find our home turned upside down, ransacked, and left in total shambles. She'd have a message from my next-door neighbor, telling her not to worry, not to talk to anyone, and for her to immediately call my sister or my dad as soon as possible.

Up to this point, I wasn't aware of the fact that my brother had also been arrested and was being escorted by DEA special agents to the MDO for further processing. Things would never be the same for the Silva family from that day forward.

I knew better than to speak in the Marshals' van, for fear they'd misconstrue my conversation with the Smith brothers. I advised Marshall and Nat not to speak either. I made it clear to both of them not to answer any questions or say a word to anyone. Period! I told Marshall that I'd be getting in touch with my lifelong friend, Vincent Flannigan, as soon as I was able to get a call to him. Vincent made an excellent name for himself as one of South Florida's top criminal defense attorneys. Luckily, and what I didn't know at the time, Vincent's specialty was defending drug offenders. Vincent and I had known each other for over twenty-five years. I knew he would not let me down.

The ride to the MDO seemed like eternity. I had a million and one unanswered questions going through my mind. How could this be happening, I asked myself over and over again. I hadn't associated with Marshall or his brothers for many months prior to our arrests. I knew better, and I even warned Marshall a year earlier that if he didn't get his act together, he and his two brothers would surely end up in jail. That was my premonition way back then. However, I never would've believed I'd be right smack in the middle of it all when the shit hit the fan.

I kept searching my mind for clues and answers. Something that would make sense, but only blank thoughts came to my mind. Nothing, whatsoever, seemed to fit the situation at hand. Nothing! I did surmise one thing was for certain, as we pulled into the MDO headquarters, this was no longer a dream, in fact, it was as real as real could be, and about to get much more real as the days, weeks, and months unfolded.

Upon our arrival, each of us was placed in separate holding cells, waiting for further processing orders. About a half-hour or so had lapsed. I heard a lot of commotion; what sounded like a familiar voice. Sure enough, as I peeked my head through the wire mesh window, in the jail cell I was being held in, I couldn't believe my eyes. There, smack in front of me, on the other side of the steel door, was my brother, Gary, and another co-defendant, Felix Nova, who would later become a fugitive from justice.

As I had later learned, Felix, a native of Colombia, eventually made bail and soon thereafter made his way back to his homeland, never to be seen or heard from again. Way to go Felix, wherever you are these days! Just as a side note, had Felix stayed around and gone to trial, along with the rest of us, he would have most likely received a harsher sentence than I did. As we later learned, during our trial proceedings, Felix had direct ties to the Colombian Drug Cartel at its highest levels.

My brother's face was full of blood, much of it was dried by now, and directly covering his right eye, with blood still oozing from what appeared to be a rather large golf-ball-size lump on his forehead. I began pounding the steel door with tears filling my eyes. My brother looked in my direction, saw my face in the window and said with a quiver in his voice, *"Bro, don't tell me they got you too!"* I simply nodded my head in despair, and as choked up as I was, I immediately asked how he got banged in the head. He replied, *"Not now; I'll tell you more when we can talk privately."*

Minutes later the five of us were escorted out of our cells to a downstairs basement and fortress-like area. We were immediately approached by S/A Sandy Jones, who introduced himself as the lead DEA case agent handling our criminal investigation.

Agent Jones looked no more like a veteran twenty-year DEA Agent, mind you, a decorated one with honors, than my cousin Sandy. Both weighed over 275 pounds, had beer-barrel bellies, pudgy faces, long curly, dirty-blonde shoulder-length hair, extremely unpretentious, and innocuous looking to boot. After the polite but stern introduction, Special Agent Jones proceeded to call each of us, one by one, to come forward, take our fingerprints, and infamous mugshots.

I finally had a few minutes to speak privately with my brother. He informed me about the incompetent, ruthless, and careless federal agents he had to deal with during his arrest and search warrant procedures. He said it was shameful how they treated him. Gary continued to inform me what fools we were not to have distanced ourselves from the Smith brothers much sooner. Like me, Gary knew one thing was inevitable, sooner or later, the Smith brothers were all going to be arrested and sent to prison for a very long time. The three brothers were addicted to cocaine and marijuana. They ingested large amounts of cocaine daily and were stoned most of their waking hours.

However, as we'd later learn, none of that mattered in the overall scheme of things. The truth was, even if we stayed completely clear of the Smith brothers, as much as a year earlier, with the conspiracy laws being what they were and what they stood for during our criminal proceedings, regardless of whether or not we disassociated ourselves from the Smith brothers long before we had, we would have, with great probability, still been indicted as co-conspirators, and most likely been found guilty of conspiracy charges, and sent to federal prison anyway. However, in my case, it would have been for a much less period of time, and I wouldn't have lost all my worldly possessions like I eventually did. *That was my biggest gripe*!

My brother informed me that he was intentionally struck over his forehead with the butt of a gun by one of the DEA agents involved in his arrest. Gary explained how the agents that stormed his apartment kept calling him by the wrong name. A name he'd never heard before. They kept calling him by the name of Felix, and my brother was trying to inform the agents that his name was not Felix.

For the record, and setting things straight, there was no search warrant issued for Gary's apartment, never mind ramming down his front door, totally ransacking it, and leaving his place in shambles with total disregard for his personal belongings, furniture, clothing, etc., or for that matter, his well-being.

When the authorities finally subdued Gary, one of the arresting officers shouted, as he picked up my brother's U.S. Passport from the kitchen table, "*I think we have the wrong guy. This guy is Gary Silva, according to his U.S. Passport, not Felix Nova. What the hell are we going to do now?*" The agent yelled out in a state of panic.

Here's the irony of it all. Years later, everyone present at the time of my brother's arrest would all have to answer, before a federally mandated mediation board, for their ruthless, overbearing tactics and excessive use of force at the time of my brother's arrest.

As a matter of fact, these same federal agents were made to pay Gary a decent sum of money for their unprofessional and overzealous behavior, which caused my brother to endure significant pain and suffering at the time of his arrest. I knew all this because I was the one who filed the Federal Tort Claim action against all six DEA agents. Talk about '*Just Desserts.*'

I tried to absorb the rest of the scenario. Gary quickly tried to share with me. However, just as we were finishing up, S/A Agent Jones intervened, and instructed us to follow him back to the holding cell area.

I was finally afforded my one call, and luckily, I was able to reach Vincent, my criminal attorney friend. I explained to him as best as possible; with the limited time I was afforded on the phone, my brother and I were in a serious predicament. Vincent's advice for

JUDICIAL WEB

Gary and I was to simply just sit tight, keep our mouths shut, don't discuss the case with anyone under any circumstance, keep strong, and he'd be by later that evening with some concrete answers for us.

Now for a little background on my lawyer friend, Vincent, one of the finest and most well-respected criminal defense attorneys in all of South Florida. Vincent had many high-profile criminal cases during his long career. He managed to win almost all of them before some of the toughest judges and juries in the state of Florida and elsewhere in the U.S. judicial system.

Vincent and I both grew up in northern New Jersey. He attended the local high school by the name of Seton Hall Prep. I attended Union High School, in a middle-class community, in Union, NJ. As fate would have it, our two high schools were archrivals when it came to baseball and wrestling.

Vincent, like me, was a varsity grappler back in the mid-1960s. I was the Varsity Captain of our undefeated wrestling team when we competed against one another's high schools in November 1963, just before President John F. Kennedy was assassinated. Vincent was also the Varsity Captain of his team.

Vincent and I met on the mats twice during our high school wrestling years. On both occasions, as I kidded him many years later, he tried everything he could do to keep his shoulders from touching the mat for a count of three. However, I must admit, no matter what maneuvers I tried to put on Vincent to lay his shoulders square on the mat beneath us, he refused to allow me to pin him. Our first match ended 13-0, my victory.

Several months later, we met again; this would be the last time we'd do so, but the competition was much stiffer this time. We were now wrestling in the District Finals, and this tournament was a gruesome one at that. I must admit, Vincent really surprised the hell out of me that day. The final score of that archrival match, after two periods of sudden death overtime, ended 6-5, once again, in my favor. I had to give it my all on that eventful day to defeat Vincent. Years later, when we finally caught up with each other, we had some very good laughs over those two unforgettable wrestling matches.

It was through Vincent's sheer determination, during both of our matches, in never allowing me the satisfaction of pinning him, that won my enduring respect and admiration toward him for the rest of my life. I believe, years later, this character trait provided Vincent with the impetus to become one of Miami's finest criminal defense attorneys.

After high school, Vincent went on to complete his undergraduate studies at Seton Hall University, and then on to Yale University School of Law, where he graduated with honors. Before I forget, while Vincent didn't have much success as a grappler, he took up boxing, and became a Golden Gloves, Featherweight Champion. Angelo Dundee, who was Muhammad Ali's trainer for many years, invited him to turn pro. However, Vincent elected the profession of criminal law instead, and boy was I happy he chose to do so.

Upon graduating from law school, Vincent landed a job in the Miami, Florida Public Defender's Office, Federal Division. He was assigned to death row inmates and racked up a very impressive career by having never lost any of his clients to the death sentence. Over the years, Vincent earned a hell of a reputation as a Public Defender, and eventually he made the career move to branch out on his own. He opened his own law firm in South Miami, Florida, which became extremely successful and remains so to this day.

Strange, as things tend to be at times, I didn't see or hear from Vincent for close to fifteen-years. However, as fate would have it, sometime in mid-1980, while my band was performing one evening, at the then famous Marriott Celebrity Roof Top Lounge, during my drum solo performance, I noticed, out of the corner of my right eye, sitting at the bar, a very familiar face. It was like *déjà vu*! I continued to stare, and my curiosity got the best of me. The band completed its set, and I made a mad dash for the bar. I tapped the gentleman, I could swear was Vincent, on his shoulder and said, "*Excuse me sir, is your name by chance Vincent?*" I couldn't, for the life of me, recall his last name, I knew Vincent was Irish, but I just couldn't remember his last name. I said: "*1963, 13-0 during the regular season and 6-5 during the District finals.*" Vincent looked at me from top to bottom. I could tell he was desperately searching his memory, but he'd obviously had one too many and drew a blank.

Even so, reflecting on our chance meeting that day, I must give Vincent credit. He replied: "*Union High School, it's all coming back to me now, Steve, Steve, right, give me a second to recall your last name; how could I forget?*" He then shouted, "*Steve Silva, I don't believe it. How the hell have you been? Of all the places to meet up again after so many years.*" We hugged each other and immediately began reminiscing about the good old days as wrestling rivals and much more. Over the ensuing years, we met and socialized many times for dinners, lunches, and parties galore.

There I was, in one hell of a jam. A jam I believed not even F. Lee Bailey or Alan Dershowitz would be able to get me out of.

As a matter of fact, I eventually managed to personally contact both of these world-class attorneys, and I even spoke directly with Mr. Bailey about my criminal case, but nothing ever materialized. What can I say? I was desperate, and I tried reaching out to some of the best lawyers I could find, but drug cases were not their specialty.

Just as Vincent had promised, he made it to the MCC (Miami Correctional Center) near Homestead, Florida, that evening. We were moved from the MDO holding facility after our initial processing was completed and then transferred to the MCC. Years later, this became the temporary home of General Manuel Noriega while he was awaiting trial for his alleged drug offenses committed against the United States back in 1991-92.

I was so happy that Vincent kept his word and visited me. He proceeded to give me the good and bad news that evening. The good news was that he arranged for a bail review hearing the following week, which was only six days away. The bad news was that I was facing very serious charges out of the District of Maryland. I was told charges, if convicted, could put me away in federal prison for the rest of my life without the benefit of parole. In other words, I would most likely die in prison. Upon hearing those crushing words, I tried to prevent myself from going into immediate shock.

Vincent assured me he'd do whatever he could for me, and the first thing was to get in touch with my daughter and explain things as best he could, about the legal issues I was facing. He reiterated to Stacy not to worry.

Vincent seemed confident the Magistrate would set a reasonable bail and he'd see me in six days at the federal courthouse for the bail review hearing. We hugged each other, and I told Vincent that my life was now in his hands. As he exited through the metal detectors toward the outside lobby area, he turned, gave me a smile, and a thumbs-up look of confidence that everything would turn out okay. However, somehow, in the deep pit of my stomach, I felt even Vincent knew otherwise, and that I was in for some very tough times ahead.

MIAMI BAIL HEARING

The van ride to MCC Miami was long and very tiresome. We didn't arrive until sometime after 7:00 p.m., on Tuesday, April 22. After we arrived we spent another two hours being processed all over again, only this time as pre-trial detainee.

Vincent had already been awaiting our arrival, just as he'd promised several hours earlier that day.

The next six days played havoc on my mind. I drove myself batty. I didn't eat, couldn't sleep, was a nervous wreck, and was mentally falling apart. My life had come to a complete halt, and everything I'd ever worked hard and strived for was in the process of being confiscated by the U.S. Government.

I was finally able to speak with my daughter. I calmed her down the best I could, reassuring her that everything was going to be okay and for her to remain strong and positive. However, deep down inside, I knew that wouldn't be the case. On the contrary, everything was about to escalate and become much worse for my brother and me.

Victoria, the mother of my son, Joshua, was totally shocked and at a loss for words when she was finally apprised of the gravity of my situation by Vincent. Being totally dependent on me for both her and our son's well-being and support, she didn't know where to go, what to do, or how to manage things with me, now locked up, helpless, and unable to give her any emotional or financial support.

As it turned out, Stacy and Victoria managed to get through the initial trauma and nightmare, which we were all experiencing, thanks to Vincent. After a few days had passed, I was eventually able to speak with both of them. We formulated a game plan to move forward and tend to this critical situation.

Friday, April 25th, couldn't have come soon enough for all of us. We were awakened at 6:00 a.m. and told to be dressed and ready to leave for court by 7:00 a.m. It was to be our initial bail hearing review and the first time since our arrest that we'd be given a chance to make bail and be back home with our family and friends. I informed the officer on duty that there had been a mistake, as our initial bail hearing review was scheduled for Monday, April 28th, not Friday, the 25th, and that I'd just confirmed this with my lawyer two days earlier. The escorting officer on duty proceeded to inform me he was only following orders and to be sure we were all dressed and ready to depart by 7:00 a.m. sharp.

We barely had time to shit, shower, shave, dress, and eat breakfast before the guards came for us in the mess hall and escorted all of us to the R&D (Receiving and Discharge) holding cell area. Once there, we were handcuffed, our waist chained, and our legs shackled. Our photos and fingerprints were taken all over again.

In the four days since our arrest, each of us must have had our picture taken at least a dozen times, if not more, and our fingerprints were inked and printed just as many times; I kid you not. I often wondered if the federal government had a vested interest in the Kodak Camera Company or some other major ink printing conglomerate, because if they didn't, they sure as hell should have.

As we took the long and depressing drive from MCC back to the U.S. Federal Courthouse in South Miami, I couldn't help but think that either Vincent had royally screwed up, or the government got it all wrong. I was betting the government would be the culprit in this mishap. Vincent was too sharp to allow this to happen to me.

As fate would have it, not only was Vincent not in court that morning, but neither was the government's counsel. In other words, it

JUDICIAL WEB

turned out to be one big royal screw-up, just as I'd originally predicted before we left MCC Miami.

The Bailiff instructed the U.S. Marshals that there was a computer glitch, and our hearing was originally scheduled for Monday, the 28th, as Vincent had correctly apprised us. However, the computer erred by not accurately making the proper entry. In other words, some government flunky forgot to enter the correct data, and now all of us would wind up suffering for his failure to do so.

The U.S. Magistrate, noting our presence in Court that day, inquired with us as to whether or not we wanted to enter our pleas of not guilty or choose to wait until Monday to do so. After careful consideration, we unanimously felt it best to wait until Monday, when counsel would properly represent us.

Our second court appearance was properly rescheduled for us to appear on Monday, April 28th, at 3:30 p.m., with counsel. My dad was there, along with his long-time friend, Anthony, my sister, my daughter, my brother's fiancée Linda, several of our close friends, my next-door neighbors, Jack and Ruby, and of course Vincent, my attorney of record for the bail hearing only.

The Bail Hearing was held in U.S. Magistrate Churnoff's Courtroom, and after a heated back-and-forth legal duel, bail was set as follows: $500,000.00 for my brother, Gary, $500,000.00 for Nat, the same for Frank. As for Marshall and I, NO BAIL. We were as dumbfounded and distraught after hearing the Magistrate utter those words. Don't get me wrong, we were happy as could be that our brothers made bail, but we couldn't believe the Magistrate denied bail for Marshall and I. There was absolutely no rhyme or reason for such high bail being set for Gary, Nat, and Frank, not to mention Marshall and I being denied any bail whatsoever.

Vincent didn't know what to make of the bail hearing either, and for the first time I began to feel that we were really in deep shit. Possibly, much deeper than any of us realized, including Vincent.

Vincent had one small bit of court business to tend to on our behalf, before we'd be whisked back to MCC Miami. He waived what is commonly known as a *'removal hearing,'* which was to be set later on during the week. Vincent informed us he did this so we would immediately be transferred to Baltimore, Maryland where we'd eventually stand trial. Vincent felt by doing this we could have our attorneys in Maryland ask for another bail review hearing, and at that time try to get Gary, Nat, and Frank's bail substantially reduced, and at the very least try to have a reasonable bail set for Marshall and I. We all agreed that this strategy made the most sense.

We wound up spending the next twenty-seven days at MCC Miami before we eventually left for the Baltimore City Jail, in Baltimore, Maryland, one of the worst rated jails in the entire country at the time.

According to federal law, we were supposed to have been transferred to Baltimore within ten days of our initial appearance before a federal judge or magistrate in order to be properly and timely arraigned. The law reads as follows: Preliminary Removal Hearings, under Title 18 U.S.C. Section 3060 (b) (1), the accused shall be arraigned not later than: 1). By the tenth day, following the date of the initial appearance of the arrested person held in custody without any provision for release, or held in custody for failure to meet the conditions of the release imposed.

Unfortunately, we soon learned that for every federal law in the accuser's favor, there's a convenient counterpart to assist the government in overcoming any obstacles it may encounter. In this case, a federal magistrate or judge could extend this time constraint in the absolute interest of justice, and/or due to extraordinary circumstances.

Since the U.S. Marshals' transportation services were busing at the seams, any motion filed by our attorneys to dismiss our case, based

JUDICIAL WEB

on undue delays, would have surely been ruled frivolous.

During my twenty-seven-day stay at MCC Miami, I made the best of my time there. I began taking extensive notes, recreating the series of events leading up to my arrest, and formulating a viable defense to discuss with my new Maryland attorney, who Vincent was instrumental in assisting my family in locating for Gary and I.

Let me share with you a little history and the general layout of MCC Miami. This detention and holding prison facility is located in the southwest section of Dade County, thirty miles from downtown Miami, Florida. It's situated off the Florida Turnpike's Homestead Extension, at the 152nd Street exit, and very close to the Miami International Airport.

Opened in 1976 as a Federal Correctional Institution for young adult offenders, MCC Miami was subsequently converted to a facility to house federal offenders awaiting trial (often referred to as pre-trial detainees).

While I was serving time there, MCC Miami offered vocational training in the culinary arts, ABE, GED, and ESL classes, computer education, also electronics, pre-release programs, social education, ceramic, leather craft classes, music, pottery and art classes, too.

MCC Miami's recommended capacity, back in 1986, was (504) male offenders only. However, with overcrowding just a few short years later, it significantly increased to several thousand federal inmates and continues growing to this day.

MCC Miami also had a prosperous UNICOR textile factory, which employed approximately 230 inmates while I was there, and likewise has expanded considerably since then. Probably well over 500 federal inmates by now.

Medical services included three full-time physicians, one dentist, nine physician assistants, one nurse, and three other health care providers while I resided there. With so many more inmates now being housed at MCC Miami, I'm certain the medical staff has equally expanded to meet the growing needs of the increased inmate population there. Religious services included two full-time staff chaplains, and several community volunteers who provided religious services for all denominations.

There were also four full-time clinical psychologists who treated the emotional and psychological needs of the inmate population.

As far as general housing goes, there was an A&O (Admission and Orientation) unit, as well as three pre-trial detention units, three work cadre/holdover units, one modular and one secure housing unit, used for disciplinary and special inmate offenders, like Manual Noriega, when he was serving his lengthy sentence there, and other high-risk offenders awaiting bail and arraignment hearings.

Most of the living quarters at MCC Miami were two-male, private units, while other areas provided small, medium, and large dormitory style living quarters.

MCC Miami, to this day, is a fully accredited facility by the ACA (American Correctional Association). When I was detained there, the staff complement was composed of (316) federal employees, which I'm certain has more than doubled, if not tripled, by now.

All of the above facts and information were taken directly from the United States Department of Justice, Federal Bureau of Prisons, 1991 Facilities Directory, which is published annually by the Federal Bureau of Prisons, 320 First Street, N.W., Washington, D.C. 20534.

All in all MCC Miami happened to be one of the finer places I'd spent my time at during my trials and tribulations within the F.B.O.P. (*Federal Bureau of Prisons, a/k/a the B.O.P.*).

Reflecting, after so many years having now passed, the best part of all was walking around the pond with my brother, while feeding the oversized goldfish our leftover food from the mess hall I'd saved for those special occasions.

It was during those walks I'd have flashbacks of my dad and I having done the same when I was growing up. He used to take me and Gary to a place called Weequahic Park, in Newark, New Jersey. We used to feed the fish, fly our homemade kites, roll in the lush, green grass, and just have a grand old time together. We even had some really great picnic outings there, too.

Boy, how I sure miss those good old days of yesteryear. I wish I could roll back the hands of time, and enjoy doing those things all over again. Sadly, with my dad and brother long gone, as of this writing, this will always remain a fond memory for me.

I'd be lying if I didn't tell you that tears would often fill my eyes whenever Gary and I would take those walks together, during our short stay at MCC Miami back in the spring of 1986.

One of my other fond memories of MCC Miami was my meeting up with a gentleman known to all as Big Jim. Back in the day, he was a senior member of a well-known biker's club called the Outlaws! What a great guy Jim was.

If you are wondering why they called him Big Jim, well, it's because he was indeed a very BIG man. I would venture to say Big Jim must have been at least 6'5" or taller, weighed every bit of two-hundred-and-fifty-pounds, if not more, sported long, dirty-blond hair, all the way down to the middle of his back, and was covered nearly from head to toe, literally, with the most exotic looking tattoos I'd ever seen. Big Jim was a true biker to the max.

Big Jim was doing a long stretch and he had a lot more years to complete his sentence. I never learnt what he was in for or how much more time he had left on his sentence since that was information you dared to discuss with Big Jim or anyone else for that matter.

As fate would have it when Big Jim learned there was a new inmate in the yard, and one who was a professional drummer, he immediately sought me out to inquire if I'd be interested in joining his country rock and gospel prison band. Of course, I immediately accepted his offer. It seems the drummer he was working with was weak and not of the caliber Big Jim was looking for to complement his ensemble. In no time flat, I was able to fit right in with the rest of the band members, all of whom were bikers, just like Big Jim. I must have stuck out like a sore thumb. They were all covered with tattoos, whereas I didn't sport a single one.

It didn't take long before we started doing shows for our fellow inmates and having a blast performing for them and the entire prison staff as well. We became so popular and the talk of the entire compound that we were asked to put on a special performance for the Warden and some of his outside guests one weekend. I must say that that performance was a blast and the highlight of my short stay at MCC Miami. Too bad it all ended in just a tad over a month of my being there.

We eventually departed MCC Miami on Wednesday, May 28, at 11:30 a.m. The weather, I recall was beautiful; it was a crystal-clear day, specially made for the long plane ride we were about to embark on. There wasn't a cloud in the sky, and the sun was already as hot as it could be.

The bus ride back to Homestead Air Force Base was quite enjoyable, with the first signs of civilization we'd seen in over a month. It was amazing to experience the things I once took for granted, like riding in a car, sightseeing, seeing the hustle and bustle of everyday life, seeing many children playing, people riding their bicycles against the backdrop of lush foliage, as we made our way to the entrance of the Homestead Air Force Base, for our next flight to Talladega, Alabama, en route to Baltimore, Maryland and the Baltimore City Jail, which was our final destination.

We wound up waiting over an hour on the bus, with no air conditioning, ninety-plus-degrees inside, parked on the runway, if you can believe that, for the U.S. Marshals' service jet, otherwise known as Pacific International Airways, to take off.

The jumbo twin-engine jet finally arrived, and we were piled in like sardines with upwards of two-hundred fellow male and female inmates from around the country. After all this time, it was rather refreshing to see a few nice-looking women getting on the plane with us. I was more surprised to see that several pregnant female inmates were traveling with us. They were off to the women's Federal Medical Center, in Lexington, Kentucky, where they would eventually give birth and, within seventy-two hours, with few exceptions, have to part company and be separated from their newborns until their sentence was completed. All of this was part of the BOP's strict inmate induction policies and procedures.

Most of these infants would be either raised by other family members, or if necessary, put up for adoption, or temporarily sent to foster homes, until they could reunite, sometimes many years later, with their mothers.

The airplane we flew in was in shambles. The seats wreaked from body odor and stale urine, and there were many missing seatbelts, which is a federal violation on the part of the FAA for failure to ensure safe travel methods for all passengers, regardless of whether they are federal inmates or just ordinary airline passengers.

Being fully restrained with handcuffs, waist chains, and leg shackles, it was next to impossible to be able to go to the bathroom, not to mention being able to even make it to the rear of the plane, where the bathroom was located, in enough time to do so.

Many inmates, mostly females, wound up wetting their pants and sometimes would even have a bowl movement on the way to the bathroom. If you were the unlucky one sitting next to an inmate that had one, you'd be SOL until we landed. Luckily for my brother and I, we never experienced these incidents during our air travels with the U.S. Marshals Service.

Several hours later, without incident, we landed at Birmingham, Alabama's domestic airport. It took about an hour to arrive there from Homestead Air Force Base.

Upon our arrival in Birmingham, we were then transferred by bus to the FCI, in Talladega, Alabama. This took us about another hour and a half to accomplish.

FCI Talladega is located in the foothills of northern Alabama about fifty-miles east of Birmingham, and one-hundred miles west of Atlanta, Georgia, off of Interstate 20, on Renfroe Road.

Unlike MCC Miami, which is classified as an Administrative, all male prison facility housing inmates with security levels 1-6, with (1) being the lowest risk factor and (6) being the highest risk factor, FCI Talladega was rated by the B.O.P. as a medium security, male-only facility. Back in 1986 it housed only male offenders with moderate to medium security risk levels.

In 1991, the Bureau of Prisons rearranged its security level classification codes. Prior to 1991, all inmates were now classified as either a 1,2,3,4,5 or 6 security level with an 'in' and 'out' custody variance classification rating. There were other inmates who were also classified with community custody levels, which enabled them to be considered for privileged halfway house benefits and accommodations, house arrest, and various other community-custody, alternative sentencing type programs, as opposed to the everyday rigors of a constant prison environment.

However, with overcrowding being what it was, it necessitated a change because it wasn't always practical or logistically feasible to maintain the 1-6 security level rating system, which the B.O.P. had in effect during the time of my incarceration. In effect, a security level 1 or 2 inmate should never be housed with a security level 3 or 4 inmate. The theory behind this reasoning was the higher the security level of the inmate, the more secure the facility needed to be.

Security levels were based upon many factors, (i.e., the severity of the offense, length of sentence imposed, quantity of drugs and/or money involved in the crime, was the crime one of violence, were there weapons involved, whether the inmate was a first-time offender, etc.). Once these elements were factored into a security grid chart, a security level computation score was derived, and the inmate housing placements were made accordingly.

The new method of computing security levels, when I first officially entered the system, as it was often referred to, that is the Federal Bureau of Prisons, remained basically the same. However, the actual levels have changed considerably. Instead of being classified as a 1-6 offender, the new method had the following custody level classifications: Community custody, minimum, low, medium, high and maximum. Also, in and out custody is still, I believe, part of the classification system today. The basic difference between an inmate who has in custody as opposed to out custody, simply means the inmate is able to work outside of the fenced in areas of the prison environment, if qualified for out custody, whereas with in custody, they cannot. So much for B.O.P. custody and security level classification history 101.

Moving on to a more thorough description of FCI Talladega, it should be duly noted that adjacent to this Federal Correctional Institution, is a minimum-male security prison camp. This is a place where inmates with a community custody level classification could, if they were foolish enough to try and do so, literally walk away, and thus escape from the facility, but pay a heavy price later for doing so, that is if they were ever caught again, and everyone who has ever attempted to do so, was. So, in other words this facility operated on an honor system since there were no fences, and only minimal security issues to deal with.

The official capacity rating for FCI Talladega was 484 inmates, but the prison population while I was a guest there was a whopping 960, nearly double the official capacity, and busting at the seams. The staff complement, while I was there, was only 344 federal employees, hardly enough staff to properly control so many inmates.

FCI Talladega was opened in 1979, and housed only male offenders from the Southeastern part of the United States. Housing accommodations included four general population units and one high-security, Cuban detainee unit. All housing facilities provided double, bunk beds. The institution provided an ABE curriculum, and also available college courses, through Talladega State College. Vocational training was also offered in the areas of heating, air-conditioning, welding, drafting, masonry, and woodworking.

During the time I was there, Talladega's UNICOR, a furniture factory, employed approximately two-hundred and twenty-four federal inmates. Medical services, while I was there, included one physician, two dentists, eight physician assistants, and seven other professional, healthcare staff members. I'm certain that the medical staff has increased substantially since I was there.

Religious services included three staff chaplains and several community volunteers, all of whom provided religious services of all faiths to fellow inmates. The institution also provided two full time clinical psychologists, who were fully licensed and accredited. So much for a quick description of FCI Talladega.

Upon my arrival at the facility, I was once again processed. Photos taken, fingerprints, name cards, the whole shebang, just like I'd experienced while at MCC Miami. Only this time the process took much longer. As a matter of fact, if my memory serves me correctly, it took me nearly four hours to get fully processed and settled in.

JUDICIAL WEB

I was a pre-trial detainee, described as an offender awaiting trial, and innocent until proven guilty, or has it now changed to guilty until proven innocent? I quickly learned that FCI Talladega was a much more secure facility than MCC Miami. It had long-term offenders who had already begun their sentences, and I was precluded from mingling with any of them in the general inmate population; thus, I was locked down in a cubbyhole environment for nearly the entire time I was there. It was like being in solitary confinement. This proved to be a very distressing time for me.

At one point, Gary and I were housed in what ordinarily was suited for a two-male cell unit. However, due to the overcrowded conditions, and exploding prison population demands, we were doubled up with two other pretrial detainees, making it a total of four in the unit instead of only two. Talk about overcrowded conditions! We were like packed sardines in that small housing unit, crawling over one another. Thank goodness this lasted only a few days until we were on the road once again and heading to the Baltimore City Jail in Baltimore, Maryland.

It was May 20th, around 2:00 a.m., when Gary and I were woken up, fed breakfast, and told to get ready for the next phase of our journey. By 6:00 in the morning, we were on our way to our next destination, the USP (United States Penitentiary), Lewisburg. What a real prison setting we'd soon find this to be.

The flight to Lewisburg, Pennsylvania, was horrendous. The scariest I've ever been on in my entire life. We boarded Pacific International Airlines at 7:45 a.m., after an hour-and-a-half bus ride to Birmingham International Airport.

The weather on this flight day was not good. It was foggy and raining, with extreme wind-turbulence, which permeated the entire airport and surrounding areas. The fog was extremely thick with forward visibility being a critical 500 feet. Any pilot will tell you that this is a very dangerous ceiling level to land a jumbo jet.

We were forced to circle the immediate airport area for approximately forty-five minutes, awaiting tower clearance to land the aircraft. As a result of the poor weather conditions the plane eventually wound up being diverted to Harrisburg International Airport, in Harrisburg, Pennsylvania, where we were finally able to land safely.

I couldn't believe we actually arrived in one-piece. Truth be told, I believe in my heart and soul the captain of the plane couldn't believe it either. You could clearly tell from the look on his face as he departed the cockpit wiping his brow, we noticed his shirt was soaking wet. We all applauded him as he and the rest of the crew exited the aircraft.

It was non-stop pouring down rain at Harrisburg International Airport that afternoon. When we finally made it off the aircraft, we were all soaking wet.

As if it wasn't enough the plane ride nearly scared me half to death, here's another good one for you to ponder over. The U.S. Marshal in charge began calling off the names of those inmates who were to deplane in Harrisburg, and who were ultimately on their way to the USP Lewisburg facility. My brother's name was called, along with the Smith brothers. However, for some strange reason, my name hadn't been called to also depart the plane.

The aircraft exit door slammed shut, the relief pilots where already on board and settled into the cockpit for the next flight to take off. The engines began to roar, and I began freaking out not knowing what the hell was going on. I was to deplane along with my brother and the Smith brothers, since we were all going to our final destination together. Something was very wrong, and I was petrified. I'd heard some weird stories during the brief time I'd been locked up since my arrest, and some of them were very horrifying. I kept trying to second guess what was going on. All sorts of weird scenarios began running through my mind. I thought the worst, since

I knew from what I'd heard through the inmate grapevine the feds could play very dirty and underhandedly, if they wanted you to become a snitch and begin singing like a canary. Something I refused, under any circumstance, to succumb to.

I desperately tried to acquire the attention of one of the Marshals on board, however, none of them were attentive or interested in what I had to say. Then, literally at the very last minute over the loudspeaker the U.S. Marshal in charge, asked, "*Is there a Steve Silva on board?*" I couldn't believe my ears. My heart was pounding a million beats per minute, waiting to hear those words uttered. I jumped out of my seat and shouted, "Yes, that's me! I'm Steve Silva, I'm not supposed to be on this plane now." I was then immediately escorted off the plane, and reunited with my brother. Gary, who was standing in the pouring rain with half an umbrella covering his head, the other half covered the attending U.S. Marshal's head, while Gary was sporting a big smile on his face.

The U.S. Marshal apologized for the screw-up, and escorted us to rejoin the rest of the detainees destined for the USP Lewisburg penitentiary.

As I quickly learned, after speaking with Gary, it turned out that my good old brother had no intention of leaving me behind under any circumstances, and immediately inquired with the Marshals' Services as to why I was still left on board the aircraft. Upon his doing so the Marshal realized he'd made a terrible mistake, and immediately sought to rectify the situation. That was a very close call if you ask me!

Boy! Was I ever so happy to see my brother's face when I got off that plane. It brought tears to my eyes, which no one could detect since the rain was pouring down all over my face at the same time.

After a two-hour wait on the bus we finally departed for USP Lewisburg, the oldest U.S. Federal Prison in existence today. Originally built by Mormons in 1894, it was officially opened as a federal penitentiary in 1932. At the time USP Lewisburg was the only high-level security federal prison on the East Coast. That has since changed, as there are several other high security federal facilities now located on the East Coast, however USP Lewisburg still remains the oldest of them all.

Now for some interesting history about this one-of-a-kind federal prison. USP Lewisburg is located in rural central Pennsylvania, outside the small quaint town of Lewisburg, which is two-hundred miles from Washington, D.C., and one-hundred-and-seventy miles from Philadelphia, two miles south of Interstate 80 and U.S. Route 15.

USP Lewisburg's security level, at the time I was there, was rated as medium to high-male, with an adjacent minimum-male camp facility. Inmates were, and probably still are, primarily from the New England and Mid-Atlantic States.

The inmate capacity at Lewisburg was rated at 976, with an actual prison population of 1,262 and growing while I was temporarily held there.

Make no mistake about it, this was the *REAL DEAL*! You would have to be a really bad ass to wind up doing time at USP Lewisburg. Some of the harshest criminals in the country were housed there.

A little more history of USP Lewisburg. Besides the inmate population capacity noted above, the staff complement was (550) federal employees, which has in recent years lessened.

Housing at USP Lewisburg included seven individual cell units and six dormitory-style housing units. It also had a maximum-security detention unit, which housed temporary status inmates, such as myself. I must say the housing at Lewisburg, when compared to other places that I was held at, was very comfortable, at least in the housing unit I was being temporarily detained at. The rooms were large, decent bedding, a clean and sanitary toilet, with showering facilities, and the food, by prison standards, I must admit was quite satisfying.

The educational training offered at Lewisburg included: ABE, GED (both in English and Spanish), and ESL programs, too. College courses were also offered through Park College, Parkville, Missouri.

Vocational training included: Certification programs in dental technology, heating and air conditioning, and commercial and residential pest control management curriculums. Also offered were apprenticeship training programs in twenty-four different trades.

The UNICOR metal factory employed 480 inmates, and was growing by leaps and bounds. The Metal Product Development Center employed approximately forty-five inmates, and likewise was expanding rapidly with the ever-growing inmate population across the U.S.A.

Medical Services were provided by two physicians, two psychiatrists, two dentists, thirteen physician assistants, and six other healthcare staff members. Correspondingly, these numbers have most likely increased since I was housed there.

Religious Services were provided to all inmates, even those in solitary confinement, by three staff chaplains, and community volunteers who provided religious services for all faiths.

USP Lewisburg also provided psychological services to its qualified inmates, through its full time clinical staff members. It's a fully accredited federal prison, in complete compliance with A.C.A. (*American Correctional Association*) standards.

There is one depressing sight that separates all other federal prisons and correctional facilities from that of USP Lewisburg, and that sight is their sixty-foot cement wall that surrounds the entire prison facility. Inmates serving long sentences there have gone stark crazy, while others have lost their life attempting to scale it. The few weeks that we were there, we never got a chance to see the giant wall from the outside yard area, because we were not allowed into the general population, but coming into the facility and when departing, it was so obviously depressing to see only that wall and nothing else past it, both from the inside and outside.

I couldn't believe my eyes when we finally pulled up to USP Lewisburg's front gate, nicknamed The Wall, as we entered this dark, cold, and gloomy looking fortress. I later learned this was the home of the infamous Jimmy Hoffa for eight years, among other high-profile, security inmates who preferred to be called convicts, many of them serving life sentences, without the benefit of parole, meaning they would never leave there alive. They would die in that god-forsaken place. The thought that I could very well wind up there, if I was to lose my criminal case, sent chills up and down my spine as we entered the prison's front yard and headed straight for the R&D (Receiving and Discharge) entrance.

Prior to my departure from MCC Miami, I'd only spoken with my new attorney via telephone on one occasion. Vincent had made arrangements with him to represent me upon sound advice from a local attorney associate of his in the D.C. area. However, not seeing my attorney, feeling depressed, and terribly frightened of the unknown, and what I could face if convicted had me very concerned. I felt ashamed of my predicament, and even more so for my two children, not to mention the shame I'd caused my parents and our entire family. I kept wishing that this was all a horrible dream, and that it would soon be over.

As I continued to dwell in my sorrow I heard a voice yell out to me, *"Hey, you over there with your head between your legs!"* I looked up from where the voice was coming from, it appeared to be from the cell next to the one I was sharing with my brother. The

JUDICIAL WEB

convict uttered, *"Kid, this prison is living hell, and if you can survive in this place, you can survive anywhere and anything, and don't you ever forget it."* I'd soon learn, truer words were never spoken. This place was a living hell, no doubt about it.

An immediate flashback had entered my mind as I tried to absorb each word this inmate just uttered. I thought of how this monster of a prison, which when looking at it from afar, consumes you with a cold chill running down your spine, and how you can't help but realize rather quickly just how serious one had to have fucked up in his life in order to get here. It was pure torture to imagine what lied ahead for me.

After our initial processing and orientation had been completed, we were then moved to a pre-trial detention cell area, and locked down for 24-hours before we'd be transported to our next and final destination, the Baltimore City Jail.

Our food was brought to us, I must say, well prepared and steaming hot, a rarity in the B.O.P. We were promptly served breakfast at 5:45 a.m., lunch at 10:45 a.m., and diner at 5:45 p.m. We had nothing else to look forward to during the day. There were no phones, no radio, no TV, no showers, no nothing allowed, but simply waiting for the next bus ride. The mattresses were ripped and badly soiled; smelled horribly, full of urine stains, infested with bugs, which were crawling inside, and they wreaked from a foul odor you could vomit from. We were issued two sheets each, hardly enough to cover the smell and bugs, one towel, one roll of toilet paper, a bar of soap, and a small tube of toothpaste and a toothbrush. There was no hot water, and the toilet seat was wrecked with filth and scum.

At first, we were informed we'd only be held there overnight. However, we soon learned we'd probably remain there over the Memorial Day weekend.

However, on May 21st, two days prior to the holiday weekend kicking in, at approximately 5:30 a.m. we were woken up, and told we'd be leaving in a few hours, which turned out to be much longer, since we didn't depart until 12:30 p.m. that day.

Once again, we experienced going through the rigorous process of fingerprinting and photo taking by the U.S. Marshals, who were ready and waiting to transport us by van instead of a crowded bus. How refreshing that sounded!

Another hour-and-a-half had passed before we were finally on our way to a fate worse than hell. A fate that would ultimately make our brief stay at USP Lewisburg seem like a '*Palace Fit for A King*' if you can fathom that!

JUDICIAL WEB

LIFE AT THE BALTIMORE CITY JAIL

The trip to the Baltimore City Jail took us three-and-a-half hours. We hadn't eaten anything since 10:45 a.m., then we were eventually fed some real slop food at the City Jail, as it is often referred to, at around 7:15 p.m., a whopping eight-and-a-half hours later.

The long ride in the U.S. Marshals' van, I must admit was quite comfortable. A lot better than any bus rides we'd taken thus far. The only problem with the van ride was the air conditioning, mixed with the cigarette smoke from the five U.S. Marshals who were assigned to accompany us, gave me a pounding headache.

The Baltimore City Jail is located smack in the middle of downtown Baltimore, Maryland. It's one of the oldest city jails in the United States, and it sure looked like it as we approached the main entrance gate.

At the time, this facility had the distinct reputation of being one of the worst city jails, as far as violence was concerned, in the nation.

I never found out how many inmates were housed at the City Jail during my stay there, but I vividly recall that the ratio of black to white inmates was better than ten to one. In other words, there was less than a ten percent white, to a ninety percent black-inmate population. Don't get me wrong, this didn't terribly bother either one of us, since neither Gary nor I was raised to be a racist in any manner. On the contrary we were always taught, as we were growing up, *to live and let live*. Period! Besides, I was in the music business for many years, and my main recording acts were all R&B (rhythm and blues) black recording artists, groups, and vocalists. At the risk of sounding like a cliché, I had many black friends, both male and female. However, the question I now had in the back of my mind, now that we were exposed to a predominantly black inmate population, would they share the same feelings toward us. We'd soon find all this out, and much more before the day was over.

We arrived at the City Jail at around 4:00 p.m. After being processed once more; yes, you guessed it, fingerprinted and photos taken again, we were then escorted to a dungeon looking area and instructed to strip down to our birthday suits (naked), where we were searched from head to toe for contraband. The attending correctional officers began making smart remarks about Marshall's long, dirty-blonde hair, which draped down to the middle of his back.

Imagine this for a moment, there we were the four of us standing stark naked in the middle of a dark, dungeon looking and horrific smelling room, while being handcuffed and our feet shackled, and stared at by four young, none over the age of twenty-five, correctional officers, all of whom were making wise remarks about the four of us by now. The officers began telling us how they read all about the millions we had supposedly made in the cocaine business. Talk about some scary shit. *"Wow!"* I said to myself, *"This is not good, not good at all."* I immediately thought if the guards knew all about our story, then how much of it did the inmates we were about to mingle with know as well. I couldn't believe that people knew all about our criminal case, all the way here in Baltimore, Maryland. How crazy was that! I was now convinced, more than ever before, that we were way over our heads and in really deep shit.

I immediately tried to change the conversation with the guards, and instead I began talking about my music career and all the black entertainers I knew and had under contract with my record company. This seemed to intrigue them. The four guards handling our intake/unit assignment phase were black, and seemed interested in learning much more about my music background and credentials.

JUDICIAL WEB

Reflecting, many years later, I must admit my music knowledge and experience may very well have been my saving grace in making my horrific City Jail life doable.

Not a single day passed without someone being injured, getting into a brawl over stupid shit, like stealing a pack of cigarettes or going on a hunger strike, or worst yet, attempting to commit suicide. You name it, it all happened at the Baltimore City Jail. I wouldn't wish on my worst enemies what I experienced and endured while doing time at the Baltimore City Jail.

I can't describe in words how humiliating it was for me to be placed inside a cage like an animal, with barely enough room to even turn around. A stainless-steel toilet seat and wash basin, no hot-running water, no air-conditioning, or even a fan to cool down our living area, with two bunk beds, whose mattresses were worse than those we slept on while we were guests at USP Lewisburg. To put it more bluntly, this ranked among the most horrific living conditions I'd ever experienced during my nearly eight years of confinement.

The temperature inside my jail cell, being only early May, would reach an average of ninety-degrees on most days. The general cell area didn't cool down until later on in the evenings, once the large hallway fans kicked in. If that wasn't harsh enough to deal with, we soon learned in late August cell temperature levels would reach a whopping one-hundred degrees or more, during the peak hours of the day.

Imagine being in your jail cell, with your cellmate, and one of you had to take a wicked dump. You'd have no choice but to do so, smack in front of your cell buddy, smell and all. This was one of the most degrading and humiliating experiences one could ever imagine. Little did I know then what experiences I would soon encounter several months later, while being a guest of the Federal Bureau of Prisons, and how much worse they'd be compared to what I experienced while at the Baltimore City Jail.

I can vividly recall how there would often be female prison guards, making their routine rounds, checking on who was doing what in their cells, and if by chance you had to go #2, oh well! Talk about being embarrassed. Luckily for me, my brother and I shared a double cell, in the beginning of our City Jail confinement, but after he made bail, it was a real test of my wits each and every waking moment to make it through to the next day.

During our first night at the City Jail, Gary and I experienced what only Hitler could have conjured up as a method of torture, during WWII in the Nazi concentration camps. I'm dead serious!

The cell next to ours was empty, and for some strange reason, every couple of seconds, the toilet continued to make the most horrendous flushing sound you could ever imagine. It would continue flushing nonstop, over and over. This went on all day and night, for two consecutive days, before someone finally came to remedy the problem. It was pure torture!

After the first few hours I began stuffing my ears with wet toilet paper, trying to muffle the sound just a little. That's how bad it was! Much to my amazement my brother slept like a log through it all, and between his loud snoring, which sounded like a freight train passing over me, while the toilet continued flushing constantly, it didn't take me long to become a total wreck. I thought I was about to have a nervous breakdown!

By our fourth day, Gary and I still hadn't had a hot shower, since there was no hot water throughout the entire jail facility, or so we were told. The guards informed us that the hot water heater had blown up, and it would be a while before it would be replaced.

My nerves were slowly beginning to become unhinged. I had no more strength or fight left in me. My spirit was on the verge of breaking. I was suffering dearly, both physically and mentally.

Gary sat me down on the bottom of his bunk and began reading me the riot act. He told me that I needed to snap out of it, or I'd wind up dying in prison. He told me that what I was doing to myself was just what the doctor ordered, the government doctor that is. They were hoping we'd crack under the stringent City Jail pressures.

I stood up from his bunk bed, thought to myself for a moment, and at that very instance it all became abundantly clear to me. Gary was absolutely right. From that day forward, all the way to the very last day of my incarceration, I heeded my younger brother's well-founded advice, and maintained a positive attitude knowing one day justice would prevail in our criminal matter.

By the fifth day, my brother talked me into taking what turned out to be an ice-cold shower. It was either that, or continue to wreak from really bad body odor, which had now permeated our entire cell.

Picture this for a moment. We soon learned that at the other end of our assigned cell block was a utility closet with a deep, washtub sink. Strange as it was, this sink had a limited supply, during certain hours of the day, of hot water. I mean *boiling hot water*! It must have been hooked up to a separate hot water heating system.

Gary and I hooked up with two black youths we'd befriended from our cell block. They showed us where two mop buckets were kept. We proceeded to fill the two mop buckets with hot water from the sink, and swiftly returned to our cell area where there was a single shower stall, which was adjacent to the inmate community bathroom.

If I should ever wind up making a movie from this story one day, this is surely one scene we'll most certainly look to include. Here I am standing stark naked inside this shower stall, which by the way had no shower curtain. Meanwhile Gary was standing just outside of the shower stall with only a towel wrapped halfway around his waist, which barely covered his ass. In one hand he held a mini-sized pail, while his other hand was holding his towel, which was too small to secure around his waist. Now here comes the hilarious part. Gary began dipping the small pail into the mop bucket, and started throwing hot water all over me, while the shower nozzle was spritzing ice cold water down my spine. What a hilarious sight to see! Everyone passing our cell block that day began hysterically laughing.

At this point during my shower, I was really good and pissed off and extremely irritated. Gary, on the other hand, was getting tired of the hot water bucket idea. I asked my brother what the hell he was doing. By this time my head was spinning, and the rest of my body was covered with shampoo suds, and my face the same. I called out for Gary to quickly throw some more hot water on me so I could rinse myself off. The next thing I remember Gary began yelling out, *"You want some more hot water? How badly do you want some more hot water, Bro?"* I said, *"Come on, stop screwing around, and give me some more hot water to rinse myself off with, for crying out loud!"* He wound up giving me some more hot water alright. Gary proceeded to pick up the entire mop bucket; the water had somewhat cooled off by now, and threw it on top of my head, which flowed all the way down to my feet. I thought I'd been hit by a tidal wave. The other mop bucket was still full. I proceeded to submerge my head into it in order to rinse off the rest of the shampoo, which was still left inside my hair. Talk about hilarious moments, this for sure would have made a classic unedited film shot.

When I finally pulled my head out of the water filled mop bucket, Gary was standing over me laughing uncontrollably. I immediately shouted: *"What the hell are you laughing at? Do you have a better way of doing this?"* Gary quickly responded, *"No, but you can get your sorry ass dried off, and fetch your brother two more buckets of hot water so I can take my shower next."* We looked at each other, and began hysterically laughing all over again.

JUDICIAL WEB

It was now my turn to get even, and you can bet your sweet bippy that's exactly what I did. For the first time in weeks Gary and I shared a little humor between us. We realized that it was good to be alive, and still be able to laugh once again. We both realized how lucky we were to be with each other, and to make the best of an otherwise very difficult and depressing situation.

We had several things on our minds, and that was for our lawyers to get us bail, fight for justice to prevail, and to gain our freedom. We knew if we had to fight our criminal case from the inside it would be virtually impossible for us to succeed. We needed to be free and able to concentrate 100% of our efforts and energy on our case, rather than having to constantly worry about just trying to stay alive in the abyss we were currently faced with. We agreed if we couldn't do at least that much, we'd have one foot in the grave, and the other was sure to follow. For now, all we were waiting on was to hear from our attorneys, who were expected to show up at the lawyer's visiting room area at any moment.

Later on that day, this would have been May 22nd at around 11:30 a.m., me, Gary, Marshall, and Nat were informed that our attorneys had arrived and were waiting to see us. The guard on duty that day, Officer Hopper, escorted us to the lawyer's visiting area. What another frightening experience that turned out to be. Here we were, four pre-trial detainees, heading to visit with our attorneys. We had walked halfway down this poorly lit, dark and gloomy corridor, when Officer Hopper shouted, *"Okay fellows, you can make it the rest of the way yourselves."*

He proceeded to direct us by saying. *"Take the corridor to the end of the hallway and then turn left, go down the stairwell until you see the guard's desk. He'll instruct you from there. Good luck fellows. I sure hope things work out for the best for you boys. This is no place for your kind at all."*

What a chill went up and down my spine after I heard Officer Hopper utter those chilling words. I immediately turned to Gary and he quickly remarked, *"He's a pussy, what do you expect! He's trying to scare us."* Just then Marshall remarked, *"Yeah, well if you ask me he's doing a damn good job of it!"* And then Gary shouted back, *"Then you're a bigger pussy than he is!"* We all looked at each other and laughed.

When we arrived at the guard's desk we were greeted by a very rough and stern looking gentleman. He reminded me of a gunslinger, beer drinking, and shit-kicking dude from the days of the Wild West. The kind of chap, if you gave him a wrong look he'd pull out his sidepiece, and whack you in a heartbeat. He asked us for our names, and instructed Marshall and I to enter the bullpen holding area, while Gary and Nat were directed to another secure holding cell across the hallway from us.

The bullpen, where me and Marshall were now gathered in, contained at least twenty other really mean-looking, motherfuckers. We were the only white boys in the entire bullpen area that morning. Pretty scary, I can tell you that. As we began mingling around, making sure to stay close together, we sensed all the other inmates' eyes were glued on me and Marshall, which was beginning to get quite scary. Now I knew why they called it the bullpen. We were the chickens in the pen, looking to be slaughtered by the bulls. At least that's how we both felt at the time.

All the seats were taken, so we wound up standing and waiting patiently until finally, after an hour had passed, our names were called for our attorney visit. The place we were escorted to wreaked from terrible body odor. It was a horrible stench. I'd bet anything most of the inmates in the visiting room hadn't showered in days, perhaps, even weeks. I knew how Gary and I had smelled after we hadn't showered for five consecutive days, so why should they be any different.

As I glazed towards the other cubicle, where Gary and Nat were comfortably sitting and carrying on a conversation between themselves, I couldn't help but think where this whole nightmare was headed. Suddenly, my mind became a total blank.

We were instructed to exit the bullpen area, and directed toward a set of reinforced, solid metal doors. Then each of us was given an assigned booth number where our attorneys were waiting to meet with us.

My attorney, David Irving, was a lawyer from a well-known and highly respected, Washington, D.C. based law firm.

Our initial meeting was rather brief. It consisted of me signing some basic retainer documents, then a brief fifteen-minute discussion followed, which ultimately led me to believe the Judicial Web being spun and ensnarling me, was now beginning to thicken rapidly.

As my lawyer had promised, he came back for a second visit later on that afternoon. I remember it was sometime after dinner around 5:30 p.m. When I saw David's face I immediately sensed that trouble was in the air. David proceeded to inform me that he had some good news and some not so good news to share with me. The good news was that U.S. Magistrate Rothstein had agreed to set another bail review hearing for the four of us the following week. My lawyer informed me that things looked favorable for Gary and Nat to make bail. However, the not so good news was the feds weren't satisfied with the pound of flesh they'd gotten from each of us in our Maryland Indictment. It now seemed they wanted even more, much more, from Marshall and I. This time the U.S. Attorney's Office, for the Eastern District of Virginia, under the auspices of U.S. Attorney Hubert, by and through his AUSA Carrie, who had also sought a True Bill (a/k/a a criminal indictment), which David had informed me would be unsealed any day now. This unscrupulous and underhanded act would now seriously deprive Marshall and I of any fair chance of making bail in Maryland.

At first, we thought it may have been a ploy, perhaps a scare tactic or strategy, orchestrated by the Maryland prosecutors to pressure us into pleading guilty in our Maryland indictment, so as to avoid another criminal prosecution in the Eastern District of Virginia. This most upsetting and depressing news totally shocked me and Marshall to our core. However, we quickly learned it was not that at all. The Baltimore U.S. Attorney's Office was generous enough to have informed both Marshall's and my attorney that the Virginia Indictment would soon be unsealed. Sure enough, several weeks later it was.

The next day Pretrial Services conducted interviews with each of us. They needed to gather pertinent information concerning our backgrounds, personal history, and past criminal records. This critical Pretrial Services Report would be used to establish a recommendation to the Court, on behalf of the U.S. Probation Department, whether or not we'd be potential candidates for bail reconsideration purposes.

Remember, Gary and Nat had already been granted bail at their initial bond review hearing in Miami. It was now a matter of whether or not the U.S. Magistrate would consider lowering our bail requirements from the current $500,000.00 each, to something more reasonable for me and Marshall.

However, for me and Marshall making bail now was seemingly out of the question. The news we'd just received from our attorneys, regarding the forthcoming Eastern, Virginia unsealed criminal indictment, was a devastating blow to our defense in our pending Maryland trial. Keep in mind the Baltimore indictment carried with it, if convicted, life without parole under the drug kingpin statute, Title 21 U.S.C. Section 848 (for running a Continuing Criminal Enterprise).

I think this is a good time to explain exactly what it meant for me to be criminally charged with the harshest of all criminal offenses, in the government's arsenal of criminal statutes. Title 21 U.S.C. Section 848 is the catch-all, Drug Kingpin Statute. U.S.C. stands for United States Code, and Section 848 is the place in the Federal Rules of Criminal Procedure where the statute can be located and fully expounded upon. The 848 Statute is often referred to as the CCE Drug Kingpin Statue. CCE stands for Continuing Criminal Enterprise.

Originally, congressional intent was intended to prosecute organized crime bosses running highly sophisticated criminal enterprises, in the enforcement of the harshest of all federal statutes. In fact, harsher than if someone was charged with having killed the President of the United States. *NO JOKE*!

Word had it that the late Robert F. Kennedy, who was the U.S. Attorney General under his brother, the late President John F. Kennedy, was responsible for getting this statute enacted into law as a retaliatory measure for the assassination of his brother.

However, as years unfolded, the intent of Congress was severely compromised and drastically changed, especially as it pertained to enforcing this criminal statute. Federal prosecutors began prosecuting people from all walks of life, even little old ladies, for the CCE offense.

In order for an individual or entity to be found guilty of the CCE offense, the following elements, back during the time of my criminal prosecution, must have been proven beyond a reasonable doubt, and the jury must be unanimous in delivering its verdict as to each of the following named elements:

1). A drug felony must have been committed under Title 21 of the U.S.C.,

2). such a felony must have been part of an ongoing continuing series of predicate violations under either Title 21 and/or Title 18, of the U.S.C. (a series, back in 1986, in most Federal District

Courts constituted three or more offenses, however, other Federal Courts have ruled two or more offenses were sufficient under the definition of '*series*'),

3). the said offenses must have been conducted in concert with five or more individuals with respect to whom one such individual occupied a position of being an organizer, a supervisor, a leader, or any other position of management over the other five or more individuals,

4). from which this said individual obtained substantial money, wealth, and/or resources.

As one would clearly conclude, I was facing a very serious criminal prosecution. As a matter of fact, there was absolutely no other criminal statute in the government's arsenal of criminal offenses, which even compared to it. Not at least when I was being wrongfully and prejudicially prosecuted for this most heinous criminal offense.

Some say being convicted of a Title 21-848 drug kingpin offense to this day, is worse than having assassinated the President of the United States, which up until recently one couldn't be executed for or even given a life without parole sentence for having committed. However, under the CCE statute, life without parole was a rather common punishment if one was convicted of having committed this heinous offense, even without personally killing anyone.

Several years after I was eventually released from federal custody, the CCE offense was updated to include a death-penalty sentence, if one was convicted under Title 21 U.S.C. Section 848 (e) (1). Making this statute now, more than ever, the harshest of all the government's criminal offenses. What made matters even worse was the known percentage of the government's conviction rate, if one elected to take his/her criminal case to trial. Imagine, a staggering 95% during my criminal prosecution days, and I'm now being told it's even higher today. Not very good odds, if you ask me.

Nevertheless, I was determined to stand trial, and if fairly and properly prosecuted I was fully prepared to take my punishment like a man. However, years later I would prove that neither of the above scenarios were true. Instead, not only was I not properly prosecuted, but I was also unfairly and wrongfully convicted of being a drug-kingpin, and made to serve a draconian sentence of 35-years without the benefit of parole for a criminal offense I was in no way, no how, guilty of.

Like I stated, prior to getting a little sidetracked, Pretrial Services came the very next day to interview each of us separately. Afterwards, we were told the interviews were just a formality for the court, and that our judicial system required it. Upon completion of our interviews we were informed by Officer Duman, a courteous, female hack (prison slang for correctional officer), that we were being transferred to different jail cells due to our being re-classified as federal, pretrial detainees. Something to do with our security and safety while awaiting trial. I guess there were concerns from the City Jail administrators, since we were still pretrial detainees, and not yet convicted felons with the sole exception of Marshall, and as such we needed to be housed under different security standards and risk factors.

Gary and I remained together, however, Marshall and his brother, Nat, were transferred to another part of the City Jail due to their younger-age differences. They were now placed in an area with other young-adult offenders ages 18-25, while Gary and I remained in the general population unit. I kind of figured this would eventually happen since the City Jail administrators wanted to keep its rape statistics down, in the wake of potentially bad press coverage, which was something the administration was dreadfully afraid of, and rightfully so.

LIFE CONTINUES AT THE CITY JAIL

After we became acclimated to our new quarters, Gary and I decided to take advantage of the daily one-hour recreation period we were afforded each day. We had to let the officer on duty know, a day in advance, if we had planned on making *yard call*, as it was coined.

During my last attorney visit, I was informed by my lawyer if I chose to mingle with the other inmates, especially during yard call, to be extremely careful of whom I decided to speak with. When I inquired with David why the sudden concern, he simply stated it was for my own good and safety. Something to do with the government possibly having placed two informants inside the City Jail to solicit information from us to strengthen their case. At first, I didn't take David very seriously. I thought his concerns were quite strange and over exaggerated. However, just as David had warned me I almost fell smack into the trap the government had deviously sprung on all four of us.

I couldn't believe it. We had our very first yard call and sure enough, while Gary and I were walking around the yard checking everything out, when out of the blue two strange looking inmates approached us. To tell you the truth I forgot their names. Anyhow, they proceeded to inform us they heard, through the grapevine, we were newcomers to the prison population, and they wanted to know if we needed anything to munch on, or maybe some cigarettes or even drugs. They said being white like us, and among the minority, we needed to stick together. They proceeded to inform us if we needed anything to just let them know, and they'd see to it that we were taken care of. Then they just casually walked away.

JUDICIAL WEB

It was pushing 3:30 p.m., and Gary would often be hungry around this time; yearning for a snack and soft drink to wash it all down with. I knew what my brother was thinking. I told him to be very cautious, and not take lightly what David had warned us about.

I must hand it to Gary, he always had more common sense than I ever had. He told me, *"Do you think, Bro, for one moment, I'm stupid enough to discuss our case with those scum bags. Give me a break, for crying out loud!"* I said, *"Okay, but you better be extra cautious anyway."*

The long and short of all this was Gary met up with the two suspected plants. He told them he'd take them up on their offer. Once yard call was over, Gary proceeded to follow both of them back to their jail cell, which was located on the other side of our cell block area. They proceeded to fill Gary up with a grocery bag of goodies, including potato chips, pretzels, candy, chewing gum, cookies, and even a carton of Gary's favorite Marlboro brand of cigarettes. Several hours later, once we were locked down for the evening, Gary and I enjoyed stuffing our faces with the bag of goodies he'd acquired, and we had a blast doing so.

The following day we went out to the yard again. Gary and I formulated a game plan to see if we could flush out the two characters we had met the day before. Our plan worked like a charm. They noticed Gary and I walking in the yard and immediately approached us. As soon as they began asking us questions about our case, which they proceeded to do immediately, we threw a curve at them, and inquired why they were so interested, after just meeting us. When they had no logical explanation in response to our inquiry, we then informed them that we were told by our lawyers not to discuss our case with anyone, much less two complete strangers. Furthermore, I informed both of them that we were also alerted to the fact that the government had supposedly planted two federal informants, inside the City Jail, to gather information in order to strengthen the government's criminal case against us. As fate would have it, when we told them all this, their faces turned red as a ripe Jersey tomato. You should have seen the expression on both their faces. I'd have given anything to have captured their facial expressions on film at that exact moment on that day.

When Gary and I went out to the yard the following morning, we couldn't find hide nor tail of those two characters. One of the hacks had informed us that during the middle of the night, the two plants were escorted out of their jail cells by two U.S. Marshals, and hadn't been seen since. Boy did Gary and I have a good belly laugh after learning that news of the day. We beat them out of a bag of goodies, and made fools of the U.S. Attorney's Office. We learned weeks later that the prosecutors in our Maryland case were livid at how easily we uncovered their two plants like we did.

Several days passed, and we still hadn't received any word from our attorneys as to how things were progressing, or if they'd received any new information concerning our criminal case.

I vividly recall how upset and depressed I'd become on the way to lunch one day. Nothing seemed to be happening. I was just feeling down and out all over again. I was very reluctant to even leave our cell, not to mention going to the mess hall to eat some real slop food again. Gary didn't want to eat alone, so I reluctantly obliged his request to join him on this particular day.

You're not going to believe this, but the mess hall, at the Baltimore City Jail, is located in the basement of a one hundred plus, year old building. To get there from our cell block area you had to exit the cell block and turn left, go down to the end of the corridor, turn right, and then down two short flights of stairs to the mess hall entrance.

Once they released F Wing, which was where our cell was located, for *feed up*, as they called it, everyone made a mad dash, like a herd of cattle, for the mess hall. You'd think they were serving something spectacular on that eventful day. The truth of the matter

JUDICIAL WEB

was whoever made it to the mess hall entrance ahead of everyone else, was first in line to be fed. That was seemingly the incentive to the daily stampede.

Some interesting facts! The stairwell leading to the mess hall was cold, gloomy looking, with chipped and blood-stained walls, fist indentations, no lighting, and the steps were full of debris and garbage. The smell and stench were so offensive you could puke. Everything from banana peels, to slices of white bread, and who knows what else was crawling on the ground beneath our feet. Graffiti was all over the staircase walls. However, the worst part of all was the inmates who were doing hard time, those offenders who were locked up with the keys thrown away, had nothing to lose by causing more chaos and tumult each day during the mess hall feedings.

These inmates were referred to as the regulars, and they manipulated the inmate population, and displayed total disrespect toward all the other inmates and prison officials, alike. If you looked at any one of those convicts the wrong way, and I mean nothing more than the slightest gaze, or if you made any eye contact with them, word had it, they'd be happy to slit your throat and let you bleed to death, right there on the mess hall stairwell. No BS! Furthermore, if any one of them learned that you were a snitch, informant, rapist, or child molester, they'd likely ram a shank into your back, and leave you for dead on the mess hall steps during those daily stampedes. Luckily, on this particular day we arrived safely, and without any incident at the mess hall entrance.

I saw all these weird and strange looking faces that I'd never seen before, and they were yelling and carrying on so loud that you literally couldn't hear yourself speak. Feeling even more depressed than I already was, I was doing all that I could to hold back my tears that were filling up both my eyes, as I glanced around the jam-packed mess hall area. Gary didn't sense any of this, because he was in front of me, and unlike me nothing really phased Gary one way or the other. Somehow, someway, Gary was able to just roll with it all. My brother seemed content as he could be, or at least he appeared to look that way. I, on the other hand couldn't help but think about my daughter, my son, also Victoria, my mom, dad, and sister, too. I had all I could do to keep myself from breaking down in the mess hall that day.

I was about to come apart, when I glanced over at my brother stuffing his face with that disgusting food, and instead I began laughing hysterically. Gary was shoving food into his mouth like there was no tomorrow. Even better yet, as if it was his last meal.

As for me, I couldn't place a single morsel in my mouth, not even if my life depended on it, that's how badly the food appeared to me. All I can recall was saving the half grapefruit they served as dessert for a snack later on that evening.

On another occasion, I vividly recall having gone to the mess hall; Gary was in line in front of me as usual. On this eventful day they were serving a special pasta soup.

It was supposed to be the special dish of the week. It consisted of fresh garden vegetables, pasta noodles of some kind, sliced potatoes, chicken chunks, and a thick semi-spicy soup broth.

As Gary's turn came up to be served, the inmate chef, who Gary had befriended, asked him how much of a portion he wanted that evening. Gary quickly responded by asking: *"How's the slop today?"* The inmate quickly replied, "The same slop as yesterday and every day," with a big grin on his face and Gary laughed. Then I added my two cents by saying, *"It doesn't appear to look all that good to me."* Gary turned and uttered: *"Bro, you wouldn't know what good was if it stared you smack in your face."* We all laughed!

Gary managed a double portion of everything, and I asked for a single bowl, which I was certain I wouldn't eat, but would wind up giving it to my brother anyway. We grabbed our trays and plastic-

JUDICIAL WEB

ware, the pasta soup, dessert, soft-drinks, and found ourselves two seats in the overcrowded mess hall on that eventful day.

I glanced around and saw everyone gorging themselves over this, supposedly, big treat of the week feast. I was thinking to myself, it couldn't be all that bad, after all, Gary seemed to be enjoying it, and it appeared everyone else did also. I decided, reluctantly, to try some. As I poked my spoon into the bowl, I hit a solid mass of what I thought was an uncooked potato, or perhaps a chicken bone. I lifted my spoon and to my surprise, it appeared to be neither. It was a dead, baby field mouse. I nearly shit! I looked over at my brother, and with the spoon in my hand and the tail of the dead mouse hanging over its side, I said to my brother, *"Bro, I hope you're enjoying your pasta soup. Look at the Cracker Jack surprise I found in mine."* He looked over at me, and then at his empty bowl he'd just woofed down, and spit the remainder of what he was chewing on out of his mouth and back into the soup bowl.

By now everyone sitting around us had laid their eyes on the dead field mouse laying in my spoon. I held it up high in the air so everyone else in the mess hall could then see it as plain as day. Next thing we all witnessed was everyone began throwing their bowls on the floor, soup and all. A huge riot broke out in the mess hall that day. Gary and I made a mad dash for the exit door and luckily just in the nick of time.

As we hurried out of the mess hall and up the adjacent stairwell, the goon squad was making their way toward the dining area to quell the disturbance I'd unintentionally created. They were in full riot gear, billy clubs, stun-guns, you name it. They were ready to kick some ass. Gary and I later learned there were several inmate casualties, the mess hall was left in shambles, and as you probably guessed by now, that was the last time they served that special pasta soup while we were there.

After that eventful day in the mess hall, I never went back there to eat again. I requested, and was subsequently granted permission to eat in my cell. Being of Jewish heritage I was immediately approved for a Kosher-style diet. Thereafter, my meals were brought to me in sealed aluminum trays, three times a day. I must say they were much better tasting and healthier than anything they were serving in the mess hall, and for that I was truly grateful. Gary reluctantly agreed to opt for the same until he'd made bail several days later, and he was once again able to enjoy our mom's home cooked meals.

We were now beginning our second week at the City Jail. We had received word that Jorge Christo, a/k/a Little G, had been arrested in Tampa, Florida back in April, around the same time frame as us. However, we weren't able to get a fix on whether or not Jorge was out on bail, or in some city jail in Tampa, or if he was headed our way.

Gary and I were cautioned by our lawyers that Jorge could very likely be a stoolie, and we were strongly urged to be extremely careful what we spoke about while around him, especially if it pertained to our criminal case, in the likely event he should ever show up at the Baltimore City Jail.

It didn't take me long to verify that Jorge was a solid dude and able to be fully trusted. As it turned out, Little G was being represented by the famous criminal defense attorney, Roy Black, of Miami, Florida. Roy's reputation was a solid one, and very well respected among criminal defense attorneys in the country. Most of all, it was a well-known fact, Mr. Black didn't represent snitches.

As luck would have it, Roy was a very good friend and professional associate of my close friend, Vincent Flannigan, also of Miami, Florida. I eventually was able to verify, through Vincent, that Little G was not a snitch and was, in fact, proceeding to trial at all costs. In other words Little G wasn't a snitch or a government informant, as we had otherwise been led to believe by our attorneys.

Lieutenant Eli, who was a living legend at the City Jail, had been following our case through the local newspapers. I'd often discuss with Eli how inept and corrupt the system had become, and how the government, more often than not, exaggerated the facts about the high-profile cases they prosecuted, in order to suit their selfish needs and self-serving interests. Many of them were trying to make a mark for themselves, and create some notoriety to further benefit their professional careers.

I always found Lieutenant Eli to be genuinely cordial, an honest gentleman, always willing to lend a listening ear whenever he wasn't tending to the multitude of problems he was constantly plagued with, each and every day at the City Jail. It took all he could muster to ensure the smooth running of the nearly two hundred year old Baltimore City Jail, and its severely overcrowded inmate population. Nevertheless, Lieutenant Eli always managed to spend a moment or two with Gary and I, from time to time, discussing our criminal case and plight with him. He, like so many others, found our criminal matters rather intriguing and very perplexing to say the least.

I asked Lieutenant Eli to please keep his ears and eyes open should Little G ever show up, and to please be sure to inform him of our whereabouts over in F Wing. He made no promises, but said he'd see what he could do, and that was good enough for me. Like I said, Lieutenant Eli was one helluva guy. He was one of the very rare individuals I'd come to meet, through all my years of incarceration, whom I fully respected, and who treated Gary and I like human beings regardless of what crimes we were alleged to have committed. Finally, I learned that Lieutenant Eli was nearing retirement status, and yearning for a little peace and quiet after a devoted and lifelong career riddled with neither.

STEVE SILVA

MEETING SUGAR BEAR AND FOOTBALL

By day six, he had become accustomed to the rigors of City Jail life. We finally settled in on F Wing and fell into a daily routine.

By now everyone in the facility had heard about us, and rumors were spreading like wildfire. People would come by our cell just to get a glimpse of us. You'd think we were some big time celebrity convicts.

Then came the personal visits by other inmates who just wanted to befriend us. Many said they'd never met a federal inmate before, especially a big time drug kingpin, as I'd been portrayed by the local media. I guess to them, and many others, being labeled a Drug Kingpin had a mysterious aura all its own that was glamorous and glitzy. Little did any of them know it was neither for me, and if convicted of this harshest of all the federal government's criminal statutes, I could very well be spending the rest of my life in federal prison, without any benefit of parole. Hardly glamorous or glitzy if you ask me!

Then, there was our next door neighbor, whose nickname was *Sugar Bear*. What can I say about young Sugar Bear! He was as big as, if not bigger than, Chicago Bear's defensive lineman, William *Refrigerator Perry* back in the day. I mean to tell you, this youngster, who was no more than eighteen at the time, couldn't fit through his jail cell door. Sugar Bear had to literally walk into his cell sideways.

When visiting with Gary and I, he took up, without exaggerating, half the cell area. Sugar Bear stood a whopping 6'11" tall, weighing a staggering three-hundred-fifty pounds, and was built like a brick shithouse. In other words, Sugar Bear was a lean, mean, fighting machine.

Sugar Bear's story was peculiar, perhaps even humorous while at the same time a rather sad one. As it turned out, Sugar Bear was originally sent to the City Jail for a misdemeanor offense. The typical black ghetto lifestyle problems that young blacks, as well as whites, encounter when they have no direction in life, no real role models to coach them, no basic education, no vocation, or any family ties. This lack of direction eventually leads people astray, and more often than not they wind up behind bars.

If you were fortunate enough to befriend Sugar Bear, like Gary and I had been able to, you'd quickly learn, after being around him for a while, that he wouldn't intentionally hurt a fly in spite of his humongous size. It just wasn't in his *DNA*.

However, if you were to rub Sugar Bear the wrong way, and believe me it would take an awful lot to ruffle his feathers, as it did the HULK if you recall, that would prove to be a much different story.

Unfortunately, for Sugar Bear, it didn't take much for someone to foolishly make fun of his big, clumsy, and goofy looking size, that is someone who was ignorant enough to do so, and thought they'd actually be able to get away with it.

One day, so the story goes, while Sugar Bear was heading towards the mess hall, someone rubbed him the wrong way. That someone supposedly called Sugar Bear a big ape, and made fun of his big head, thinking he couldn't get out of his own way when hearing those sly remarks shouted at him from afar. Sugar Bear told Gary and I that he quickly responded by asking the name caller if he wanted to have his face rearranged. At which time this moron was heard to yell back, *"Try rearranging your own face, you could surely use a new one."* Well, the rest of the story, shall we say, was history for that loudmouth inmate. Sugar Bear lost his cool and proceeded to pick this guy up by the seat of his pants and began to rearrange his face. The poor guy was covered with blood from head to toe. As if that wasn't enough satisfaction, Sugar Bear next threw this guy, who he told us weighed every bit of 200 pounds, right out the second-story plate glass window; through the rusted and already weakened steel-security bars. Luckily, for Sugar Bear, by some miracle, the inmate survived the fall and beating. He was subsequently charged with assault and battery with a deadly weapon. The deadly weapon was Sugar Bear. You see, unbeknown to any of us at the time Sugar Bear was training to become a professional, heavyweight boxer, and thus his hands were registered as lethal weapons. Therefore, if charges were ever filed and he went to trial and was subsequently convicted, that would make matters even worse for Sugar Bear at time of sentencing.

Believe it or not, the charges were ultimately dropped as a result of several stand up inmates who witnessed the entire incident, and explained by way of their depositions, that Sugar Bear was minding his own business when this other inmate had provoked him, and thus the court ruled in favor of Sugar Bear's defense. A clear case of self-defense. Sugar Bear had one hell of a defense attorney to have pulled that one off.

The only punishment Sugar Bear eventually received was being placed in what was called administrative detention, a/k/a lock down or solitary confinement, loss of all commissary privileges, no visitors (except from his attorney), and he was allowed only one hour a day of recreational activity by himself. This punishment was imposed upon him for a period of 90 days. This ultimate City Jail punishment was due to Sugar Bear's disrupting the orderly running of the City Jail. Not too shabby of a punishment, if you ask me, especially for rearranging someone's face.

Luckily for Gary and me, Sugar Bear was fond of both of us, especially Gary. You see, they both had something very much in common between them. They both very much enjoyed eating.

Then there was Football, not the game, but another fellow inmate whose story earned him this unusual nickname.

One afternoon Gary and I were on our way to the medical clinic for some required routine blood tests. These tests were routine for all newly arriving inmates. The usual AIDS, TB, Herpes, etc. screenings. The clinic was so backed up it took nearly two weeks to finally get to us when we were supposed to have had these test results within twenty-four hours of our arrival at the City Jail. Anyhow, we passed this fellow inmate in the hallway and asked him which way to the Hospital Clinic. He proceeded to tell us how to get there, and we thanked him. Just before we started on our way, Gary asked the inmate his name, to which he promptly and proudly replied, they call me Football. Gary began to laugh and said, *"I didn't ask what sport you liked. I asked what your name was!"* The inmate, once again, but this time without a smirk on his face, sternly replied, *"I said Football."* Gary and I looked at each other, sort of befuddled, and further inquired as to how he managed to acquire such a unique name like Football. *"Funny you should ask,"* he replied. *"Personally speaking, I don't even care for the sport, nor have I ever had any interest to play, or for that matter even care to watch a football game."*

Then, without any further communication between us, he proceeded to take off his baseball cap, which he was wearing at the time, and low and behold, and to both Gary and my amusement, he bent over, and while moving his head from left to right, shared with us the reason why he was called Football. Not only was his head shaped very much like a football, but the letters *FOOTBALL* were neatly tattooed into his scalp. Boy, did we all have a good laugh after seeing this most unusual oddity.

Football proceeded to share with us how he was born with this deformity at birth, and how he vividly remembered being given this unusual nickname, which he's carried with him ever since.

After chatting a while longer, we learned that Football's real sports were baseball and basketball. He was by far the best basketball player in the entire City Jail, and believe me, there were some pretty darn good players that he competed against. No one could touch Football in a one-on-one game. No one! And if you were lucky enough to have him on your team, you could always count on winning the game. Football was good enough to play with the pros. Unfortunately, this would be an unobtainable dream. Football's criminal career got in his way, and he'd be spending a considerable number of years behind bars for the crimes he'd committed.

Reflecting on things now, the City Jail was one hell of a life experience for me. One I'll surely never forget, and shall remain embedded in my memory for the rest of my life. I learned some very valuable lessons about life behind bars. I acquired a genuine sense of self-worth and values. I learned how very important it is to have a loving and caring family. So many of the inmates I met throughout our ordeal were deprived of that for the most part, which placed them in precarious predicaments, which for many would keep them behind bars, if not for the rest of their lives, at least for the best years of their lives, something I was now facing, myself.

It is truly amazing what liberties we, as Americans, often take for granted sometimes, especially when one's loss of freedom, and the greater pleasures of life are threatened beyond our control; no longer within our means to do anything about.

At the end of the day, and I can share with you firsthand, the Baltimore City Jail is one place you never want to put on your bucket list of places to spend any time at. Take it from me! *NEVER! NEVER! NEVER!*

Our lawyers sent word, soon after the Memorial Day weekend was over, we could expect another bail hearing to be scheduled.

JUDICIAL WEB

Sure enough, Memorial Day weekend 1986 had come and gone. It was now Thursday, May 29th; we were told our hearing would take place on Friday, May 30th at 2:00 p.m. sharp.

STEVE SILVA

SECOND BAIL REVIEW HEARING

It was Thursday, May 29, 1986. Our second bail review hearing was scheduled for Friday, May 30, at 2:00 p.m. For some reason, I was feeling very depressed. I'd been feeling restless, and the cool night's breeze kept me awake as it made its way through the second floor of the jailhouse. The steel barred, glass-covered windows were left wide open, and the only thing between my jail cell and the cold night's air was ten to fifteen feet of floor space. We were only issued two thin sheets, one to cover the mattress, and the other to cover ourselves with no blanket.

You'd think that in the month of May, especially in the Northeast, one could manage without any blanket, however, the weather had become so unpredictable, that no one knew what to expect. Morning came, and our cells were unlocked, as usual, at 6:45 a.m. I picked my head off my pillow and felt an excruciating pain shoot down the middle of my neck, back, and right leg. I was once again crippled. The sleeping conditions were the worst one could ever imagine. With my past medical history, as a result of several auto accidents, none of which were my fault, and the severe chronic lower back and neck injuries I sustained as a result of my high school and college wrestling days, coupled with my strict martial arts training, back in the day, I was literally a physical wreck.

This morning was especially hard on me. In addition to my chronic, agonizing neck and back pain, I'd become moody and very irritable. I was thinking about my two children. Stacy was all alone with no one to turn to. She was only eighteen, and while she was independent and self-sufficient for her young age, she'd never been completely left on her own before. Stacy always knew how and where to reach me at all times. Even if I was out of town on business, she always had a means to reach me on my cell phone, or wherever I might be staying. These options were no longer available to her.

As close as Stacy and I had been during those precious years while I was raising her as a single parent, she now found herself all alone; with no family locally to turn to, and the guilt feelings I was experiencing about all this was beginning to settle in. If it wasn't for the few close friends Stacy was fortunate to have around her, she'd surely have been in bad shape.

My deep thoughts then turned to Victoria, who fulfilled one of my greatest wishes in life. She gave birth, in late March 1985, to Joshua, a healthy, whopping ten-pounder. Boy was that an experience of a lifetime to witness. I couldn't believe my eyes when the doctor said, *"It's birthday time, a baby boy."* I stared at the doctor, now holding my son by the heels of his tiny feet, and became very emotional. *"Just what the doctor ordered,"* I uttered underneath my breath. I was suddenly overwhelmed with joy, and felt my entire body uncontrollably shaking. I was finally blessed with a healthy, new-born son. A son who would now carry forward the Silva family namesake. Up until then there had been no heir to do so.

Finally, the one treasure in my life that made me feel whole once more had come true. I'd been through so much pain and unhappiness, for so many years, after having suffered the terrible loss of a stillborn son from my first marriage. Something no parent should ever have to experience. I never thought I'd be able to put that tragic event behind me. However, as I later learned in life, *'Time heals all wounds.'* It usually really does! With these precious thoughts engulfing me, as I awoke on this particular day, I started to realize it might be a very long time before I'd be free to enjoy my family's presence once again. I began to feel empty and lonely inside, and started weeping all over again.

Gary was still sleeping, snoring away as usual. I decided to make a few calls, and catch up on my diary writing while waiting for our attorneys to visit with us. They were due to arrive shortly.

Gary finally awoke and slowly got his act together. We munched on some commissary food while waiting for our attorneys to show up. It wasn't until 6:15 p.m. when we finally got word that our attorneys had arrived. The officer on duty gave Gary and I our visitor passes, and instructed us to report immediately to the visitor's lobby.

After pacing the lobby floor for a good half-hour, while patiently waiting to be called for our attorneys to visit with us, we were finally escorted to meet with them.

I must admit my attorney really looked sharp, but he appeared to be very tired. He got right down to business, and informed me what I could expect at our bail hearing the following afternoon. We spoke about strategies for the hearing, and I'd asked David about some questions I had of my own.

Seven-o-clock came, lawyers' visiting hours were over, and David had to leave. We said our goodbyes, and I headed back to my jail cell. Gary's lawyer was supposed to show up on that same day and time, but he never did, so Gary wound up accompanying me back to our jail cell.

On the way back to our jail cell we saw a fellow inmate we'd seen earlier in the week, while we were having routine blood tests performed. This fellow inmate had both of his wrists wrapped with gauze and surgical tape. The word around the compound was the kid tried to commit suicide by slicing his wrists with a homemade, makeshift knife, which was readily available for sale all over the prison compound.

However, this time when we saw him his shirt was ripped off and all bloody. His entire body was cut up with razors like marks 10" to 15" long. There had to have been at least fifty knife marks all over this fragile, blond-haired, blue-eyed, young white boy's small-framed body. Worst part of all, he was handcuffed, feet shackled, and made to stand still while yelling like a crazy man, "*They tried to kill me! They tried to kill me! Please, someone help me! Help me!*"

As we got closer to this wild-sounding inmate, we also noticed his face was badly sliced. At that instant moment, as we passed by the prison infirmary, we looked at one another and at the two attending officers on duty in total shock. We'd both speculated that this inmate could've been razor sliced by someone he may have either rubbed the wrong way or perhaps he was a government snitch. However, we later learned, through the grapevine, this young boy was scared to death of being sodomized by other inmates. To avoid this almost certain fate, he decided to try and fake a suicide so that he'd be placed in solitary confinement at the prison's psychiatric, twenty-four-hour lockdown ward.

After the first wrist-slicing episode, the jailhouse psychiatrist didn't feel this inmate's motives were self-destructive, if you can fathom that, and ordered him placed back into the general population.

We learned the following morning when everyone was instructed to return to their cells immediately and a 24/7 lockdown was initiated, that this inmate was found dead in a pool of blood and officially ruled a suicide. However, the word around the jailhouse was that this young inmate, who didn't look a day over eighteen, was a big snitch, and that he received his so-called just desserts, having chosen to take his own life. The 24/7 lockdown was swiftly reversed once it was determined that the inmate's sudden death was ruled a suicide and that there was no hanky-panky involved.

After lights out, Gary and I discussed my attorney visit and our upcoming second bail hearing. The next thing I heard was my brother's famous snoring sounds. So much for another sleepless night for me. I began to silently laugh, and with my ears plugged with wet toilet paper once again, I closed my eyes and eventually fell sound asleep.

I needed to take a breather for a few days, four to be exact, in order to reflect on the disaster that took place on Friday, May 30, 1986, the day of our long-awaited second bail review hearing. I mean it took four days for me to get a hold of myself and try to understand what really transpired that day in Federal Courtroom C. Never would I have believed that this great country of ours, with all its freedoms and our *'Justice For All'* motto, could have had its standards so violated in that courtroom on that eventful day.

If the government could've gotten away with what I'm about to share with you so early in my *quest for justice* to prevail, I'm afraid to think what the future holds for all of us. I was now convinced, more than ever, that I was in for the battle of my life. I realized that for me to prevail in my quest for justice, it would truly take a miracle.

Let me begin by saying that I was extremely nervous on Thursday, the night before we were all due in court. My head was pounding, I couldn't eat a thing, and my mind was preoccupied with a million and one thoughts. I read portions of the Old Testament, something I rarely did. I read Joshua, and finally went to bed after reading Hebrews. I vividly recall it taking me a while to get into the Bible reading mode. However, after reading Psalms it became much easier for me to do so.

I remember laying the Bible on my chest, as I stared up at the severely cracked and peeling ceiling a few feet above my face. The apprehension was tearing me up inside as I closed my eyes and tried to fall asleep. I was terrified and fearing for my life.

Gary was on the lower bunk, his happy-go-lucky self as usual, but he was also somewhat concerned about the unknown future, which laid ahead for us. The difference for Gary was that he already had bail set for him, and he was only looking at the possibility of getting it reduced by the Magistrate. However, I was being held without bail, and it seemed doubtful that things would change for me.

JUDICIAL WEB

We had about thirty-minutes or less before lock-down for the evening. I suddenly remembered I hadn't done my wash for the rest of the weekend. I jumped off my top bunk, and started to gather all my dirty clothes, both mine and Gary's. Gary looked at me like I was crazy. He said, *"Hey bro, what the fuck are you doing? Have you lost your fucking mind, we're going home tomorrow, forget about all that shit."* I replied, *"From your mouth to God's ears."* Gary told me if I washed the clothes I had in my hands, I'd surely not be going home, and we left it at that. I heeded my brother's sound advice, put the clothes bucket down, and placed it in the corner of our cell. However, as I did so a strange feeling I couldn't quite explain came over me. I felt the very next day I'd be washing those dirty clothes I'd left behind in the corner of our jail cell. Nevertheless, I heeded Gary's wishes and good intentions. I went back to my top bunk, said goodnight to him, and within minutes Gary was in la la land, snoring away like a bear.

Many fellow inmates came by to wish Gary and I good luck with our court appearance in the morning. They all said they truly hoped we didn't come back. Since Gary was already sound asleep, they said they'd be back in the morning to say goodbye to him.

Sure enough, at the crack of dawn, 6:30 a.m. to be precise, the guard came to our cell to wake us. *"Court day,"* he yelled! *"Get dressed and be ready to roll in thirty-minutes."*

I had no problem getting myself up. I was awake practically all night reading the Bible, reflecting on my life, and wondering if I'd ever make it past all this adversity I was now facing.

Gary, finally got up shortly after I did. We looked at each other and he said to me, *"Hey bro, we're getting the hell out of here today. Do you hear me?"* I had a knot in my stomach, and a pounding headache from the night before. I replied softly, *"Well bro, for sure at least one of us will be leaving this hell hole today,"* very well knowing that that someone was Gary, and not me. Just prior to leaving our jail cell, we were visited by several fellow inmates who wanted to say their goodbyes and wished us farewell.

It was amazing for Gary and I to have all these inmates come by to say goodbye to us. Many of them were hardcore convicted, African American criminals, with records a mile long. After all, who were Gary and I to have them treat us like this! We were the minority white boys on the cell block. We had only been there a little less than two weeks. Some of those inmates had been in the system for many months, even years, however, for some strange reason they truly had warm feelings for the both of us. Gary and I were very touched. Being in prison under such extreme hardship, with the harshest conditions one could imagine, and to know we were still able to acquire a feeling of security and friendship with these hardened criminals, was simply astonishing.

After we said our goodbyes, we got dressed, had breakfast, and just prior to leaving both Gary and I simply stared at each other. As we walked out of our jail cell and slammed tight the solid, steel grilled gate, the last thing I remembered glancing at was that bucket of soiled clothes in the corner of our cell. I said to myself, "*I sure hoped my brother was right on this one,*" reflecting on what he had told me the night before about not doing the wash that evening, confident that we wouldn't be coming back. I left everything in our jail cell, and told a fellow inmate to divide it all up, the left-over commissary items, books, clothing, etc., amongst all our friends, but with one stipulation, that they'd do so only if I didn't return by 7 p.m., thinking I'd be back long before then if things didn't go right for me.

Upon leaving the cell area, Officer Dorsey gave us our passes and we headed downstairs to be received by the U.S. Marshals Service, who in turn would transport us to the Federal Courthouse in downtown Baltimore for our long awaited second bail review hearing.

JUDICIAL WEB

We met Marshall and Nat, who had been separated from us ever since we were reclassified two weeks earlier. They really looked like they'd been through hell and back.

We turned in our bed sheets, towels, and other soiled laundry items, and we were then directed to sit down in the bullpen, with upwards of fifty or more other inmates, all of whom shared similar legal issues. Mind you, this bullpen area was made to comfortably seat no more than twenty five inmates at a time. I could honestly state, with conviction, we were packed like sardines inside that bullpen area that day, with no ventilation, no a/c, not even a ceiling fan to cool us off.

The four of us stuck together like birds of a feather. We were the only Caucasian inmates in that entire holding cell area on that eventful day. After spending about an hour and a half inside, we were finally called out one by one, handcuffed, our waist and legs shackled, and conveniently escorted to the U.S. Marshals' van where we were then transported to the U.S. Federal Courthouse, on West Lombard Street in downtown Baltimore, Maryland. As the van rolled underneath the giant, solid red-steel-enforced doors, and exited the City Jail, the anxiety I was experiencing at that moment was unimaginable.

The ride through the city of Baltimore was refreshing, as we entered civilization once again. In this short but exhilarating ten-minute ride to the Federal Courthouse, I was reflecting on my entire life, and the blood in my veins was beginning to boil. I was having a hard time controlling my fears, anxiety, and the emotions that had now consumed me. The stress I was now experiencing was unbearable. I guess you could say, without a doubt, I was more fearful of the unknown than anything else, and I visualized that pail of dirty laundry in the corner of my jail cell.

I tried my best to stay focused, and heed the words my brother uttered before we departed for our upcoming second bail hearing.

However, truth be told, reality was beginning to set in. I was facing a life sentence, without the benefit of parole, for a crime I was in no way guilty of.

We arrived at the courthouse at 8:45 a.m., and our hearing was scheduled to take place at 4:00 p.m. The waiting seemed to last forever. We were informed that Pretrial Services, along with their investigators, wanted us at the courthouse as early as possible in order for them to be able to conduct individual interviews with the four of us, to determine whether we were bondable candidates.

These investigators were supposed to be impartial, and unbiased federal probation officers who were appointed by the Court. Their main function was to independently evaluate our backgrounds, and make recommendations to the Court as to whether they felt we were a bondable risk or not. Our lawyers informed us that not all investigators were above board, honest, and trustworthy. In other words, there were those who were fair, honest, and impartial, and then there were those who were not. Guess it was like anything else in life, you have those individuals who are decent and honest, and who take their respective life's work seriously, and then there are those who are biased, crooked, and who thrive on taking advantage of the system by usurping their official positions and power over others. *"What else was new!"* I mumbled to myself.

Once we arrived at the courthouse, we exited the Marshals' van and was escorted through a secret underground elevator, which took us to the fourth-floor inmate-holding area. Upon our arrival we were placed inside a rather small holding cell along with five other pretrial detainees, who were also awaiting their Court appearances. On that day, the tension in that room was so real that no one dared to utter a single word or even look at another inmate the wrong way. It was so depressing to witness the anxiety we all experienced, in that tiny area, on that eventful morning.

The U.S. Marshal in charge read our names one by one. We were then individually escorted to another area of the building, where we had our photos and fingerprints taken by a gentleman named Charlie. We later learned that Charlie was the resident fingerprint expert. Seems Charlie had been around for many years and knew his craft quite well.

As Charlie fingerprinted each of us, it was remarkable. He told us things only we, or someone very close to us, would have known about. For instance, Charlie told my brother that he knew Gary liked to read a lot, which was accurate. He knew Gary loved to go fishing, that he once had come into a lot of money, and when Gary was younger, he had a fishhook caught in his left index finger. Gary told Charlie that he was right in every instance, with one exception, he never came into a lot of money, and they both had a good laugh.

On our way back to the holding cell, Charlie told us there were 650,000 computer combinations and categories of fingerprints, and with the new system the government now had in place, it could pretty much detect, with extreme accuracy, an individual's entire life's history from a proper set of fingerprints.

Once back at the holding cell area, we were served lunch and settled in for a long wait, which lasted nearly six hours before we were finally escorted to the Magistrate's Courtroom.

As the clock passed 4:00 p.m. we all started getting edgy and began wondering what the hell was going on. What seemed to be the delay? Everyone began speculating. Gary and I thought Magistrate Rothstein's docket was so backed up that we'd wind up having to come back the following day. We dreaded the thought of going through this ordeal all over again. Marshall and Nat sat quietly, staring at the walls around them, with bland expressions on both their faces, and not really knowing what to think or say.

Finally, at approximately 4:55 p.m. we heard the familiar chain-link sounds in the nearby hallway; we knew it was now time to meet our fate. The four of us stood up and wished each other good luck. The holding cell door opened, and one by one we were asked to step out into the hallway to be properly restrained. *"Silva brothers,"* yelled one of the Marshals. *"Over here,"* Gary and I, simultaneously, yelled back. *"The Smith brothers,"* hollered the other U.S. Marshal. They proceeded to handcuff and waist-chain us, avoiding the unnecessary leg shackle restraints, since we were only going down the hallway to the Magistrate's Courtroom.

I can't begin to explain how my heart ached when that courtroom door swung open, and I saw my dad, daughter, and sister, sitting there somber as they could be. Also, in the Courtroom were the Smith brothers' family, the pretrial investigators, the court reporter, Assistant U.S. Attorneys, Andy Nolan, Greg Wells, Special DEA Agent Sandy Jones, the local press, a slew of courtroom deputies, and local spectators, too. I knew one thing for sure, this wasn't a dream, but rather a very real, living nightmare!

Our attorneys had arrived just as we were being seated, and the bailiff announced, *"All rise, the Honorable Magistrate Rothstein presiding."*

"Be seated," the Magistrate ordered.

The atmosphere in the Courtroom was a cold, damp, and eerie feeling. It was now time for the fireworks to begin. What it all boiled down to was whether my lawyer would be able to convince the Magistrate of the overreaching and otherwise overzealous objections from the government's counsel, that I was neither a risk of flight, nor a danger to society, the two prerequisites one must satisfy before the Court can even entertain granting someone a reasonable bail request, which up until now I was being denied. As a matter of fact, not only was I not afforded a reasonable bail, but I was being held without any bail. *Period!*

First the Court heard from Steve Arlan, the defense attorney on behalf of Nat Smith (for purposes of his bail hearing only). Then Mr. Wells gave his account as to why the government opposed lowering

Nat's bail. Next came David Irving, on behalf of my brother (also, for bail review purposes only), and then the prosecutor uttered his underhanded version of why my brother should, likewise, be denied a lower bail. Then David addressed the Court on my behalf. I thought David did a plausible job for both Gary and I that day. His arguments were well executed in my humble opinion. I felt certain the Magistrate would set at the very least, a reasonable bail for my brother.

The Assistant U.S. Attorney (AUSA), Gregory Wells, addressed the Court and began to completely humiliate me with such lies and misstatements of facts, which we later learned were personally communicated to him by Jon Gerritt. This prejudicial rhetoric had infuriated me to a point that I wanted to burst into a rampage. However, I did my best to maintain my composure, as I watched the Magistrate listen to Mr. Wells' colloquy, while glancing over at me and my counsel from time to time.

Mr. Arlan next addressed the Court on behalf of Marshall Smith, who was eventually retained as his trial counsel, with a similar plea as cleverly used by my attorney. The Magistrate listened attentively as Mr. Arlan concluded his legal argument on behalf of both Nat and Marshall.

Mr. Wells once again addressed the Magistrate, trying to convince him that in no way was Marshall deserving, as a second time drug offender with a prior criminal record a mile long, of any bail consideration whatsoever. It appeared as though Mr. Wells was obsessed with making certain that Marshall and I would receive no bail considerations but rather we'd be immediately returned to the Baltimore City Jail.

Time was running; it was now pushing 5:20 p.m. I still couldn't get a clear sense of what was happening or how things would turn out for all of us.

In a surprised announcement, the Magistrate after having heard all legal arguments, both pros and cons, stated: *"I've already made up my mind as to one of the defendants before me, and I will take a fifteen-minute recess in order to decide on the other three defendants now before the Court."*

The next fifteen-minutes seemed like eternity. We all kind of stared at one another and speculated as to what the Magistrate's rulings were going to be. Everyone pretty much concurred that if anyone had a chance of making it to the street, Gary was the most likely candidate. The best issue Gary had going for him was his chronic poor health and medical history, and the mere fact that my parents would assure the Court, that Gary would remain in their custody throughout his entire pretrial proceedings.

The Magistrate entered the Courtroom, nearly fifteen minutes to the second, and stated he was now ready to proceed with his final rulings. He started first with Nat, and when he finished stating his reasons, he ordered Nat to be released on a $100,000.00 personal signature bond, which required no money or personal property to be pledged on his behalf.

Next came Gary; it was nip and tuck with his fate. This was due, in part, to the negative accusations alleged against Gary by the government's prosecuting attorney. However, as I alluded to earlier, with Gary's extensive, medical history, coupled with all his present medical conditions would wind up being the deciding factors that swayed the Magistrate to lower Gary's bail from $500,000.00, as previously set, at our initial Florida bail hearing, to a $250,000.00, personal, signature bond. Like Nat, Gary wasn't required to pay any bond-deposit fees, or pledge any personal property, either. The Magistrate, as he read off Gary's bond conditions, stated on the record that Gary was to report to his pretrial probation officer twice a week and that he'd be subjected to weekly drug testing as his probation officer saw fit. Furthermore, Gary was restricted to traveling only within the state of New Jersey, and he was forbidden to travel to Florida under any circumstances. Gary was ordered to reside in

JUDICIAL WEB

the full-time custody of our parents until trial, at which time he could then reside with our sister, who lived in the general area of the Federal Courthouse in Baltimore, Maryland, or he was permitted to reside in a local hotel, with either one of our parents. For Gary, one thing was for certain, this sure beat the hell out of going back to the City Jail.

Finally, it was my turn to learn of my fate. The Magistrate began to speak: *"This was, indeed, a very hard decision to make. In fact, it was a very close call at that. While the Government's case was rather convincing, as far as Mr. Silva's involvement was concerned, especially as it pertained to the alleged conspiracy, Mr. Irving's fine rebuttal was equally compelling as to his client's family ties, character, past, and personal history, etc. However, whenever there is such a close call as this particular case seems to be, I'm usually inclined to give the benefit of the doubt to the Government. I listened very intently to the counsel's fine rebuttal on behalf of Mr. Silva. While I'm convinced that the Pretrial Services Report (PSI) is accurate in all aspects, and has strongly urged this Court to grant Mr. Silva a reasonable bail consideration, coupled with Mr. Irving's fine showing that the defendant did, in fact, have an ongoing legitimate music enterprise and a rather successful relationship in the music industry, nevertheless, it is my opinion, after weighing all the evidence presented by both sides, due to the seriousness of the charges alleged by the Government's counsel, and the many persons that Mr. Silva has come to meet while on his professional business travels abroad, he could very likely be a risk of flight and therefore not available to stand trial. Therefore, we shall continue to detain Mr. Silva, without bail, and he is hereby ORDERED to be taken back to the Baltimore City Jail upon the conclusion of these proceedings."*

It was now Marshall's turn to get hammered. Surely, with him being a second time drug offender, his extensive prior criminal record, his chances of making bail were slim to none, especially after the Magistrate had just finished slamming me like he did.

Boy, I wouldn't have wanted to be in Marshall's shoes that day. Here I thought the Magistrate really came down hard on me.

You had to have been there to have witnessed it firsthand. The Magistrate came down on Marshall, after his lawyer's brief rebuttal, like a ton of bricks. He tore into Marshall's past, then stated on the record that it was obvious Marshall hadn't learned his lesson the first time, and that he'd be headed straight back to the City Jail, right along with me, until the time of the trial. I turned toward Marshall and for the very first time, in the nearly six years I'd known him, he began to weep uncontrollably. I knew the feeling all too well. However, for Marshall, the worst was yet to come. We thought our lawyers, as promised, would be able to work out a compromise with the Government's Counsel if things went sour and we were denied bail once again. This was what we were told they had already worked out with AUSA Wells. We were promised, as an alternative to being brought back to the City Jail, that we would both be housed at the local halfway house, called Volunteers of America (VOA), which was only a ten-minute drive from the Courthouse. However, as fate would have it, we were informed by our lawyers that the Government's Counsel, at the last minute, conveniently changed their minds, and even denied making any such promises. So, back to the Baltimore City Jail we went.

I must admit, all things being equal, our lawyers really fought vigorously for the two of us on that eventful day. It just wasn't a lucky day for Marshall and I. The one concession we were granted from the Magistrate's final ruling was for Marshall and I to remain housed together, despite us being reclassified by City Jail officials. However, it was days after our return to the City Jail I'd yet to see *hide nor hair* of Marshall.

In the meantime Magistrate Rothstein had now set the final date, of July 17, for our formal arraignments, where we'd plead not guilty to our alleged criminal offenses.

JUDICIAL WEB

Once we were safely transported back to the City Jail, our lawyers paid us a quick visit. It was not yet 7:00 p.m., and visiting privileges had not yet been terminated for the evening. Our attorneys informed us that they had planned on working together on an appeal of our bail denial to the judge who was scheduled to try our criminal case. His name was the Honorable Judge Moore. David informed me that he'd know more on Monday, and for me to hang in there and stay strong. As we shook hands through the black, steel exit door he uttered the words, *"It's not over until the fat lady sings."* I couldn't help myself and smiled as I replied, *"It's not over until she takes a wicked dump."* We both had a hearty laugh, and it was a jovial way to end an otherwise disappointing and very exhausting day.

After David had left, I made my way back to my cell. It was just about 7:00 p.m., and sure enough staring me right smack in my face was that bucket of dirty clothes I'd left behind nearly twelve-hours earlier. What a depressing sight to see. I should have taken that bet with Gary.

At that exact moment, I quickly decided to make the best of an otherwise very troubling situation. I paid a visit to the coin operated pay phone down the hallway from my cell, and placed a collect call to my sister's home to see how Gary was doing. This was the first time that Gary and I were separated from one another since our initial arrest. Luckily, I'd caught my dad just prior to him and my mom leaving for their long drive back home to New Jersey.

I was able to speak briefly with my dad, and he informed me that Gary was in tears having to leave me fend for myself at the City Jail. Gary told our dad earlier that day, on their drive back to my sister's home, he wished that he was back there with me, that's how truly bad he felt. He knew the hell I would soon have to face by myself, without the benefit of him at my side. That's one helluva brother for you. We really had a chance to become very close with one another due to our unfortunate circumstances, and certainly this would be an experience that we'd never forget for as long as we both lived.

Fate, I guess, does have a very strange way of dealing with peoples' lives, and in this instance, between Gary and I, it was truly amazing. You see, until our arrest on April 22, 1986, Gary and I hadn't seen or spoken with one another for an entire year. We were having a feud over our horse racing business, and our differences on how things should be handled between us. Being stubborn as I was, I never gave Gary much credit for any of his ideas, or his commonsense tactics in a field in which he was much more knowledgeable and experienced than I had ever been. So, one day Gary just said the hell with it all, threw in the towel, and I never saw or spoke with him again, until we met face to face, on that eventful day, at the Dade County Jail's Federal Detention and Holding Cell. We found this to be quite amusing since we lived less than a mile away from one another at the time of our arrests.

I must say, while reflecting on all this, when we first saw one another that somber, Tuesday, mid-morning, we found ourselves both in total shock. I can remember my brother's face, full of dried blood, with a good size lump in the middle of his forehead. What a horrible experience to have witnessed, despite all the time we had been away from one another, and then to have both of us thrown into such a tenuous situation was depressing beyond words. A situation before it was all said and done, would wind up having us fighting the battle of our lives.

Back to the phone call with my dad. We spoke briefly before Gary got back on the phone. Talk about weird feelings. Here we were, less than twelve-hours ago sharing the same jail cell, and now I'm speaking with my brother, talking to me from my sister's house phone. We continued speaking for a few more minutes until my time was up. Gary told me how much he'd missed eating good food once again, one of my brother's favorite past-times, which both of us had been missing ever since we were arrested many weeks earlier. My ten-minute phone privileges were just about up. I wished my brother well, told him we'd speak again soon, and back to my cubby hole I went.

JUDICIAL WEB

I didn't feel like speaking with anyone. I took a quick shower, returned to my cell, and tried to get some shut eye. As I closed my eyes and began to reflect on the entire day's events, I couldn't help but silently weep. I'm ashamed to say, but I continued doing so until there were no more tears left to shed, and eventually fell into a deep, somber sleep.

I was now back at the Baltimore City Jail without Gary, and uncertain as to what was going to happen next. Talk about being scared, would be putting it mildly. Let me tell you, in all honesty, without Gary around I remained scared to death now more than ever before.

Many questions were now lingering in my mind. Would I be stuck here, at the City Jail, until my trial was over? Should I plead guilty to something I knew in my heart I wasn't guilty of, for the sake of making it all go away. Would I be fortunate to have another bail hearing any time soon? These were questions I was pondering, which I desperately needed answers to immediately.

The next morning, David paid me a surprise visit. We got a chance to go over some strategies for my bond appeal before Judge Moore. He was the trial judge recently assigned to hear my criminal matter.

David proceeded to share with me one of the things that really hurt me from making a bond at my prior hearing. It was the last statement uttered by Mr. Wells, as communicated to him through DEA Agent Sandy Jones, all of which was a total fabrication of the truth. In other words, one big lie!

Agent Jones informed Mr. Wells that he'd received word from Jon Gerritt about a drug deal, involving sixty kilograms of pure cocaine, that I had supposedly used my thirty-four-foot Silverton, cabin-cruiser to haul the load in. He further stated that I was even bragging about it to Gerritt. After hearing this information from Agent Jones, Mr. Wells immediately communicated it to the Magistrate, in open court, and I was dumbfounded listening to all those fabricated lies. I couldn't believe what I heard during that bail hearing. I began to laugh uncontrollably, which might have been a big mistake, rather than remaining calm, cool, and collected.

However, the reason for my outburst was simple. My yacht had been without its two inboard engines for nearly six months. They were being repaired, all of which was well documented. The vessel was docked behind my residence, and hadn't been moved in many months. I informed David that this rhetoric was a totally fabricated lie, which was conjured up by both Agent Jones and Jon Gerritt.

I urged David to vigorously refute this issue during the bail hearing. However, being caught off guard and totally surprised, there wasn't much he could do, or even anything he could offer the Court as evidence in order to provide an accurate response to the government's falsely presented testimony. After all, this was not a trial setting, and at the end of the day, it would all boil down to the word of Agent Jones and the prosecutor's communication to the Court, compared to David's unconvincing explanation on my account, without any concrete evidence to back up my side of the story.

If you were a Las Vegas odds maker, who would you have likely placed your money on, me or the government prosecutor, as to who was going to win that argument before the Court? If you chose the government prosecutor, you guessed right. *NO BAIL!*

ARRAIGNMENT DAY

I awoke feeling ill on Wednesday, June 4, 1986, at around 6:30 a.m. that morning. I guess it was a combination of depression setting in once again, coupled with the anxiety of the upcoming arraignment, scheduled for Friday, June 6, at 2:00 p.m.

The weather outside was miserable, raining and very gloomy. I tried my absolute best to shake loose my depressive state of mind, as I desperately wanted to maintain a positive attitude going into the important arraignment and bond appeal stages of my criminal case. However, no matter how hard I tried to fight it, I just couldn't get myself together. I was a complete and total mess.

I tried thinking of Friday's upcoming court proceeding in a positive manner, and reflected on the telephone conversation I had earlier with my brother and dad. My dad was saying that he was getting ready to bring out his WWII, U.S. Army uniform, which he'd kept preserved in a special, mothball closet in our basement, and give them a fight they'd never forget. It was finally beginning to settle in. The federal prosecutors and law enforcement personnel were trying desperately to punish me for electing to exercise my Constitutional rights and go to trial, rather than pleading guilty and becoming a snitch for them.

By now they all knew that I was not a candidate for their snitch camp. Their motive for keeping me at the City Jail and fighting vigorously to keep me from acquiring a reasonable bail was pure and simple. They were hoping that a few more weeks of the brutal conditions, and the living hell I was experiencing would cause me to crack up and eventually cave in. That was their game plan. They were not only looking to take away everything I'd ever worked for in my life, but they were also looking to keep me behind bars for the rest of my days if I didn't fully cooperate with them.

Later that day I received word from my attorney that everything was pushed forward until the following Monday, June 9th. Seems as though the Magistrate's docket was overloaded for Friday, and he couldn't hear our arraignments until Monday. I also learned the trial judge had agreed to hear our appeal bond arguments on the same day, and boy was that music to my ears.

As things now stood, we'd be arraigned on Monday, June 9th at 2:00 p.m., in front of Magistrate Rothstein, and then at 4:00 p.m., barring any unforeseen circumstances, we'd be in front of the Honorable Judge Moore, who would hear both Marshall and my appeal bond arguments.

The upcoming weekend promised to be an exciting one for me. I was expecting visits from my daughter and infant son, who I hadn't seen since I left Miami in early May. Stacy was already in Maryland staying with my sister and parents, who had driven down from New Jersey to lend their moral support and help me maintain a positive attitude going into Monday's court hearing.

My son and his mother were traveling from Sarasota, Florida, and they were due to arrive at the Baltimore International Airport early Friday evening. I arranged with my brother and dad to pick them up and bring them, along with my daughter, to visit with me at the City Jail on Saturday morning.

The weekend went by swiftly, and it was refreshing to see family again, especially my daughter and one-year-old son, Joshua. The visit itself was rather restrictive, but I had a wonderful time seeing both of them again. It was just what the doctor had ordered. I desperately needed a boost of encouragement to hold me over and get me through the next phase of my criminal ordeal.

Monday, June 9, 1986, I was woken up at 5:45 a.m. and told to be

JUDICIAL WEB

ready within 45 minutes. The officer on duty had informed me the U.S. Marshals would soon be there and that I needed to make sure I was downstairs at the bullpen area by not later than 6:30 a.m. *"Silva, don't be late!"* the guard yelled out.

Marshall met me at the bullpen, and together we waited for the U.S. Marshals Service to escort us back to the Federal Courthouse. Would you believe, we didn't leave the City Jail until 9:15 a.m. Talk about punctuality! They apologized for being so late and told us they had a flat tire, a typical bullshit excuse if you ask me.

I recalled it was a beautiful day, sunny, a whopping eighty-five degrees, and as we departed the City Jail once more, Marshall and I looked at one another and I said, *"Here we go again, Marshall. I sure hope this is our last day in this rat hole."* We slapped each other a high five and away we went.

For some reason I was feeling a lot more positive, especially after just seeing my family. I also felt more confident as we approached the Courthouse, thinking things might just turn out differently this next time around. I was counting on our lawyers having researched the legal issues and to adequately make a viable argument before Judge Moore, hoping we'd be successful in finally being granted a reasonable bail for both me and Marshall.

Prior to entering Courtroom C, the U.S. Marshals, who had escorted us, proceeded to remove our leg shackles and handcuffs. We were then directed to take our proper places next to our lawyers, who were already seated and awaiting our arrival.

Once again, the Courtroom was filled with our family members, the media, the prosecutors, and a slew of spectators, all of whom were curious to see the government's big fish of the day.

The Magistrate entered, and without getting into too much detail the entire proceeding was over and done with in ten-minutes. So much for the arraignment portion of our criminal case. Marshall,

Gary, Nat, and I, all pleaded not guilty, and then Marshall and I were taken directly back to the federal pretrial holding cell area. We were now awaiting our previously scheduled 4:00 p.m. bond appeal hearing, in front of Judge Moore.

As I was being escorted from the Courtroom, by the U.S. Marshal's Service, I couldn't help but notice my mom and dad's faces as I passed by them. I'll never forget how terribly distraught they both looked. I couldn't even look directly into their eyes. I was so ashamed of what I'd put them through.

Words could never express how I felt on that day, as I left the Courtroom and passed by both my parents. Despite all this, my dad managed to give me one of his famous winks, and my mom cracked a tearful smile. Then there was Gary who was bubbly as always, and he managed to give me a double thumb up while my sister and daughter were trying their very best to understand it all. I gave them all a smile and told them, *"Keep the faith, somehow, someway, things will all work out."*

At exactly 4:17 p.m. Marshall and I were brought to the second floor, Courtroom #3. We were staring at the huge oakwood doors, when the U.S. Marshals once again removed our leg chains, handcuffs, and then proceeded to open the entrance door, and directed us to be seated next to our attorneys table, which was empty, since our attorneys had not yet arrived.

As we were being escorted to our appropriate seats, the U.S. Marshals wished us good luck, and hoped things would finally work out for us. Reflecting, I can now state with conviction and certainty, I truly believed they both genuinely meant it.

This Courtroom was set up just like a T.V. reality show. Judge Moore was already present when we walked into the Courtroom on that eventful day. Judge Moore was in the very front part of the room, six feet off the ground, looking directly down at us. To his right was the twelve-seat jury-member box; the four alternate juror

JUDICIAL WEB

seats were directly behind it. Then there were the lawyer's and defendant's tables, which were situated directly in front of the presiding judge's podium. Last but not least, to the left of the judge's podium was a table reserved for the Assistant U.S. Attorneys.

Behind these two tables was the area where the potential witnesses would be called to testify, and directly behind them was a huge area for family members, spectators, and of course, the media and press personnel to be seated.

By now, the entire courtroom was nearly full. Both Marshall's family and mine were present, the government's attorneys and our counsel took their respective positions, and there were a number of spectators and press personnel present as well. Talk about butterflies! The last time I recalled having them was in high school during the last bout of the regular wrestling season, where I was the Captain of our undefeated wrestling team, and I was defending my undefeated 12-0 wrestling record. Thirty-two years later, I was experiencing the same kind of butterflies here. Only this time, they would have a completely different meaning. It was like Deja Vu. This time the butterflies were out of fear for my life, not for defending my undefeated high school wrestling record. Which, miraculously still stands some fifty-nine years later. I won that final match, taking my undefeated record to 13-0, and since then, way back in 1964, no one has ever been able to match it.

Our attorneys finally showed up and made their way over to the defense table where Marshal and I were seated; we shook hands and the proceeding began. I took a deep breath and while doing so, I glanced over at my family, gave them a smile, and winked at my dad. Our lawyers informed us to just listen carefully, and assured us that everything would turn out just fine.

I couldn't help but notice the table in front of me, which hosted an abundance of music related paraphernalia my folks brought with them for the hearing. This material ranged from music recordings, while our studio was opened, records we produced and distributed around the country, also photo albums of the concerts and artists I produced, and much more.

I had the strangest feeling, and I was trying to visualize how it would all play out once our actual trial began, which wasn't that far away. As I began processing all this in my mind, the Bailiff announced the proceeding was now officially in progress.

David made his opening statement first, followed by Marshall's counsel, and then the prosecutors spoke. When all was said and done, and Judge Moore heard all the arguments on both sides, he rendered his final rulings.

Judge Moore simply stated, as far as he was concerned, the Baltimore City Jail was no place for Marshall and I to be further housed, regardless of the alleged criminal charges lodged against both of us by the government. In Judge Moore's final summation, he stated that a proper bail should be posted in the amount of $250,000.00 for each of us.

Judge Moore went on to further stipulate, and so ordered accordingly, that the said bail was to be secured by property and/or cash, and that we would be sent to the Volunteers of America (VOA) Halfway House, in downtown Baltimore, as soon as the proceedings were concluded, and all the proper paperwork was fully executed. End of story, so we thought!

The VOA, being a halfway house, was 100% better than the Baltimore City Jail. No bars, no security, no jail cell, no more sleepless nights, due to poor sleeping conditions, the horrific bedding, and no more cockroaches crawling all over the place, to worry about any longer. In other words, freedom at last. What a sigh of relief. I was finally able to exhale after hearing those words uttered from Judge Moore's mouth. We'd now be permitted to leave the premises, but only if accompanied by our attorneys or a representative of their firm, and then only for the purpose of going to their office to prepare for our forthcoming criminal trial.

Judge Moore also ordered drug-testing to be conducted on a regular basis while housed at the VOA. We were also informed that one positive drug test, and we'd be immediately sent straight back to the City Jail, no questions asked.

Upon hearing Judge Moore's final ruling, the prosecutors were fuming and stormed out of the Courtroom. They seemed good and pissed off. However, we just kicked ass, and won our first monumental victory! We'd been charged with the worst federal crime in the government's arsenal of felony penal codes. Up until then no one, as we soon learned from our attorneys, was ever granted bail, or ever dreamed of being sent to a halfway house for the crimes we were alleged to have committed and subsequently indicted for in the Eastern District of Maryland. *Never!*

You may now be scratching your head, and asking yourself why? As you know by now a Title 21-848 CCE offense requires a minimum mandatory ten-year sentence, to a maximum of life imprisonment, without the benefit of parole, and the loss of all of one's criminally forfeited assets upon conviction. With that much time facing an accused defendant, the inference was one would likely flee if given the opportunity to do so.

If not for Judge Moore's judicial fairness during our second bond hearing, and his ability to prevent the prosecutors from trying to railroad us by insisting that we were a risk of flight, and that we should remain incarcerated at the Baltimore City Jail, that's exactly where we would have been headed once the hearing was over.

However, we both came from very respectable backgrounds, upstanding families, and a good overall education. Hence, Judge Moore decided to take a very risky chance with us.

Judge Moore went on the record and stated: *"I'll feel awfully sorry for the both of you, should you decide to flee, and choose not to show up for trial."* I quickly, without any hesitation in my voice replied," *Your Honor, we'll surely be there, and thank you from the bottom of my heart for taking this chance on us. We won't disappoint you. I can unequivocally make this promise on behalf of Marshall and myself."* Judge Moore than glanced over at Marshal, who quickly nodded his head, and promised the Judge that he'd do the same.

We'd soon be released to our lawyers' custody. That meant we'd no longer be handcuffed and foot shackled, and we'd be free to leave the courthouse as soon as all the paperwork was finalized. I turned around and with a broken voice told my family I loved them. I noticed my daughter sobbing, because she had thought I'd be able to go directly home with her. She was especially sad, because I wouldn't be able to attend her high school graduation, which was less than 10-days away. However, little did my daughter know just how lucky I really was on that day, and that I didn't have to go back to the Baltimore City Jail and face that horror any longer.

I don't believe anyone in my family, with the exception of my brother, really knew how fortunate it was for Marshal and I to have been released to a halfway house. Not to mention the VOA only had two empty beds waiting for us on that eventful day. We thought we'd have to wait until there was space available at the VOA, and that could have literally been weeks away. Talk about a very lucky break for us. For me it was a miracle!

Gary informed all the family about what had just happened, and although I wasn't totally free, for the time being anyway, I was at least one step closer to getting there. I felt if I could prove myself at the VOA, and stay clear of any trouble, not do anything foolish, like attempting to escape, that I would eventually stand a good chance of getting completely free on bail, with no restrictions within a few weeks' time. However, according to our lawyers, that was only wishful thinking.

After we were escorted by the U.S. Marshals out of the Courtroom, we were once again handcuffed, leg shackled, and taken back to the holding cell area where Marshall and I thought we'd be released to our lawyers' custody, and headed to the VOA Halfway House. Boy were we in for a big disappointment. About fifteen-minutes later we found ourselves on our way back to the Baltimore City Jail, without any explanation whatsoever. We never heard from our attorneys as to what was happening to us. We were both dumb-founded and freaking out!

We arrived back at the City Jail all bummed out, signed ourselves back in, and were issued the usual one pillow and pillowcase, two-bed sheets, two washcloths, two towels, and a toiletry packet, all over again.

We soon learned that the paperwork necessary for our releases was not signed by Judge Moore. We were told that it was too late in the day by the time the hearing was over for the Judge to do so, and there was no one to properly process our release forms. However, I had a different take on what had just happened. I figured it all out on my own. This was just one more ploy the prosecutors played to get us back to the City Jail. I felt if I had to spend one more rotten night there, knowing that I was leaving the very next morning, and hopefully never to return there again, that I could handle this last-minute twist of fate. Luckily, I was able to get some commissary items that evening. I told my fellow inmates I wanted to share it all with them. I wanted to have a going away party, and that's exactly what we did.

The party was over swiftly, and all my commissary food was devoured. But I really didn't care, it was my last night in that rotten hell hole, and I'd be leaving it all behind in the early morning. I felt bad for my fellow inmates. However, I knew the long road ahead for me was bleak, my future was uncertain, and looked very grim, at least for the time being.

Upon returning to my cell, I was greeted by a young inmate named Danny. He was my new roommate; a kid who had just turned seventeen years old. I had a prior roommate named Earl after my brother was released on bail. Apparently, they moved Earl to a local psychiatric hospital for medical evaluation. He was truly a nut case!

Earl had a lot of mental health issues, and was plagued with demons he was unable to cope with. He had no business being in the City Jail with all his serious baggage. I was glad that he was finally getting some much needed professional psychiatric help.

My personal opinion, for what it's worth, after having lived with Earl for nearly two weeks, aside from some fantasies he'd shared with me about Jesus and Satan, Earl seemed, at least on the surface, quite normal. I don't know what kind of chemical imbalance was plaguing him, but I did learn that Earl lacked a proper childhood, and a normal father/son relationship.

Now Danny, my new roomy, a young, blond-haired, green-eyed, boy, who if dressed up in a sequence outfit, and handed a guitar and microphone, could've been the next teenage heartthrob in the country. However, instead of choosing a righteous path in life, Danny chose to get himself into a shit load of trouble at a very young age. Danny was charged with possession of a dangerous substance called *Toley,* which was a potent construction type glue-based chemical, the use of which corrupted the morals of a minor. The minor was his eleven-year-old friend.

Danny informed me this glue-based substance, when placed inside of a plastic baggie and sniffed, after about five minutes, makes a person hallucinate so badly, that if you were reading Penthouse or Playboy, you'd swear the exposed naked women were right there performing your wildest sexual fantasies. Certainly not appropriate for any eleven-year-old boy to be experiencing. I kept thinking I'd

JUDICIAL WEB

be leaving all this madness behind me in the morning as I drifted off and finally fell asleep.

At 6:15 a.m., the next morning, Officer Dorsey came by and informed me that the U.S. Marshals would be picking me up at 9:00 a.m. Little did she know I was ready and fully dressed to leave the night before. I never unpacked, and I was more than ready to go. I said my goodbyes, and hoped in a sincere manner I'd never have to spend another night in that City Jail ever again.

I headed for the Classification Desk and turned in my pillow, two sheets, towels, and a handful of prison-issued clothing items. I was then directed to the federal-holding cell area where I met up with Marshall. We waited patiently to be taken to our new temporary home at the VOA.

Eight-o-clock came, nine-o-clock passed us by, and by now we were the only ones left in the holding cell. Something just didn't feel right to me, and we began feeling very nervous. Sure enough, around 9:15 a.m. we were informed by the duty officer that we weren't going anywhere that day, and for us to return to our cell area at once. Marshall and I looked at each other in total shock! We couldn't believe what we'd just heard. Something must have gone drastically wrong at the Courthouse.

As we gathered our belongings we passed two U.S. Marshals who had been patiently waiting for their orders to transfer us, and I asked them what was going on. One of the Marshals, named Doug, mentioned to me that it was something to do with a technicality in posting our family's properties for bail. I inquired with Doug as to how long he thought it would take to get this matter resolved. Doug informed me that it could be hours or perhaps even days. He really didn't know jack-shit, and was just looking to shoot the breeze and make small talk with me. I guess out of pure boredom they were both ready, since early morning, to transfer us to the VOA as originally planned for.

When I returned to my cell area, Officer Dorsey and everyone else were quite surprised to see me again. I made my way back to my cubby hole, feeling bummed out and depressed.

The next thing I did was make a phone call to find out what the hell was going on. I tried to reach my dad in his hotel room. My sister answered the phone and proceeded to inform me that everything was alright, but there was a hearing scheduled in front of the Magistrate at 11:00 a.m. to formally post the release of the properties. I told my sister that it all sounded very strange since it was now 10:00 a.m., and Marshall and I were just sent back to our jail cells and told we weren't going anywhere. Gloria told me she didn't know why they did that and for me to just sit tight for a little while longer, and everything would work out just fine. So, that's exactly what we did.

As I went to lie down, I couldn't help but feel depressed, terribly disappointed, and in deep despair. After all, how much more disappointment could one person take? As I began to doze off, I heard Officer Dorsey yelling for me to pack my things once again. She said the U.S. Marshals were finally ready to take us back to the Courthouse. I didn't know whether to believe Officer Dorsey or not. Perhaps she was playing a joke on me. But my common sense told me otherwise. Off I went, hoping this would finally be the real deal once and for all. Sure enough, the Marshals were waiting for us to enter the security area. They proceeded to pat us down, and we then needed to sign some paperwork for our releases all over again. The Marshals took our final thumb prints. We checked out with the cashier, collected our belongings, and what little money we still had left in our commissary accounts, and immediately headed for the federal courthouse once again.

Upon leaving the steel-grilled front gate, Marshall and I turned and looked at the ugly green and red steel doors, which everyone must pass through upon entering and leaving the Baltimore City Jail. Over the top of this door were the words: Reception Diagnostic

Classification Center. Just at that precise moment, Marshall and I looked at each other, and then glanced back at the sign, as we walked out into the prison parking lot.

Unlike the day before, when the weather was simply wonderful, today, Tuesday, June 10, 1986, was a cloudy, gloomy, and drizzly kind of day. Were we feeling gloomy. *Hell no!* We were so happy that we were actually getting away from some of the worst conditions we'd ever experienced in our entire lives.

I felt from that day onward, no matter what the outcome, things would only get better and not worse. Boy would I soon be in for a rude awakening, thinking things would only get better. That was wishful thinking, on my part, and would soon be swiftly erased from my mind.

We were escorted back to the federal courthouse, this time in a brand new 1986 Chrysler, Newport, and immediately taken to the fourth floor for the final paperwork signing for me and Marshall's official releases to the VOA Halfway House.

We were placed in the holding cell for about fifteen to twenty minutes, at which time we were brought upstairs to the Magistrate's courtroom. Upon entering, my mother, father, brother, sister, and daughter, were all sitting there looking somewhat happy. Marshall's grandmother and mother were both there as well. Our lawyers were front and center, along with the two Assistant U.S. Attorneys. The only person who didn't show up that morning was the U.S. Attorney for the District of Maryland. He must have been still cooling off from the day before, when Judge Moore granted us bail, and ordered us to be sent directly to the VOA.

The Magistrate went over everything, and then instructed us on how the bond was to be posted, and the stipulations as to its forfeiture. It was going on 12:30 p.m.; Magistrate Rothstein had a 1:00 p.m. hearing on another case. Accordingly, the signing of our bonds was reset for 2:30 p.m., in order to give everyone a chance to eat lunch, and have the paperwork ready to be executed upon everyone's return.

Back to the holding cell once more. Around 2:15 p.m. we were brought back to the Magistrate's chambers, hopefully, for the very last time being handcuffed and foot shackled, before being released to our lawyers. Once inside the Courtroom, Magistrate Rothstein went over our bond conditions with our lawyers and family members. Marshall and I then reviewed and signed off on the necessary documents.

Then came an unexpected and unpleasant surprise. There was some sort of a detainer placed on Marshall, from two years ago, in another county in the state of Maryland. Something to do with some sort of misdemeanor drug charge, and those charges had to be satisfied before Marshall could be eligible for acceptance at the VOA. Without this detainer lifted Marshall would be headed back to the Baltimore City Jail, where he'd remain until time of trial. I felt really bad for Marshall's predicament.

Magistrate Rothstein and Marshall's lawyer, Steve Arlan, tried desperately to get around the matter, but it was to no avail. It seemed no one in the '*Just Us*' department wished to be denied their pound of flesh, and this incident was no exception to that unwritten rule. Marshall was now in for some more harassment, only this time by state, rather than the federal authorities. The U.S. Marshals proceeded to escort Marshall from the Courtroom, and as he departed I could sense his deep despair.

The next thing I recall was immediately being greeted by my parents, daughter, brother, sister, and away we all went with my lawyer, David, to his office in downtown Baltimore. Free at last, for the first time in several months. Boy did that feel awesome!

Once we arrived at David's office, we unwound for a few hours before David took me to the VOA to be officially registered. Cars, buses, trucks, shops, and the awesome smell of food, from the nearby restaurants were such a wonderful delight. What an experience that turned out to be for me. It was like I was in the jungle for a while, and then suddenly I found myself in paradise. However, I couldn't help but have mixed emotions, because of Marshall, and I kept wondering what his fate would now be. I asked myself whether Marshall was going to be able to make it through this last bit of torment. Would Marshall be able to hold up and not cave in on me; perhaps cut a deal with the government, and then become a cooperating witness against me. Was this possible? In my mind, I quickly answered myself with a big *"YES!"* Of course, anything was possible. These were the two persistent thoughts that occupied my mind in recent days. No telling what was going through Marshall's mind after this latest setback. Time for me to sharpen my skill set and brace for the worst.

Just to digress for a moment, before leaving for the VOA, I spent two hours with my family at David's office. We used his conference room to speak about some family matters that needed to be addressed. I also knew that some realities had to be dealt with. For one, David would now want to discuss his fees, since he got me out on bond. I feared that my parents wouldn't be able to afford his services. Without a competent attorney to represent me, especially with the kind of charges I was now facing, I wouldn't stand a snowball's chance in hell, at any trial. After all, if convicted, I would be facing a minimum of ten-years, to a maximum of life, without the benefit of parole. I was literally fighting for my life!

I was beginning to feel bummed out all over again. I got the feeling from my family that I wasn't going to be able to afford David's legal services or retain the lawyer of my choosing. I had less than ten days to advise the court of my retained counsel and time was running out fast, nine days and counting. The government's counsel had me ensnarled in their web, right where they wanted me. All my assets were pledged, including my sister's condo, in order to post the $250,000.00 necessary to bail me out of jail. All our family's assets were now either being pledged or seized to secure bail bonds for my brother and I. Now, what was I supposed to do.

The government figured it this way, they could paralyze you through their criminal seizure and forfeiture statutes, by having the court grant the government the right to seize all your assets, through criminal forfeiture proceedings, under the Drug Kingpin, 848 CCE statute. They would then ask the Court to set a high bond, hoping you'll be unable to post one, and if you're fortunate enough to be able to do so, it will wind up costing so much money, when all was said and done, that you'd have no funds left to properly retain a decent lawyer to represent you.

The kind of specialized attorneys, who tackled cases such as ours, were reaping anywhere from $75,000.00 to $100,000.00 or even much more, back in 1986. Most lawyers required upfront payment in full, while others required half their fee up front, and the balance before trial, with absolutely no guarantee of producing a positive outcome.

Without proper resources to fund adequate legal counsel, in these complex criminal cases, one would stand a very good chance of being found guilty. Especially, if he/she must resort to a less competent defense counsel, or perhaps a court appointed public defender who might be unwilling to put forth the necessary effort to have at least a fifty-fifty chance of a favorable outcome.

The government now has you right where they want. Ensnarled in their *JUDICIAL WEB*. Their game is to get you to plead guilty, sometimes through the plea-bargaining process to a lesser charge, which is well within their legal power and right to do so. Perhaps, if you have enough meat and potatoes to offer them, information that is, they could then justifiably ask the Court to significantly reduce your sentence for pleading guilty, agreeing to provide pertinent information, by becoming a witting government informant, stoolie, or rat, as they are often referred to among inmates doing time on the inside.

The government will look to also have you forfeit all your assets and worldly possessions, through your alleged ill-gotten and unlawful gains, all in an effort to have you provide them with a bigger fish than you. Here I was, at this very ebb, at a terrible disadvantage. That's the game!

My parents had to leave for their long drive back to our family residence in Northern New Jersey. They informed me they'd be back to visit soon, at which time we could then discuss, in further detail, retaining David as my attorney of choice. We said our goodbyes and off they all went.

David and I then left for the VOA. The ride there was rather short; we had spoken some words, but I could sense David was in a hurry; he wanted to get me there and then go about his business. I couldn't blame him one bit. I assured David, upon our arrival at the registration desk, I'd make every effort to expedite my getting registered rapidly so that David could leave and get on with his pressing issues of the day.

I was next in line to be registered, I bid David farewell, told him I'd see him in the morning, and asked him what time I needed to be ready for him to pick me up. For me, the earlier the better. He shouted back that he'd be there by 10:00 a.m. I nodded and waved goodbye.

The VOA's facilities are similar to those of the Salvation Army. In other words, a non-profit organization with minimum self-funding capabilities. Most of its funding comes directly from donations, mainly from Maryland taxpayers. I also learned there was federal grant funding available for the asking. However, there were strict guidelines in place for this funding source to be met in order for this sort of funding to be made available to the VOA. Namely, a smooth running ship had to be maintained at all times, and keeping a low profile with no reported violence or escapees, a/k/a walkaways being reported to the media was mandatory.

As I quickly learned, after being there for a short while, this was a real juggling act with the many high profile convicted felons on probation, others waiting for trial, like myself, and others awaiting sentencing. This was not an easy task, by far, for those staff members running this halfway house facility.

JUDICIAL WEB

LIFE AT THE VOA

The VOA was a very old, dilapidated, yet quaint, but rather rundown facility in dire need of extensive renovations. Since the city of Baltimore had bought up all the waterfront property, which was where the VOA was now located, plans called for it to be moved to a newly renovated hotel facility, in downtown Baltimore. Consequently, nothing was done to improve the existing facility while I was a temporary resident there. None-the-less, it was 100% better than the Baltimore City Jail, which was notorious for having the reputation of being one of the worst city jails in the country. From my own personal experiences, I couldn't have agreed more. It was horrendous beyond comprehension. I don't know how much longer I could have held on staying there.

The VOA offered better food, and the beds were much more comfortable. Unfortunately, there was no air conditioning in the main sleeping quarters, however they had these industrial size fans, which kept the living quarters somewhat tolerable during the hot summer days and nights. Also, unlike the City Jail, there were no guards to worry about, just social workers, and no fences or walls, of any sort, to make you feel you were living in a hostile prison environment.

In other words, if one was thinking of escaping they could just walk out the front door if they chose to do so. In that respect being at the VOA was so much better, both mentally and physically, than being in that rat-hole City Jail. Nevertheless, it was still very lonely, somewhat depressing, and although a much lesser form of incarceration, it was still confining with very strict conditions I'd now have to fully abide by.

I was next introduced to my case manager, who would be handling things for me while at the VOA facility. A pleasant, young-looking woman by the name of Regina. She appeared to be in her late 20s, a sort of Barbara Streisand look-alike. We talked for a while about my background, case history, family, and children. I showed Regina some photos of my family, and then I had to fill out some paperwork for her. She then provided me with a VOA Rules and Regulations booklet to read over, sign, and return to her in the morning.

Next on the agenda was my mess hall visit, where I had my first decent meal in some time. Real mashed potatoes for a change, string beans, and some tasty beef stew. Peaches, in thick puree, for dessert, and freshly squeezed lemonade to wash it all down with. The meal was simply scrumptious. I was in seventh heaven! What a meal compared to the slop food we were being fed over at the City Jail.

After dinner I was paged to report to the main office. I put my dinner tray away and headed downstairs. When I arrived, I was informed within two hours I'd be requested to take my first piss-test. I was assigned a locker and bed number on the fourth floor. I made my way back upstairs, located my bed, and decided to lay down and take a catnap.

Two hours had passed, I awoke and made my way back downstairs to the lab to try and provide the duty officer with a urine sample, for drug-testing purposes. I was further instructed that if I couldn't provide an adequate urine sample, I'd have to do so first thing in the morning. This would insure that I complied with the VOA's drug-testing orders, which eventually became the case.

I had a very restless night's sleep, with all kinds of thoughts entering my mind, until I just closed my eyes and dozed off.

Morning came quickly, 6:30 a.m. rise and shine; by 7:00 a.m. our beds had to be made. Breakfast was served daily from 6:30 to 7:30 a.m. Fresh scrambled eggs, bacon, orange juice, coffee, and/or chocolate milk. A far cry from the City Jail's breakfast menu.

Then came the pee-testing ordeal. The testing hacks, as they are referred to at the VOA, call it a Piss test. No joke! That's how they all referred to it, including the female hacks.

Let me explain the importance of this piss test. One of the main criteria for being able to continue in the VOA's program was that you have no contact with any drugs or alcohol while you resided at their facility. Seems the only way to control this restriction was through frequent piss testing.

The chemical found in marijuana is often referred to as THC, otherwise known as tetrahydrocannabinol, which remains in the body in detectable amounts for up to forty-five days or more in some instances, while cocaine remains in the body for up to seventy-two hours. Alcohol can remain in the body for up to forty-eight hours. Hence, through the random sampling of urine, in any of these three main testing areas, they can detect a negative or positive result. If the result is positive, just one time, you are booted out of the program, and immediately sent back to the City Jail. That's why the piss test was so vital and strictly enforced.

Of course, I had no problems with any of these testing requirements since I didn't drink alcohol, I knew better than to fool around with drugs, and thus run the risk of being sent back to the City Jail, something I would never risk at any cost. One thing I might add is that this piss test was embarrassing, very degrading, and really made you wonder whether this was still the U.S.A. or the U.S.S.R.

I followed Terry, the administrative officer, to the designated testing room where he went over the entire procedure with me in detail. I was handed a small, clear-plastic sterile-bottle, with a red twist-off cap. The bottle was the size and shape of a small four-ounce, orange-juice container. I was told to pull my shorts and underwear down to my knees, my tee-shirt up past my chest and face Terry directly. I was then instructed to hold the bottle with my left hand, and urinate into the bottle as Terry was staring directly at me while doing so. The bottle must be filled at least halfway, or the sample provided would not pass muster with the lab. Upon completing this humiliating task, I was then directed to place the red cap on the bottle, and hand it back to Terry. The bottle was then held in plain sight for me to see, and I then washed my hands. I was next asked to sign some papers and Terry attached a sticker to the bottle with my name on it. There was a metal vault located behind the testing area, where all specimens were placed for immediate shipment to one of the several testing laboratories around the country. My specimen, along with the necessary paperwork, was then placed into a plastic bag, and secured with an elastic band. I was instructed to open the shoot, and drop the package down into the sealed metal vault. It was now out of the hands of the VOA, with no further responsibility, and off to its final destination later on that day.

The reports are usually returned within a week to ten days, and if there are any discrepancies, and/or a positive reading, the counselor gets in touch with the offender/resident and discusses it with them in complete confidentiality.

In case you're wondering about the strictness of this testing procedure during the actual testing process, residents, unsupervised, used to do such things as neutralize their urine specimen with salt or vinegar when urinating while still being on drugs, thus providing a false-negative result. To avoid this mishap, the authorities at the VOA saw fit to change their policy, and would no longer have unsupervised testing procedures.

Also, other residents with drug addictions would often pay good money to those who didn't take drugs or consume alcohol to take their piss tests for them, thus passing their tests with flying colors, while the untested resident could still remain high on drugs. Hence, even more of a reason for the VOA clamping down on unsupervised piss testing.

I couldn't believe what I had just experienced. I mean it was so de-

JUDICIAL WEB

grading for me, I can only imagine how it must have been for counselors like Terry. I felt like I was some sort of laboratory animal being experimented on. However, I got through that ordeal without incident and headed back upstairs for lunch. Afterwards, I went out back to the dock area for the very first time. I would now like to share with you some inner thoughts that I experienced that day.

I finished my lunch and was informed I could go out back, unescorted, and sit by the water watching the boats go by in the Baltimore Inner Harbor. *Boy was I excited!* I was like a little boy having been rewarded for finishing his lunch.

There I was, walking around outside of the VOA building through a yard full of junk cars, all banged up, and pretty much destroyed, while making my way towards the waterfront dock area, some fifty or so feet away. I was all alone, and as I approached the area, which appeared at any moment to likely fall apart, I began to sigh. I couldn't hold back my tears any longer. I must have cried, non-stop, for at least a good fifteen-minutes. I was crying for many reasons. I cried for my freedom, at last. I cried out of fear, fear of the unknown. I cried because I was happy to be out of the Baltimore City Jail, and I cried because for the first time in over two months I felt like a human being once again, rather than some animal locked away in a cage. I really let it all out on the dock that day. Thank goodness there was no one around to see or hear me do so.

It was a beautiful, sunny day, and I was eventually able to come to grips with myself. I sat on a broken-down, wooden picnic table facing the Inner Harbor and pondered. The picnic table was infested with tiny black ants, as I watched them scattering all around me through my tear-filled eyes. I also noticed some smaller sized boats passing by, and the warm summer breeze felt so good on my face, coupled with the salt air, that I just lost myself in deep thoughts of the past.

While enjoying the sun's rays, I began thinking about all that had transpired since that terrible day back in April when the axe fell on my life, I noticed out of the corner of my right eye an image that appeared to be Marshall's attorney. I had tried to call him all morning to find out what had happened to Marshall, but I was unable to reach him. As I turned toward the image, I realized that it was, in fact, Steve. I immediately sprung off the bench, wiped the tears from my eyes, and ran towards him. Steve told me with a big smile, "*Your roommate is upstairs having lunch.*" I couldn't believe the words I just heard! I could hardly wait to see Marshall, and learn what happened to him after we shook hands in the courtroom the day before.

I made my way to the second floor mess hall area, and sure enough there was Marshall eating lunch, while facing the street and looking rather bummed out. I knew by the look on his face, and his body posture, he'd been through hell for the past twenty-four-hours. As I greeted Marshall, we both smiled and slapped each other with a high five. After Marshall had finished his lunch, we spoke about his ordeal after I'd last seen him on Wednesday afternoon. We discussed how we were going to raise the funds our lawyers needed to handle our criminal case. We knew the criminal charges we were facing were serious, and that this was certainly not a routine case by any means. We needed competent and well experienced counsel, which we felt we had. However, there was no chance of my coming up with the necessary funds to satisfy David's requested six-figure fees. I was literally flat broke.

Upon speaking with my attorney friend, Vincent, from Miami, I learned about a new criminal case involving my similar situation. Something to do with a defendant's right to proper counsel and the government seizing all his assets, thus depriving him of a counsel of his choosing. After carefully analyzing the issues at hand, the trial judge ruled in favor of the defendant, and ordered the government to unfreeze some of his assets so that he was able to afford his counsel of choice. I asked Vincent to send David a copy of the ruling. Perhaps we could convince Judge Moore to apply the same case law in our criminal proceedings.

JUDICIAL WEB

All this was weighing heavily on my mind. We were also informed that a superseding indictment was due to be handed down by the government and that there were new charges filed against us stemming from our original indictment, which was now rumored to be coming under a separate one, out of the Eastern District of Virginia, directed at Marshall, me, and possibly Gary as well. It seemed never ending for all of us!

I don't understand, and perhaps I never will, how our government could use the testimony of individuals already convicted of distributing drugs, using drugs, and making millions of dollars doing so, just because they gave up someone else when that someone else could be innocent of the alleged crimes they were ultimately convicted of, and the liars are either never prosecuted, or they are eventually released from prison, or their sentences are significantly reduced by becoming a government informant. This was incomprehensible for me to digest. Yet this was exactly what transpired in my criminal case, while these same circumstances remain the same to this very day.

Several individuals, we were now being told, most of whom were previously convicted felons, some of whom had already spent time in federal prison for their respective crimes against society, who cut deals with the government, and had fully cooperated, were able to get me, my brother, Marshall, and his two brothers, among a host of others, on hearsay testimony alone, arrested and placed behind bars.

There were no drugs, money, or illegal weapons found at any of our homes that were searched. Furthermore, there were no drugs, money, or weapons found at any of our business locations or warehouses that were also searched. Yet, despite all this, I'd been earmarked as a drug kingpin for allegedly operating a continuing criminal enterprise, which if convicted could send me to federal prison with a life sentence without the benefit of parole.

This wasn't something to be taken lightly by any means. It was a dramatic chain of events in all regards. My thoughts and worst fears were now running rampant, and there was nothing I could do to change the trajectory of what was to follow. A living nightmare like none other.

CI #4

Now, if that wasn't enough, one confidential informant known only to us at the time to be CI#4, as listed in our indictment, would turn out to be not only a very close friend and business associate of mine, but he was also like a second brother to me. He told me things about his life, in the strictest of confidence, a word of which I've never breached nor betrayed to this very day. Imagine, I would soon learn he was the one who had betrayed me to save his own neck from being criminally indicted. He was the one that informed the government, by way of false and perjurious statements, about me, my brother, and others, which were subsequently used to secure criminal indictments and convictions against me and many others.

In other words, I was made the subject of a grave injustice because of CI #4's perjurious testimony during his grand jury and subsequent trial testimony in my criminal proceedings.

Now for some hard-core facts surrounding CI #4's involvement in my criminal case. CI #4 was the worst kind of informant one could have in a trial such as ours. He was a decorated, ten-year veteran of the Broward County Sheriff's Dept., sometimes seen riding in his squad car, while other times cruising on his Sheriff's motorcycle.

In December 1978, an incident occurred involving the manslaughter of an African American youth, allegedly committed by CI#4's fellow police officers. The problem for CI#4 was he eye-witnessed the entire event, while riding his motorcycle on that particular day. It was CI#4 who became one of the state's main witnesses against his fellow officers, who were alleged to have committed this most heinous act. This criminal case was highly publicized over major TV networks, and got local and national media coverage for quite some time. The District Attorney, who prosecuted the case, would later become the top legal advisor during the Clinton administration.

As a direct result of CI#4 having changed his testimony at the time of this highly publicized trial, which significantly differed from his grand jury testimony, all the defendants were acquitted, which subsequently resulted in multiple civil lawsuits, mass rioting events, causing multiple deaths, and millions of dollars in property damage throughout South Florida.

That was to be the end of CI#4's tenure at the Broward County Sheriff's Department. CI#4's life was subsequently threatened, presumably by fellow law enforcement officers, his home was burned to the ground, which was believed to have been caused by unknown arsons, as a vengeful act against CI#4.

The next thing I'd learned was that CI#4 took up flying, which was a favorite pastime of his. I also learned that CI#4 had accumulated, in a very short time, a luxurious home in an exclusive part of Miami Beach, Florida, which was fully equipped with a professional tennis court, large swimming pool, jacuzzi, sauna, a weightlifting-training gym, and even a helicopter pad. He owned two new Mercedes, one for him and the other for his wife. If that wasn't enough, CI#4 also owned several small, single-engine airplanes and a 42' Bertram yacht, which he was half owner of. All these assets were acquired within three years after leaving the Broward County Sheriff's Department.

In May of 1983, CI#4 was arrested in Columbia, South Carolina for illegally transporting, possessing, and distributing ten kilograms of cocaine. In other words, CI#4 was depicted as being a big time drug smuggler and multimillionaire.

Guess that explains how CI#4 was able to purchase all those expensive assets and toys that he'd often bragged about. A classic one-time good cop turned bad cop kind of story. At least that's how the

JUDICIAL WEB

local media portrayed it after he was caught and arrested in South Carolina with ten-kilos of pure Colombian cocaine.

This was a very bad time for CI#4. His life was threatened with the possibility of going to federal prison for a very long time. All that CI#4 had illegally acquired in his life, from his drug smuggling escapades, was now at risk of being confiscated by the U.S. Government. Remember this adage and don't ever lose sight of it for the rest of your life, Once a cop, always a cop! It's as pure and simple as that.

CI#4, through his contacts and his $350,000.00 in cash payout, was able to beat his criminal case and was acquitted of all charges. Unfortunately, CI#4 wasn't as lucky regarding the civil forfeiture proceedings brought against his aircraft, which was used for his drug smuggling operation, as it was subsequently forfeited to the government. Some would say this was *JUST DESSERTS!* After all, the government had to get a piece of the pie for playing ball with CI#4 and his legal team, and thus granting him a *Get Out of Jail Free Pass*, right.

Several years had passed, and CI#4 continued with his exploits in the drug netherworld. The stories he would share with me were fascinating. Some of them bordered on being literally unbelievable, but I was a very good listener. CI#4 would often take me into his strictness of confidence. He'd share with me some of his many smuggling escapades. Here's one I vividly recall, but not sure if it was true or purely fabricated.

It was early fall, months after the Columbia, South Carolina arrest, when CI#4 was called to pay the debt to his FBI buddies who helped him escape going to prison for a very long time. Remember, those were the witnesses who supposedly assisted him at his trial while backing up his alibi, which ultimately led to his acquittal.

During this time frame, the FBI and DEA were at odds with one another, each trying to outdo the other by seeing who could catch the bigger drug kingpin, or make the bigger drug bust. It was even coined 'The Bigger Fish' game. The tension was so bad for a while that the bigwigs in Washington were called in to mediate their differences. It was all over the nightly news, and often made the subject of featured articles in many of the major newspapers across the country.

We now know, years later, the DEA and the FBI would often withhold information from one another concerning major drug-cartel investigations they were simultaneously working on. The result of which cost the American taxpayer millions of dollars in unnecessary spending, due to this fiasco.

It was this scenario, and these ego-juggling antics, which led CI#4 to be called upon by the same FBI agents who helped him with his South Carolina drug bust, to try and pull off an unbelievable, daredevil, drug smuggling act.

As CI#4 related the story to me over lunch one day at a quaint seafood restaurant called the Banana Boat, off State Road 84, in North Fort Lauderdale, Florida, I couldn't help but wonder, who CI#4 really was. Was what he had shared with me that day, factual or pure fantasy. If it was factual, it would certainly explain how he was able to beat the system, when he miraculously escaped a very harsh federal prison sentence for his Columbia, South Carolina drug bust.

CI#4 told me that he was asked to set up a drug deal to make his FBI buddies look good to the media and their bosses in Washington, D.C. He told me they needed a large load of cocaine so when the bust took place, the FBI would look good in the headlines the next day. I know this must sound absurd, but this was the gist of the story CI#4 communicated to me during our lunch date.

CI#4 proceeded to make all the necessary arrangements, with one condition, when the bust took place none of the Colombians would be apprehended. In other words, only the drugs would be seized. I guess this was to ensure that CI#4 would not wind up floating in some Everglade, alligator infested canal, never to be seen or heard from again. This was the appropriate punishment by Colombian Drug Cartel's standards for being an informant, which in one form or another would often prove to be the case.

On the day of this infamous drug smuggling event, CI#4 boarded his aircraft, at a local airport in South Florida, and headed for a remote airstrip, deep inside the jungles of Bogotá, Colombia. His co-pilot was sent by the Cartel to insure the 125 kilos, worth millions of dollars, landed safely at its purported Miami, Florida destination.

All players were now in place. As the sun began to set over the Florida Everglades, CI#4 and his co-pilot began their descent towards a hidden airstrip, where they'd be met by FBI agents ready to catch their prey, the load of cocaine that is.

As CI#4 landed and began to exit his aircraft, an eerie feeling came over him. He couldn't help but think how easy it would be for him and his co-pilot to be wasted in the middle of nowhere, never to be seen or heard from again.

They unloaded the 125 kilos of pure Colombian cocaine they'd successfully landed with, and loaded them into the station wagon that was conveniently awaiting them.

As CI#4 continued to relay the story to me, he said he then got back into his aircraft, taxied down the grassy runway, and took off heading for the Executive Airport in North Fort Lauderdale, Florida.

The plan was for the co-pilot to take the station wagon with the load of cocaine to its final destination. According to CI#4, as he later was informed by his FBI buddies, as the co-pilot pulled out onto the main highway, heading south toward Fort Lauderdale, he was pulled over by a Florida State Trooper. It seemed that one of his taillights was burnt out. Not able to speak a word of English and considerably frightened, the Colombian co-pilot began running from his vehicle and into the nearby woods before the State Trooper was able to apprehend him. Shortly thereafter, the FBI agents involved with CI#4's prearranged drug-bust operation, converged on the vehicle and conveniently took over the investigation.

According to CI#4, the news media ranted and raved all about the FBI's big drug bust the following day, but no arrests were ever made. The co-pilot eventually made his way back home to Colombia, and CI#4 was completely absolved of any wrongdoing or hanky-panky by the FBI. The Colombian Cartel's leader, who was his employer for this large load of cocaine, never questioned CI#4 about the incident. All in a day's work CI#4 related to me as he picked up our lunch tab. We parted with a high-five and went our separate ways. CI#4's debt was paid to his FBI buddies, and for the time being, it was clear sailing; back to business as usual for everyone.

In the years that followed, CI#4 had supposedly become a government informant for the DEA, and he began setting up drug busts, turning in his cocaine connections, his good buddies, and close friends, two of whom would be me and my brother, Gary.

For CI#4, he didn't care much about placing his entire family in life threatening jeopardy. It was common knowledge that once the Colombian Cartel bosses became aware of someone's indiscretions and government informant status, they'd find them and deal with them accordingly. Most often they'd wind up torturing and killing the informant and his entire family. These guys didn't play games. They were ruthless individuals who made certain those that crossed them would pay dearly for doing so.

However, CI#4's philosophy was that if you've done something criminally wrong in your life, get caught doing so, and then had the chance to save yourself by turning in whomever you could, even innocent victims, by lying about anything and everything you've done wrong, then that was the only way to beat the system.

Remember, once a cop, always a cop! I wished I'd known then what I'd painstakingly learned years later. CI#4 was the worst kind of informant you could possibly have in a trial such as mine.

By early 1986, the word on the street was that CI#4 was looking at a life sentence, without the benefit of parole, if he was brought down on another drug smuggling operation. As I'd later learned, this was the reason CI#4 was eventually forced to become a government informant in my criminal case.

I kept asking myself, why! Why did CI#4 see fit to lie about not being a drug kingpin? He was granted full immunity from prosecution; he was required to tell the truth. Instead, CI#4 decided to conveniently replace my name for his during his formal proffer, and the many subsequent debriefing sessions with government prosecutors.

CI#4 went on to inform the government's interrogation team all about his alleged criminal activities, but he conveniently claimed I was his boss, and that I arranged everything from A-Z. It was this strategy, coupled with his false and perjurious testimony, all to my detriment, that once again temporarily provided CI#4 another free, *Stay Out of Jail'* pass. However, CI#4 failed to realize this would eventually prove to be his last and final attempt to do so.

STEVE SILVA

WHAT A DIFFERENCE A DAY MAKES

Monday, June 30, 1986, it's been a while since I had the desire and mental stamina to open my diary and begin writing again. I tried doing so on several occasions, but my thoughts and feelings were numb, filled with emptiness and depressing thoughts.

Father's Day had come and gone, and it was the worst I'd spent since first becoming a father, some 18 years earlier. With the exception of my daughter, no one remembered good old dad on my special day. Joshua was too young to speak with me, as he was only a tad over a year old at the time.

Stacy and I spoke briefly that Sunday. She told me how much she missed me, and that she was glad to have me as her father, despite the terrible things the government was saying about me. As the tears rolled down my cheeks I told Stacy how much I would always love her, and to remain strong; that somehow we'd get through all this heartache soon.

I was sure glad my mom and dad were still alive, and able to help care for my daughter. They were able to provide her with the emotional support and guidance she'd need in the ensuing months, especially with our trial being just around the corner. It wouldn't be easy, but our family was strong and determined to see justice prevail. Little did they know then, what a travesty of justice laid ahead, and what we were really up against.

Stacy told me how much she missed me being at her High School Graduation ceremony a week earlier, and she only hoped that I'd be there for her college graduation, which was only four years away. That remained to be seen. I couldn't make her any concrete promises

JUDICIAL WEB

either way, and I knew down deep inside that must have really hurt her. Imagine missing your child's high school and college graduation ceremonies.

As we said our goodbyes, and I hung up the phone I couldn't help but feel very disheartened. I have raised my daughter, as a single parent, since the tender age of nine, and here she had just turned eighteen years old, had graduated from high school, and neither her mother, nor I were there to see our daughter accept her high school diploma. What shame my daughter must have harbored in her heart on that eventful day.

I'd just finished a span of two weeks at the VOA filled with all kinds of excitement and unpleasant surprises. There was the pending superseding indictment, and the exposure of confidential informants, especially CI#4, that we were made privy to.

I became terribly distraught after finally learning who CI#4 was. I asked myself, over and over, how could he have done this to me, especially after all I'd done for him and his family over the years of our close friendship. Talk about being a poor judge of character. This went way beyond poor. This was so alarming and pitiful it turned my stomach inside out, and made me sick to my core.

The mutual feelings we shared between our families and between our two daughters, my personal talks with his young son, who CI#4 was beginning to have serious issues with, and the close friendship I thought we both shared, while all of his other close friends had seen fit to desert him. All this made me even more angry and bitter than I'd already been.

Can you imagine how I felt when my lawyer informed me if it wasn't for CI#4s false-allegations and perjurious grand jury testimony, I wouldn't have been indicted for being a drug kingpin under a Title 21, Section 848 (running a continuing criminal enterprise) statute.

No wonder I was unable to sleep, think straight, or eat deliciously prepared meals at the VOA over the past several weeks. My entire outlook on life had been totally shattered.

My parents, brother, sister, and daughter visited me the week after Father's Day. We enjoyed eating delicious sandwiches from the local delicatessen they were allowed to bring into the VOA over that weekend. We discussed the case and the criminal charges lodged against both Gary and I. However, despite all this, I was still unable to shake my depressive state of mind.

The following weekend Marshall's mother, brother, Nat, and Marshall's fiancé, Fran had all came to visit him. They invited me for some home cooked food that Marshall's mom had baked especially for her son, a roasted chicken dinner, with all the trimmings. To top off the festivities, Mrs. Smith brought a home-baked ginger cake, which was out of this world. Marshall later informed me that this was a Smith family tradition, the home-baked ginger cake that is.

It was nice to see Marshall feeling somewhat relieved and in good spirits for a change, as he too was feeling lonely and very depressed upon his arrival at the VOA.

Our lawyers came to pay us a visit the following Monday. They brought us some more bad news, as if we didn't already have enough to worry about. They informed us that we were about to be indicted in another federal drug conspiracy, this one out of the Eastern District of Virginia, on similar drug charges to the ones we were now facing out of the District of Maryland. The new charges lodged against us were due to the snitches in our Maryland criminal matter. Apparently, they also implicated us in the newly unsealed Virginia indictment.

Our Maryland lawyers informed us that unless we could convince the judge in our Virginia case to consolidate the charges in both venues, and thus try the entire case in Maryland, we could find ourselves in deep shit. We'd be exposed to two separate trials, in two separate venues. This legal maneuver, perpetrated by the Maryland prosecutors, would be next to impossible to overcome. They were hoping we'd cave in and plead guilty, which we came extremely close to doing.

Marshall and I looked at one another. We knew we were fighting an uphill battle. One trial was bad enough, but to think about having to face the heat in a second one, was more than either of us could possibly imagine or endure.

Our lawyers informed us that things didn't look good. Judge Ellis, in our upcoming Virginia proceeding, was a real stickler when it came to drug cases. He most likely wouldn't agree to consolidate our two cases, not to mention the Assistant U.S. Attorney in Virginia was vehemently opposing our request as well. Monday, July 28, 1986, was the date set for us to be arraigned in the U.S. Federal Courthouse, in Fairfax, Virginia.

Picture this scenario. We were finally granted bail in Maryland and no longer being held at the Baltimore City Jail. However, we were now facing the possibility of being sent to a Virginia federal prison, and forced to begin the bail review process all over again. Talk about an unimaginable scenario turned into a living, and inconceivable nightmare.

If that wasn't enough, here's the icing on the cake. In addition to being hit with another criminal indictment in Virginia, our lawyers were now informing us the Maryland indictment was soon to be superseded by another indictment, which would now include additional criminal charges of IRS tax-fraud violations.

The government usually supersedes an indictment when they feel they have new evidence that is stronger, and thus assist in giving them a better chance of gaining a conviction. However, in our criminal cases, as far as our lawyers were concerned, it was just the opposite. They felt the entire original indictment was too weak, and the government needed more evidence to secure a stronger legal position against us, in hopes that we'd eventually look to cave in and ultimately do what most all federally accused defendants wind up doing, that being they plead guilty and fully cooperate before the trial day, thus sparing the government a long and drawn out trial in two separate courtrooms. This was a clever chess move on behalf of the Maryland government prosecutors.

Talk about feeling down and out. I don't think I ever recalled feeling as depressed as I felt during this time in my entire life. I didn't want to speak with anyone, not my lawyer, family, or daughter.

My parents told me there was no way they could afford the legal fees my attorney was asking, especially due to this new legal development. The government had already seized all my assets, and I felt like I didn't have a prayer in the world to devise a way to defend myself properly, which was just what the prosecutors had hoped for.

Marshall felt the same way, and he just wanted to put it all behind him, plead guilty, take his punishment, and be done with all of it. That's how bad it got for him. He was a two-time, convicted felon, and if found guilty, he was facing a possible life sentence, without parole. I knew then that Marshall was beginning to lose it. I watched him literally wither away, both mentally and physically before my very eyes. He was already seeing a Court ordered psychiatrist, and taking heavy doses of mood-altering meds, including (75) mg of Elavil, four times per day. Marshall became a walking zombie. Luckily, I hadn't gotten that bad just yet.

Perhaps as a result of my strong family ties, my commitment to seeing truth prevailed, that I, unlike Marshall, was a first-time offender with no prior criminal record whatsoever; the fact that I was a father of two beautiful children, who I knew would never have forgiven me had I chosen to plead guilty, especially to a crime I was in no way guilty of, provided me with the resolve to refuse to give up, and I thanked my lucky stars above that I had all this going for me.

I remember, while going through my locker at the time I was pondering all this heartache, a book fell out and hit me over the head.

JUDICIAL WEB

No joke, this really did happen! I went to pick it up and placed it back inside my locker, because reading a book at the time was the furthest thing on my mind. I glanced at the title, *"For the Defense,"* by F. Lee Bailey. I began reading the cover, and a little of the introduction, but then put it down. I just wasn't in the mood to read. Then, over the loudspeaker, I heard my name being called for a telephone call. We were allowed to receive calls on the ground floor pay phones. Whenever a phone call would come in for a resident we were paged over the public address system, and literally had less than a minute to drop everything and get to the first floor to take the call. There were four floors at the VOA, and I was on the top floor when I was paged. To make it down to the pay phones in less than a minute, from the fourth floor, was a real challenge, especially if one was in the middle of doing something, which would often be the case.

I made a mad dash for the first floor, and luckily made it in time to answer the call. I learned it was Vincent, my lawyer-friend from Miami. We spoke for a long time, must have been over an hour, and he let me spill my guts out to him. When I was all done crying the blues, Vincent reminded me about a new case, recently decided out of the Fourth Circuit Court of Appeals. The Defendant/Appellant, Leon Durwood Harvey, through his counsel, argued before the Fourth Circuit Court of Appeals, that Harvey was denied his Sixth Amendment right to a counsel of his choosing, since the Government moved to seize and subsequently forfeit all of Harvey's assets, thus denying him the ability to pay the lawyers he had retained with some of those assets, regardless of whether or not they were being alleged to have been illegally acquired as a direct result of Harvey's drug smuggling enterprise.

The judge in Harvey's criminal case, after careful consideration, had denied the government's pre-trial Motion to Forfeit. Thus, allowing Harvey the ability to utilize his assets to pay the legal fees to his attorney of choice. The only caveat the District Court placed on the record was, so long as the property and/or funds being transferred to Harvey's attorneys was not a sham or a fraudulent transaction, he'd be allowed to use them to pay his attorneys' fees.

The government disagreed with the lower court's denial of its forfeiture motion, and appealed to the Fourth Circuit Court of Appeals, challenging the District Court's ruling. Six months later the appellate panel rendered its published opinion. The Appeals Court Affirmed the District Court's Order, which prohibited any and all current attorney fees from being forfeited, without prejudice to the government's rights to further proceedings to seek forfeiture of any other property and/or funds transferred as attorney fees, in any sham or fraudulent transactions made by the defendant/appellant, Harvey.

Not to confuse anyone, let me digress for a moment and provide a quick rundown on the different courts within our Federal Judicial System. Each state has at least one U.S. District Court, where civil and criminal cases, as well as constitutional issues are litigated. There are eleven U.S. Circuit Courts of Appeals, which cover all fifty states; all U.S. territories, and then there's a Federal U.S. Circuit Court of Appeals, located in Washington, D.C. These Circuit Courts of Appeals also hear issues of a constitutional nature, both in federal and state courts.

As stated above, each of the U.S. Circuit Courts of Appeals is strategically located around the country, and includes several states. For instance: The U.S. Circuit Court of Appeals for the Fourth Circuit (the federal court, which ultimately presided over my criminal and civil issues) is made up of Maryland, Virginia, West Virginia, North and South Carolina, respectively.

The U.S. States Supreme Court is our country's highest Court. It's where the buck stops, and it's the final legal authority of our Nation. In other words, it's the law of the land. If a case is decided one way or the other by the U.S. Supreme Court, it can only be changed or altered by an act of Congress, which is extremely rare. The only other relief the accused would have, is by way of a presidential pardon or act of clemency, granted by the incumbent president, from a civil or criminal, federal conviction, or by the governor of any of our fifty states, involving a state's civil or criminal conviction, or via possible post-conviction relief.

So, to recap, the case Vincent had reminded me about, United States vs. Harvey, was decided by the Fourth Circuit Court of Appeals. In this case, during pre-trial proceedings, the government petitioned the U.S. District Court claiming that Harvey's assets should be forfeited, and he shouldn't be permitted to utilize them to pay for his legal defense.

This proffer was made by way of a formal motion, claiming that the assets were tainted, having been acquired by drug revenues, and thus they didn't belong to Harvey, but rather to the U.S. Government. The judge determined that this would violate Harvey's Sixth Amendment right to a counsel of his choice, and denied the government's forfeiture motion. The Government appealed the case to the Fourth Circuit Court of Appeals. However, after waiting six long months, the Fourth Circuit, in a unanimous decision, Affirmed the District Court's ruling. Since the Fourth Circuit's ruling was not yet rendered, at the time of my criminal matter, we were between a rock and a hard place. If we rolled the dice and chose to use the District Court's ruling in Harvey's criminal matter, not knowing if the Appellate Court would affirm or overturn the lower court's ruling, we'd be SOL if the ruling was overturned. On the other hand, if the Appellate Court affirmed the lower court's ruling, and thus allowed Harvey to utilize his assets, even if they were illegally acquired via his alleged illegal, drug escapades, and we chose not to file a challenge to the government's similar motion before Judge Moore in my criminal proceeding, which could very well prove to have been a drastic mistake. Like I stated earlier, I was between a rock and a hard place.

As a result of the Harvey ruling, by the District Court for the Eastern District of Virginia, a decision was made by my attorney, after conferring with Vincent and several other prominent legal scholars, that a hearing should immediately be requested before Judge Moore, who was then handling the pretrial proceedings in our criminal case.

The motion was filed by my attorney, and surprisingly Judge Moore granted us a hearing on Monday, July 28, 1986, at 9:00 a.m. The purpose of the hearing was to determine whether my seized assets could be released, and thus allow me the opportunity to retain an attorney of my choice. Sounds familiar!

Coincidently, the date set for the hearing was the same day that I was to appear before Judge Ellis, in the Eastern District of Virginia, for arraignment proceedings on my second criminal indictment. What a juggling act our lawyers had to maneuver to get Judge Ellis to postpone the arraignment hearing, so that we could keep our hearing date with Judge Moore, on that same day.

I had a few days to kill until I would know something definitive, as to how things would all turn out. I decided to catch up on some reading. I remembered my sister giving me the book, *"For the Defense,"* by F. Lee Bailey, the one that fell out of my locker and hit me over the head. I never got around to reading it while I was an inmate at the Baltimore City Jail, so I felt now was a good time to do so. I was intrigued by Mr. Bailey's life, ever since I was a freshman, back in 1965, after hearing a lecture given by him when I was attending Monmouth College, now renamed Monmouth University, which is located in Long Branch, New Jersey.

I took a refreshing shower and afterwards began to read, non-stop, into the wee hours of the following morning. I couldn't put the book down. The following day I continued reading, and later that evening I was able to finally finish one of the most fascinating and intriguing, true-life stories I've ever read in my life. Well, maybe except for this one!

I was truly moved by the many compelling aspects of Mr. Bailey's life. Especially his astute legal mind and track record as a marvelous criminal defense attorney, all of which inspired me to write him a

JUDICIAL WEB

letter outlining my current legal predicament. It took me the better part of the following day to complete my thought process and write that letter. By the time I completed the fourth draft, I knew it was ready to be mailed. I wanted my letter to be well written and grammatically correct, and in the mail it went.

While I was working one day at my new assignment at the VOA, which was answering the phones in the Administration Office, a call came in that I happened to answer. The party on the other end of the line asked to speak with Mr. Silva. I informed the party that I was Mr. Silva, in a somewhat state of surprise since I wasn't expecting to ever receive a telephone call from the outside in this manner. The party quickly replied, *"Hold please for Mr. Paul Rashkind."* I later learned that Mr. Rashkind was Mr. Bailey's partner and a good friend of Harold Bluestein, my personal injury attorney.

I'd spoken with Harold several weeks earlier about an accident case he'd been litigating for me. I mentioned to him that I'd written to Mr. Bailey, at which time he informed me that he was good friends with him and his partner, Paul Raskind. Nothing more was ever mentioned about the matter. Boy was I ever surprised at the chain of events that followed after I answered the phone that day.

Paul and I spoke for a good fifteen minutes. He informed me he was calling from their Boston office, and that they'd recently opened an office in South Florida. He proceeded to inform me that he was going to have the papers I forwarded to Mr. Bailey sent to Miami for his personal review and follow up. At first I didn't know what to say or how to react. I was flabbergasted! I thanked Paul for calling me, and when I hung up the phone I was literally speechless and on cloud nine. I didn't know who to call first!

While all this was going on, the past week was a rather hectic one for our lawyers. On Wednesday, July 23rd, all eight defense attorneys met in Judge Moore's chambers to discuss the trial date, and any anticipated problems or delays that might arise.

STEVE SILVA

After several hours of back-and-forth bickering, Judge Moore decided that Monday, October 20, 1986, would be our official trial date. It was apparent that Judge Moore wanted to be certain that our case would be tried in October because he was planning on retiring at the end of the year; he didn't want our case to run into the following year, if at all possible.

During the in chamber's meeting, both mine and Marshall's lawyers broached the subject of our being released from the VOA to the third-party custody of our parents. Surprisingly, as it may sound, we were informed by our lawyers that Judge Moore didn't have any issue granting our lawyer's request. However, leave it to the prosecutors, they vehemently opposed any such order, and made it known to Judge Moore that the in chamber's meeting was strictly to determine the trial date and not our release from the VOA to the street. Consequently, Judge Moore had no other choice but to stand mute on any further discussion about the matter, and so at best our hopes of being completely free were short-lived. The only thing it did do for us was to set up the possibility for our lawyers, at some future date, to file a proper motion before Judge Moore to render a ruling on the VOA release issue, which I was truly grateful to hear.

Another weekend passed, and I spoke with my parents and daughter and shared a few good laughs with them. To pass some time I did number's painting, which I thoroughly enjoyed doing, and I finished reading another book, an autobiography by David Brenner, the comedian, called *"Nobody Eats Tuna Fish,"* a humorous rendition of a young man's life, which I very much enjoyed.

On the following Monday, I awoke, shit, showered, shaved, and got neatly dressed for another day at the VOA. The sun was shining through the dark, shade-drawn window, in the dormitory area. However, I was feeling kind of down, despite the beautiful weather outside, while wondering if I'd ever get out of this life-altering mess I was experiencing. Would I ever be able to live a normal life once again. Would I be spending the next ten or more years in federal prison, as a casualty of the War on Drugs. What would become of

JUDICIAL WEB

me. Would I be deprived of seeing and enjoying the youthful years of my only son, Joshua. Would I not live to enjoy dancing at my only daughter's wedding. Would I not live to hold in my arms and kiss my future grandchildren. All these questions, and many more were lingering in my mind, as I made my way to work that morning. I couldn't help but feel deep despair every waking moment as I began another day at the VOA.

While I was trying to take my mind off these many unanswered questions, I was paged to the front desk to pick up my legal mail and some beautiful photos of Joshua sent to me by his mother, Victoria.

I took my lunch break, and for the next half hour I just stared at the photos of my young son. I was wondering if I would have to continue to be emotionally tortured by not being able to see Joshua grow up. Would my only memories of my son be by way of some instamatic camera lens.

After my lunch break, I returned to the administration office and continued my workday. It must have been around 1:00 p.m. when the phone rang, and I answered it. I said, *"Good afternoon, may I help you?"* A soft-spoken woman's voice answered and said, *"May I speak with Steve Silva, please."* I quickly replied, *"One moment,"* as I was trying to second guess who the caller could possibly be, since I didn't recognize the voice.

Somehow, don't ask me how or why, I just knew at that moment my prayers had been answered. I was about to speak with one of the greatest defense attorneys of modern time. Yes, I was ready! I gained my composure, pushed in the flickering hold button, and said, *"This is Steve Silva, can I help you?"* Once again, the mild-mannered, soft-spoken voice said, *"Please hold for Mr. Bailey."*

A few seconds passed and then, with the most distinguished voice, *"Mr. Silva, this is Mr. Bailey."* I quickly responded, *"I don't believe it, my prayers have finally been answered."* Mr. Bailey replied,

"Well, I don't know about all that, however, I felt I owed you at least the courtesy of a phone call. Tell me a little more about your criminal matter." I inquired with Mr. Bailey if he'd read over the documents and the detailed letter I'd sent him, outlining the main issues of my criminal case. He quickly responded and informed me that he hadn't done so as of yet. He wanted to first speak with me, and acquire a feeling as to what my case was all about. I proceeded to give Mr. Bailey a quick scenario of my indictment. We spoke for a few more minutes; however, having sensed Mr. Bailey was pressed for time, we ended our brief conversation. Mr. Bailey asked me to call him back once Judge Moore ruled about my assets being released to pay my legal fees. By that time, Mr. Bailey told me he would have read over all my paperwork, the blueprint of my criminal matter, and then decide on the feasibility of taking on my criminal plight. I thanked Mr. Bailey for calling me and hung up the phone in total shock!

I thought to myself, I just spoke with one of the finest defense attorneys in the country. One who will certainly go down in the annals of modern-day jurisprudence, as being a truly remarkable human being, and a champion spokesman of Lady Justice.

To you Mr. F. Lee Bailey, even though nothing ever became of our brief five-minute conversation, I truly want to thank you for the great lift in spirit you provided me on that extraordinary day, which I will certainly never forget. Especially, for having renewed my confidence and faith in myself when everyone else said I was wasting my time writing to you, and by proving them all wrong when you called and spoke with me that day. From the bottom of my heart I truly wish to personally thank you for your call.

As things eventually turned out, after careful consideration, with so much going on and the uncertainty of my ability to even consider being able to afford the legal services of Mr. Bailey, and the many discussions with my family and close attorney friend, Vincent, we collectively decided having Mr. Bailey represent me wouldn't be in my best interest. I didn't need the added publicity or the speculation

JUDICIAL WEB

from the U.S. Attorney's Office as to how I was able to afford such a high-profile attorney to represent me.

As this day had now ended, I couldn't help but think that positive things were about to happen for me. A new light had been cast upon me from this wonderful accomplishment. Sweet dreams were mine that night, and as I fell asleep, I silently uttered, *"The pen is mightier than the sword."*

Once again I'd like to digress, take a writing break, and share a poem I was inspired to write after my call from Mr. Bailey concluded. It goes like this:

I DID IT ALL

I did it all and I stood tall,
I never thought I'd take a fall.
Then one day in early spring,
the feds came and said I led an
enormous cocaine ring.
On that fatal April day in spring,
I was taken away and asked to sing.
My life has never been the same,
I'm very truly much to blame.
To think at 40 I did it all,
until the feds came and took it all.
and what a hardship I've caused us all.
I've traveled the globe twice over,
performed on cruise ships the world over,
I've been to dozens of islands under the sun,
where I've shared my music talents with everyone.
Been an author, inventor, salesman, a horseman, too,
I've sold real estate in Florida, even Timbuktu.
Been a Notary, a Freemason, and Rotary Club member,
even owned recording studios and record companies, too.
Then one day it was all over,
Big Brother came and said,
Steve Silva move over.

STEVE SILVA

*Left me nothing,
not even to start over.
Yes, this is my story,
it's very sad but true.
I did it all and I stood tall,
I never thought I'd take a fall.
Now all that's left,
is my will to survive,
and my strong desire,
to stay alive.
For my children, Stacy & Josh,
I know this must all sound very harsh.
But I promise you both,
When this is all over,
I'll bounce right back,
and be ready to start over.
I did it all and I stood tall,
I never thought I'd take a fall.
Where there's a will there's a way,
and I hope and pray,
my jury will come to feel the same way.
Steve Silva NOT GUILTY!
NO WAY! NO HOW!*

LIFE AT THE VOA CONTINUES

Here's some of what was happening on the outside world regarding Marshall's brothers, Nat and Frank, and my brother, Gary, who were all out on bail for the past several months.

Frank, the middle brother, is a 6'1" tall, slender, good-looking, talented guitar player, and an aspiring songwriter, too. Frank relocated to Los Angeles just prior to our arrests. He began performing with a heavy-metal rock group out there. He was asked to join the band after making a name for himself, while attending a well-known music institute in LA. As far as I knew, Frank was perfecting his craft, hoping to become a famous musician one day.

Next, I'd like to introduce to you, TCIB (which stands for, The Cat Is Back), the one and only, Nat the Cat, otherwise known as Nathaniel C. Smith. Nat was the youngest, most talented, and wildest of the Smith brothers. Like his brother, Frank, Nat was a very talented young man. He was twenty-six at the time of his arrest, 5'7" tall, good looking, with long, dirty-blond colored hair, green eyes, like a cat, good natured, and a free-spirited individual. Nat's true talents had yet to be unleashed; he didn't know where his true potential and talents would take him in life. Nat was a fine drummer, but in my opinion, a better vocalist, front man, and a potentially gifted songwriter if only he'd put his mind to it. The problem with Nat was that he lacked discipline and patience. I think he might have had ADHD (Attention Deficit Hyperactivity Disorder), and didn't know it. I had noticed a lot of changes in Nat over the years I was around him, some good and others not so good. However, I truly believed once this mess was behind us, Nat had the potential of becoming a successful musician and songwriter, too.

Unfortunately, Nat, unlike Frank, had his music career placed on hold as he was currently helping his mom, who was going through some trying times in her life. She and Nat's dad had recently been divorced, and she was forced to vacate their farmhouse of fifteen-years, because of their divorce settlement. Since Frank was in LA at the time, and Marshall was still at the VOA and unable to move freely, Nat felt it best to lend his mother some moral support, by staying with her, until the trial was over.

Then there was Grandmother, Mary Smith, the pillar of the entire Smith family. Mary had recently suffered the loss of her husband, Paul, and having been very close to all her grandchildren, from her only son, Mary, too, needed some moral support from Nat in order to help her through her depressive state of mind, which was seriously affecting her quality of life as well. After all, the arrests of her three grandchildren were very embarrassing, especially at her age, and while still mourning the sudden and unexpected death of her husband, for over 50 years, she had to remain strong for everyone.

Nat had his work cut out for himself having to deal with all these problems, as well as those of his own. After all, Nat was facing a stiff federal prison sentence if convicted of the crimes he was indicted on. I'm sure, like the rest of us, this weighed very heavily on his mind.

Last, but by no means least, there was my brother, Gary. What can I say about my bro. The one thing I can honestly state with certainty, had Gary not been released on bail when he was, more than likely, with all his severe, ill-health issues, he never would have survived as long as he did. In other words, with the conditions being what they were in the Baltimore City Jail, with the poor medical attention, and the lack of proper medical treatment for Gary's life-threatening, thrombophlebitis illness, his blood disorder, and diabetes, he surely would have died in prison, or at the very least lost both of his badly infected legs.

I was very grateful that Judge Moore had compassion, and agreed to allow Gary to make bail, which then allowed him to acquire the proper medical treatment for his serious and well-documented medical ailments.

Gary, being naturally lazy and barely self-motivated, often relied on me to kick him in the ass, from time to time, in order to get things done, especially when it came to taking care of his many health issues. Now that I was no longer around to keep after him like I did, thank goodness Judge Moore allowed Gary to make bail, and remain under the care and custody of our parents pending the outcome of our forthcoming criminal trial.

Imagine at thirty-seven years old, and still being under your parents' wings. I guess you could say that was Gary's fate. Gary stood 6'1" tall, weighed a hefty two-hundred and fifty pounds, with brown hair and brown eyes. Gary's greatest assets in life were, he had a heart of gold, was very good natured, possessed impeccable common sense, and a better friend in life you couldn't have asked for. Talk about a sense of humor. Gary loved making people laugh, as it came natural to him.

My brother's favorite pastime was eating and guzzling six cans of Diet Pepsi every day. Gary could consume, in a single day, more soda than anyone I've ever known. I believe that this contributed immensely to his ultimate demise in life. I'm sad to say, in his later years, he paid a very dear price for doing so. Gary said he liked drinking Diet Pepsi, because it gave him the greatest burning sensation whenever he'd guzzle it.

I would often tease my brother by telling him if he really wanted an unbelievable burning sensation, one he'd never forget, he should try guzzling some freshly brewed jalapeno pepper juice.

Without any exaggeration, I've seen my brother down a two-liter bottle of Diet Pepsi, at one sitting, without any problem. Talk about eating, Gary ate like there was no tomorrow. We had a standing joke between us.

I told Gary, I believed he'd rather stuff himself with food than make love to a beautiful woman. You know what his response was. *"You're 100% right, bro!"* Imagine that! I guess that's where we drew the line and differed greatly.

I often wondered where Gary acquired his eating and drinking habits from, until I asked my dad one day. He told me that his father, our grandpa, Hymie, may he rest in peace, was a brute of a man during his day. He said it would be nothing for his father to sit down at the dinner table and consume an entire head of fresh lettuce, half-a-honeydew melon, two whole large, sweet onions, a half-a-loaf of bread, a whole broiled chicken, a huge portion of boiled potatoes, mixed veggies, and then wash it all down with a quart of ice-water or freshly brewed prune juice, which was his favorite drink. My dad's mother, my grandma, Fannie, may she also rest in peace, loved to drink lots of water. All hours of the night, she'd drink fresh juices, soda water, and ice-water, too.

So, as you can see, Gary must have inherited these two traits from my dad's parents, and together it turned him into a human eating, and drinking machine.

Enough of my brother's bad habits, here's a few of his better ones, which in my opinion, far outweighed his shortcomings. A genuine Taurus; true to his zodiac sign, with a heart of gold, and the patience of a saint. But cross Gary just once, and you're in big trouble. I mean, Gary wasn't the kind to try and do you any physical harm, instead, he'd just wipe you off, and have nothing further to do with you. He just wasn't one to be taken advantage of, although many tried.

My brother would often go out of his way to help you, and always gave you a fair shake as long as you treated him fairly and with honest and utmost respect. He demanded that from others, like me, all the time. Gary was not materialistic, in the least, nor the jealous type, and he always enjoyed sharing with others.

The one trait I considered to be Gary's greatest was his impeccable common sense. No one that I've ever met in my life, to this very day, has matched this innate and intuitive ability that my brother possessed. So many times, I can readily recall Gary saying to me, *"I told you so, bro,"* and more often than not he was right on the money.

Gary's knowledge of sports, especially football, baseball, basketball, and thoroughbred horse racing, was incredible. I vividly recall an event I'd like to share with you regarding my brother's exceptional skills at professional NFL handicapping.

One winter, we decided to take a trip to Las Vegas, several weeks before the Super Bowl game, back in 1972. Gary decided to play a Pick Ten Win a Million card. He needed to pick and win all ten NFL games being played over that eventful weekend, to win the one million dollar Grand Prize. P.S., Gary picked and won the first nine games, and came within seconds of winning the tenth and final game, for the Grand Prize of a whopping, one-million-dollars. We stayed glued to the TV that entire weekend, as each game was being played, while stuffing ourselves with gourmet food, and just having a great time together.

I really didn't pay much attention to Gary possibly winning the Grand Prize, until late Sunday afternoon. He was nine for nine, going into the Sunday afternoon's game number ten. We were both in total shock-mode. Here's how it all played out.

It was Christmas Day, 1972. The Kansas City Chiefs were playing the Miami Dolphins, for the Conference Championship. As fate would have it, whoever won that game, would eventually go on to play in Super Bowl VII.

Gary liked the Chiefs, who was the underdog. The game rules for the one-million-dollar Grand Prize were no handicap points were given to either team. Whoever had the most points at the end of the game would be declared the winner.

All Gary needed in order to win the Grand Prize was for the Chiefs to hold on for another minute and thirty-seven-seconds, and Gary would have won the cool, one million smackaroos. However, on that eventful day Murphy's Law raised its ugly head. Truth be told, it just wasn't meant to be.

As fate would have it, the score was tied at 24/24, at the end of the fourth quarter. By the end of the first overtime, the score remained the same. Then eighty-two minutes and forty-seconds into the game, now in double-overtime, the Chiefs made it all the way down to the thirty yard line, well within field goal range, for their seasoned placekicker to easily score the three points the Chiefs needed to clinch the game, but he missed by literally a few inches, as the football hit the right goal post, and bounced out of bounds. Can you believe that!

The Dolphins, with less than a minute left on the game clock, drive the ball all the way down to the thirty-seventh yard line, and Garo Yepremian, the Dolphins' star, place kicker, steps onto the field, and kicks the winning field goal, making the final score 27-24, and down the tube went Gary's million dollars. Talk about a thrilling, nail-biting, experience!

Boy were we good and bummed out! We came so damn close to winning that million dollar, Grand Prize. Miami, that season, went on to defeat the Washington Redskins to win Super Bowl VII, 14-

7, their first Super Bowl victory. I never quite understood why my brother picked the Chiefs to win over our home team, Miami Dolphins. I guess he had his reasons. What can I say, you win some and lose some, right!

Here's the irony about this entire story. It does have a happy ending after all. Even though Gary and I were both fuming after Garo clinched the game for Miami and caused Gary to lose that big payday, we both got over it, and had a great rest of the day and evening. We saw a wonderful magic show featuring the famous David Copperfield, and stuffed ourselves at the fabulous Bellagio dinner buffet.

The following day, Gary bounced right back into action. He won the Monday night game with a parlay, winning the game outright and then hitting the over/under bet, which covered all our expenses for the entire trip, plus left-over pocket change to boot. So, all in all, we lost the million, but we still came away winners, which few vacationers can boast or brag about, after leaving *SIN CITY* and returning back home safe and sound.

What more can I say about my brother, Gary. I'm sure I could easily fill the rest of these pages with all the good things my brother had done for me, my daughter, our family, and all his loyal friends over the years.

Unfortunately, Gary is no longer with us. He lost his battle to live, from his many life-threatening, medical ailments, which finally took his life on May 29, 2008, at the young age of 59. My life has never been the same, since!

Now that I've covered, as best I could, the activities of both Marshal's brothers and my brother, Gary, I'd now like to share with you a little bit about some of the infamous residents I'd come to befriend, while a temporary resident, at the VOA's halfway house.

STEVE SILVA

I'm certain you've heard of the word mafia, or the expression mafioso, at one time or another in your life. Most people would agree, whenever hearing those two words or reference being made to them, they are usually equated with violence, murder, evil, and horrible images.

I have a surprise to share with you! The word mafia, as listed in the Ninth Edition of the New Collegiate Dictionary, © 1986, [page 715, definition #3] states: "*a mafia is a group of people with similar interests and backgrounds, prominent in a particular field or enterprise; often known as a clique.*" This is exactly what I'd been indoctrinated into when I was first introduced to the mafia, a/k/a Little Italy, as I later came to learn while I was a resident at the VOA.

The members of this VOA mafia family were Patsy, Georgie, Tony, and Armando. You know the well-known slogan, "*When E.F. Hutton speaks, everyone else listens!*" These kind-hearted gentlemen changed that saying around to, "*When the VOA mafia members speak, everyone at the VOA listens.*" Well, not exactly, but it was just that things that were recommended to get done, did indeed, eventually get done.

Here's a typical example of exactly what I mean. The fourth floor of the dormitory, at the VOA, was exclusively utilized for housing federal prisoners, that's where me, Marshall, Patsy and his posse, along with twenty-five other residents slept.

It was now the middle of the summer, and there was no air conditioning. Needless to say, our sleeping conditions were unbearable, especially during the daylight hours, when many of us would likely be taking an afternoon nap, reading a book, or just catching up on writing letters and postcards to friends and family members. So, the VOA mafia boys decided enough was enough. Temperaments were boiling, tension was mounting, and the VOA residents were

JUDICIAL WEB

getting very agitated by the day. *"Time to put an end to all this,"* Georgie said. *"We need air conditioning here and we need it now!"*

Don't ask me how, but Georgie was able to get approval from the VOA Administrator, and within a week's time, the fourth-floor of the VOA acquired two new 33,000 BTU a/c units. From that day forward, it was a pleasure to reside at the VOA, especially on the fourth floor, for all of us. I can't begin to share with you how much everyone appreciated Georgie being able to pull this off.

Then there was Patsy, born in southern Italy, whose parents were also of Italian heritage. Patsy really knew how to live. I came to know him when we first arrived at the VOA, and like Marshall and I, being federal, pre-trial detainees, Patsy was also assigned to the fourth floor. Upon hearing Patsy's distinguished accent, I knew he was from Italy or of Italian descent. Italy was one of my favorite places to visit, whenever I was traveling through Europe. It's a very lovely country, and one I'd enjoy visiting again one day.

On several of my international music trips to the world famous Midem Music Festival, in Cannes, France, held in January of each year, I would often stopover in Italy on my way back home to consummate many of the music publishing contracts I secured while at Midem, for my recording artists, that I represented over the years.

Having acquired a little bit of knowledge of Italian culture, its people, customs, and traditions, I felt confident about starting a conversation with Patsy upon meeting him at the VOA.

As the days passed, Patsy introduced Marshall and I to the ins and outs, the dos and don'ts of the VOA. For this we were both very grateful. Many days we'd sit out back on the dilapidated patio-dock and have lunch together, while watching the boats go by in the Inner Harbor. This is where we'd have our daily gatherings with

Patsy and the boys. We'd talk shop for many hours after work, and listen to each other's heartaches and humorous comments of the day. I thoroughly enjoyed those long talks I had with Patsy, and can honestly say I used to look forward to them each day while I was at the VOA.

Patsy, on several occasions, would make me lunch when I wasn't in the mood to do so myself. He packed a 5'4" solid frame, with a sharp mental attitude and strict disciplined state of mind, which I came to admire. He was a true gentleman. Patsy was known to be a very mellow, easy going, type of dude. It was rather hard to ruffle his feathers, but by the same token, Patsy took no shit from anyone, not even from any of the VOA staff members.

When Patsy was right, he was right, and he'd stand his ground, no matter what. Sometimes he was treading on thin ice, being threatened to be sent back to the Baltimore City Jail for his tough stance on things that mattered to him.

Never once did I see Patsy or for that matter any of the VOA mafia members ever eat in the VOA's dining room. I found that quite odd, but later learned the real reasoning for them not doing so. They always managed to have their food specially prepared and sent in each day. Boy, did they know how to eat. I knew this firsthand, because I was often invited to join them, and what a feast we'd have. Talk about eating like a King!

What can I say about Tony! He was a fifty-two-year-old young man, who at first glance one might mistake for a real tough guy, based on his Willie Nelson look-a-like appearance. However, once you come to befriend Tony, you'd quickly find him to be as nice and pleasant of a person you'd ever wish to meet. Like Patsy, Tony was also instrumental in helping me and Marshall adapt to the rigors of the VOA's lifestyle, since he'd already been through their initial indoctrination several months earlier.

I learned that Tony suffered much through his incarceration and criminal ordeal. The day after his arrest he'd learned that his only son, who had just turned twenty-five, had committed suicide. Talk about an extremely traumatic experience for anyone to suffer under ordinary and normal circumstances. However, with Tony being incarcerated at the time it was as if he died also. He later told me, with tears running down his face, as he vividly recalled the incident, that his son blew his brains out with a 38-caliber semi-automatic revolver having placed it into his mouth and pulled the trigger. Tony seemed to think that his son must have felt somewhat responsible for his father's predicament in life, and the pressure became too insurmountable for him to cope with any longer.

Tony also learned that his son was heavily addicted to opioids, and was fighting desperately to overcome his addiction at the time of his dad's arrest. When Tony got word about his son's suicide, he felt so depressed and was unable to do anything about it. What made matters even worse, due to his present state of incarceration, Tony wasn't even allowed to attend his son's funeral. Imagine that! Then, as if that wasn't enough tragedy and emotional trauma to endure, having just lost his only son, Tony got word, several weeks later, that his only brother had died of a sudden, fatal, heart attack.

Minus one loving son and a brother, while feeling such great despair, Tony nevertheless rose above it all, and was able to fight back with all the mental, emotional, and perseverance he could muster, in order to prepare for the fight of his life and his eventual freedom. Tony's crimes involved alleged possession and distribution of small quantities of cocaine and marijuana. However, according to Tony, the prosecutors twisted the facts, as they are often known to do. Consequently, with Tony's extensive criminal history, the government's attorneys felt they had and open and shut case. However, when it came to trial day, a rather lucrative deal was struck between the government and Tony. Tony received only a five-year prison sentence, his wife was given probation, as part of the plea bargain arrangement, and Tony and his wife were required to forfeit nearly a million dollars in accumulated assets. I guess Tony was rather pleased with the government's plea-bargaining offer. If convicted, Tony was facing forty to fifty years in federal prison for the criminal charges he was indicted on.

Tony survived, and he taught me quite a valuable lesson in life, *"Only the strong shall inherit the earth, and if in your heart you believe in yourself and your cause, then you too shall survive."*

Some say that Tony received such a sweet deal because he became a government informant, and sold his soul to the devil. I never learned whether this was true or not. However, should this have been the case, Tony would have to live with himself, and his actions for the rest of his life. In my humble opinion, Tony suffered plenty with the loss of his only son, and brother. And for this I say, *"To each their own."*

Next on the member's list was none other than Georgie, the originator and Grandmaster of the VOA's Mafia clan. Georgie decided who was in and who was out, as far as being a member of his elite family, especially when it came to the parties they would throw from time to time. You want to talk about eating, those boys really knew how to chow down. We had some pretty big feasts while I was there.

Georgie was a charming, and rather astute individual, in his mid to late 40's, stood 6'5" tall, and weighed a whopping 280 lbs. with all his clothes on. He was built like the ROCK, a/k/a Dwayne Johnson. Georgie had a very peaceful personality, and maintained a calm, cool, and collected air about himself. However, if you ruffled his feathers, look out, because the floor and walls would rumble as if a tornado had struck the building. Yet, Georgie could be as gentle as a lamb, or at times as angry as a bull in heat. He was usually the mediator of the mafia clique, and for that matter the entire fourth floor, which consisted of about forty residents at any given time. If there was a problem, Georgie would usually be the one, most likely, to resolve it amongst the residents. And as far as any problems we might have had with the staff, Georgie was our officially appointed spokesman and mediator as well.

Georgie was incarcerated for extortion, drugs, wire fraud, and money laundering. He was indicted on fourteen counts, in more than five states, and was looking at spending the rest of his life behind bars. However, after a hard-fought legal battle, coupled with some clever plea bargaining, and a ton of money spent on his legal team, Georgie was finally able to minimize his losses, and was now awaiting sentencing, in late August 1986, where he was hoping to receive a three to six year federal, prison term. Not too shabby for all that criminal conduct, wouldn't you agree!

Last on the list of VOA mafia-members was a young man by the name of Armando. I really didn't know much about Armando. We only shared a casual hello and goodbye from time to time. However, I observed that Armando was highly respected by the other members of the so-called VOA's, Mafia family. Armando was at the VOA for a short period, by the time Marshall and I had arrived. He claimed that his wealth and financial security were acquired in the construction and housing development industry. Armando was in his late 20's, well dressed, outspoken, and a rather handsome dude. His crimes stemmed from IRS tax evasion and tax fraud charges, which he was eventually indicted, convicted and subsequently sentenced to federal prison for ten-years. He was also slapped with a restitution fine of $250,000.00, the maximum penalty under the law, for the crimes he was found guilty of.

Armando was waiting to be transferred to a federal prison, and was granted permission to stay at the VOA until the U.S. Marshals were ready to transfer him to his new home. Despite Armando's incarceration at the VOA, he led everyone to believe he was still very wealthy and worth millions. I trust he will begin paying back his fair share of taxes to Uncle Sam from here on out. My intuition tells me that the IRS will make sure of that, and they'll be watching Armando's finances for many years to come.

That pretty much wraps up the Italian mafioso family, clique, clan, call it what you'd like, at the VOA, and those individuals that I'd come to meet and spend time with while I was detained there.

I guess, if I was to sum it all up, I'd have to say between all the VOA's Mafia family members combined, they had potentially more exposure in sentencing years at the time, than the entire history of our country; a sum of money legally or illegally acquired, and assets confiscated in the multi-millions of dollars. However, despite all their combined indiscretions, they possessed hearts of gold, enough to overfill the vaults in Fort Knox, Kentucky.

MY BIG SURPRISE VISIT

July 30, 1986, was another lovely, sunny day at the VOA. I hadn't written anything of interest in my diary since late June. However, today I got the inspiration to pick up my pen and begin writing once again.

It was Wednesday afternoon, around 4:30 p.m. and I decided to find myself a comfortable seat in the visitor's lounge area, looking to catch up on the past twenty-three days of events I'd been lax in writing about. I had seven hours before all the lights went out, which took place during the weekdays by 11:30 p.m., and on the weekends at midnight.

On Monday, July 28th, my brother, Marshall, and I, were preparing to enter not guilty pleas in the Eastern District of Virginia, before the Honorable Judge Brown. We also learned that the other seven co-defendants, as named in our Virginia indictment, were there to enter their respective pleas as well. Some of these individuals I hadn't seen in over five years, while others I'd never laid eyes on in my entire life.

All the lawyers and family members of the accused filled the courtroom that day. It was jammed packed with many press and news media personnel, too.

The hearing was scheduled to commence at 9:00 a.m. sharp. By 9:30 it was all over, if you can believe that. Everyone pleaded not guilty, as was expected. We were made aware by our lawyers that most of the defendants would eventually change their pleas to guilty, in exchange for plea bargaining deals they'd already secured with government prosecutors, which called for their full cooperation and testimony in our upcoming Maryland trial. In other words, for everyone else, except for my brother, Marshall, and I, it was all a big show and total BS, as far as we were concerned. Our Virginia trial date was now set for Monday, September 22, 1986, exactly one month to the day away from our October 20th, Maryland trial date.

The only hope left for us now was to try and convince the trial judge, in our Virginia case, to allow us to consolidate our two criminal cases, otherwise we wouldn't stand a snowball's chance in hell of prevailing in either. This was just what the government's prosecutors had hoped for.

I hadn't seen my brother in several weeks, and when he and my mom appeared at the courthouse, I was shocked to see Gary without his mustache. He's sported one for the past fifteen years or more. Gary's face looked pale without his mustache, but as the day wore on and I got accustomed to seeing him without it, he really did appear much younger looking.

At the arraignment proceeding I was represented by my Maryland attorney's Virginia law firm. They had sent a well-respected criminal defense attorney by the name of Jerry Kramer. Jerry and I met briefly before the arraignment hearing; we went over some pertinent issues before he entered his appearance on my behalf. While my brother had his Virginia court-appointed lawyer, by the name of Bob Cook, to represent him. This was Bob's first criminal case. Marshall had his Maryland attorney, Steve Arlan, representing him.

JUDICIAL WEB

We were uncertain of several pressing issues going into the Virginia arraignment hearing that day. For starters, we were concerned about whether the judge was going to allow us to post the same bond, as we had already posted with the trial judge in our Maryland upcoming trial. Remember, our bail was already set at $250,000.00 for each of us. Or was Judge Brown going to play hardball with us, as he was notoriously famous for doing, and thus cause us to post additional bail, which at this point would have been next to impossible for any of us to come up with. If this latter scenario became the case, we'd be conveniently sent directly to a Virginia federal prison, or perhaps right back to the Baltimore City Jail, courtesy of the U.S. Marshals Service, until the Virginia trial began. I thought to myself, another nightmare was now brewing all over again.

However, as things eventually turned out, we were fortunate to have been granted permission, by Judge Brown, to utilize the same bail as we posted in Maryland for our upcoming Virginia trial.

My beloved mom, bless her heart and soul, was patiently waiting outside the Courtroom entrance during our Arraignment proceeding. She couldn't stand the pressure or the suspense any longer. It had gotten way overbearing for my dear old mom and rightfully so. Both her and my dad had already been through hell and back with Gary and my legal matters.

As Gary and I exited the courtroom with our lawyers that day, our mom just stared at the both of us from afar, and she began to break down and cry uncontrollably in front of everyone. It was very embarrassing, but it was what it was. Nothing Gary or I could do about it, except hold and hug our mother warmly, and look her in the eye and assured her that everything was going to be just fine. At least that was what we wished we could have conveyed to her at that moment to calm her down. She was a wreck! She asked why this was happening to us, and what did she do to deserve all this anguish, at this late stage of her life. Mom went on to say how our dad would never make it through the trial, and that this would certainly be the end for both of them.

I was numb and didn't know what to do or say. Mom was really taking it badly, I could see it all over her face, her swollen, teary eyes and her look of total despair, coupled with the very real prospect of her two sons going to federal prison, had really gotten to her that day.

We just placed our arms around our mother and tried our best to console her by assuring her that one way or another, everything would turn out just fine. However, little did I know then, as I was uttering those comforting words to my mom, what misery Gary and I were in store for.

I felt so sorry for our mom. She was very distraught and the thought of having not one son, but perhaps both her sons in federal prison, was enough to rattle her brain big time!

I thought to myself what if I was convicted and received a long sentence, say ten years or more, and during my incarceration I lost one or both of my parents. I began to sigh silently heavily. My entire life was in turmoil. I began thinking how my son would grow up not knowing who his father really was, other than someone he was told to call dad, who he hardly ever saw or knew, and my daughter married one day with children, my grandchildren, that I would hardly see or be around to watch them grow up. With

JUDICIAL WEB

all these overwhelming thoughts, tears began to roll down my cheeks. I could no longer control my hidden emotions.

My mom noticed my tears and hugged me. I told her I'd be alright and soon we both calmed down. My brother, as usual, cracked a few jokes to lighten things up a bit and we all had a hearty laugh. While we went outside for some fresh air, our lawyers were wrapping up the final paperwork to ensure our release on bail in the Virginia Indictment, at least that's what they had led us to believe they were doing.

Just then, the bailiff summoned us to go back inside the courtroom, as a complication had developed. Judge Brown was now asking us to post the property and funds we'd already posted in Maryland, through the signatures of our family members, in the Virginia case as well. Since only my mom was present and not my dad, or sister, Judge Brown demanded that my parents and sister sign the necessary bail release forms before Gary or I could be released on bail.

In Marshall's case, his mother, grandmother and his fiancée's parents, who posted property for his bail in Maryland, were also required to now execute bail release documents before Judge Brown would release him as well. However, as fate would have it, they were all out of town and not available either. Judge Brown was very adamant and demanded that we be detained until all the necessary paperwork was properly executed before any of us would be released on bail.

Fortunately, the prosecutor in our Virginia criminal case agreed with our lawyers' request to do a proper and timely filing of the necessary documents, in compliance with, Judge Brown's Court

Order, by 5:00 p.m. that day. Judge Brown further agreed to a compromise in that he'd accept telegrams from those family members who were unable to make it to the courthouse by 5:00 p.m., due to such short notice. Gary, Marshall, and I were then escorted to the local processing and detention area, on the basement floor of the Courthouse. Upon our arrival, we were once again photographed, fingerprinted, and requested to fill out a host of forms regarding our family history, education, criminal records, etc.

While I was being processed my attorney, along with my mom and brother, was able to get in touch with everyone, and miraculously arrange for the necessary paperwork to be completed prior to the 5:00 p.m. deadline.

Luckily for me, my sister was just getting ready to leave her apartment when our mom called her. She was leaving to spend the weekend at the beach with friends. Had our mom called a minute later, Gary and I would have spent the next several days in a Virginia prison hellhole, rotting away until this was all sorted out.

Marshall's grandmother and mother managed to meet his lawyer at his downtown Baltimore office that same afternoon. Upon their arrival they signed the necessary documents. Marshall's fiancée's parents were successfully contacted and were able to telegraph consent from their Florida residence, too.

My poor mom had to travel from the courthouse in Richmond, Virginia, all the way back to Baltimore, Maryland's U.S. District Courthouse. Her original plan was to head directly back to our family residence in North Jersey, on an already pre-paid train ticket, but of course those plans had to change in order for her to be able to sign the necessary paperwork for both Gary and I, so that we could both be released on bail before 5:00 p.m. that evening.

My sister wound up having to cancel her weekend at the beach with her friends, and she had to drive all the way to Baltimore, from her home in Bethesda, in order that she, too, could sign the necessary documents required of her on our behalf.

By 3:00 p.m. the required paperwork was completed, and we were now headed back to Baltimore ready for phase two to begin.

At 4:30 p.m. another hearing was scheduled with Judge Moore, our Maryland trial judge, at the Baltimore Federal Courthouse. The purpose of this hearing was to determine whether Marshall and I would be able to have our previously seized assets released by the government so that we'd be able to continue to afford our retained lawyers in both our criminal proceedings. Or would we be forced to accept court-appointed counsel to defend us in what was now the battle of our lives.

We both knew if this was to become the case, we might as well throw in the towel now. Our case was so complicated that only an experienced criminal trial attorney could properly defend us, and thus give us the best defense we could possibly hope for, not some wet behind-the-ear rookie, or an inexperienced public defender.

As we entered Judge Moore's chamber, our lawyers told us we had a one in three chance of a favorable ruling and that they'd give it their best shot. That's all Marshall and I could have asked of them.

Gregory Wells, the government's lead prosecutor, made a desperate attempt to convince Judge Moore to rule against the release of our assets to pay for our legal fees. He proceeded to inform the judge that he was certain we had lots of undisclosed assets, money in the millions of dollars within which to amply pay our attorneys. Our lawyers objected to the prejudicially rendered statements by Mr. Wells, and then in an eleventh-hour tactic, our lawyers offered for both Marshall and I to take the witness stand. This legal, and very risky maneuver would allow our lawyers to cross examine us under oath, and prove that we had no other assets other than those the government was already fully aware of.

Mr. Wells was dumbfounded! He couldn't believe that we opted to take the witness stand. To make matters even worse for him, after we did, Judge Moore was totally convinced that we were telling the truth and, in fact, both rendered indigent.

As a direct result of our testimonies, Judge Moore ordered the immediate release of all our assets to pay our legal fees, and then all hell broke loose in the courtroom that day. Mr. Wells was livid by Judge Moore's surprise ruling, and our attorneys were in their glory, loving every minute of our first major victory.

However, I saw it all in a different light. I believed Judge Moore's ruling was a victory of truth for Marshall and I, and whether or not Mr. Wells wished to believe us, we were flat broke and in desperate need of this big break.

We still had a long road ahead of us. The Virginia consolidation hearing was soon approaching; we were still uncertain whether Judge Moore, who we were quite pleased with thus far, was going to stay on as our trial judge. We heard rumors, through our lawyers, that Judge Moore was looking to retire soon and take senior status. As such, he would surely not entertain a trial, such as ours, that could last for several months as the government's prosecutors and our lawyers were anticipating.

My mom, brother, and sister were happy for me as they all left for home with peace of mind for the time being. At least for now, we all knew that I could afford the attorney of my choosing to represent me in my continued quest for justice.

It was July 4th weekend, 1986. I was excited because I was expecting a visit from my son and his mother, Victoria, who I hadn't seen in several months.

Victoria and Joshua arrived late Thursday evening and they checked into a local hotel minutes away from the VOA.

The next morning, I spoke with Victoria, and she informed me how tough the trip was for her and our son. She told me she'd be at the VOA before noon, as she had to feed and bathe Joshua before visiting with me.

Reflecting on it all, I must say Victoria was a real trooper to have traveled all the way from Florida with our son to visit with me. I was forever grateful for her doing so.

I was waiting on pins and needles for them to arrive when the cab pulled up to the front entrance, and they entered the facility. They didn't see me at first, but I saw them. I was later told that Victoria had to sign in and have her bags checked by security. I sneaked up behind Joshua, who was clinging to his mother's shorts, and I said, *"Joshua, who's the best little boy?"* He immediately turned around, as did Victoria, and my little guy ran into my arms. With tears rolling down my cheeks, I picked Joshua up and held him tightly against my chest. I gave Victoria a big hug and kiss, and we all made our way to the VOA's Visitor's Lounge. Joshua had his head buried in my left shoulder with both of his arms wrapped tightly around my neck. He stayed that way for the next half hour or more and never once lifted his head. He just seemed to really miss me, which I was kind of surprised about since I had been wondering all along if he'd even recognize me anymore.

After a while, Joshua finally lifted his little head, looked around to see where he was and began poking and touching my face with his tiny fingers. He touched my mouth, eyes, nose, and ears, too. He couldn't stop touching my face, and I couldn't believe I was finally holding my son in my arms. The visit was short, as Joshua was getting restless and cranky. Victoria knew it was best she left and got our son ready for bed. We said our goodbyes, and Victoria took a taxi back to her hotel room, as it was a rather long and very exhausting day for her and our son.

That evening Victoria and I spoke on the phone. I told her that I would see her and Joshua in the morning, after my lawyer picked me up, and then he'd swing by to fetch them from their hotel.
At around 11:30 a.m. the next day, my lawyer and I picked Victoria and Joshua up from their hotel and made our way to David's law office. We spent a good part of the day there. I needed to go over some important documents with him, and since his office was adjacent to the hotel where Victoria was staying with our son, he offered to have me spend some private time with my family. I felt once again like a human being, a feeling I'd missed for a very long time.

JUDICIAL WEB

We spent some quality time together, but my only regret was that time was flying and we'd be saying our goodbyes before long, not knowing when I'd see Victoria and Joshua again.

At 5:15 p.m., David suggested he'd take me and my family back to the VOA, as he had dinner plans with his wife and needed to get going soon. On the way back we stopped for some Chinese takeout that we wound up chowing down at the VOA Visitor's lounge.

Before long, it was pushing 9:00 p.m. and Joshua was getting cranky. Victoria felt it was time to leave, as she still had to pack, get our son to bed, and then get up early to catch her flight back home.

I carried my son outside, where a taxi was waiting to take Victoria and Joshua back to their hotel. I handed Joshua back into Victoria's arms and kissed him gently on his forehead and cheeks, not knowing when I would see him or Victoria again. As I laid my eyes on Joshua, now comfortably sitting in his car seat next to Victoria in the backseat of the taxi, I looked at both of them with sadness in my heart. Joshua also seemed very sad and confused, too. I think he knew what was happening, and that he wouldn't be seeing me again for a very long time. The look Joshua gave me that day, with his squinting eyes, was enough to bring tears to mine. I'll never forget that moment for as long as I live.

As the taxi pulled away from the curb, I waved goodbye and tried my best to contain my emotions. I wiped the tears from my eyes, and smiled as they disappeared down the main street on their way back to the hotel.

The next morning, Sunday, I was awakened by the resident manager and told I had a phone call. I quickly dressed and dashed down the four flights of stairs to answer the phone. It was Victoria calling me from the airport to let me know she and Joshua had arrived safely at the airport and were soon ready to board their flight back to Florida. I told her I was happy to hear from her and deeply appreciated her visit and for making the extraordinary effort to bring our son to see me. I hung up feeling depressed all over again, and headed back upstairs to shower and get ready for another long day.

At around 4:00 p.m. I tried placing a call to see if Victoria had arrived back home. The phone rang three times, and Victoria finally answered on the fourth ring. I was so happy to hear her sweet-sounding voice and my son, who was yelling in the background. I was at peace once again, knowing they'd arrived back home safe and sound.

The next day, however, I awoke feeling ill with knots in my stomach, and once again feeling down. I just couldn't shake my depressed state of mind. I kept thinking about Stacy, Joshua, Victoria, and my mom and dad. I decided to take a stroll out back and get some fresh air. As I passed the visiting room, on my way outside, I noticed the brown and white wooden horsey Joshua had been playing on just a few days earlier. I broke down once again. I felt trapped, with nowhere to go, waiting for my two trials to be over, and learn of my destiny one way or another.

After an hour or two of breathing fresh air and just being alone; no noises to deal with, I reported to my assigned work area for another workday ahead of me.

JUDICIAL WEB

As I stated earlier, regarding my decision to not have Mr. Bailey represent me, for reasons I've already expounded upon, I still needed to get back in touch with Mr. Bailey, as promised, and let him know of my decision not to retain him.

Having Mr. Bailey represent me, while it all sounded so surreal to even be able to make that happen, I felt it might intimidate the prosecution team, leaving the judges in both our criminal cases more inclined to side with them, as a means of balancing the scales of justice, so to speak. Plus, the jurors would be less inclined to believe that I was, in fact, indigent and flat broke while wondering how I was capable of hiring the legal services of such a high-profile lawyer as Mr. Bailey.

I finally mustered the courage to call Mr. Bailey's South Florida office and spoke with his secretary. She informed me that Mr. Bailey was in Tampa on another high-profile criminal case and wouldn't be back until the end of the week. I left her a message to relay to Mr. Bailey. I told her that I'd follow up with a letter to him, which I did later that day. I never heard back from Mr. Bailey or anyone else from his law firm.

On that Wednesday, July 9th, at around 3:00 p.m. I met with Marshall, his lawyer, and David. We discussed some alternative strategies and certain options, which both our lawyers felt we still had available to discuss. I didn't like how the meeting was going, and quite frankly, I was getting increasingly upset by the minute. Our lawyers informed us that the government's position was unyielding and that they wouldn't budge an inch off the Title 21 Section 848 CCE felony charge against either of us.

We were further informed that we were the meal tickets to future promotions and huge raises for the head DEA agent and both prosecutors in our criminal case if they successfully secured convictions and/or guilty pleas from us. Our convictions on the CCE 848 charge would reap a mandatory minimum of ten years, without the benefit of parole, in federal prison, with a maximum sentence of life, without parole, plus the loss of all our seized assets, most of which would be used to pay our legal fees, and fines in the millions of dollars, too.

There was no way to go for me but to fight to the very end. I was determined to have a jury of my peers decide my fate. Our lawyers informed us that the best offer the government was prepared to make was fifteen years without parole, the loss of all our assets, based on full cooperation, by pleading guilty to the Title 21-848 Continuing Criminal Enterprise offense.

The bigger insult was that we had to decide to accept this ludicrous offer by Friday, July 11, just two days away. I looked at Marshall; he looked at me, and then I stared into David's eyes. I uttered in a stern, calm voice, *"Tell the prosecutors, both son-of-a-bitches, and their hatchet man, Agent Jones, what and where they can shove that kind of bizarre plea offer. Tell them to shove it where the sun doesn't shine!"* I was furious! During the remainder of that meeting, nothing further was mentioned about plea bargaining, but rather for us to prepare for trial full steam ahead.

The only thing weighing heavily over us now was the Virginia indictment and whether we'd be lucky enough to get the judge to consolidate our two cases as previously requested. The motion was set to be heard in the Virginia federal courthouse in front of Judge Brown, just two weeks away. If we couldn't convince this judge to rule in our favor and order both our criminal proceedings

JUDICIAL WEB

to be consolidated, we'd really have a major battle on our hands, and in that case, I wasn't sure there would be much of a chance we could prevail with our more pressing and pending Maryland criminal trial.

A STROKE OF GOOD LUCK

Our second trial was scheduled for Monday, October 27, 1986, in Baltimore, Maryland, only two months away. The Government was doing us dirty, as they were looking to place undue pressure on us. They wanted their pound of flesh by giving them our guilty pleas, which they were desperately seeking. By doing so, they'd save themselves the time, effort, expenses, and the trouble we'd otherwise cause them by bringing us to a lengthy trial, and then run the risk of losing their case against us.

The prosecutors were going to do everything possible in order to convince Judge Brown, in our Virginia case, to deny our motion for consolidation. If the judge sided with the government, we'd be forced to consider cooperating with them in our Maryland case, very well knowing we wouldn't be able to withstand the pressure of two federal trials. That was their well-planned strategy and ultimate goal.

The Virginia criminal indictment was a joke. Out of the thirty counts as charged, we were listed in only four of them, and they were for possession of cocaine, not the more important conspiracy count. The prosecutors were keen on steering clear of charging us with any conspiracy count in Virginia. They knew had they done so, they'd be forced to dismiss our Maryland indictment, as our constitutional rights, based on double jeopardy protection, under the Fifth Amendment, coupled with our collateral estoppel rights, would have been unquestionably violated.

JUDICIAL WEB

It was all keenly orchestrated to force us to plead guilty in our Virginia criminal case. The government, as we'd soon learn, always strived to have its cake and eat it, too. That's why our lawyers were so adamant about our motion being right, with i's dotted and t's crossed, so that we'd have the best chance at our upcoming Virginia consolidation motion hearing. This would be the last road block the government could use short of foul play.

I submit to you, what I considered to be an absolutely flawless Consolidation Motion, brilliantly prepared and argued by my lawyer, and had you been Judge Brown that day, listening to David's most convincing argument on my behalf, I'm 100% certain that you'd have agreed that his argument was very persuasive. David fine-tuned his brief, and sent it off to Judge Brown for his review and final ruling on our hearing day.

We attempted to convince Judge Brown that since the two cases, the one in the District of Maryland, and our Virginia case, were one in the same, and in the interest of judicial fairness and economic savings, both cases should be consolidated into one. Either a single trial in Virginia, encompassing all the counts listed in both indictments, or a single trial in Maryland, doing the same.

I was still at my lawyer's office on Wednesday, July 9th, around 6:00 p.m., waiting for my brother to arrive. Gary was visiting with his public defender, along with the prosecuting attorney and Sandy Jones, the head DEA agent on both our criminal cases. They were both interested in speaking with Gary. It seems they were interested to learn what my brother knew about the conspiracy and our co-conspirators in our Virginia case and whether Gary would be interested in a plea bargain for his cooperation in both cases.

They wanted Gary to give them information about Marshall and my involvement in the conspiracy, and a host of other players they believed my brother had knowledge of. They informed Gary in exchange for his cooperation and truthful testimony they'd recommend he be granted immunity from prosecution, he wouldn't have to serve any prison time, and he'd spend the next three years on federal probation. Gary couldn't believe how desperate the government was, and how low they were willing to go in order to gain a conviction, turning one brother against another.

For me, the irony was had I had a crystal ball and the ability to see what was coming, how distorted and prejudicially rendered our criminal trial turned out, I'd have gladly advised my brother to cut a deal with the government, save his ass, and tell the truth about my alleged criminal involvement. Because, at the end of the day, had this been the case, and reflecting on all that transpired during our upcoming trials, Gary would have been able to save my ass as well, and the real culprits would have been prosecuted and given lengthy sentences rather than me. However, my fate wasn't going to be that easy to resolve.

Upon my brother's arrival at David's office, he shared the entire story with David and me. He discussed in fine detail what had transpired between him, his lawyer, the government's prosecutors, and the head DEA agent in our criminal cases. Gary informed us how the government ran their little snitch speech by him and how he then looked at his lawyer, then over at the two prosecutors, who were both sitting comfortably in their recliner chairs, along with the DEA Case Agent, and then shook his head in disbelief; didn't say a further word, and politely got up and walked out of the informal, proffer interview. Gary informed David and me that he couldn't believe what he had just experienced.

He said he was now convinced, more than ever, that the government was still fishing for more evidence against us, and if they had to stoop that low to use him to gain a conviction on me, something was drastically wrong with their case against us. At least, that was Gary's common sense on the matter.

Gary spoke with me briefly in private. We both expressed our deep concerns, and he told me in his jovial demeanor that we had a tough battle on our hands. However, he also believed if we stuck together and remained strong and steadfast, we stood a fighting chance to prevail.

As tears began rolling down my cheeks, I told Gary to watch over my daughter as best he could and to take care of his health, as he was not well at all. We talked about the good old days when we were growing up and all the crazy things we did together in our youth. Gary tried to convince me that somehow, someway, we were going to see each other through this living nightmare. We took an oath, right then and there, that we'd not let them beat us no matter what. *No way! No how!*

Our meeting finally ended, and my brother hopped into a taxi and headed back to the train station for his three hour ride back home. Gary and I hugged each other. I proceeded to tell him how much I appreciated his comforting words, common sense wisdom, advice, and unselfish support, despite our past differences over the last several years. He said, *"Later, bro, chin up; remember, it's not over until the fat lady sings!"* I cracked a smile as he left for home, and David proceeded to drive Marshall and I back to the VOA. He told the two of us to hang in there, to stay strong, and that he'd be back to visit with me in a few days.

All that night and through the next day, I tried desperately to get some answers sorted out in my mind. I had many unanswered questions I still pondered over and wanted closure on.

I was feeling down and in deep despair, and everyone at the VOA noticed it written all over my face. I could no longer hide my deteriorating mental state. The walls were closing in on me. The thought of spending the rest of my adult life in federal prison, locked away in a jail cell for something I was in no way guilty of, really got to my mind, body, and soul. I began to feel like I was ensnarled in a spider's web, with no way out.

I knew in my heart I was not guilty of being a drug lord, as defined in the Title 21-848 Drug Kingpin statute, for which I was wrongfully charged, and subsequently convicted of. The worst part I believed was that the government prosecutors knew it, too. However, they were in too deep and wouldn't be able to make things right, for fear it would cost them their careers and prohibit them from becoming federal judges one day, which was the ultimate goal for many Assistant U.S. Attorneys. Unfortunately, for me, the government was in over their heads. They were already in bed with the wrong culprits, and made certain inferences to the Washington Bureau Chiefs, within the Department of Justice, proclaiming they had an open and shut case against me and the others indicted in my criminal case.

In order to secure an indictment on a CCE offense, one must convince the Department of Justice, through the U.S. Attorney General, back in 1986, that is, that the allegations and evidence against the alleged CCE defendant were solid and would stick beyond a reasonable doubt. So, in order to reverse this charge, unlike any other federal, criminal statutes, it must go the revered route. That is, the challenge must be so overly convincing as to prove to the U.S. Attorney General that the evidence wasn't strong enough to sustain a CCE conviction beyond a reasonable doubt, and thus should be dismissed from the indictment.

No one likes to admit being wrong, even if it means saving years off a person's life, based on an erroneous indictment charge and the subsequent wrongfully imposed sentence. I'd now come to realize this was exactly the case surrounding my criminal plight.

I began asking myself why everyone in our case couldn't just tell the truth about what part or role they played in their alleged criminal acts, and take their punishment like men, instead of being a bunch of low life snitches, telling lies about me in order to save their own asses from going to prison. After all, why should the system allow them to go free, even though they had gotten caught doing illegal acts that had nothing to do with me or my alleged criminal activities.

As the day began winding down, and nightfall was beginning to settle in, I tried to second guess how the next few days would unfold.

David was planning on making a last ditch effort to have the prosecutors dismiss the CCE count against me in our Maryland Indictment. We were seeking a more favorable plea bargain, something a much more reasonable than the fifteen years without parole, which the government had originally offered me several weeks earlier.

A few days passed, and David called me at the VOA. He let me know that on Monday, July 14th, he was scheduled to meet with

Mr. Wells and Mr. Nolan, as well as the U.S. Attorney and Sandy Jones, the DEA case agent. Together they would discuss what, if anything, could be worked out that would be more favorable for me, and he would call me as soon as the meeting was over. I wished him good luck and waited with bated breath to learn the outcome of his meeting.

Around 5:30 p.m., I received a page over the loudspeaker to come to the first floor for a phone call. I knew it had to be David calling me to discuss the outcome of his meeting. My heart was pounding as I made my way from the fourth-floor dormitory to answer the call. As soon as I heard David's voice say, *"Steven, how are you?"* I knew I was a cooked goose.

David proceeded to inform me he'd spent the better part of two hours trying to convince my prosecution team I was not a drug kingpin. However, none of them bought it. As a matter of fact, David told me under no circumstances was the government going to come off the CCE count, and the best offer they'd now entertained was no longer fifteen years without parole, just a few weeks earlier, but was now twenty years, without parole. I was shattered, speechless, and numb, all at the same time.

After only a few minutes had passed, and I was able to gain my composure, I informed David that I was sorry, but I couldn't talk anymore and hung up the phone.

The next day I received another phone call from David. He informed me that he couldn't sleep all night and felt terrible about the outcome of the meeting from the day before. He wanted my permission to call the U.S. Attorney one last time and see if they'd be receptive to meeting with me. David thought, perhaps I could do a better job of convincing the government's prosecution team that I was not a drug kingpin under the CCE-848 statute, and by doing so, they'd cut me a much better deal upon speaking directly with me.

I was extremely reluctant, and my first thoughts were that I would not subject myself to any such arrangement. I thought it was a set up, and that David was selling me out. That's how deranged my mind became. I trusted no one. However, at the same time, I was very desperate for a break. I informed David if he felt this would be to my benefit, then by all means to set up the meeting.

I guess I came to grips with reality, and nothing ventured, nothing gained, right. At least that's what I wanted to believe. The only stipulation I insisted from David, as to my willingness to meet my adversaries, was I wouldn't be required to be a snitch. I wasn't interested in being labeled a rat, and I would only speak the truth regarding my culpability, and exactly my role in the conspiracy; nothing more. David agreed with my plan, and would set up the appointment for me to meet with the prosecution team.

Later that same afternoon David called to inform me the meeting was set for the following day, July 16th, Wednesday, at 10:00 a.m. sharp.

David thought this was a really good break for us. The U.S. Attorney was letting us know the door was still open, and this was my chance to set the record straight, once and for all. Upon doing so they'd realize I wasn't who they thought I was, and hopefully cut me a better plea bargain deal than was now on the table. I had the challenge of my life cut out for me. I was unable to sleep for the rest of the evening. So much was going through my mind. I didn't know if David was setting me up, baiting me, or what to believe anymore. After all, David was an ex-Assistant U.S. Attorney, from the very same U.S. Federal District I was now being prosecuted in. As a matter of fact, both Mr. Wells and Mr. Nolan worked underneath David's command when he was the Assistant U.S. Attorney, not all that long ago. I'd also learned my criminal case was David's very first as a Defense Attorney. For me, that was a rather scary scenario. Like I stated earlier, I didn't know what to expect. I had no other choice but to roll the dice, and hope for the very best outcome.

The next morning couldn't have come quick enough. I shit, showered, and shaved by 9:00 a.m., and was waiting anxiously for David's arrival at any moment.

As fate would have it David was running a tad late, and called his contact at the U.S. Attorney's Office to let them know of our brief delay. David was finally able to scoop me up, and I made it to the meeting by 10:30 a.m.

While riding in David's car, on our way to meet with everyone, David informed me that this was a once in a lifetime chance. He proceeded to let me know how fortunate we were to have the U.S. Attorney for the Eastern District of Maryland, the one source that could erase the CCE-848, Drug Kingpin charge with the stroke of a pen. I should have known then and there I was being conned.

David suggested that I try my utmost to remain calm, cool, and collected, but most of all to be 100% upfront and honest, while at the same time convincing. He wanted me to come across as being humble, sincere, and not make it appear like I was snow-white, during my explanation of exactly what my role was in the overall conspiracy.

I asked David what protections I'd have, and how could I be certain what I told the interviewing members of the prosecution team wouldn't be used against me at the time of trial, in the event things didn't pan out. I needed to learn what assurances I would be afforded that nothing I said during my interview could be used in any way, shape, or form to hurt my brother or me later down the road. I also wanted to know what they'd be prepared to do for me in return for my being candid and 100% truthful. I was looking for a commitment from the government to drop the drug kingpin count from my Maryland Indictment.

David informed me that this would be an informal proffer session. However, should the prosecution team believe the information I'd provided them was true and accurate, then a formal proffer session would be forthcoming. I began to get the picture, I was getting the short end of the stick. David told me there'd be no tape recordings of the proffer session allowed by either of us; only hand-written note-taking would be permissible.

What if the information I shared with the government wound up being of no interest to them, or they felt that I wasn't 100% truthful and upfront with them. I wanted assurances that nothing I briefed them on could be used against me during my trial. However, I questioned David's strategy because I couldn't comprehend how this could possibly be to my benefit. After all, I could go into the meeting and tell the government everything they wanted to learn about my individual culpability surrounding the conspiracy, its alleged conspirators, and then depart the meeting with nothing concrete offered to me after all was said and done.

I was smart enough and didn't fall for that bullshit trap because that's exactly what transpired. I used some common sense for a change. The Government sure tried to make a complete fool out of me during their informal proffer session. If I hadn't smelled something very fishy from the moment I entered the conference room, where the meeting was being conducted, the prosecutors would surely have taken full advantage of me.

After only fifteen minutes of my trying to convince everyone that I was nothing like they'd portrayed me to be in their overreaching indictment, they all stood up and thanked me for my time and informed David they'd be back in touch with him in a few days. I shook hands with everyone present that day, thanked them all for allowing me the opportunity to speak candidly with all of them off the record, and we then departed the meeting room. *"What a complete and total sham,"* I uttered to myself as we exited the building.

I got into David's vehicle and we headed back to the VOA. David mentioned he felt confident that things went rather well, and we'd have to now wait to hear back from the U.S. Attorney's Office with their reconsiderations if any.

However, I had a completely different take on the outcome of the meeting. On the contrary, I believed that the government's attorneys had only one goal, which was to use me for what ended up being the minuscule information I provided them regarding my individual involvement with the alleged conspiracy, and that the whole thing turned out to be for their own amusement and sole benefit. They had absolutely no intension, whatsoever, of making any kind of deal with me.

Two days later, on Friday, July 18th, at approximately 5:00 p.m., David paid me a surprise and unexpected visit. I really didn't know how to read his face when he confronted me. But it didn't take me long to realize my suspicions were right all along. David informed me that the entire prosecution team had decided that the CCE-848 count in the Maryland indictment wouldn't be vacated. He continued to advise me that the government didn't feel any of the information I'd provided them during the informal proffer session was worthy of belief. Furthermore, they were not prepared to budge off their earlier plea bargain of twenty years, without the benefit of parole, plus a recommended court-assessed six-figure fine, full cooperation, and the loss of all my assets through an uncontested civil forfeiture proceeding.

Needless to say, the first thing that came to my mind was that I was betrayed by my lawyer. I felt I got royally screwed by David's poor judgment and ill-founded advice. I didn't have anything further to say. David, on the other hand, proceeded to inform me with a stern look on his face, to hang tough, and there was still plenty of time for something good to materialize. However, for me, this sounded like desperate rhetoric, with really no substance or genuine concern for what our next move was going to be.

I began to get the eerie feeling that David really didn't want to take my case to trial. He was hoping I'd plead out, and he'd be done with me and my criminal plight, which he now knew was going to be a very long and drawn-out trial. Something I strongly believed he was hoping to avoid at all costs.

David once again uttered to me, as he was exiting the front door of the VOA, not to give up just yet, and that he still had a few more aces up his sleeve. I said under my breath, without him being able to hear me, *"Who is he bullshitting!"* Then I yelled back, *"Sure, David, safe travels getting back home."* He waved and off he went.

Now feeling low and angry, at the same time, I decided to retire for the evening, missing dinner, and laid down on my pillow for another restless night ahead. The only peace of mind that I had to console myself, as I began to doze off into la-la land, was the mere fact that my parents and daughter had planned on visiting me over that weekend, and I was very much looking forward to seeing them once again.

The next morning, I awoke with knots in my stomach. The anxiety that I was experiencing was mounting. I began suffering from a severe headache, something I rarely had experienced in my life. I was worrying about our upcoming Virginia Consolidation Hearing, now only six weeks away. I wondered if we lost the consolidation motion, then what! We had no other game plan to fall back on.

Marshall was expecting his family that weekend, as they were coming to celebrate his milestone birthday. Marshall's mom promised to bake him some homemade goodies, and he invited my family and me to join them.

As it turned out, my parents and daughter arrived at the same time as Marshall's mom and his fiancée, Fran, so we all sat together for a while to celebrate Marshall's big 30th birthday bash at the VOA.

My family's visit was just what the doctor ordered. We spent a splendid two days together. We spoke about various topics, from my daughter's welfare and her college plans to my parents' health and my current state of mind.

My dad tried his best to cheer me up and encourage me to stay strong and optimistic, but his efforts to do so were in good faith at best. He knew the odds were stacked heavily against me and getting worse with each passing day. I put on a fake smile and hoped for some miracle to make things right.

My mom and dad were not all that religious, but they had recently found a renewed interest in prayer. My dad preached for me to keep faith in my heart, that everything would turn out just fine. However, I knew better, but I didn't want to upset him any more than I knew he already was. After all, he had to carry the heavy burden of the entire Silva family on his shoulders, and at sixty-eight years old, with his health issues, that was not an easy burden for him to bear.

My mom talked to me about her fears and other family issues. She shared her concerns about me, and my brother and how she wouldn't be able to live if we were both convicted and sent to prison. A reality just around the corner from potentially happening. I didn't know what to say or how to console my sixty-two-year-old mom at that moment. I knew that my mom and dad were suffering deeply from all they had to deal with.

I can't imagine what must have been going through their minds having to face the reality of both their sons going to prison with one of us, more than likely, for a very long time.

My mom and dad had both suffered and miraculously survived

several bouts of life-threatening cancers over the years, and now having to cope with all this stress, surrounding our criminal ordeal, was way too much for them to bear.

Before I knew it, the weekend was over, and I found myself once again in a dreary state of mind.

During the middle of the following week, I received another call from David. We spoke about the upcoming Consolidation Hearing. He informed me we had a fifty-fifty chance of our motion being granted by Judge Brown. I told David they weren't such bad odds; they could have been much worse, and we laughed.

Then, literally at the eleventh hour, luck was finally going to go our way. We were informed that Judge Brown, who was originally assigned to our Virginia case, was no longer the presiding judge. We were informed that a much more lenient judge was now in charge of our fate, and that because of this change, our chances were now moved to better than fifty-fifty that our two cases would be consolidated. I was cautiously optimistic about this new and exciting development. We'd soon learn if luck was now on our side as the big day was finally upon us.

Both Marshall's and my lawyer attended the hearing without us. We were told we weren't required to be there. Not sure if that was a good sign or not, but we accepted our lawyers' advice and hoped for the best.

I awaited David's call with knots in my stomach from the moment I awoke at 6:00 a.m. It was now 10:15 a.m. and still no call. The hearing was scheduled for 9:00 a.m. sharp, and David informed me that it wouldn't last more than an hour at best. I couldn't concentrate on anything else. I was anxiously waiting to receive David's phone call and learn of our fate one way or another.

It was around 2:00 p.m. when I was paged to the downstairs lobby phone. It was David, and he informed me of the bad news. After strenuously arguing our case for consolidation, the new judge took a twenty-minute recess to deliberate; after he returned to the bench, he delivered his final ruling. He denied our Motion to Consolidate. I can't explain how devastated I was to hear those words uttered from David's mouth. I was speechless, knowing the ramifications of the Judge's final ruling. I felt as though my entire life had just came to a screeching halt. I thanked David for his efforts, despite the negative outcome, and for his phone call as he had promised. I hung up the phone without any further conversation.

I returned to the fourth floor to locate Marshall, who was lying in his bunk bed, and proceeded to share the bad news with him. He took it very badly. With this new twist of fate, we knew we had to now come up with another game plan. However, I had made it known to Marshall that we were all out of aces. I told Marshall, *"The government must be in their glory after hearing the judge render his decision."*

Fast forward to what transpired next, which was nothing short of an eleventh-hour miracle for both of us. Instead of putting us through two trials, our lawyers were able to work out a plea bargain in our Virginia case, whereby we'd agree to plead guilty to one count of distribution, which carried a five-year maximum sentence. However, if we were found guilty on any counts at our upcoming Maryland trial, the distribution count from Virginia would run concurrently with any sentence given by the judge in our Maryland case. If, however, we were found not guilty of any counts in our Maryland trial, we'd serve only two years in a federal prison work camp for the Virginia distribution count. Under the circumstances we were now facing, that arrangement seemed very fair and plausible.

Our lawyers worked very diligently to prepare the paperwork for our final review and execution. Once this tedious process was successfully completed and totally out of the way, we began to concentrate on our upcoming Maryland trial, which was only a few weeks away.

JUDICIAL WEB

THE MARYLAND TRIAL

With the Virginia criminal matter behind us, our lawyers were now able to concentrate on preparing for our upcoming Maryland trial. We had a lot of work ahead of us and not much time to put it all together. We had to decide on witnesses to call for the purposes of testifying on my behalf. We also desperately needed a sensible game plan that would generate a favorable outcome when all was said and done.

As the weeks neared our trial date, now set for jury selection to take place on Monday, December 15, 1986, at 9:00 a.m., I began to get a sense that Marshall was acting very strange towards me. His lawyer was picking him up on a regular basis and when I would question him about it, he'd shrug it off and would tell me he was preparing for his case. However, I felt, deep down in my gut, otherwise. My worst fears were about to unfold.

I spoke to David about my concerns, and he did some further research. Sure enough, he confirmed what I had been feeling for some time now. Marshall had decided to join the enemy's camp. He became a government informant, a rat, a snitch, call it what you want, but this was a devastating blow to our criminal defense, with jury selection scheduled only a few days away.

Marshall knew for certain I was no drug kingpin. However, now faced cooperating with the government's prosecution team, he'd be pressured into saying anything they asked of him in order to save his neck come time of his sentencing. After all, Marshall's criminal record read like a who's who in the drug netherworld. He already had multiple drug felonies on his rap sheet. He was facing a life sentence, without parole, if convicted on the Title 21-848 CCE (drug kingpin) offense, and with the three-time felony loser act, recently enacted into law under President Herbert Walker Bush's Administration, Marshall was looking at life either way. At the end of the day, I really couldn't blame Marshall for taking a plea deal and agreeing to testify against me. He had no other choice.

This was devastating for me, and David knew this was the case. What made matters even worse was that Marshall had to testify against his two brothers, Frank and Nat. That is unless he could convince them to plead out and do the same as he'd chosen to do, which is exactly what transpired a few days later.

Our criminal indictment began with eight defendants, and come December 15th, when all was said and done, we were down to only three of us. My brother Gary, my other co-defendant Jorge Christo, and myself. One other co-defendant, Felix Nova, jumped bail. We learned through the grapevine he made it safely back to his homeland in Santiago, Chile. Another co-defendant, Eduardo Torquet, was severed from our trial on some technicality. We were informed he was negotiating a plea deal just before our trial was to begin. However, at the last minute, Eduardo changed his mind, and several months later he stood trial by himself. He was convicted on multiple charges and sentenced to twenty-five-years, without parole. I guess Eduardo decided it was better to go to trial and take his chances, rather than be labeled a snitch, while serving time in federal prison. Being Colombian, Eduardo made the right choice for himself. He knew, all too well, what the consequences would have been if he'd chosen to become a snitch, and then wound up doing time in a federal prison.

Now, the only ones left to stand trial were Gary, me, and Jorge Christo, a/k/a Little George. Little George was fortunate, and was financially able to hire a very well known, high profile, criminal defense attorney, from Miami, Florida. One, I'm certain many of you have heard of. His name was Roy Black. Roy was involved with many high-profile cases, such as the OJ Simpson murder trial, often appearing as a commentator on national news channels for this highly publicized criminal case.

Another high-profile criminal case, in which Mr. Black served as lead counsel, was William Kennedy Smith's rape trial, the nephew of the late President John F. Kennedy. It was his sister, Jean Smith's son, who was alleged to have raped this young girl while taking a stroll together on a beach in Palm Beach, Florida. As fate would later unfold, besides Smith's full acquittal, Mr. Black wound up marrying one of the jurors in that trial.

Mr. Black was of great legal counsel to our entire defense team during our criminal trial. He was a team player, and he knew the stakes were high for all of us if we were found guilty as charged. Roy also felt the government wasn't playing by the rules, and as such the odds were stacked heavily against us.

I would now like to delve into the trial proceedings and give you an idea of what I was up against. Marshall now had the task of not only saving his own ass, but also his two brothers. He needed to convince the jury that I deserved to be convicted under the drug kingpin statute. Remember, that conviction brings an automatic mandatory ten-year sentence, without parole. A big win for the government. We knew Marshall's testimony would be crucial to the government's case in securing a Title 21-848 CCE Drug Kingpin conviction against me.

During Marshall's testimony he lied and exaggerated about the truth of my involvement in the drug conspiracy. He was unable to face me, even once, during his lengthy testimony. Marshall knew all too well he was doing the government's dirty work for them. The government's prosecutors grilled Marshall for two full days while he took the witness stand. Then came David and Roy's grueling cross-examination. We won some much needed brownie points with the jury and the Judge, who seemed very attentive to what Roy and David were able to extrapolate from Marshall's cross-examination.

David and Roy felt confident any ground the government's counsel might have reaped after their direct examination of Marshall was lost once they completed their cross-examination of him. Marshall couldn't keep his story straight from one answer to another. He was heavily medicated, with a host of psychotropic drugs geared to calm his nerves, while also on suicide watch. In other words, Marshall was a walking zombie. He was unable to discern fantasy from reality. We all felt confident that the jury would discard anything that Marshall had to say against us during his trial testimony.

Moving right along, the government placed a host of other witnesses on the witness stand, from business associates of mine to government agents from the DEA, FBI, and other local law enforcement officials, all of whom were heavily involved in the undercover surveillance, and the overall investigation of our criminal matter.

Then came the bombshell the government had been holding out for last. They placed under oath CI#4. You remember the decorated ex-Fort Lauderdale law enforcement officer, turned drug smuggler. His direct testimony went on for two straight days. Next, there was another two days of grueling re-direct testimony by David and Roy, and then the government's prosecutors decided to recall CI#4 back to the witness stand, to testify some more. Thus, once again we had another crack at CI#4 on redirect. It was truly a circus to bear witness to.

CI#4, who was now identified as Jon Gerritt, a/k/a Doc, my one-time very close friend and partner in several music related businesses, had chosen to totally distort the truth, and commit perjury in the highest regard. Again, as I mentioned earlier, I was later able to prove the government's lawyers knew or should have known about Doc's perjured testimony during my criminal trial, but instead, they chose to remain silent and do nothing about bringing this to the attention of Judge Moore or to our attorneys. Instead, they conveniently and prejudicially chose to keep it a secret, and allowed Doc to continue fabricating the truth about my involvement in the drug conspiracy. Doc proceeded to place me as the boss, the kingpin, of the entire organization, and at the end of the day, the jury obviously bought it, hook, line, and sinker. This was a subversion of perjury in its highest regard, perpetrated by the government's prosecutors to further taint the truth and eventually gain a wrongful and illegitimate conviction against me, which nearly cost me spending the rest of my adult life in federal prison.

Our trial lasted a whopping twenty-four days, from start to finish. However, taking into consideration holidays, especially Christmas and New Year's, plus weekends, and the bad weather days, including two major snowstorms, one was named one of the worst blizzards in the last 50 years, the trial stretched on for seven weeks in duration, or forty-nine days to be precise. Jury selection began on December 15, and the jury found the three of us guilty, of all charges, on Monday, February 2, 1987. So much for Judge Moore's retirement plans.

I'll never forget how I felt after the jury foreman read the verdict. I was now facing a minimum-mandatory sentence of at least ten-years, without parole, for the CCE-848 drug, kingpin conviction. I was also found guilty of conspiracy, possession, money laundering, and distribution convictions, too. All totaled; I was looking at over sixty-years in federal prison. Talk about a scary punishment!

Judge Moore was notorious for handing down stiff sentences for drug offenders, and especially those convicted of being drug kingpins, under the Title 21 CCE-848, a federal criminal statute, which carried a minimum-mandatory ten-year sentence up to life, without any benefit of parole.

I was numb to my core, as the U.S. Marshal handcuffed me, and escorted me immediately out of the courtroom. As I departed, I glanced over at my entire family, weeping and in total shock. My mom was removed from the courtroom because she began crying uncontrollably, and my dad did everything he could do to constrain her outburst. He had to deal with the thought of both his sons now in federal custody, and about to be sentenced to a considerable amount of time in federal prison. I can only imagine

JUDICIAL WEB

what was going through his mind, as the verdicts were handed down. My young daughter and sister were embracing one another, and were both crying out of control. My brother-in-law and daughter's fiancée were doing all they could to console them, but understandably unable to do so.

Our lawyers were overly surprised at what had just happened. Especially, in lieu of the perjured testimony by the government's star witness, and equally surprised that the jury was unable to see through it all.

I had insisted that I take the witness stand and set the record straight, but I was strenuously advised against doing so by my lawyer, my brother's lawyer, and Jorge's lawyer, too. Roy had his reasons for voicing his strong opinion on this issue; however, in retrospect, I firmly believe had I not followed my lawyer's advice, it may have resulted in a much different outcome. I should have opted to take the witness stand on my own behalf, and told my side of the story, which none of the jury members were privy to.

Judge Moore set our sentencing date for Tuesday, April 14, 1987, at 9:00 a.m. sharp. Once again, we had our work cut out for us. We had meetings with pre-sentencing officials from the Department of Justice, who were to gather as much information as they could to present to Judge Moore so he could review, prior to us being sentenced, mitigating circumstances, such as our family and employment history, our backgrounds, and education, etc. It was a long and very involved process, but much needed, as a first-time offender, especially in my case, facing a life sentence, without parole. During our lengthy trial proceeding, I needed to prove to Judge Moore that I was not what I was purported to be. A task I now felt would be next to impossible to accomplish.

Our lawyers planned to file an emergency motion with Judge Moore, in order to allow us to remain out on bail until sentencing day, which was two and a half months away. It seemed it was not clear, after the verdicts were handed down, whether Judge Moore would still allow us to remain out on bail, rather than be sent back to the Baltimore City Jail until our April 14th Sentencing Date. The U.S. Marshals had already escorted us from the courtroom to the holding cells, awaiting further instructions from the Judge.

Call it luck, fate, or perhaps even a miracle. Judge Moore had the Bailiff summons our lawyers and the prosecutors, moments after he'd already exited the courtroom. He instructed the Bailiff to direct everyone to his Chambers. The lawyers were scratching their heads, not knowing what to expect next.

After everyone had reconvened inside Judge Moore's Chambers, he informed the prosecutors and our lawyers, that he saw no reason why he should revoke our bail and that Marshall and I should be allowed to remain at the VOA, and Gary could continue to stay with our parents until sentencing day. However, the prosecutors seemed very dissatisfied with this arrangement. They argued since I was facing a mandatory ten-year sentence, without parole, if not longer, that I was now a definite risk of flight. They also argued that Marshall, having testified against me as a cooperating government witness, could not reside in the same facility where I was staying. The VOA wouldn't approve of this arrangement as well.

When all was said and done, Judge Moore had made his final ruling as follows: He overruled the government's argument that I would be a risk of flight. He mentioned in his ruling that had I been so, I would have fled long before now. He also was aware that if I were to flee, I would leave my parents in grave financial trouble, as they would lose their home, and on top of that, my sister would lose her home as well. Also, Judge Moore was kept fully informed by regular updates from the U.S. Probation Department, who oversaw my parole conditions at the VOA, and that I had been a model resident since my arrival.

Then came this unexpected and most shocking news blurted out of Judge Moore's mouth. He agreed with the Government's position about having Marshall and I stay at the VOA together. He believed that this would not be a comfortable situation for him or the VOA. He ordered I be released to the custody of my sister and her husband, and that I'd be allowed to stay at their home and make regular visits to my attorney, in further preparation of my forthcoming sentencing hearing. The government prosecutors were extremely livid. They threw a tantrum in Judge Moore's chambers, which they were reprimanded for doing. My lawyer was in his glory but kept his poker face and gave a smirk to the government's two prosecutors.

Meanwhile, Marshall was already being escorted back to the VOA by the U.S. Marshals Service. Jorge was also allowed to remain out on bail and returned to his Mom's custody while awaiting sentencing. Gary was sent home with our parents. I was able to fetch my things from the VOA and drove back to my sister and brother-in-law's home in Silver Springs, Maryland. My daughter came with us and sat in the back seat to comfort me.

I couldn't believe this was happening; the ride back to my sister's home was a somber one at best. I was now facing the reality that I'd be spending the next ten plus years in federal prison, and this really got to me. I broke down on the drive home, and couldn't control my emotions. All kinds of thoughts were running rampant through my mind. How would my daughter handle not having her father around anymore in her life.

I'd been raising Stacy as a single parent, and soon she'd no longer have me around to rely on anymore. How would my parents be able to handle all this, with both their sons locked away in federal prison; with me gone for at least ten years or perhaps even a lot longer. We finally made it back home, and all I wanted to do was get some much needed rest. It was a very depressing, exhausting, and very stressful day.

SENTENCING DAY

Soon after I was found guilty, I wrote another poem I'd now like to share with you. Facing a life sentence, without the benefit of parole, I penned these words from my heart and soul.

THE INJUSTICE IN JUSTICE

Once I thought our judicial system was truly great,
but now I think it's always been so damn fake.
Lady Justice sure seems blind,
she's about to give me a lot of time.
Doing time, I'll be going out of my mind,
why does justice have to be so blind?
One thing's for sure; it's a known fact,
the injustice in justice is just that.
If I get no relief from filing my appeal,
I wonder how that's all going to feel.
Hard to swallow this legal system of ours,
it's so far-fetched, it's like living on Mars.
My son who just turned two, and knows not I,
because I keep telling him one great big lie.
He often asks why I don't come home to play?
I keep telling him one day soon I hope and pray.
Until then in these four walls I lay day after day,
hoping to be back home with my family soon one day.
The injustice in justice is such a crime,
soon I'll be doing a whole lot of time.
Why does justice have to be so blind?
One thing's for sure it's a known fact,
the injustice in justice is just that.

I've already thoroughly outlined, in the opening pages of my book, what exactly transpired at my sentencing hearing, and how I made the absolute best allocution anyone could have mustered to a judge, who was so prejudicially biased and utterly convinced that I was everything the government's prosecution team alluded I was. There was no way that Judge Moore was going to show me any sympathy or for that matter any consideration, other than impose upon me a draconian sentence, in order to satisfy the government's blood thirsty sentiments in seeing me sent away to prison for a very long time, if not for the rest of my life with no chance of parole.

The U.S. Probation Office presented to Judge Moore the PSI (Presentencing Investigation Report). I must say it was very well written, and while there were some misstatements and typos, all and all it was a very clear picture for Judge Moore to learn that I had a prosperous and legitimate life. I was well educated, with two Master's Degrees, an accomplished musician, and had always been gainfully employed, having earned a decent income from all my music endeavors. I was a good father having raised my daughter, at a young age, as a single parent. Accordingly, I was very satisfied with the PSI report, which would be presented to Judge Moore prior to him sentencing me.

The only thing was, I don't think it mattered one way or the other what the report had stated and/or recommended to the Court. I felt I was going to get hammered no matter what.

Next up at the plate was the government's lead prosecutor, Mr. Wells. He spoke briefly before the Court and went off on all the people's lives I ruined with my drug enterprise and baby's that died because of my drug dealing empire. Then he turned the mantle over to his associate, Mr. Nolan, who ran rampant with his allegations about my criminal enterprise, and how it impacted the people of Western, Maryland, and the harm I'd caused, through my cocaine distribution network. Mr. Nolan ranted and raved for well over twenty-minutes, while the news media was having a field day

JUDICIAL WEB

taking notes on everything that was being stated in the courtroom that day.

Both Mr. Wells and Mr. Nolan had presented their side, which was riddled with lies and prejudicial language. All of this made me boil inside and want to scream out loud at the same time. By then I was convinced that anything I had to say on my behalf would have, no doubt, gone in one ear and out the other in Judge Moore's mind.

It was now our lawyers' chance to speak on our behaves. Gary's lawyer spoke very briefly, and concluded his plea to the Court for a lenient sentence for Gary, based on his ill-health, low culpability in the overall conspiracy, and him being a first-time offender. Gary's lawyer was hoping Judge Moore would give him a light sentence, commensurate with the sentences the other small-time defendants, in the Virginia conspiracy, had received.

Honestly, even though Gary's lawyer's allocution on his behalf was short, sweet, and to the point, I felt he did a fine job of laying out the basis for which Judge Moore could perhaps give Gary probation, and thus allow him to tend to his serious health issues. Unfortunately, for Gary, that was not in the cards. Judge Moore sentenced him to fifteen-years, for his conspiratorial roll. Needless to say, Gary was devastated. I might add what makes this such a draconian sentence for Gary, was the mere fact that Gary wound up opting to go to trial in the Virginia criminal case, and he was found not guilty of the one possession count he was charged with, and he walked out of the courtroom a free man. However, his luck ran out with his Maryland convictions. I felt terrible for my brother. I knew my parents were now grieving badly.

Roy Black next argued on behalf of his client, Jorge Christo. He did an excellent job presenting his plea to the Court, to grant his client a lenient sentence, as he was also a first-time offender. Roy argued that Jorge had severed his relationship many years prior to the indictment and subsequent arrest of Marshall, his one-time close friend and business associate, and that it had been several years since the two of them even communicated or did business with one another. Jorge was involved as a real estate agent in South Florida, and doing very well for himself. He was engaged and about to get married, start a family, and he didn't deserve a stiff sentence for his minimal roll in the conspiracy. However, like Gary, Judge Moore wasn't buying any of Roy's pleas for leniency, on behalf of his client, and sentenced Jorge Christo to ten-years in federal prison, with the benefit of parole after serving only a third of his sentence. As things turned out, Jorge did pretty well for himself. With good behavior time credits, he'd be released in a little over three years. Hopefully, his fiancée would be willing to wait for his release before they tied the knot, which I believe she ultimately wound up doing.

Finally, it was my time to rise and shine. Judge Moore listened to my fifteen-minute allocution before the Court, but I knew in my heart it was going in one ear and out the other. He was bored out of his mind, and couldn't wait for me to conclude my allocution, so he could proceed to pass his draconian sentence upon me.

Remember, the government was asking for sixty-years, and I was freaking out that Judge Moore could impose such a sentence, but to me anything over ten-years would be more than I could ever endure. At least, with a ten-year sentence I'd have some light at the end of the tunnel. I'd still be able to pick up the pieces and make a new life for myself.

Then came the long-awaited bombshell that everyone was waiting for. Judge Moore pounded his gavel, and in a split second my life was turned completely upside down, and mangled like a metal car-crushing machine. *"Steve Silva, I sentence you to thirty-five years in federal prison, without the benefit of parole."*

Those were the harsh words uttered by Judge Moore, Senior District Court Judge for the District of Maryland, on Tuesday, April 14, 1987. Since then, I've tried to muster all the energy, knowledge, willpower, and courage to prove I wasn't guilty of the harshest felony offense, in the government's entire arsenal of criminal statutes, for which a jury of my peers had otherwise found me guilty of.

Remember, the prosecutors wanted Judge Moore to sentence me to sixty-years without parole. They wanted him to throw the key away on me and throw away the key he did. Thirty-five years without the benefit of parole, was a life sentence for someone of my adult age. I'd have to serve a minimum of twenty-four years in prison if I was granted all the good time behavior credits I'd be entitled to. I'd be a shattered (73) year old man by the time I was eventually released from federal prison, if I was even lucky enough to survive such a lengthy term of incarceration.

I thought to myself if I managed to stay healthy enough to endure such a stiff sentence, that upon my eventual release I would still be able to enjoy a few good years with my family and friends before I died, and this would be all I could hope for. Nevertheless, it was extremely difficult to process what had just happened to me. As far as I was concerned my life was over and done with at that very moment.

As had been expected, the courtroom erupted. There was pandemonium everywhere. The government got their pound of flesh, and they now had their meal tickets to potential federal judgeships. They were considered heroes on this day. The media also had a field day, writing all about my thirty-five-year, non-probable, sentence on that eventful day.

My parents were in a state of shock. My daughter and sister were speechless, and I could hear my daughter crying, while my sister held her tightly in her arms to console her. My daughter's world was about to be turned upside down. She would now have to relocate from our government forfeited home in South Florida, after she graduated from High School, to Maryland, live with my sister, and attend a college in the local area, which she eventually wound up doing.

We were now officially sentenced, and Gary, me, and Jorge were immediately taken into federal custody by the U.S. Marshals Service. We were handcuffed, foot shackled, and escorted out of the Courtroom. Several hours later Gary and I were whisked off in the U.S. Marshal's Bureau of Prison's jet, and headed for MCFP in Springfield, Missouri (Medical Center for Federal Prisoners). That's where many inmates with medical or special needs are sent to. Gary and I were kept together for the time being. He had several serious medical issues that needed to be treated and tended to daily, and I was dealing with herniated discs in my lower back, which prevented me from walking more than a short distance at any given time. This automatically qualified both of us to be sent directly to the Federal Hospital Unit, in Springfield, Missouri, and so off we went.

The jet ride was frightening! I thought we were going to crash several times. The turbulence was horrific, and I've done a lot of airline traveling in my day. Even the U.S. Marshals were showing signs of nervousness, and had begun displaying overly cautious reactions, due to the severe turbulence we were experiencing.

Imagine being 30,000 feet in the air, handcuffed, feet shackled, and unable to move about, or even go to the bathroom for that matter. Several prisoners on that flight pissed in their orange jumpsuits. I kid you not! When we finally landed, several hours later, it was pitch dark. As we exited the airplane and on to the tarmac, we waited for the BOP buses to arrive and take us to our new home away from home. It was April and still very cold in Springfield when we arrived. We only had our short sleeve, light weight, orange jumpsuits, and blue slip-on sneakers, which were a size too big for me. I was having a hard time, between my back issues, the oversized sneakers, with both feet shackled, and walking with the other inmates who were lined up in military style rows, heading to the buses that had now arrived, and were waiting for us to board.

This entire experience was more than I could bear. Gary was a few feet ahead of me and he seemed to be managing with his bad legs.

He kept telling me, as we were approaching our bus ride and about to board, his concerns about eating when we finally arrived. That was what was mostly on Gary's mind. Eating! Can you believe that! I had to laugh, and told him we'd be lucky to get bread and cheese sandwiches, with tap water to wash it all down. He didn't like my reply one bit. You want to know the honest truth? That's pretty close to what they served us on our arrival at the hospital's inmate, R&D (Receiving and Discharge) unit. They proceeded to serve us American cheese sandwiches, with a bag of chips, and a small carton of OJ.

As for Gary, he was able to eat as many of those sandwiches as he desired. They were there for the taking. I could barely finish my one sandwich, while my brother managed to grab a handful that night, which made him a very happy camper for a while.

LIFE AT THE FMC

Before the name was changed to MCFP, it was called, while we were there, Federal Medical Center, or FMC Springfield, Missouri. I heard, through the grapevine, they'd improved the facility in recent years. MCFP operates as a bona fide hospital facility now. When we were doing our time there, it was a joke. It was more like a run down, Red Cross facility, with limited supplies and medical equipment. These weren't the professional medical conditions you'd expect to service legitimately ill, special needs, and handicapped inmates. Believe me, it was far from being that.

I found myself filing TORT claims against the BOP, for failure to provide adequate healthcare for both my brother and I, along with many other inmates that were doing time at FMC. I'm proud to say my minimally acquired legal skills, at the time, were seemingly enough to have the BOP make major improvements to their hospital practices and facilities. At the end of the day, my intervention became extremely beneficial to both the inmate population, as well as the medical staff at FMC. I became an instant hero, but not without consequences, as I would soon experience.

Several weeks after we arrived at FMC, and I was able to raise all that ruckus, in spite of the results I was able to accomplish for everyone, the officials at the BOP were not happy about my having pressured them into doing what they otherwise should have done many years earlier, and they conveniently decided to punish me in their own special way. I regret now ruffling their feathers, and forcing them to retaliate against me.

One night, without any warning, I was visited by two U.S. Marshals. I was told to pack all my things, get dressed, and they'd be back to fetch me in ten minutes! When I asked them where I was going, and why I was leaving FMC, they told me, *"You know why Silva, and if you don't, that's on you, get dressed and be ready to roll in ten minutes."* That was the extent of their reply. I wasn't able to get word to Gary since he was in the hospital unit and being treated 24/7 for multiple health issues. I left word with my roommate to make sure he got word to my brother in the morning, so he could follow up with my lawyer and our family to learn why this had happened to me.

Ten minutes later I was escorted out of FMC, once again handcuffed, foot shackled, and off we went, but to where I had no clue. No one would tell me. I was shitting in my pants. Talk about scary, this was way beyond scary. This was panic-attack time to the max! Remember the prison movie *"CON AIR,"* starring Nicolas Cage and John Cusack, especially the airplane ride! That's what I was about to experience.

This totally unexpected move, in the middle of the night, and the way this was secretly carried out, could have been a screenplay for a modern-day movie thriller. (*The kidnapping of a high profile government inmate, who was needed to solve a serious crime committed against our government, and they needed this inmate's assistance to intervene and take care of this imminent problem*). It was that scary for me to experience.

By the time the morning had arrived, Gary was made aware of my disappearance. He immediately jumped on the phone to try and reach my lawyer, who was still representing me on my direct appeal. If anyone could get to the bottom of this issue, it would be David. At least that's what Gary had thought. Unable to reach David on his first try, he then tried contacting our mother. When she heard Gary's voice, and the horror story he'd informed her about, she panicked and said she'd contact the BOP in DC to try and find out where I was sent and why. Gary already had suspicions about what was happening, so he chose not to further complicate the issue with our mom, and instead instructed her to make the calls to try and contact David, until she had successfully reached him.

Mom was some trooper. She got on the phone and raised holy hell with the BOP Director's secretary, in DC; then she had David make a follow up call with someone she had spoken with earlier during the day. She assured David she'd get to the bottom of what had happened to me and report back to him, promptly.

A few hours later a call was placed to David's cell phone; he was informed that due to the overcrowded prison population that those inmates who were not in need of a high level of special medical attention, had to be removed in order to make room for other very sick inmates. At first, David had no choice but to accept that underhanded explanation. However, he changed his position once he finally was able to speak with me the following day, upon being relocated to the FCI (Federal Correctional Institution) in Texarkana, Texas, where ninety percent of the inmate population spoke only Spanish, and few if any, at least when I was serving time there, spoke any English, or very little at best.

Texarkana, at least back in the late 1980's, was a relatively small federal prison facility. It was located in a very remote part of Texas. I felt very uncomfortable from the moment I set foot inside that facility. And to add insult to injury, they were no way, no how, able to tend to my serious back injury issues.

Once I was able to communicate all this to David, he was able to relay this information to the BOP. I'm happy to say several weeks later I was headed back to FMC, where I was once again reunited with my brother. Boy was Gary ever so happy to see my face again, and I was equally elated to see his.

The problem for me now was the Warden was fully aware of my ability to manipulate the system, and thus overcome any adversity, which eventually signaled trouble for me as the weeks unfolded. This Warden was not someone you wanted to rub the wrong way.

And that's exactly what I was able to pull off by being sent back to his facility, where he was the captain of his ship, and he saw me as a potential threat to the stability he tried to maintain at FMC.

I did my utmost to mind my p's and q's and stay low-key, but apparently it wasn't enough. I didn't know it, but it turned out that the Warden was attached to holding on to his grudge against me. He was determined to find an iron clad way to get rid of me once and for all, with assurances I wouldn't be coming back there any time soon, if at all.

Gary and I were being treated for our legitimate, medical issues, and life now seemed just fine for the two of us. Gary was eventually moved from the hospital section to the general inmate population, where I was situated. At least we were housed on the same floor, making it much easier for us to work on our appeal, and see each other on a daily basis. We sat and ate in the mess hall together, and made the best of our time while at FMC.

Let me digress for a moment and share with you an interesting story. At first, you may think it to be quite amusing, however, once you've given it some deeper thought, I believe you'll soon change your mind. The situation I'm about to share with you was quite serious, and if it wasn't handled properly, it could easily have turned into a disaster, and a grave embarrassment for the Warden, the Director of the BOP, as well as the U.S. Attorney General, during the time of my incarceration at FMC.

This was an event involving one of the highest profile inmates, at the time, in the history of the BOP. The amazing part of the story, I'm about to share with you, is that my brother and I were made privy to it, through a fellow inmate at FMC. If not for Gary's intuition and common sense, there very likely could have been a major prison riot, with massive casualties and consequences, while we were serving time at FMC, not to mention a national news story.

Here's how it all unfolded. Gary befriended this monster-size-looking inmate while walking the yard everyday to get some exercise for his legs. He had to walk very slowly, while most all the other inmates were speed walking and would briskly pass him by. Unlike Gary, because of my bad back, I wasn't able to walk much at all. So, I would accompany him to the walking track, sit myself down on a nearby bench, and watch Gary take his daily stroll around the track, and then we'd head to the mess hall for lunch together. That had become our routine for several weeks now.

This modern-day, giant-looking, mild-mannered gentleman stood 7'5" tall and claimed to weigh 550 lbs. He was only mildly obese. No joke! As I said, he was a living giant. His face looked scary, and he had a big scar, which ran from ear to ear, on the top of his bald head.

Every day, like clockwork, this inmate walked the track from early morning to mid-afternoon. He'd walk with his head down while he shuffled his feet, and he'd slowly move his long, hairy, dangling arms, with the same rhythm as his feet movement. Somehow, he took to liking Gary, and they befriended one another. They even made it a point to begin walking the track together a few times a week. They didn't say much to one another, as Gary noticed this inmate seemed somewhat illiterate and he wasn't much for making conversation. He'd smile at Gary from time to time, sporting a big grin on his face, with an eerie and devilish look in his eyes. Leave it to my brother, Gary, to befriend this extremely peculiar inmate.

Some of you may recall the name Andre Rene Roussimoff, a/k/a Andre the Giant. Andre stood 7'4" tall and weighed a whopping 560 lbs. That was nearly the exact height and weight of this inmate, who became Gary's new yard-walking buddy.

Imagine facing someone on the football field who was 7'5" tall and weighed 550 pounds, with nothing but meanness and evil in his

JUDICIAL WEB

eyes. If I was a quarterback I wouldn't want to see those eyes staring at me, I can tell you that.

On this particular day Gary was walking with Ed. I was sitting on one of the many benches lining the outdoor walking track, reading one of my *Jeffrey Archer* novels, a gifted author, I might add. Gary stopped by the bench and introduced me to his friend, Ed, but he was called Mr. Ed by everyone else.

I reached out to shake Ed's hand, but my hand was like a small child's compared to Ed's. That's how huge his hands were. If you compared Ed's body size to that of Shaquille O'Neal, the famous NBA superstar, back in the day, Ed would dwarf Shaq's physique. Ed was 4"s taller and weighed over 225 more pounds than Shaq, who stands 7'1", and currently weighs around 325 lbs., on a good day.

Rumors began circulating around the prison compound that the person Gary had befriended, by the name of Ed, was supposedly the *Texas Chainsaw Massacre Killer*, who was finally apprehended in 1974 for his gruesome chainsaw, styled murders. Remember, I said rumors. Supposedly, he couldn't stand trial due to his insanity plea and was subsequently sent off to FMC, where he was given a full frontal lobotomy, which ran from ear to ear, and was visually seen on the top and sides of his huge, oversized head.

Now for the rest of the story, as the late great *Paul Harvey* would always say during his weekly, nationally syndicated radio broadcasts.

When inmates would zoom past Ed, while he was taking his daily stroll at a much slower pace along the inside path of the walking track, some inmates chose to get stupid and looked to antagonize or tease Ed. They'd make chainsaw-like sounds as they walked or ran past him.

On this sunny afternoon in late May, Gary and Ed were taking their routine walk, when they lost the energy to walk any further. A bunch of inmates started humming the chainsaw sound. I could sense the commotion in the distance as it resonated louder and louder. I immediately noticed that Ed was getting upset and very agitated by the chainsaw sounds he heard. He was about to become unhinged, but luckily Gary was able to talk him out of doing so.

Gary began feeling very uncomfortable since Ed was already serving a life sentence without parole and was the subject of a full lobotomy several years earlier. Gary well knew that Ed could still reason, especially when certain inmates would make fun of him. I immediately thought this was not good and could turn into a disaster, especially if Ed acted like the *Hulk* and finally lost his temper. Luckily, he remained calm and collected, and he and Gary found the energy to keep on walking one final lap.

Those inmates had no idea, to this very day, how lucky they were that Ed just brushed them off like he did, thanks mostly to Gary's intervention. Perhaps, if Gary wasn't with Ed to calm him down, those antagonizing inmates could have all been seriously injured, if not mutilated or killed on the track that day.

To make matters even worse, this crazy Warden decided to play on that evening, of all evenings, the newly adapted *Texas Chainsaw Massacre* movie thriller, in the main auditorium, for all the inmates' amusement. Imagine that!

I did everything in my power to beg the Warden not to play this movie. I insisted that if he did, the blood spilled would be on his hands. I tried to make sense with the Warden, but I wasn't getting through to him. To avoid a possible disaster for him and his reputation, which was excellent, so I'd been told, I suggested he place Ed in lock down status for the remainder of that evening, and come up with some lame excuse why that was necessary.

At the end of the day, the Warden heeded my suggestion. As a result of his doing so, nobody was hurt, and the Warden prevented a possible catastrophe, which he'd have surely paid a heavy price for had he not heeded my sound advice.

The next day, Ed and Gary were back on the track, walking slowly together, as if nothing had ever happened the day before. However, as fate would have it, Gary and I were unable to ever verify whether Ed was actually who he was rumored to be.

The weeks flew by, and Gary and I were getting rather antsy. We thought that we needed a change of scenery and climate. It was very cold in Springfield, Missouri, almost all year round. Gary preferred a change of seasons, and I preferred a much warmer climate. I never did fare well in cold climate environments.

In the meantime, our lawyers were working diligently on our Appellate Brief, which was due to be submitted for its review by the Fourth Circuit Court of Appeals, in the coming weeks. I was hoping to secure a hearing date before the Fourth Circuit to reverse the Jury's guilty verdict, especially on the Title 21-848 CCE count. This form of Post-Conviction Relief, as I would later learn, was next to impossible to prevail on. Better than 95% of all appellate challenges are never granted a hearing, and those that are, less than 5% ever receive a favorable ruling. Unlike my brother, Gary, I've never been a serious betting person, but if you asked me, those were some pretty stiff odds to overcome.

POST-CONVICTION RELIEF ERA

I would now like to shed some insight as to the nature of post-conviction relief, and the limited options I now had left in my legal arsenal's continued quest for justice to prevail.

Let me take you through the process so that you'll have a full understanding of exactly what I was up against, and the slim odds I had of overcoming my ongoing criminal ordeal.

First, we start with an investigation; then a grand jury is convened, and if the evidence presented is enough for the grand jury to issue an indictment, then the next step is the issuance of an arrest warrant, then the defendant is arraigned, and he can plead guilty or not guilty to the charges lodged against him or her. If a not-guilty plea is entered, which usually is the case, then a trial date is set by the judge assigned to the case, usually within a reasonable period of time as set forth by the U.S. Constitution's Sixth Amendment. A prong of which clearly states: *"Without exception, in all criminal prosecutions, the accused shall have the exclusive right to a speedy and public trial, by an impartial jury of his or her peers, in the State and district wherein the crime shall have been alleged to have been committed."*

During the pre-trial period there is the discovery process where evidence is exchanged on both sides, depositions may be taken, interrogatories are requested, and from all this evidence gathering a strategy is prepared for both the defense and prosecution sides to proceed to trial.

In federal criminal cases, such as mine, you're first tried in a U.S. District Court. All the states have at least one U.S. District Court,

JUDICIAL WEB

while others may have several. The size and population of a state often determines how many U.S. District Courts there may be in that particular state. Criminal cases are usually tried in the U.S. District Court nearest to where the alleged crime was originally alleged to have been committed, or alternatively where the grand jury's indictment was initiated from.

In some criminal matters, such as ours, when there are multiple jurisdictions involved, there can be multiple trials in one or more different jurisdictions. In our particular case, the alleged crimes were committed in Florida, Virginia, and in Maryland. Florida is where the alleged conspiracy was first born, and then the alleged distribution network extended to Maryland and Virginia.

The U.S. Attorney's Office, for the Southern District of Florida, felt there wasn't enough evidence to try us in their district. So, the U.S. Attorney's Office, for the District of Maryland, conveniently chose to pick up the ball, convened a grand jury there, and reaped their pound of flesh with the issuance of a multi-count, criminal indictment to be tried in the U.S. District Court for the District of Maryland. That's how we all wound up in Maryland's Federal District Court system. Then, when a superseding indictment was handed down, in the Western District of Virginia, from alleged distribution drug crimes, which crossed state lines from Maryland to Virginia, we wound up with a second criminal indictment in Virginia's Federal District Court system.

After a criminal case is successfully tried and verdicts are handed down by the presiding judge, if the trial is before a judge only, called a bench trial, or in my case by a jury of my peers, the case is finalized, and punishment is rendered, usually by way of a prison sentence, which is handed down by a federal judge to the guilty defendant(s). But, as the often used saying still stands, *"It's not over until the fat lady sings."* The next phase of the judicial process moves our criminal matter to the designated appellate court system.

Most guilty verdicts are, more often than not, appealed to the next highest federal court, called the Court of Appeals. There are currently ninety-four U.S. Federal District Courts in the country, with thirteen U.S. Federal Circuit Courts of Appeal, including one assigned for the District of Columbia, and of course the one and only U.S. Supreme Court, the highest court in the land, where the buck stops there as they say.

Accordingly, a criminal matter runs its usual course through our Federal Circuit Courts, which is a long and arduous process, and could take as much as a year or longer to resolve.

In my criminal case it was 18 months before everything was ruled upon and finalized. An 18 month time frame is common, especially if there's an Oral Argument Hearing ordered by the court. That was something we were desperately hoping we'd be granted.

Next step, which is an option that the defendant has available to him, and for which must be exercised if the defendant has plans to seek post-conviction relief, he or she must always first exhaust all appellate court filings before exercising any post-conviction relief challenges to his or her conviction. Standard legal procedure, as it's often referred to.

The final step, in seeking justice, is off to the U.S. Supreme Court, where a defendant's challenge to his or her conviction is faced with even greater odds against prevailing, and where the words slim to none are often uttered amongst legal professionals.

The U.S. Supreme Court receives petitions, which are called Writs of Certiorari, both in criminal and civil matters, by the thousands, which are selectively chosen and heard by the justices, from the first Monday in October, continuing until usually late June or early July, during each sitting term. So, you can only imagine how extremely difficult it was to have your criminal or civil matter reviewed, and then set for oral argument, by the highest court in the land. From my personal experience it was slim to none!

JUDICIAL WEB

Now that one has thoroughly exhausted their appellate rights, they are left with a few more bites of the apple of justice. This is where Post Conviction Relief comes into play. An extraordinary specialty of criminal law, which is practiced by only highly skilled, professionally trained, and well experienced criminal lawyers. These lawyers must not only be knowledgeable of the ins and outs of our criminal justice system, but they must also possess the exceptional research and writing skills, which enables them to find that one, or perhaps two reversible flaws in a defendant's prosecution, which could be argued once again before the U.S. District Court, where the initial trial was conducted for the sole purpose of seeking a new trial, or at the very least a resentencing hearing. Usually, this takes place by way of what is termed an Evidentiary Hearing.

Imagine how difficult this process can be. You're going back to the same court with often the same federal judge who heard your case several years earlier; where you were found guilty by a jury of your peers, sentenced by the same judge who you're now asking to reopen your case, set aside the jury's verdict, and grant you a new trial or a reduced sentence based upon some flaws that you must now argue and convince the judge, beyond a reasonable doubt. Talk about the odds of winning this argument! Forget about slim to none anymore. This goes far beyond slim to none. This would now require divine intervention and/or a much needed miracle.

Let me be clear here. This post-conviction relief process is rarely ever granted, and in my case I probably had a better chance of winning the Florida Lotto, Mega Million, or Power Ball lottery, than prevailing on any post-conviction relief proceedings afforded to me.

My criminal case was highly publicized, so out of the ordinary, involving many government officials from the hierarchy of the DEA, FBI, U.S. Attorney General's Office, both U.S. Attorney's Offices for the District of Maryland, and Virginia; even the White House's involvement, under President H.W. Bush's overzealous *War on Drugs* and his *Zero Tolerance* tactics, as well as President Clinton's

1994 Crime Bill and his *War on Drugs* stance, all of whom had their hands, one way or another, in my criminal matter.

Having Judge Moore overturn my drug kingpin conviction, and re-sentence me would have created much havoc, a huge embarrassment, and potential loss of many justice department professionals, from corrupt DEA agents, who intentionally mishandled my criminal investigation, and who saw fit to falsify records in order to seek and gain an otherwise unjust conviction, to the subordination of perjury perpetrated against me by the government's prosecution team, including the dereliction of duty from the U.S. Attorney for the District of Maryland, and the misguided and mislead Judge Moore, who was biased in many of his harsh rulings against me, as a direct result of being duped by the government's dirty pool antics, and their prejudicial and biased prosecution of me during my criminal proceedings. The odds of me prevailing from any such post-conviction relief afforded to me, would certainly take a miracle to now overcome.

The two remaining legal maneuvers, after exhausting a Direct Appeal review, and a Writ of Certiorari, under post-conviction relief standards, in a last ditch effort to overturn an otherwise unjust conviction in U.S. Federal District Courts, are either by way of a Rule 33 Motion for a new trial, or a Rule 2255, a/k/a as a Writ of Habeas Corpus.

Under a Rule 33 Motion for a new trial, the proper language that is used to determine whether a convicted felon qualifies for such post-conviction relief or not, is as follows: 1) upon a defendant's motion the court may vacate any judgment, and grant a new trial in the interest of justice, 2) any motion for a new trial, under a Rule 33 filing, must be timely filed, within three-years after the finding of guilt is rendered, or within one year from the denial of a Writ of Certiorari to the U.S. Supreme Court. However, if an appeal is still pending, a court may not grant a motion for a new trial pursuant to Rule 33, until the appellate court remands the case back to the district court of original jurisdiction, 3) if the Rule 33 Motion is based on newly-discovered evidence, the prevailing threshold must reach the level, if proven, and viewed in light of the evidence as a whole, which would otherwise be sufficient to establish, by clear and convincing evidence, that no reasonable factfinder would've found the defendant guilty of the offense(s) as charged, and lastly, 4) due to a new Constitutional rule of law, made retroactive to cases on collateral review by the Supreme Court, which were previously unavailable. These were the legal standards and guidelines set forth during my criminal ordeal, and pretty much remain the same today.

The second and final bite of the apple of justice, which is afforded a defendant under post-conviction relief proceedings, is known as a Rule 2255 motion, also referred to as a Writ of Habeas Corpus. A Latin term meaning bring the body, or present the body. In other words, in the world of legal jargon, bring the body before the court.

A writ of habeas corpus requires a person to be brought before a judge or court, especially for investigation of a restraint of that person's liberty, and is also used as a legal right of the accused, against unlawful and/or illegal imprisonment.

Under literally, this last-ditch effort for post-conviction relief, a convicted felon, in custody under sentence by the court; established by an Act of Congress claiming the right to be released upon the grounds that the sentence was illegally imposed in violation of the Constitution and/or the laws of the United States, or the Court was without jurisdiction to impose such sentence, or that the sentence was in excess of the maximum authorized by law, or is otherwise subject to collateral attack, may move the Court, which imposed the sentence, to vacate, set aside, or correct the said sentence.

My allocated time frame to effectuate this post-conviction relief process had several distinct variables. The one that was most applicable in my criminal case surrounded the first date, which the facts supporting the claim or claims presented could have been discovered through the exercise of due diligence, when filed within one year from the first date of discovery.

I would like to rehash here a bit and go back in time. David completed my Appellate Brief, which I felt he did a decent job preparing; listing the potential reversible issues we felt would most likely grab the Fourth Circuit Court of Appeals' attention, and held the best chances of us reaping an Oral Argument before the court's three-judge panel. The appellate brief was timely filed on April 19, 1988, and the waiting process began. Weeks and months had passed with still no word from the Appellate Court.
It took over eight months before we received the appellate court's final ruling. Our Oral Argument request was denied, and the Fourth Circuit, in their unanimous decision, *AFFIRMED* the lower court's ruling, on December 29, 1988. In essence, the Appellate Court had *DENIED* our motion for a new trial, based on the issues we had raised on Direct Appeal.

The walls of faith were rapidly closing, and reality was swiftly sinking in. I would be serving the remainder of my thirty-five-year sentence in federal prison. I knew the chances of prevailing with any Writ of Certiorari, to the U.S. Supreme Court, would be a waste of time and money. We timely filed the Writ of Certiorari, and waited another ten months before the U.S. Supreme Court sent us a one sentence *DENIAL* notice. I was also informed that David was now officially removed from my criminal case, and wished me good luck with my post-conviction relief efforts.

I can vividly recall some twenty-eight years later, how I felt on that day when I received word that David was no longer going to be involved in my criminal case. Any hope I had left to overturn the injustice I was served by our '*Just Us*' government, I now felt was totally diminished.

Since I was no longer represented by counsel I filed, on my own behalf, my Rule 33 Motion for a new trial. I based my assertions on a strong belief that I was denied a fair trial due to gross prosecutorial misconduct surrounding the government's known, or should have known use of perjurious testimony by their star witness, Jon Gerritt, during my criminal proceedings, which was enough for the jury to have found me guilty of being a drug kingpin.

My problem was the evidence presented, at the time, was not convincing enough for Judge Moore to grant me a hearing, and thus the motion was denied, without prejudice. This meant that I could seek to re-open the case and file a Rule 2255 motion once I had further convincing evidence to warrant the Court to do so.

Needless to say, this was not going to be an easy task, not by any stretch of the imagination. The odds of my being successful were once again heavily stacked against me, and next to impossible to overcome. Back to the drawing board once again it was.

DOING TIME GOING OUT OF MY MIND

Another year had passed; time seemed to be flying by rapidly for us. Our Direct Appeal and Supreme Court challenges were all behind us, and my Rule 33 Motion for a New Trial was also denied. Gary and I settled in, for the time being, trying to adjust to prison life.

Gary and I were both still residents at the FMC in Springfield, Missouri, and tired and bored of the depressing environment we were subjected to daily.

Many inmates came and went, and some even died right in the beds next to where Gary and I were also housed. These were some of the most sick and indigent people I'd ever laid eyes on in my entire life. I mean these were hardened career criminals, with murder rap sheets, rapists, child molesters, habitual felons with life sentences, you name it. There were also those with missing limbs, colostomy bags, even completely blind inmates, who were all housed in this medical prison facility.

I put my mind and efforts into getting Gary and I out of there, and transferred closer to home, as soon as possible. The problem was, Gary needed constant medical attention for his many serious and life-threatening ailments, the only other place, at the time, in the entire BOP was a place called FCI Fort Worth, where they had a medical ward for inmates with chronic medical needs. After much research and letter writing, I learned that being transferred there was next to impossible. The waiting list was a mile long, but that didn't deter me. I strongly believed, where there's a will, there's a way! My newly adopted nickname became '*Perseverance Silva.*'

As fate would have it, I learned through the grapevine, FCI Fort Worth had a very decent music program, and they were always looking for musicians to perform concerts for their resident inmates and prison staff members. Word had it the Warden there was a die-hard music lover, and was constantly searching for inmates who were eligible to be transferred to his prison facility, especially if they possessed professional music talent. I also learned, every year the warden put on a live music concert with top country music legends who volunteered to perform for the inmates there. The best part was that the opening acts were performed by inmates, who warmed up the inmate audience before the headliners performed.

I felt this was our meal ticket to FCI Fort Worth! I immediately jumped on it and began a letter writing campaign to the Warden at FMC. Remember, he had it in for me when I forced his hand and I was shipped out, only to return a few days later. I thought perhaps this was a way for him to get rid of me for good this time. I felt if I presented the situation properly, he'd arrange for Gary and I to be transferred to FCI Fort Worth, and he'd have some empty beds to fill for two new and more desirable inmates.

I sent another barrage of letters to my mom to solicit her help in contacting other outside personnel, who were influential and could make this happen. I even sent a special letter to the Warden at FCI Fort Worth, hoping he'd take interest in my professional music talents, and send for both Gary and I as soon as possible.

Several weeks passed, and then one afternoon I heard my name being paged over the inmate's PA speaker system. I was told to report, immediately, to the administration building's front office. I wasn't sure what that was all about, because usually when inmates are called to the admin office, it's more often than not, bad news. It's usually to inform the inmate that a loved one has died, or a family member was seriously ill and wasn't expected to live. My walk to the admin office was riddled with terrible fears and frantic jitters. My only consolation was Gary wasn't being paged, and if something terrible happened to our parents, we'd both be called to the admin office. Then I thought maybe it was my daughter who was seriously injured in a car accident, or something dreadful had happened to her or perhaps my younger son, Josh. What if it was Gary, who was in the hospital section, and I hadn't seen him since the evening before. All these scenarios were running frantically through my mind.

When I arrived at the admin office, I was instructed to go down the hallway to the Warden's Office. I wasn't sure what to expect next.

The Warden greeted me with a smile and instructed me to sit down on the couch opposite his desk. He then proceeded to inform me that he had received a letter from the Warden at FCI Fort Worth. Apparently, he'd inquired about having me transferred there ASAP. There was a big time annual music event, which was going to be presented to the bigwigs at FCI Fort Worth, and other personnel from the surrounding Federal Prisons. The Warden very much needed someone with my professional music background to coordinate it all, and put together a kick-ass sounding opening-act band for the headliners, who were going to be Waylon Jennings, his wife, Jessi Colter, and Kris Kristofferson. I was dumbfounded, to say the least. I uttered under my breath, *"Where there's a will, there's a way!"* I felt very fortunate to be the recipient of another unexpected triumph.

The Warden wanted to know how I managed to pull something like this off. I pondered my response carefully, and informed him that I had no idea. Perhaps it might have been divine intervention. He laughed and asked me if I was willing to be transferred. I replied with a big smile, but I needed the assurance that my brother would also be able to accompany me. The Warden quickly responded, "No!" When I asked him why, he flatly stated that the medical facilities at FCI Fort Worth were not adequate to handle Gary's serious medical needs. I chose not to engage in any further conflict with the Warden, and thus jeopardize my chances of being transferred to FCI Fort Worth, which I was desperately seeking to accomplish. I felt confident that once I arrived there and proved my worth to the Warden, he'd be able to arrange to have Gary transferred there in due time.

After I'd left the Warden's office, I immediately arranged to meet and speak with Gary at the hospital ward. He was thrilled for me to move on and have a much needed change of environment, not to mention the opportunity to play music once again. Gary and I heard FCI Fort Worth was one of the finest federal prison systems within the BOP. It was a splendid facility, with a host of amenities, unlike most other federal prisons, at the time, in the country. The music program there was the finest in the system. The meals were supposedly awesome. The recreational center had some of the finest weightlifting equipment one could ask for in any professionally equipped, outside gym facility. They also had a large auditorium where their inmates produced shows, movie nights, and even bingo events.

Off to FCI Fort Worth, Texas I went. Upon my arrival, I was immediately greeted by the Warden, introduced to his official staff, and asked to make a list of things I needed to put the band together, and he let me know he was counting on me to pull this off for him. We only had a month before the concert was to take place. That wasn't much time to put everything together. I had no choice, but to rise to the challenge and make it all happen.

I immediately put the word out all over the compound, and auditioned some fine musicians who were already performing on their own, but lacked direction, or the discipline to hold rehearsals and form a tight-knit, kick-ass band. Something that came quite natural for me to accomplish, which I'd done many times over in my life.

By the time the month was up we had a music group that was great sounding, with a young and very talented guitar player and vocalist. He was able to imitate, to the amazement of all the other band members, *Waylon Jennings*, who would be performing live on the same stage as us. I was going to do my nifty drum solo and bring the house down, like I often did in the outside world many times over. We were ready, willing, and able to make this night for the Warden, his invited guests, and the entire FCI Fort Worth inmate population, a night they'd well remember. I forget the exact date of the concert, but it was a spectacular evening, the sky was crystal clear, sunset was upon us, and the outside concert was about to kick off. The stage was built professionally by an outside promotion company the Warden hired with professional lighting and a remarkable sound system. All was good to go!

I must admit I got the jitters after noticing the area was totally engulfed with the entire inmate population. There must've been a thousand or more inmates, outside guests, security guards, fire rescue, and off-duty policemen, anxiously waiting for the event to begin.

The Highwaymen were scheduled to land by helicopter in a nearby field, and then escorted to the stage to jam and rock the place. My band was already set up and ready to start the festivities with our own versions of some of The Highwaymen's favorite hit songs.

We performed five songs, and then I did my five-minute drum solo bringing the house down, and the Warden was in his glory. We received a standing ovation from our fellow inmates as they hollered for more. We were permitted to perform two more rock 'n roll hits, one was *Midnight Hour* and the other was *Evil Ways*, by *Carlos Santana*. I couldn't help but indulge myself with a second drum solo to Evil Ways, which ended our spectacular performance on a high note, with another inmate standing ovation.

Then entered The Highwaymen. They complimented us on our performance, and asked that we remain on the stage to play one of the songs they'd heard us perform earlier while on the way to their dressing rooms. It was one of their hit songs, called *"Desperados*

JUDICIAL WEB

Waiting for a Train." After we finished, Waylon, and Kris congratulated each of us with firm handshakes, and we left the stage while they took over. These musicians were a class act. They performed for nearly two hours without a break. The Warden took me aside and thanked me for taking care of business. He proceeded to inform me that I'd made his day, with a big smile on his face. That was my opening to ask him if he'd consider doing me a favor. He replied in the affirmative, but only if it was within his power and authority to do so. I told him I'd come by to speak with him in the morning, he agreed and we left it at that.

When the show was over, Waylon approached me as I was taking down my drum set. He wanted to know how much longer I would be doing time. I looked at him and asked why? Waylon proceeded to inform me that they were losing their drummer after their next tour, and he wanted to know if I'd be interested in joining their band for their next concert touring dates. I told Waylon that I wasn't sure when I would be available, and asked him for a means to get in touch with him upon my eventual release. I got Waylon's info, thanked him for his genuine offer and further interest in my music talent. Too bad I couldn't have made that happen, as I was just starting my thirty-five-year, non-parolable, sentence, and I didn't know how much more time I'd have to serve before I'd see the outside world again. I will forever cherish that wonderful feeling I experienced that evening.

The next morning, I made my way to speak with the Warden. After some small talk and our reminiscing about the concert performance the evening before, I got straight to the point. I asked the Warden if he could try his best to get my brother to FCI Fort Worth so we could be reunited once again. I informed the Warden how very important it was for me to be with my brother, and that I would never have left him at FMC if I didn't feel I could do a wonderful job here musically, and once that was accomplished, I was hoping I could ask him (the Warden), if he'd consider rewarding me in kind by trying his best to find a way to have my brother transferred to FCI Fort Worth.

The Warden was very understanding; he made no promises, but he'd see what he could do. We shook hands, and I informed the Warden that that sounded fair enough. I left and headed straight for the mess hall before it closed for the breakfast meal. I felt confident if the Warden was able to have my brother transferred, without any complications on his part, he'd be more than willing to do so.

Several weeks had passed, and I'd learned from my mom and dad that Gary wasn't happy with me not being around for him. He was feeling down and wanted to know if I had made any progress with getting him transferred to be with me. I informed my mom and dad I was working on it, but it would take a little more time. I explained to them that Gary's complicated medical issues were a problem, and the treatment he was receiving at FMC Springfield wouldn't be the same as he'd be able to receive at FCI Fort Worth, and we left it at that.

I wanna say, it must have been a week or so later, while I was sitting in the mess hall chowing down lunch, with my back facing the front entrance, when I felt a tap on my right shoulder, while at the same time I heard my brother's very distinctive voice asking me if he could sit down and enjoy lunch with me like old times. I immediately turned around; it was Gary alright. We hugged each other, and I was freaking out that my brother and I were reunited once again. With a big grin on my face, I said to myself *"Thank you Warden for making this possible."*

Gary was immediately assigned to the hospital ward, where he received adequate medical treatment, twenty-four-seven. I was able to visit him daily, and we often ate lunch and dinner together.

Meanwhile, I landed a job in the inmate law library during the weekdays, while on the weekends I was able to continue with my music activities. Time was passing swiftly, and I was desperately trying to make some inroads on finding a solid game plan to file a winnable Rule 2255 Motion, which would be my very last chance, short of a Presidential Pardon, or commutation of my draconian prison sentence, to free myself from all this madness, and the dreadful thought of having to spend the next twenty-plus years in federal prison.

I gained an awful lot of legal knowledge while working with other jail-house lawyers, as they were called, and I eventually became an astute one of those guys, myself. I spent countless hours in the inmate law library. It was there I gained the confidence that there was hope and light at the end of the tunnel for me. I uncovered a host of inconsistencies, while combing through my voluminous grand jury and trial transcripts, which thankfully I was permitted to receive from my lawyer. We're talking about thousands of pages of transcripts. Piece by piece, little by little, the puzzle began to take form and come together. I was astonished at what I was able to uncover.

In the meantime, let me share with you what I was trying to do to get Gary released from his lengthy fifteen-year sentence. Like me, Gary had lost all his appeal rights, and his Rule 33 Motion for a new trial wasn't something he wished to pursue. We both knew what the outcome would be from doing so. Instead, I embarked on a little known legal maneuver based on Gary's severe and well documented health issues, coupled with the inescapable fact that if Gary continued to be incarcerated without outside professional medical intervention, his life would likely be severely endangered. Besides his bout with diabetes, Gary had a weird blood disorder, and his life-threatening thrombophlebitis, which severely affected both his lower limbs could cause both legs to be amputated or worse yet, he could get a blood clot at any time, which could end his life instantly.

With all this going on, and Gary now confined to a hospital bed, I filed a Rule 35 Motion with Judge Moore, on his behalf. This motion, back when we were incarcerated, was used for a reduction of sentence, which the lower court judge could entertain at any time, based on unusual circumstances, such as poor and life-threatening health issues, which Gary was certainly more than able to prove to the Court, and for which a federal judge could order his immediate release.

I felt Gary met all the qualifications for immediate relief, pursuant to a Rule 35 Motion. Hopefully, to time served and immediately released from incarceration. Remember..."*Nothing Ventured! Nothing Gained!*"

I did extensive research before composing, and eventually filing the pro se motion with Judge Moore. We had all of Gary's medical records from both the outside doctors and those from FMC and FCI Fort Worth. The documentation was voluminous, but it verified in undisputable and distinct detail, Gary's life-threatening medical condition. I boxed it all up and forwarded the Motion to Judge Moore's attention. By this time Gary had already served close to three-and-a-half-years of his otherwise fifteen-year sentence, for which, with good behavior credits he'd only had to serve a five-year sentence. So, for Judge Moore he was only giving my brother a get out of jail pass, about a year-and-half earlier than he'd otherwise have to serve to complete his sentence.

Between you and me, Gary never had much faith in Judge Moore granting him any relief, being the strict conservative judge that he was. He had a reputation for having no mercy, whatsoever, and rarely, if ever, had Judge Moore granted a Rule 35 Motion to vacate or reduce an inmate's sentence, no matter what the alleged circumstances may have been. However, I was a firm believer there was always a first time in life for everything, including Gary being granted early release, based on the Rule 35 Motion I prepared and submitted on my brother's behalf.

JUDICIAL WEB

It took several months for Judge Moore's law clerks to sift through all the voluminous documents that accompanied Gary's motion, but at the end of the day, it was determined, even after the government prosecutors strenuously argued to the contrary, that Gary needed emergency medical treatment, or he'd risk dying in prison.

Judge Moore ordered Gary's immediate release from FCI Fort Worth; within several days of the Court's order he was released, and was soon back home with our parents. Gary was now able to continue with his much needed outside medical treatment. You know from reading a prior chapter, what Gary's fate was and how he lost his battle to live. At least I was able to make sure my dear brother wouldn't die in prison.

As for me, I continued to piece together my Rule 2255 Motion, but I knew if I filed it on my own, it would likely fall on deaf ears, and would prove to be a big mistake. I needed to hire a local lawyer from the Maryland, DC area to champion my cause. More on all this in the chapters to follow.

Without Gary around anymore, I decided it was time for another change of scenery. Besides, I wanted to try and get closer to my home state of Florida, and be able to have regular visits with my son and his mother, who I'd not seen in over five-years. I knew my transfer request would be a difficult one. FCI Tallahassee, which is where I wanted to be transferred to, was next to impossible to get to from Texas. The waiting list was much greater than having made my transfer request to FCI Fort Worth. I was hoping that I could count on the Warden to assist me once again with my new transfer plans.

I'd learned from the Warden's secretary, that my transfer request was being reviewed and actively under consideration, however, at this time FCI Tallahassee wasn't accepting any new inmates, especially from the southwest region, and with my lengthy sentence, being a medium security rated federal prison, it was unlikely that

I'd qualify to be transferred there any time soon. The best they might be able to do, according to the secretary, was to get me back to FCI Miami, which wasn't a place I was interested in going at all. I'd been there and didn't like that environment one bit. It was brutal. Lots of gang related issues, racial tension all the time, and just not a place conducive for me to continue doing my time at. I needed to have unfettered access to the inmate law library, which I heard FCI Tallahassee was noted for, and that was my goal. I had no choice but to remain patient, and wait to see what door opened next for me, while hoping and praying for an approved transfer to FCI Tallahassee in the foreseeable future.

The weeks and months passed, and still no word on my transfer request. I began to grow impatient. Too much time had passed, and I yearned to be back in Florida, hoping to have regular visits from my son, his mom, and perhaps my daughter as well.

I continued working in the inmate law library, and established a reputation for being a top jail-house lawyer, helping many inmates with their criminal cases and even having some luck getting relief for several of them, while I was serving time at FCI Fort Worth. I was proud of myself for being able to help other inmates get released from their prison sentences, based on the technicalities I found while researching their criminal matters. It was the most rewarding experience for me, and I loved every minute of it. Maybe I missed my calling, and should have been a criminal lawyer.

While at FCI Fort Worth, I managed to befriend several high-profile inmates. One in particular, whose name I've chosen not to reveal, was the Godfather of a very famous, mafioso, crime-family, located in the northeast. He was serving a lengthy sentence for his racketeering endeavors, and supposedly he was linked to the JFK assassination and follow up conspiracy. This crime boss was a true gentleman, and treated me and Gary, while serving time with us, with the utmost respect. We enjoyed lengthy conversations with him, and other Italian inmates he surrounded himself with.

While suspicions still remain about this inmate's veracity, and his possible involvement with the Kennedy Assassination and surrounding conspiracy theories, this subject was forbidden to ever be raised when in the company of this Godfather and high-profile crime boss.

This next event, which I'm about to share with you, will sound so farfetched, that you'll think it's 100% fantasy. However, I assure you that what you are about to read is beyond a shadow of a doubt, both 100% accurate and truthful. The problem, once again, will be that I am not at liberty to reveal the name of the individual (inmate) that I'm about to refer to. However, I promise you, he was real, and may still be alive to this very day. Let's begin!

The time frame for this event took place in or around October of 1991. It was close to 4:00 p.m., which was the usual time, in every federal prison throughout the U.S. when they would conduct what is called a standup count of the inmate population for each prison in the BOP. This was to ensure that everyone was accounted for, seven days a week, come 4:00 p.m. If not, all hell would break loose, nationwide, within the BOP's administrative system. This daily maneuver was taken very seriously by all the prison guards, the administrative staff, each inmate, in each and every federal prison, and especially the Warden of each federal prison, within the entire BOP.

If the inmate population count was off by even one inmate, the count would be repeated all over again. Sometimes it could last for several hours, and other times only a few minutes. In some instances, an inmate would be missing, whether he was lying dead somewhere with a shank stuck in him, or he escaped. In those rare cases, the entire prison population would be placed in what was called, lock down status. Sometimes this would last several hours or even several days, in the event someone had actually escaped, was seriously injured, or even found dead. I experienced several of those nightmare events during my prison stay. I can honestly tell you; it was absolutely no fun and most horrifying to have bear witness to.

On this particular chilly day in October, while everyone was scrambling to get back to their assigned bunks, and ready for our daily standup count, I heard my name being paged over the PA system, which could be heard throughout the entire prison facility. The guard on duty that day instructed me to head directly to the Warden's office. Here I went once again. I thought to myself, what now! Maybe another music concert was in the works. I should have been so lucky. It was nothing like that at all. This was serious business, and I was about to be placed into the very thick of it all.

Apparently, as the compound was shut down for the routine 4:00 p.m. standup count, a new federal inmate was seen being escorted by U.S. Marshals into the Warden's Office. The intriguing part about this inmate's entry into FCI Fort Worth, he was wearing a black hood over his head so that no one could initially identify or recognize him. I didn't see this take place, but many other inmates facing the admin building, while waiting to be counted, saw exactly what was going on. All sorts of rumors started flying. Something the Warden became overly concerned about.

So, here I am about to enter the Warden's office once again, but this time the circumstances were completely different and very surreal. This was much different than my very first Warden's meeting. I knew this was serious stuff. The Warden welcomed me into his office with a somber look on his face, unlike the jovial demeanor exemplified when we last met. He proceeded to mention that a high-profile inmate had been temporarily assigned to his jurisdiction, and that after a careful analysis of all fifteen-hundred plus inmates currently being housed at Fort Worth, there were only a handful of qualified inmates who were chosen, with exemplary records, to become the roommate of this extraordinary, high profile inmate.

JUDICIAL WEB

I couldn't wait to learn the identity of this mystery inmate, and so I just mentioned to the Warden with a very stern face, *"How about we cut to the chase, Warden, and kindly inform me who this mystery inmate is?"*

Without any hesitation, the Warden blurted out that the inmate was none other than a previously sitting federal judge, who had recently been convicted, back in May of 1991, after having been found guilty by a twelve-member jury for bribery and tax related crimes. Supposedly, this was the very first time a sitting federal judge was ever sentenced to federal prison, within the entire history of the BOP. The judge's sentence was handed down in late August. His bail was revoked, and he was immediately remanded to the custody of the U.S. Marshals Service, and ordered to begin serving his fifteen-year sentence at FCI Fort Worth, in Dallas/Fort Worth, Texas.

I questioned the Warden as to what all this had to do with me, and wanted to know why I was summoned to his office. His reply was very short and brief. He was a bit taken back by my having questioned him. He then looked directly into my eyes and said, *"Because you've been hand-picked by me and my staff, after a careful review of your inmate record, along with five other nominated inmates. After much deliberation and scrutiny, it was a unanimous decision that you'd be the best fit for the judge to have as his roommate, until such time that we can move him to a federal prison camp facility, which I anticipate will be as soon as possible."*

I was speechless! On one hand, I was somewhat reluctant to learn that I was chosen by the Warden to be the judge's roommate. However, in the back of my mind, I was also thinking, this may be a golden opportunity for me to pick this judge's brain, befriend him, get some good sound legal advice from a federal judge, and perhaps, after all was said and done, the Warden would see his way clear, once more, to repaying me in kind, and I'd soon be on my way to FCI Tallahassee. I thought to myself, how sweet would that be. But the age-old adage still remains, I'm sure you're all fully familiar with…*"When something sounds too good to be true, it usually is."* Right! As you will soon read, that's exactly what transpired when this federal judge officially became my roommate.

After that day's standup count was successfully completed, and everything was back to normal, it turned out that several high-profile inmates were able to put two and two together. They began spreading vicious rumors that I was a snitch. They used the proof of my being called to the Warden's office during lockdown and the 4:00 stand-up count, which provided me the opportunity to sneak across the compound and speak with the Warden. This created a lot of problems for me. However, my reputation amongst my fellow inmates was flawless. I helped many inmates with their legal issues, and by doing so, I made some pretty solid, standup inmate contacts, who saw fit to watch my back and make sure nothing unfortunate happened to me.

Luckily for me things calmed down, and it was back to business as usual. In the meantime no one initially recognized the judge, and I never revealed who he was or what circumstances led him to wind up being my new roommate. My prior roommate was gone. He was taken back to court for an evidentiary hearing, which I helped him prepare, pro se (on his own, as a friend of the court). I was happy for him, and thought I'd be enjoying the benefits of having a room all to myself, at least until his return.

That was short lived, since the judge moved into my room, and much to my surprise seemed to have adapted quite well to prison life. During his stay with me, we both shared our legal knowledge, and I was even asked by the judge to review his appellate brief, which was being prepared for him by one of the best law firms in the country. I told the judge I'd be quite honored to do so.

Hold on to your seats everyone! This story is about to get juicier! As fate would have it, I quickly determined this judge was not at all astute about the appellate process, or even post-conviction relief procedures. I found myself educating this federal judge about his own legal issues, and even found an issue that his big-time lawyers had surprisingly failed to raise for the judge on his direct appeal. The issue was called '*vouching*.' When I suggested to the judge to have his lawyers try and add this winnable issue to his appellate brief, the judge decided to put me on the phone with his lead appellate counsel and discuss it directly with him. The phone call lasted about five minutes, at best. I couldn't get a word in edgewise with this hot-shot, egotistical attorney. He was no more interested in speaking with a jail-house lawyer, than the man on the moon. I figured as much and communicated this to the judge, after we finished our brief conversation and I hung up the phone. The judge was quite upset because he'd come to respect my legal acumen, even though I wasn't a lawyer and worse yet, I was a federal inmate serving time just like him.

Now for the P.S. to this remarkable story. The judge lost his Direct Appeal. I shared with him his fate upon carefully reviewing his appellate brief submission. It was weak and stood no chance, whatsoever, of being worthy of the Fifth Circuit Court of Appeals' consideration, for any kind of post-conviction relief the judge was seeking. I believe that the judge knew this as well.

In the meantime, as fate would have it, someone in the inmate population got wind from the outside that a federal judge was incarcerated at FCI Fort Worth and what his name was. It didn't take long for this news to spread like wildfire throughout the entire inmate population. What made matters even worse, the inmate who found out and spread this news, was supposedly the brother of a defendant this judge sentenced to thirty-years in federal prison, several years earlier. She was in the process of filing her Rule 2255 Motion, asking the court for relief based on the judge having been indicted and now convicted of accepting bribes, in exchange for handing down reduced sentences to those who could afford to pay the bribe money, and she stood a very good chance of winning her freedom based on this newly discovered evidence. However, now serving time at the same facility as this federal judge, this inmate had been overheard making verbal threats to harm the judge for giving his sister such a harsh sentence, just because she wasn't in any position to bribe the judge, and reap a reduced sentence, as he'd done for many others while sitting on the federal bench as a U.S. District Court Judge.

Then, one evening, shortly after this news had spread all over the prison compound, in the middle of the night, two U.S. Marshals came into our room, awoke the judge, and that was the last I'd seen or heard from him ever again. Word had it that he was immediately shipped out to a nearby federal prison camp, and continued to serve out his remaining sentence there. However, I learned through the grapevine, several years later, the judge had finally filed his Rule 2255 Motion to vacate, set aside, or reduce his sentence. The one main issue he supposedly used, in further support of his motion for relief, was none other than the issue of vouching. Remember, that was the same issue I'd initially suggested his hotshot lawyer use on his direct appeal, which he categorically refused to file.

Even after all these years having passed, this still brings a huge smile to my face, and much joy to be proud of. Had this federal judge insisted his high-profile lawyer included the vouching issue on his Direct Appeal, he would have stood a much greater chance of being released a lot sooner than he otherwise was. The last I heard, his Rule 2255 was granted, and he was supposedly resentenced to time served and was freed at last. Imagine that! So much for my astute jailhouse lawyering skills and sound advice.

Now for the best news of all. I'm guessing, it must have been several weeks later, I'm walking around the compound with some fellow inmates, when I heard my name being paged loud and clearly over the PA system. *"Inmate Silva, report to your unit supervisor immediately."* What now, I thought to myself.

Remember, whenever an inmate is paged over the prison's PA system, it usually means only one thing. An immediate family member has died or was gravely ill and the clergy staff member is there to console the inmate. But this page didn't have me report to the inmate chaplain's office. This page had me report to my unit supervisor. Could this be the news I'd been patiently waiting for? I made a beeline to my unit supervisor, and upon my arrival I was greeted by a U.S. Marshal as well as the on-duty unit supervisor. I was told to pack my things, and that I was being transferred, but I wasn't informed where I was headed. I thought that this was rather strange. Where could I be headed other than FCI Tallahassee. I was packed in no time flat, and headed for the inmate receiving and discharge area. I tried to get a handle on where I was headed from the U.S. Marshal, who was escorting me, but he remained silent and wouldn't give me a straight answer.

Once I was processed and ready to depart FCI Fort Worth, the Warden showed up, which was unprecedented and a total surprise for me. He proceeded to shake my hand, and thanked me for being a role-model inmate. He gave me a quick wink, and I knew then where I was definitely headed. FCI Tallahassee, here I come! I couldn't believe it. I was elated beyond words. This meant I'd finally be able to see my estranged son, and have regular visits with both him and Victoria. Maybe I'd even be able to have a visit from my daughter, Stacy, too.

DIESEL THERAPY

My trip to FCI Tallahassee wasn't without incident. It was terribly uncomfortable, and quite scary at times. The U.S. Marshal Service made several stops along the way to our final destination. Being handcuffed, foot shackled, while 30,000 feet up in the air, on a run down, dilapidated, government jetliner, wasn't something favorable to experience. We were informed, prior to boarding the plane, if we had to go to the bathroom we needed to do so before we boarded. If not, tough luck, because we were told we wouldn't be able to do so once we were seated inside the aircraft. There were several inmates who pissed and even shit in their pants, because they weren't allowed to go to the bathroom once we were airborne.

It was nightfall by the time we'd left Fort Worth, and landed safely at Tallahassee International Airport. We were escorted off the airplane and transferred to an inmate, transport bus, which took us directly to the prison facility. I don't remember exactly when we finally arrived, but it was late in the evening, the compound was already shut down, and most of the dormitory lights were also shut off.

After we'd exited the bus, and entered the inmate receiving and discharge entrance, we were then fully processed and escorted to our temporary housing quarters. It was now the wee hours of the morning, and all of us newly transferred inmates were thoroughly exhausted and ready to catch some much needed shuteye.

Let me give you a heads up on what the words fully processed entailed. We were instructed to strip down to our birthday suits, and being stark naked with a government issued towel wrapped around our waist, and a small bar of soap, we were then escorted to a nearby

JUDICIAL WEB

communal showering area, and while being watched by two male prison guards, we were told to shower quickly. After we dried off, we were then issued a pair of boxer shorts, a tee-shirt, an orange jump suit, a pair of blue and white slipper-styled sneakers, a pillow, a top and bottom bed sheet, two small bath towels, two wash clothes, two rolls of toilet paper, one toothbrush, a small tube of Colgate toothpaste, and two bars of soap. That was considered our inmate receiving toiletry and care package.

It took us a few weeks to learn the do's and don'ts of this prison facility, as each federal prison I was sent to, during the nearly eight years of my confinement, all had different rules and regulations, depending on the security levels of each prison setting. Since I was serving a lengthy sentence, my security levels fluctuated between medium and high. Unfortunately, for me, I was sent to many high level security prisons, rather than medium ones, all around the country. Talk about a one-of-a-kind learning experience, this was all that and much more. I was doing time with some of the harshest career criminals in the country, many of whom were serving life, double, triple life sentences, without any chance of parole. That's the kind of unimaginable environment I was exposed to as a guest of the Federal Bureau of Prisons.

I experienced a nationally televised inmate riot that occurred at the infamously known, maximum-security prison, at USP Atlanta, Georgia. Here's a list of notable current and former inmates that served time at this federal penitentiary. The well-known crime bosses *Whitey Bulger, Meyer Cohen, Al Capone*, to name a few, then there was the famous fraudsters, *Jimmy Burke (one of the master minds of the Lufthansa Jewelry Heist of 1978), Henry Hill (also one of the Lufthansa Heist culprits, which the Wise Guy novel was written after, and the famous Goodfellas movie was born from), Frank Abagnale (notorious check forger portrayed by Leonardo DiCaprio in the 2002 film, Catch Me If You Can), Carlos Ponzi (inventor of the financial fraud, otherwise known as the infamous, Ponzi Scheme), Michael Vick, Big Meech, Bernard 'Bernie' Madoff,* let's not leave out the infamous, *Jimmy Hoffa*, and there were many others, too numerous to mention.

USP Atlanta is also used as a federal, transfer-prison facility. Meaning, inmates pass through there like a revolving door on their way to their final prison housing and confinement destinations.

Now, is as good a time as any to explain what the title of this chapter stands for. Diesel Therapy, to an otherwise lay person, can be a bit deceiving while reading my book. However, I can assure you, it's far from being anything pleasant you'd ever wish to experience in your life. Let me explain!

After I settled into my routine at FCI Tallahassee; while waiting patiently for a decision from an attorney, who I decided to have champion the last bite of my apple of justice, and whose practice was in the Baltimore, MD area, I chose to engage in taking on a lot more of my fellow inmate's, legal challenges, and to help as many inmate's worthy of my research and jailhouse legalese as possible. I guess I took on more than I could chew. However, I enjoyed the work and my efforts were well rewarded. I was rather fortunate to have won many legal challenges, with some having generated small results, while others were monumental victories for those inmates I felt were dealt a raw hand of justice, like myself, and through my assistance the wrongs were rightfully overturned. Some inmates were awarded a new trial, others a reduced sentence, while in some rare instances, inmates I assisted were immediately released from incarceration. Some of my finest jailhouse lawyering was accomplished at FCI Tallahassee.

In other words, I became a big thorn, and an embarrassment to the government. They obviously got wind of my jailhouse legal reputation, as it had followed me all the way from FCI Miami, Florida, to the Baltimore City Jail, Baltimore, Maryland, to the Federal Medical Correctional facility in Springfield, Missouri, to FCI Fort Worth, Texas, and now to FCI Tallahassee, Florida. You could say I'd made the rounds in just over a couple of years being behind bars. However, if I had a crystal ball, and knew what harsh consequences were about to follow from helping all those needy inmates, I seriously doubt I'd do the same all over again.

So, here we go as I'd alluded to above. I finally settled into my routine, and got to know the lay of the land as they say. The inmates at FCI Tallahassee enjoyed a different mentality and environment when compared to everywhere else I'd been thus far. It was much more laid back with a lot less racial tension, no gang related issues, and everyone just seemed to have gotten along much better there. It was a well-organized, well-kept prison facility to be doing time and housed at. I really liked being at FCI Tallahassee. Plus, I was able to have several visits from Josh and Victoria, which were a big plus for my moral and mental state of mind.

I was working non-stop, between the law library job I was very lucky to snag soon after my arrival, and my music endeavors on the weekends, similar to my routine while at FCI Fort Worth.

The weeks and months past, and I was deeply ingrained with several inmate's legal matters. Suddenly, out of nowhere, I found myself the victim of what federal inmates otherwise coined *Diesel Therapy*, which was known as severe punishment for doing something the BOP had profusely discouraged and frowned upon. You guessed it, doing legal work for other inmates.

The inmate law librarian's job description called for inmates to assist with legal research, while helping less-competent inmates with their legal issues. Unfortunately, for me, it didn't include giving legal advice, writing briefs for them, or assisting them in any manner with getting them out of prison, or actually writing motions to the courts on a fellow inmate's behalf. All of which, I guess you could say, I was unwittingly guilty of. My motives were only with good and honest intentions in trying to assist others who I believed were treated unfairly by our judicial system, and who had no way mentally, or financially to fight against the injustices they were unjustly served. I didn't feel I was doing anything wrong at the time. However, the BOP and others in the Department of Justice felt otherwise. Unlike the BOP, I enjoyed helping the less fortunate and downtrodden.

I was subsequently stripped of all my law library privileges, and prohibited from doing any more legal work for any more inmates. I was now only allowed to do research on my own case, during the hours allocated for inmates to do so, which was only a few hours a day. That was a very harsh punishment for me to endure. I needed as much time in the inmate law library as I could possibly muster. My soul ambition was to continue working on my legal issues, and thus assist my new counsel with pertinent research for my 2255 Motion, which was soon to be filed with Judge Moore in the next few months. As far as I was concerned this action went far beyond punishment for me. This was clearly, without a doubt, a violation of my constitutional Eighth Amendment right against cruel and unusual punishment.

I researched this issue extensively, and chose to file a motion before the court against the BOP and its entire establishment. My ego got the best of me, as this was something I should have thought long and hard about before doing. But it was too late, as the damage had already been in motion with the filing of my brief in the DC Federal District Courthouse, Washington, DC.

Here's the next thing that happened, I was visited by my unit supervisor, while I was in the law library doing some research on my criminal case. I was instructed to follow him to my room, while he informed me, I was about to have, what was infamously called, an inmate shakedown.

My room was torn apart, my bed was turned upside down, all my personal belongings, legal papers and my toiletries were boxed up,

JUDICIAL WEB

and I was shipped out that same day, to where I hadn't a clue. No one would tell me, and that was very disturbing and frightening news. I'd heard the term diesel therapy and what it entailed, but I never thought I'd experience being a victim of this torturous and unimaginable punishment by the BOP.

This deplorable, demeaning, and unusual action was usually restricted and perpetrated upon inmates who displayed disruptive behavior and who disrespected prison authorities while serving their federal sentence. It wasn't intended to be used strictly for routine disciplinary measures.

Here I was, in one fell swoop, uprooted, once again, but this time I wasn't sure what the outcome would be. Remember, the last time I was uprooted I got my family involved, and it was for health reasons that things had swiftly turned around. I knew this wouldn't be the same case this time. This was punishment for me helping others beat our *'Just Us'* legal system, which was hell bent on doing whatever was necessary in order to gain convictions against downtrodden and less fortunate defendants, many of whom were serving time for either crimes they were absolutely not guilty of, forced to plead guilty to, or they were handed draconian sentences, as I was, based on overzealous prosecutors and biased judges, like I'd been made a victim of.

I can't even begin to share with you what happened next, but I'll try my best to do so. I couldn't make any phone calls to alert my family about what had happened or where I was headed. I'd no idea what would become of my legal papers, and my personal items that were hastily boxed up during the shakedown and the searching of my room. I had several inmates' legal work to now place on hold until I could figure out a way to continue to assist them, if at all. Of a much bigger concern for me was all my legal work was now in serious jeopardy of not being timely and properly filed. It was a nightmare beyond all nightmares.

I was shipped from one prison to another, and placed in twenty-four-hour lock down status, with only one hour per day to get some much needed fresh air, while being confined to a 10' by 10' barbed wire fenced in outside area, all to myself, to exercise, or just walk around in circles.

My family knew I usually called them every other day, and I never allowed more than a few days to pass without contacting someone in my immediate family. When my family hadn't heard from me in over a week, they became concerned, and began calling to inquire what was going on with me. They couldn't get any straight answers from anyone. Not even the Warden, which I later found out was the new Warden, since the old Warden had retired during my diesel therapy bus tour, compliments of the BOP.

It was now going on a month, and I'd made the rounds to some of the most notorious federal prisons in the country. Here is a list of all the federal prisons I was in and out of, some for a day, and others for a few days or more, before my family was finally able to get to the bottom of my whereabouts, and then got things pretty much all sorted out for me once and for all.

I was housed at the *USP (United States Penitentiary) Atlanta, GA, USP Leavenworth, Kansas, USP Lewisburg, PA, USP Terre Haute, IL.*

Once I made the USP run, I was next shipped off to visit *FCI Petersburg, VA, FCI Allenwood, PA, FCI Butner, NC, and FCI Texarkana, TX.*

All in all, while on my diesel therapy bus tour, I had visited and stayed at a total of eight BOP facilities. All in a period of just over (30) days. Pure torture! That's what it was.

I recall a most unpleasant event, which took place while on my diesel therapy bus tour, when I was transferred to FCI Petersburg, VA. We pulled in there during the middle of the night, and the prison staff wasn't expecting us until the following morning. So, they weren't ready to accommodate our bus full of inmates that evening. They had no place to house us. They needed to improvise and build a make-shift area for the twenty-five of us to be able to sleep for the night, until they could sort things out in the morning.

There was this old wing in the prison that wasn't used to house inmates in a very long time. It was run down and in total disrepair. The rooms were full of cobwebs and they smelled terrible. There wasn't another choice for us to stay except maybe on the hard-concrete floor for that one evening. Since that was not an option, I found myself locked in one of those putrid prison cells, sleeping on a mattress that was torn and infested with some sort of tiny, black insects, which I tried desperately to contain with the white sheet I was issued to cover the mattress with, and another to cover myself. Mind you, no pillow, and to make matters even worse, my toilet didn't flush.

I tried my best to sleep, but wasn't able to do so. I noticed in the corner of my cell a bunch of cockroaches scurrying around. Due to poor lighting, I couldn't determine why they were doing so. That is until I looked closer and saw several small mice chasing after them. I guess they were looking for a late-night snack. Talk about being rattled. This incident shook me to my core.

In the meantime, unbeknownst to me, while all this was going on, my brother and sister were making headway getting through to the proper authorities to get me back to FCI Tallahassee as soon as possible. They finally found out the details of my whereabouts, and supposedly why all this had happened to me.

I can't recall exactly when, but shortly after my FCI Petersburg experience, I was informed I'd be heading back to FCI Tallahassee at any time. Needless to say, that was music to my ears. I promised myself once I got back there, I'd toe the line and keep to myself. Furthermore, I would denounce all my jailhouse lawyering skills, and strictly focus on my Rule 2255 Motion. That was my main objective, and exactly what I promised to effectuate once I was safely back at FCI Tallahassee.

The trip back to FCI Tallahassee was without incident and upon my return I was greeted by many of fellow inmates who were all hoping I would return for one purpose and one purpose only. You guessed it, to assist them with their legal issues. Unfortunately, I had no other choice, under the circumstances, but to let them all down. I couldn't risk another hell bent diesel therapy wild and life threatening adventure.

FCI FORT DIX

I made it safely back to FCI Tallahassee, and learned a costly lesson while being on that diesel therapy bus tour. It was one hell of an extraordinary and horrific experience. One I'll surely never forget for as long as I live.

The weeks and months kept flying by, and I was coming up on the eighth year of my incarceration. I finally retained my Baltimore post-conviction attorney, Jerry Rutledge, to handle my Rule 2255 Motion, which was my very last shot at gaining my freedom, and the reversal of my thirty-five-year (non-parolable), drug kingpin sentence. Many circumstances transpired in the years leading up to retaining Mr. Rutledge.

Let me digress for a moment. Things back home in New Jersey started to fall apart with our family. My mom was diagnosed with her second breast cancer, while my dad was battling his recent colon cancer diagnosis, after being officially in remission from his bout with bladder cancer, several years earlier. Gary was having bad health issues, too. Our family was in bad shape. When I spoke with my brother, he suggested that I try to get closer to home. He felt FCI Fort Dix, which was only an hour's drive away from our home in North Jersey, would be just what the doctor ordered for the family.

After doing further research I learned that I was eligible to be transferred there, and I set my mind on doing so. I didn't know how the Warden would react to approving my transfer request, due to the prior events, which caused me to get on the wrong side of his administration. Nevertheless, I still believed it would be worth my efforts to try and do so. I was convinced it was a good idea to make this transfer request, which would also allow me to be closer to my new attorney, and I would finally get to see my mom and dad who I'd not seen in nearly eight years. Being in poor health, they were unable to visit with me as I was incarcerated in prison facilities far away from home.

Things started to ramp up on the legal side of my case. We learned from reliable sources that something remarkable was in the making. Apparently, there was breaking news about the one source the government heavily relied upon to convict me of being a drug kingpin. Remember the government's one and only star witness in my criminal case. The main witness who I claimed had lied, connived, and totally deceived the prosecutors, DEA, FBI agents, my entire jury, and especially, Judge Moore. The infamous Jon Gerritt, whose nickname was *Doc!*

I recall being contacted by Vincent, the Miami criminal defense attorney and longtime friend of mine. He asked me to hang tight and don't do anything irrational. Apparently, Vincent received word, through reliable sources, that Jon Gerritt was supposedly indicted by the same prosecutors who had prosecuted me, and that this revelation would eventually assure me of at least a new trial, if not a substantial reduction in my sentence. He said he'd soon get the particulars, and be back in touch with me. I was stunned, and jumping for joy after hearing this startling revelation and unbelievable news. If this information was true and accurate, what a twist of fate this would turn out to be for me and my family.

After several weeks of letter writing, including to the Warden at FCI Fort Dix, and BOP officials in Washington, DC, along with a list of all my accommodations and recommendations, which were made on my behalf to insure the transfer request became a reality, I finally received word there was a very strong possibility I'd be transferred within the next few months. The current holdup had something to do with my security level being reclassified in order for me to be transferred to Fort Dix, and then there was a waiting list issue I needed to be placed on.

JUDICIAL WEB

I waited for what seemed like eternity. However, it actually only took eight weeks before I was approved for my transfer, which was music to my ears. I felt sad about leaving FCI Tallahassee, and no longer able to see my son and Victoria, but I had no other choice. My other family members needed me closer to them, and I made the decision to honor their request to do so. I wasn't seeing Joshua or his mom all that often, and not that I used that excuse to make the move, but that did play into the equation somewhat.

I was kind of surprised the Warden went along with my transfer request, as he had to have approved it, but I felt at the end of the day it really didn't matter to him one way or another. I guess he was happy that I was no longer a thorn in his side, and even more elated to having finally gotten rid of me.

So, once again off I went, and some three hours later the U.S. Marshal's private jet landed at Newark International Airport, in Newark, NJ. The Fort Dix prisoner's transfer bus was waiting to transfer me straight to the prison facility. By the time we reached the R&D entrance we'd been on the road for a tad over an hour.

FCI Fort Dix is located in the quaint township of Browns Mills, NJ, with a sparse population of under twenty-thousand local residents. This prison facility was, at the time, the largest single federal prison in the United States by its number of inmates, which according to Wikipedia.org, accommodated roughly four thousand low to medium security level federal inmates, and another roughly five hundred inmates at the nearby prison camp facility. FCI Fort Dix is located approximately forty miles from Philadelphia, PA, and was an hour's drive from my parents' home in Northern New Jersey.

Upon my eventual arrival at FCI Fort Dix, I had to make a huge adjustment. This wasn't like any other ordinary prison I'd ever been incarcerated at. Fort Dix was huge, and once upon a time it was one of the largest U.S. Army bases in the country. It took several years to convert the facility into a federal prison under President Clinton's

Administration. Construction was still ongoing while I was there. The housing dormitories were like large Army barracks, just like you'd seen in the movies. Inmates were housed in bunk beds with no air-conditioning, only large standup fans, which hardly cooled the area off, with several hundred inmates living in each dormitory. It wasn't an environment that I was at all happy about, or felt I'd be able to adjust to any time soon. The two prior prison facilities I'd been housed at were rather luxurious, when compared to the bunk bed dormitory-style living I would now experience.

Time passed, I made some decent inmate acquaintances, took up painting again, and joined a 50's rock 'n roll band. Since this was a lower security prison environment, the correctional officers were much more mellow and compassionate, than the high-level security prison facilities I'd previously served time at.

On November 6, 1993, after being at Fort Dix for a few months, I finally received a surprise visit from my parents. It was Saturday and the weather outside was rainy, cold, and filled with cloudy skies.

During their visit, my dad shared a story with me that was kind of nostalgic for him. On this very same day, raining and cold as well, fifty-three years earlier, he was drafted and subsequently indoctrinated into the U.S. Army. His reporting station was, of all places, you guessed it, the Fort Dix U.S. Army Base, in Fort Dix, NJ.

How strange it must have felt for my dad, may he rest in eternal peace, to have survived his tour of duty, during WWII, only to return to the very same place he was discharged from, more than a half-century later, to visit his first-born son, now incarcerated at the very same place, which was once one of the country's largest and most prestigious U.S. Army Camps in the nation. Needless to say, my mom, may she also rest in eternal peace, began to cry, as my dad recalled his Army days prior to and after the war had ended.

It's important I keep things in perspective. It was finally confirmed,

JUDICIAL WEB

on April 27th, 1990, Jon 'Doc' Gerritt was, indeed, arrested and indicted for, among other criminal offenses, having committed perjury during his four-day testimony at my criminal trial. He was also indicted on a drug conspiracy, importation and distribution of large quantities of cocaine and marijuana, interstate travel in aid of racketeering, and last but certainly not least, a Title 21-848 CCE Drug Kingpin Offense. How's that for *JUST DESSERTS!*

Doc was now looking at spending the rest of his life in federal prison, without parole. Imagine the overwhelming adrenaline rush I felt upon receiving this miraculous, and unimaginable news. I can't describe in words how I felt at that instance. I became numb to my core. I realized at that very moment, after waiting all those painstaking years, my nightmare would soon be over.

There was no doubt in my mind that this monumental, exculpatory news virtually guaranteed me a new trial, and at the very least a resentencing hearing, more than likely to time served, and I'd soon be reunited with my family and loved ones.

Unfortunately, as fate would have it, I soon learned it wasn't going to be all that easy. As a matter of fact, it turned out to be an entire year of bitter litigation, with the government's prosecution team, the courts, Judge Moore, and a host of other unforeseen issues and circumstances that ensued, before my eventual release from my 35-year, without parole, prison sentence I'd been unjustly serving, going on eight years by this time, would be over.

During all this time at Fort Dix, I wound up doing extensive research for my attorney, who would soon file my 2255 motion, based on newly discovered evidence from Doc's recent indictment, his trial, and convictions on all counts, including having committed perjury during my criminal proceedings.

I'm happy to say, and this was the final nail in Doc's coffin, at sentencing, the judge slammed the book at him. His judge gave Doc a 35-year sentence, without the benefit of parole, for also being a drug kingpin, under the same Title 21, 848 CCE statute he was instrumental in getting me convicted of, with his perjurious testimony, during my criminal proceedings. Imagine that!

At the end of the day, Doc, with his good time behavior credits, wound up serving 22-years in the slammer, nearly three times more than I wound up serving. Talk about *JUST DESSERTS*. This news finally allowed me to sleep peacefully, once again.

Let me walk you through the series of events that soon followed. After Doc was sentenced, he was sent to FCI Butner, NC, where he remained there and served his entire lengthy sentence. Doc was able to save close to fifteen-years off his original sentence, having been awarded good-time behavior credits for his exemplary inmate status. However, all that time spent away from his family had surely cost him dearly.

The most disappointing and disheartening part of my story is, had Doc told the truth from the very beginning, not committed perjury during his trial testimony at my criminal proceedings, but rather plead guilty to what he was guilty of, and still struck a plea-bargain with the government for immunity, so long as he told the truth and nothing but the truth, I wouldn't have been convicted of being a drug kingpin, given a thirty-five years sentence, without parole, Doc would have been given a reasonable, or perhaps no prison sentence at all. He would never have served 22-years behind bars, like he wound up doing, and the government would still have gotten their pounds of flesh, but at least the end results would have been much fairer and more balanced for Doc and I.

Instead, Doc took the low road rather than the high one, costing him the better part of his adult life behind bars for doing so. The greed factor raised its ugly head once again!

When I reflect on all this, having not spoken with Doc since he testified against me back in 1986, going on thirty-seven years now, I often ponder what his thinking would be today. If I could simply ask Doc just a one word question, I wonder what his answer would be. My one word question would be, *WHY?*

What happened next, in my continued quest for post-conviction relief, was the timely filing of my Rule 2255 Motion to vacate, set aside, or correct my sentence, by my attorney. Believe it or not, with the same Judge Moore, who was now turning eighty-five, and still sitting on the federal bench. Truly an amazing feat to have accomplished.

I was anxious to be back in front of Judge Moore, and be able to place on the record, once and for all, the words I uttered during my sentencing allocution, when I looked Judge Moore straight in the face and told him, *I'LL BE BACK!* I now yearned to face Judge Moore once again, and remind him of the promise I made when I uttered those same exact words in his courtroom, nearly eight-years earlier. Even more so, I couldn't wait to witness the expression on Judge Moore's face, upon seeing me at the Evidentiary Hearing, which was pretty much guaranteed I'd be granted very soon.

Judge Moore eventually had no choice but to grant our motion for an Evidentiary Hearing, and subsequently set it for Monday, November 29, 1993, at 9:00 a.m., to be held in Courtroom C, the same Courtroom 'C' that he sentenced me from, eight plus years earlier.

Since Mr. Rutledge was going to be out of town and unavailable the weekend prior to our scheduled Evidentiary Hearing before Judge Moore, he requested my presence in Baltimore the week before so we could meet face to face, and discuss our last minute strategies for our upcoming hearing.

My family made plans to be present at my scheduled hearing, which was estimated by my lawyer to last at least two weeks, for a total of nine actual court days not counting the weekends.

It was early morning on Monday, November 8, 1993, when I was informed by the correctional officer on duty that day to pack up all my belongings and report to the R&D Unit, by not later than 7:30. I couldn't believe my ears when the officer uttered those words to me.

I wasn't planning on leaving for at least another week, if not longer. I hadn't begun packing anything in my final preparation. I was now being told to pack up all my belongings, and report immediately to R&D. Boy, was I in a state of frenzy. It wasn't until 11:30 p.m. on that same Monday evening, before I was once again suited up, handcuffed, leg-shackled, and on my way to Baltimore, Maryland, at least that's where I thought we were headed. The other federal inmates traveling with me, in the same run-down bus, were headed to the Federal Penitentiary, in Lewisburg, PA, now renamed USP (United States Penitentiary). We were informed we were being taken there to drop off and pick up other federal inmates who shared our common destination. I hated the confinement being in lockdown status, with a six-and-a-half-hour bus ride ahead of me, before eventually reaching USP Lewisburg that evening.

The bigger, unexpected surprise was upon our arrival at USP Lewisburg, instead of dropping off and picking up prisoners, as we were told would be the case, we were instructed to exit the prison bus and soon told that we were going to be held overnight at the USP, due to inclement weather conditions that prevented us from traveling to our final destination, the Baltimore City Jail.

This was devastating news for me to learn. I had a hearing date scheduled for Monday, November 29, at 9:00 a.m. sharp. I needed to be back in Baltimore as soon as possible so I had ample time to meet and discuss the strategy of my upcoming hearing with my attorney. This layover could very likely drag on, for who knew how long, before we'd be back on the road and heading to Baltimore. This had me overly concerned and quite upset; the worst was still yet to come.

The one thing I vividly recall, while being previously housed at USP Lewisburg, was their 60 foot walls that surrounded the entire prison

JUDICIAL WEB

complex. Once you entered this prison facility, it was like being in a concrete cage, with nothing but these gigantic walls surrounding you. Everywhere you turned and everywhere you looked, was a giant 60' wall. This would be the perfect *TRUMP BORDER WALL* scenario, which President Trump (#47) would still love to see erected along our southern border. However, for me, it was so depressing and demoralizing to view and experience all over again.

Our overnight stay, as I'd predicted, turned into a week and then another week. By now it was pushing Thanksgiving Day. I was frantic! My hearing was only days away.

As fate would have it, there was a stabbing of two prison guards during our brief overnight stay, which was now being thoroughly investigated, causing the entire prison facility to be placed on lock-down status. We learned through the prisoner grapevine, that one prison guard had died of multiple stab wounds, while another was rushed to the local hospital and remained in critical condition.

Word had circulated quickly that the inmates in the high-level security section had been complaining about the poor plumbing, lighting, and the lack of fresh air in their cells. They decided to retaliate, since no one was paying attention to any of their requests to improve their basic living conditions.

Many of the high-security level inmates who were involved in this stabbing incident were already serving life sentences, many without parole, so they presumably had nothing to lose. Killing a guard or two wouldn't result in any further capital punishment for those inmates involved.

Finally, things began to settle down, and lock-down status was lifted two days before Thanksgiving, which fell on November 25th that year. I was back on the prison bus, headed to the Baltimore City Jail, where I'd be spending my Thanksgiving holiday.

The only consolation was this would likely be the last Thanksgiving

Day holiday that I'd be spending behind bars. At least that's what I was led to believe after my lawyer and I had finally spoken the following day, after my arrival at the City Jail, on Wednesday, November 24, 1993.

As D-Day was rapidly approaching, feeling apprehensive and full of anxiety, I continued to remain cautiously optimistic, and my resolve was as strong as ever. I was confident that this final bite of the apple of justice would prove victorious for me, and that my continued quest for justice, after the long and arduous nearly eight years of patiently waiting, would finally pay off.

MY EVIDENTIARY HEARING

For those of you who may not be familiar with the legal terminology of what an Evidentiary Hearing is, allow me to elaborate for a moment.

An Evidentiary Hearing (EH), from a legal perspective, is any court proceeding that involves witnesses giving testimony under oath. In criminal matters, particularly those involving felonies such as mine, evidentiary hearings are standard operating procedures, however, by the same token, they are extremely rare to come by.

At an EH, the presiding judge hears arguments from both the prosecutor(s) and defense counsel to determine if there is enough evidence to have the defendant's motion, in my case, my Rule 2255 Motion to vacate, set aside, or correct one's sentence, ruled on in favor or denial of the said motion.

The extenuating and unusual circumstances, which I alleged, and would have my attorney vigorously argue on my behalf in my Rule 2255 Motion were as follows:

1). The government included false information, supplied by Jon Gerritt, in its application for a search warrant of the defendant's home.

2). Gerritt's perjured grand jury and trial testimonies deprived the defendant of his due process of law, in further violation of his Sixth Amendment right to a fair trial, by a jury of his peers.

3). The Government's impermissible vouching, as it pertained to the credibility of its star witness, Jon Gerritt, during its closing arguments.

4). The Government's inexcusable failure to timely provide exculpatory evidence and discovery relating to Jon Gerritt.

5). The Court sentenced the defendant, in part, based on Gerritt's perjurious trial testimony.

6). The Defendant was wrongfully and prejudicially convicted, under the government's Title 21, Section 848 CCE criminal statute, based on perjurious trial testimony of its star witness, Jon Gerritt.

On Monday, November 29, 1993, a few weeks after my parents paid me a surprise visit, while housed at the Baltimore City Jail, I was escorted by U.S. Marshals back and forth to Court, for the next nine days, to attend my long awaited EH.

During the nine-day EH Judge Moore heard testimony from both prosecutors, the DEA's head case agent, my trial counsel, David Irving, and several other government witnesses who Mr. Rutledge called to the witness stand. Then the big bombshell came, which nobody, not even Judge Moore, saw coming! I finally decided enough was enough. I chose, on my own behalf, with the full approval of my lawyer to take the witness stand, and after all these years finally have my day in Court.

The media covering the hearing was in a frenzy, and I was loving every minute of it. Some of the very same reporters who were present to slam me in the press, after I was convicted and sentenced by Judge Moore, were now present at my EH, nearly eight years later. They must've been in total shock seeing me take the witness stand, and finally being able to set the record straight so many years later. I'll now extrapolate more on my EH testimony below.

The primary issue addressed at the hearing was the history of the government's relationship with Jon Gerritt. In this regard Mr. Wells, the lead prosecutor, and the head DEA case agent, Sandy Jones, both testified they became aware of Jon Gerritt in mid-year 1985, at which time a grand jury subpoena was issued upon him.

JUDICIAL WEB

An attorney for Gerritt then contacted the U.S. Attorney's Office for the Southern District of Florida, indicating Gerritt's willingness to cooperate.

In the meantime, the conditions at the Baltimore City Jail had gotten much worse since the last time I was there, more than seven plus years earlier. It was literally a living hellhole, and currently listed as one of the top ten worst prison facilities in the country. Being a predominately black populated prison, I was one of the few white boys to be housed there. Having already spent considerable time at the Baltimore City Jail, I knew, just like before, I'd have no problems fitting in, and being accepted by all my fellow inmates, who immediately took a liking toward me.

The nine-day hearing was a remarkable turnaround from the last time I was in Judge Moore's Courtroom. It seemed that everyone present knew what was about to transpire, even the Judge, who had a somber look on his face during the entire proceedings. I think Judge Moore had finally realized the Government's Counsel had royally screwed up, and there was nothing he could do to save them from drowning this time around. In other words, they were cooked geese.

My lawyer had a field day, having placed both prosecutors, Mr. Nolan, and Mr. Wells on the witness stand and grilled them, under oath, without mercy, while I was having my own field day watching them sweat and fess up to the wrongs they perpetrated against me, and how they tainted the jury, and deceived Judge Moore with their known or should have known use of perjured testimony given by their star witness, Jon Gerritt, during my criminal proceedings. Truth be told, they should have both been indicted and tried for the criminal offense of subornation of perjury.

Mr. Rutledge also called to the witness stand Sandy Jones, the head DEA case agent in my criminal case. Agent Jones proceeded to make a complete fool of himself, while under direct examination by Mr. Rutledge. He was an embarrassment to the DEA and the Court for allowing his CI#4 to pull the wool over his eyes, and for that matter everyone else in the U.S. Attorney's Office for the District of Maryland. My attorney called a few more witnesses on my behalf, and then as stated earlier had me take the witness stand, which surprised everyone, including Judge Moore. None of the government's prosecution team were prepared for this surprise move by Mr. Rutledge, which we'd carefully strategized. I made the final decision that this was going to be my day in Court, and I refused to be deprived of my doing so, at all costs, this time around. I waited for over seven years to face the government's prosecution team and especially, Judge Moore. I needed to speak my peace and set the record straight, once and for all.

Before I share with you how I addressed the Court, and exactly what I stated on the record for everyone in the Courtroom to hear, on that eventful day, I wish to have you read what Judge Moore had to say after he heard all the testimony from the government's prosecutors, the head DEA case agent, the U.S. Attorney, for the District of Maryland, several other government witnesses, and let's not forget my two full days of testimony.

Here's what Judge Moore stated on the record, which brought tears to me and my family's eyes, who were all present during my entire nine-day Evidentiary Hearing. They had also been waiting seven plus years for this day to finally arrive. We all listened attentively to Judge Moore's ruling.

"In summary, absent Jon Gerritt's perjured testimony, the Court finds that the jury probably would've acquitted the defendant of the CCE charge. Accordingly, that conviction will be vacated, and a re-sentencing on the remaining counts shall be ordered."

Needless to say, the government had the choice to appeal Judge Moore's ruling, and perhaps even try me once again on the CCE offense. However, they knew better than to attempt to do so. Without Gerritt's testimony, the second time around, they could never have secured another CCE conviction against me, and even if they contemplated doing so, the issue of double jeopardy would prevail, since Judge Moore had vacated my conviction and thirty-five year no parole sentence in his Final Order. So, that option was off the table for good. The only option left for Judge Moore, as far as my lawyer was concerned, was to impose a significantly reduced sentence, which would immediately set me free. I'd already served the maximum sentence on my fifteen-year conspiracy count, which was one-third or five years with good-behavior credits. Since I made it a point to keep my nose clean, and was considered a model inmate, during my seven plus years of confinement, I would've been awarded the good-behavior credits, and since I'd already served seven plus years, I was already more than two years over my mandatory release date. The Government knew this, and so did Judge Moore.

The following day the Baltimore Evening Sun had a front page article, after Judge Moore vacated my CCE conviction, my thirty-five-year, non-parolable sentence, and he ordered I be re-sentenced based on the evidence presented during my Evidentiary Hearing. Here's how the article read, which finally set the record straight once and for all…

FEDERAL JUDGE AGREES TO RESENTENCE DEALER

BALTIMORE-A federal judge has agreed to resentence a drug dealer who appealed his 35-year prison sentence because a police officer had lied on the witness stand during his trial.

Steve Silva (alias) was convicted in 1987 and sentenced to thirty-five-years in federal prison, without parole, for operating a Western Maryland drug ring.

Prosecutors argued that there was sufficient evidence to convict

Silva even if the testimony of a former Fort Lauderdale police officer was disregarded.

Senior U.S. District Judge Moore, this week vacated Silva's conviction for the continuing criminal enterprise offense and subsequent conviction, and re-instated Silva's conspiracy conviction.

The maximum sentence Silva could receive under the sentencing guidelines is 15 years. The Judge will resentence Silva prior to December 31st.

And that's how the headlines appeared for everyone to read and re-read, especially the government's entire prosecution team, including the U.S. Attorney who mishandled the case from the very beginning.

What a tumult this reversal caused. At the end of the day, I learned from the grapevine, a total of nineteen other criminal cases were overturned, and either thrown out, or re-sentencings were conducted all over the country. Apparently, Doc must have been pretty darn busy testifying in many other criminal proceedings, for which they, like myself, were entitled to a new trial, and/or a resentencing hearing.

Word had it that this caused a big shakeup in the U.S. Attorney's office for the District of Maryland. Many would be, or otherwise expected promotions, which were due to be handed out prior to my EH and Judge Moore's final ruling, had been placed on hold. When the smoke had finally cleared there were a total of nineteen other criminal cases, just like mine, that had been overturned with many wrongfully and prejudicially convicted inmates, who were entitled to be immediately released from federal prison, and a bunch more waiting on resentencing hearings, just like mine.

If you think this matter was over and done with, think again. It was the beginning of another unimaginable nightmare for me.

I'll now share with you what I stated on the record to Judge Moore,

JUDICIAL WEB

after I was thoroughly grilled by Mr. Nolan, Mr. Wells, and Judge Moore, who also saw fit to vigorously grill me. He tried his absolute best to trick me, but he should've known better.

This was to be my day in Court, and no one was going to deprive me of making a spectacle of myself, no way, no how this time around! I was allotted ten minutes to make my closing statement, and I addressed the Court as follows:

"Your Honor, members of the Court, my family, and to all those present in this Courtroom this afternoon, including the media, who I hope gets it right this time.

Your Honor, thank you for this opportunity to address this Court once again. It's taken me seven plus long and arduous years to make it back to your Courtroom, and to finally set the record straight.

One thing about this great country of ours, is our American Jurisprudence and Judicial System of Government. Unlike many other nations around the world, our rule of law, governed by our Constitution, provides a legal forum for an aggrieved party, such as myself, who's been victimized for a very prolonged and drawn out period of time, but who is still able to bring to the attention of this Honorable Court, that a grave wrong and injustice has been perpetrated against me.

Another undisputed fact is that as great as mankind has become, we are all born with one very distinct, and common fault. We are not perfect! That is to say, we are all capable, among many other things, of making misjudgments, mistakes, and committing wrongdoings.

I'm certain that everyone in this courtroom here today, at one time or another, has made a mistake, perhaps a misjudgment, or even a wrongdoing, at least one time in their life.

However, some of us choose to correct their wrongdoings, immediately upon committing them, while others choose to ignore them, or perhaps wait until a proper time for one reason or another. Then there are those who never choose to do so. Instead, these individuals opt to take their mistakes and wrongdoings to their graves.

During the course of this lengthy, nine day, evidentiary hearing your Honor has heard an awful lot of mistakes that were made, either directly or indirectly, by way of sworn testimonies, as well as corroborated evidence, from the very same government officials that saw fit to wrongfully prosecute me, and had you and the jury convinced that I was a drug kingpin, and deserved to be sent to prison, for basically the rest of my adult life, without the benefit of parole.

For instance: Mr. Wells, the lead prosecutor, during my criminal proceedings, informed you that he had probable cause to indict Jon Gerritt, prior to having completed his testimony during my criminal proceedings.

I submit to you, Your Honor, this was not just a mistake, this was an intentional, grave injustice, perpetrated upon me. I would also submit, Your Honor, there were many other similar instances where mistakes were made, and wrongdoings committed by other government officials involved in my criminal investigation, prosecution, and subsequent conviction, which to this day, no one has been held accountable for.

Another incident that comes to mind was that of DEA Agent Sandy Jones. During his EH testimony before this Court, Agent Jones testified, under oath, that he also knew after Jon Gerritt had completed his trial testimony, during my criminal proceedings before Your Honor, seven plus years ago, that Jon Gerritt had committed perjury, in the highest regards, and yet Agent Jones chose not to rock the boat, or come clean with his mistake and wrongdoings, by not bringing it to the attention of my defense counsel, during my trial, or for that matter to anyone else in the U.S. Attorney's Office handling my criminal matter. Why?

We heard from many other witnesses that my lawyer had grilled on direct examination, all of whom testified under oath, that they, too, committed mistakes and wrongdoings during my criminal proceedings. But in my case, they waited way too long to do so, thus denying me a fair and just trial by a jury of my peers.

Let's not forget the testimony of Mr. Andy Nolan, the government's co-counsel prosecutor. Mr. Nolan, my true and loyal adversary, had committed grave mistakes and wrongdoings, during my criminal trial. Mr. Nolan misrepresented to this Court, as well as to my jury, many material facts he knew, or should have known were false, and were never brought to anyone's attention, not to Your Honor, my trial counsel, or anyone else in the U.S. Attorney's Office for the District of Maryland, and especially to the jury, who were deprived of the benefit of knowing about these gross errors, which were committed during my criminal proceedings.

Where Mr. Nolan's egregious conduct got even worse, Your Honor, was during my Appellate Process, during his Oral Argument before my three-judge appointed panel. Mr. Nolan proffered to the panel that the government's star witness, during my criminal trial, was credible and trustworthy, and had testified truthfully, during all aspects of my criminal investigation and his trial testimony, but nothing could've been further from the truth, and Mr. Nolan, surely at the time of my Appellate process, and especially during the Oral Argument phase, knew or should have known about his star witness having committed perjury during my criminal trial.

Your Honor, these wrongful acts, as far as I'm concerned, were intentional and prejudicially perpetrated upon my Appellate Panel, all of which further deprived me of a fair review of the trial *record, and thus caused me to lose, once again, my quest for justice to prevail in my criminal matter."*

At this point, with my time running out, I wanted to look Mr. Nolan in the face from the podium I was using to address the Court. I directed the following allocution to him. I had rehearsed these lines over and over again, but being a bit nervous, I still couldn't keep them to memory. Hence, I kept referring to my written notes.

I stated as follows: *"Mr. Nolan, I came all the way back to this Courtroom, and the Baltimore City Jail, with much built up animosity, dissension, and disgust, in my mind, body, and soul, as to how you and your entire prosecution team had denied me a fair and just trial before this Honorable Court, and a jury of my peers. However, I'm here to say, I'm leaving here today with a clear mind and conscience after nearly seven plus years of my incarceration, that I've learned to forgive you and the entire prosecution team for all the pain and suffering you and your cohorts have caused me and my entire family, especially my young son, and daughter, by depriving me of their love and affection for all these lost years I dearly missed spending with both of them.*

I know I'm probably the most disliked person in the entire U.S. Attorney's Office for the District of Maryland, and rightfully so. After all, no one knows better than you the avalanche of letters and allegations I've alleged against you and the entire prosecution team, in the way and manner you've all mistreated me, and the corrupt mishandling of my entire criminal matter. However, I'd like to state for the record, and I mean this sincerely, over the past nine-days of this Evidentiary Hearing, despite all of the dissension and animosity between us, I've come to respect you as my adversary, something up until now I've been unwilling, and unable to admit, or accept doing. However, it's most evident you've truly become a seasoned prosecutor, and most respectfully I commend you for this accomplishment.

And last but certainly not least, we have my testimony before Your Honor, and this entire Courtroom. The Court has heard from me, and the many mistakes that I've openly admitted to while on the witness stand, under sworn oath. I've testified 100% truthfully, without hesitation, when questioned by both my lawyer, the government's counsel, and Your Honor.

Your Honor, I know talk is cheap, and the words that one utters are often merely just that, words. I decided to take the witness stand, this second time around, for my own peace of mind, and to set the record straight once and for all.

I wanted the Court to learn, after all these years have passed, the true nature of my culpability in my criminal case.

I wanted the government's prosecution team to know the many missing pieces of my true involvement in my criminal case. Likewise, I wanted the government's prosecution team to know the many flaws that surrounded their criminal investigation, the wrongful acts committed by their star witness, Jon Gerritt, and the false testimony perpetrated against me by the head DEA Case Agent, Sandy Jones, all of which severely prejudiced me during my criminal proceedings, which ultimately lead to my conviction of the harshest criminal offense in the government's arsenal of felony statutes. A punishment, upon conviction, that comes with an automatic, minimum-mandatory, non-parolable sentence of ten-years, for which you've sentenced me to thirty-five years, without parole, that I've now already served nearly eight years of that draconian sentence.

Another well-founded and most important reason for my taking the witness stand had to do with my family, especially my young daughter, whom I'd been raising as a single parent, prior to my arrest.

I needed to let my daughter know who her father once was, and who's now standing here before you today. Stacy has surely suf-

fered plenty over the years of my confinement, having been deprived of my love, affection, guidance, and my ability to be there for her all these missed years. I know this was more than my young daughter could possibly bear. I really don't know how I'll ever be able to make all this up to her. I guess only time will tell.

For my beloved parents, who sat through all the pain and agony these past nine days of my Evidentiary Hearing, not to mention the last seven plus years of my incarceration, I'll never be able to undue the hurt, humiliation, pain, anguish, and the amount of suffering I've caused them, and for which they've had to endure all this time. For this, I'm deeply remorseful, and utterly ashamed. I only hope I'll be able to, in some way, share with them some happiness in their remaining golden years upon my eventual release from prison.

As for my brother, Gary, and sister, Gloria, who I know every time they lay their head down to sleep at night, wondering how their big brother is doing, and whether or not we'll be able to one day, once again, enjoy the close relationship we once shared, I can only say, stay tuned, it should be soon.

My brother, of all people, knew how hard it was for me to make the decision to take the stand here today, and once and for all speak my peace, very well knowing the possible consequences of my doing so.

Your Honor, there comes a time in a man's life when he must own up to the wrongs he committed against society, if he ever expects to become a productive human being once again in his life. Being remorseful isn't enough; actions speak louder than words.

Like "Truth crushed to the earth will rise again," I truly believed in my heart and soul, that "No lie can live forever." This has finally been proven, beyond a reasonable doubt, with the tell all outcome of the fate of Jon Gerritt, who is now serving the same exact sentence, for the same drug king-pin conviction as I've been serving these past seven plus years.

Because of this event, my prayers have finally been answered. It's now seven plus years later, that I now find myself with this extraordinary and rare opportunity to be brought back before Your Honor, to set the record straight once and for all. For this, I'm truly grateful.

Your Honor, I fully admit as you have heard me testify during these past four days of grueling cross examination, by the government's prosecutors, as to my involvement in the drug netherworld. I furthermore fully admit, with deep remorse, what I did during the years between 1983-1985 or thereabouts, was undeniably wrong, and a part of my life I'd very much like to turn the page; place behind me, and pick up the shattered pieces so I may once again have the opportunity to start my life anew. I am deeply remorseful for all my past indiscretions, wrongdoings, misjudgments, and for the crimes I've been duly found guilty of.

In closing, I pray upon this Court, based on all the evidence that has been presented during my nine-day Evidentiary Hearing, and now made an official part of my criminal record, that I be granted a second chance to prove I can become a productive member of society once again.

Believe me, Your Honor, I am a changed man, and not the same Steve Silva that stood before you, nearly eight years ago. I state this before Your Honor, with the utmost conviction in my heart.

I wish to thank Your Honor for allowing me this lengthy time to address the Court."

What happened next, you'll surely find it hard to believe, process, or even comprehend!

Judge Moore called a recess, after my allocution was finished, he informed Mr. Rutledge and the Government's prosecutors he wanted to take a lunch break, and for everyone to return at one-o-clock sharp.

I had hopes of being released that day, based on the mere fact that I had already served more than enough time on my remaining felony convictions, since they were all run concurrent with one another, which allowed me, along with my good-time behavior credits, to only have to serve one-third of my largest remaining sentence, which was the conspiracy count. Since the maximum time I could have spent for the conspiracy conviction was fifteen-years, one-third of fifteen, was only five-years. Since I'd already served more than seven years, I was under the impression I'd be immediately released, right then and there, from the Courtroom, and set free as a bird at last.

However, I was soon in for another big disappointment in my life. I'm talking Disappointment, with a capital D.

Lunch break was over, and everyone was gathered back in Courtroom C ready to hear what Judge Moore had to say.

"*All rise,*" uttered the Bailiff. Judge Moore entered his Courtroom, looked at everyone, and with a grim, stern-expression on his face, looked directly at me. If looks could kill, I'd be dead. Oh! Know! I didn't know what was coming, and neither did my attorney. The prosecutors looked stunned as well. I'm thinking, what the hell did I do wrong! I spoke from my heart. I testified, under sworn oath, the whole truth and nothing but the truth, so help me *GOD*.

What Judge Moore uttered next, was nothing short of another miscarriage of justice perpetrated upon me, all over again. Can you believe Judge Moore had the audacity, the unconscionable nerve, to inform Mr. Rutledge that he needed more time to review the entire record, absorb the prior nine day EH proceeding, along with my transcribed, hearing, testimony transcripts, coupled with the government prosecutors' and the DEA senior, case agent's hearing, testimony transcripts, which would take at least a month or more before the hearing transcripts would be made available to him. I was dumbfounded. What next! Where was I going to be shipped off to, while I awaited Judge Moore's decision on the fate of my release from prison.

Yep! You might have guessed it, back to the Baltimore City Jail all over again, where I would lay and rot for another eight weeks. It took Judge Moore four weeks after he received the entire hearing's transcripts, and then another four weeks for his clerks to assist in writing his fifteen-page opinion.

Mr. Rutledge met with me several times during my eight weeks stay at the City Jail. He couldn't apologize enough for what was happening. The only consolation he shared with me was that Judge Moore wanted to make 100% certain his i's were dotted, and his t's crossed before he'd set me free. He said in that same breath, I caused a lot of damage to the entire U.S. Attorney's Office, and that heads would be flying and prosecution members who handled my criminal prosecution would lose their prestigious jobs, some would be demoted to much lower rankings within the U.S. Attorney's Office, and word had it that the senior, head case Agent, Sandy Jones, was on his way out the door, too. The powers to be, looked to make Agent Jones their fall guy, scapegoat, sacrificial lamb, call it what you'd like, but truth be told, those phrases were all appropriate in describing Agent Jones' culpability. After all, Jon Gerritt was his stoolie. He knew or should have known that his star witness was not credible and committed perjury in the highest regards, and that he, of all government personnel, should have been leery of all this from the get-go.

So, here's what transpired next, in a nutshell. After spending another grueling eight weeks at the Baltimore City Jail, under even worse conditions than I'd experienced seven plus years earlier, but luckily without incident, or any harm done to me, I was brought back to Courtroom C to hear what Judge Moore had to say with his final ruling, and my fate, which he held in the palm of his hands.

My family was there, all over again. The media was present and of course the U.S. Attorney's Office personnel, packed the Courtroom on that eventful day.

Judge Moore didn't waste any time. He proceeded to read aloud his ruling, and everyone listened very attentively.

At the end of his twenty-five minutes of boring rhetoric, it all boiled down to Judge Moore not doing what he otherwise knew he had to do. He didn't wish to scorn the government's prosecution team. He wasn't about to make fools of them, and he had his mind made up, he wasn't going to let me off the hook that easily either.

Judge Moore had the nerve, the gall, the balls, to minimally admonish the government's prosecution team, with minor jabs, as to how they mishandled my criminal investigation, and their subsequent prosecution tactics during my criminal trial. It was a joke! A total disgrace what had transpired in Judge Moore's Courtroom that day. Another hellbent miscarriage of justice was about to be perpetrated upon me all over again.

Judge Moore proceeded to illegally sentence me to the maximum sentence on my reinstated conspiracy conviction of fifteen-years, and then he chose to sentence me on two other felony counts, of five years each, that he ran consecutive to the fifteen-year conspiracy sentence, for a newly imposed sentence of twenty-five years. I couldn't believe my ears. My lawyer had words with Judge Moore, and read him the riot act. He proceeded to inform him that he'd not only imposed an illegal sentence upon me, but also his actions were unconstitutional, and a further violation of my Sixth Amendment rights. I'd already served all of the underlying, five years, concurrently run sentences, and the only sentence left to give me was the fifteen-year conspiracy sentence, for which I'd already served the required one-third maximum sentence for. Meaning, I should've been immediately released from the Courtroom that day, and sent home with my parents. But, unfortunately once again, that's not the way things had turned out.

Judge Moore proceeded to defy his prior ruling, in that my thirty-five-year, without parole sentence be vacated, and that I'd be re-sentenced appropriately on only the re-instated conspiracy charge. However, Judge Moore decided to completely ignore his own ruling, during the conclusion of my Evidentiary Hearing, and did as he saw fit once again.

I wasn't about to let Judge Moore get away with his illegal, unprecedented, and unconstitutional actions; thus causing me another miscarriage of justice. Mr. Rutledge felt the same way.

BACK TO THE FOURTH CIRCUIT

Here's how things quickly unfolded after Judge Moore passed his wrongfully and illegally imposed sentence upon me.

The US Marshal's Service escorted me back to the holding cell where my lawyer joined me. I rattled off several directly on point cases I'd committed to memory just in case this very event transpired. I informed Mr. Rutledge to immediately file another emergency appeal to the Fourth Circuit, and to use the cases I just provided him for their immediate review. He fully agreed with me and promised to promptly do so.

My parents and our entire family were in total shock, and left the Courtroom without being able to speak with me. I felt terrible for my daughter and my parents. I later learned that my daughter was planning her wedding date around the hopes that I'd be free at last, and thus able to walk her down the aisle, but that dream was now totally shattered. Devastation set in quickly, but I wasn't about to give up. I was convinced, beyond any doubt, Judge Moore got it all wrong, and his resentencing me to 25-years was vindictively, prejudicially, and unconstitutionally imposed.

I was determined not to allow this egregious act of injustice get me down. I needed to do something legally to fight back, and that my quest for justice prevailed. Furthermore, I needed to ensure that my long awaited freedom was imminent.

I knew my fate was now in the hands of my lawyer, and his ability to convince the Fourth Circuit Court of Appeals to conduct an emergency hearing, and set the record straight once and for all.

I now knew I'd be headed back to Baltimore City Jail, where I'd most likely remain until my emergency motion was filed and heard. What I didn't anticipate was what was about to happen next.

I spent two sleepless nights at the City Jail and then, in the middle of the early morning, before sunrise, on that second day, I was escorted by the US Marshals Service, back to good old FCI Fort Dix. Imagine that!

However, before I was abruptly removed and transferred back to FCI Fort Dix, I had time, while at the City Jail, to write my emergency appeal brief points for Mr. Rutledge to incorporate into his final draft. Don't laugh, but I had to do so on toilet paper, since I was not permitted, while in holding status, to have access to any utensils, such as paper or any writing tools. I was lucky to have been able to borrow a fellow inmate's pencil and began writing, strictly from memory, the cases and the verbiage that would set the stage for my next challenge to Judge Moore's, vindictive, and illegally imposed sentence. My lawyer needed to provide the Fourth Circuit with iron clad case law, which was directly on point with the issues surrounding my emergency appeal. By doing so there'd be no question how they'd have to rule, and thus overturn Judge Moore's bias and wrongful interpretation of the sentencing laws, which had been in place for decades, and engraved in stone by the Fourth Circuit's precedents.

No joke, but I used nearly a half-roll of toilet-paper, and the entire pencil that I'd borrowed to jot down my notes. Now came the task of making certain I had a way to get all this to Mr. Rutledge as soon as possible.

Luckily for me, I had an unexpected visit from my daughter and sister. They wanted to learn what had transpired with my illegally imposed twenty-five-year sentence, which Judge Moore had just handed down to me.

I met them in the visitor's lounge, a dingy, small cubicle with poor lighting, and after I'd been through the standard, padded-down search, we were able to spend only fifteen-minutes together. I stuffed the toilet-paper, carefully wrapped up into my underwear and made sure it was well concealed. Yes, I took a big chance, but I had no other choice. My time was running, and I had a bad feeling that I wouldn't remain at the City Jail for much longer. I didn't know when Mr. Rutledge would be able to visit with me again. So, it was a godsend that my sister and daughter visited me when they did. As fate would have it, the following morning I was on my way back to Fort Dix.

I was able to pass my toilet paper notes, without incident, to my sister with instructions to get them to Mr. Rutledge that same day. Luckily, his office was only an hour away, and on my sister's way home. Boy, what a relief that was.

As previously stated, my premonition turned out to be right on the money. Just as I had informed my daughter and sister, the very next day, after their surprise visit, I was shipped out, early morning, and on my way back to Fort Dix.

The bus ride to Fort Dix was another rattled experience, and one riddled with trauma and unforeseen excitement. Halfway back to Fort Dix, the bus broke down during the morning rush hour traffic, being handcuffed and foot shackled, we were made to sit and wait inside the bus, with little ventilation, except a small, infrequent, breeze that whisked across my face every few minutes. It wasn't until several hours later that the US Marshal's transport bus arrived. We were then escorted from the broken down bus to the new one, in single file, one by one. We were drenched in sweat, while the tensions were brewing among us inmates and the guards as well.

It was close to nightfall by the time we eventually made it back to Fort Dix. Since the mess hall was already closed we were offered a quick snack, which consisted of two cheese sandwiches, a container of milk, and two chocolate chip cookies to hold us over until morning. We were stripped-searched and processed all over again. By this time I was totally fed up, and frustrated as I could possibly be.

Several weeks had passed, and still no word from the Appellate Court on my emergency motion. In the interim I had a few brief visits from my brother and dad, which helped pass the time for me.

Another interesting event I'll now share with you was my face to face meeting with, allegedly, the Don of all Don crime family bosses in the history of the mafia. The infamous, notorious, and well known gentleman, *John Joseph Gotti, Jr.*, a/k/a *Teflon Don*.

Mr. Gotti had a brief stay at FCI Fort Dix, and had worked in the laundry room, sorting laundry and passing out towels, sheets and pillowcases, to fellow inmates. That was his work detail every day. When I went to the laundry room, upon my return from my resentencing hearing, to be issued my allotted bedding and towels for the week, Mr. Gotti had greeted me with my supply pack. We spoke briefly about my horrific resentencing experience, how I was grossly mistreated by the sentencing judge, and how crooked I felt our *'Just Us'* legal system had become. Mr. Gotti seemed genuinely interested in listening to my story, but wasn't the least bit surprised. We shook hands, and he wished me the very best of luck with my appeal, and I wished him the same with his criminal matters, which supposedly had placed him behind bars for the rest of his life, with no possibility of parole.

I must say, I found Mr. Gotti to be a true gentleman, and one hell of a stand-up guy. He had the personification of standing firmly on his principles by never allowing anyone, or anything, to intimidate him in any manner whatsoever. He was just doing his time and wanted to be respected and left alone. That was the impression all of us had after meeting Dapper Don, which was another nickname Mr. Gotti went by.

Mr. Gotti's stay at FCI Fort Dix was short, as he was having some medical issues that required special treatment, and he was expecting to soon be transferred to MCFP in Missouri, where I'd also spent time at. I offered Mr. Gotti some inmate to inmate friendly advice on what to expect upon his arrival at MCFP, and wished him the best of luck with his medical and legal issues.

Mr. Gotti eventually died, supposedly, of natural causes, on June 10, 2002, while serving his life sentence, without parole, at the Medical Center for Federal Prisoners, in Springfield, Missouri. Supposedly, while incarcerated, Mr. Gotti was stricken with esophageal cancer and at the end of his life he was hardly able to speak, had difficulty swallowing, and lost a considerable amount of weight before he eventually passed away.

Weeks turned into months, and the Fourth Circuit Court of Appeals was taking their sweet time, and there was nothing Mr. Rutledge or I could do to hasten their decision making process. In the meantime, I continued to serve time I should never have had to serve. I was furious and growing angrier with each passing day.

It became increasingly more difficult for me to sleep at night. I laid awake staring at the ceiling above, and wondering when this ongoing nightmare was all going to end. After all, Jon Gerritt was serving, and justifiably so, my 35-year prison sentence, without parole, while I continued serving my illegally imposed 25-year sentence, even though my drug kingpin conviction and 35-year, non-parolable sentence was ordered vacated by Judge Moore, and yet, after having fully vindicated myself, and won a monumental court battle against all odds, I was still incarcerated. Why?

Talk about the *Injustice In Justice* and the *Judicial Web* that continued to ensnarl and prevent me from being set free. This was the epitome of my relentless quest for justice to prevail, which would become yet another hard fought legal battle from which I was determined to conquer and eventually overcome.

The cold and brutal winter months were here. A new year was rapidly approaching, and I was about to celebrate my forty-sixth birthday, after nearly 8-years of confinement.

The big sixty-four-dollar question I kept pondering over and over, was whether or not I'd be spending another New Year's celebration behind bars, with my fellow inmates, or would a miracle intervene, which would finally set me free, and allow me to spend it with my family and loved ones.

I knew from my years behind bars if the Court was going to rule, and grant the relief prayed for in the motion we filed with the Fourth Circuit Court of Appeals, they'd do so prior to the end of the year. The courts, in general, make it a point to try their best and clear their calendars as the end of the current year approaches, so they'd have a fresh start as the new year unfolds. So, if anything favorable was going to happen for me it would have to be very soon.

I recall having a brief telephone conversation with Mr. Rutledge several days prior to December 25, 1994, Christmas Day. He informed me he felt confident that a favorable ruling by the Fourth Circuit Court of Appeals was imminent, but questioned why it was taking the Court so long to rule. It was now going on five months since my resentencing hearing, and Mr. Rutledge felt with the motion we filed being cut and dry, and with all the supporting case law, in further support of the single issue we raised, a ruling should've been handed down long before now. He couldn't wrap his mind around why it was taking so long for an opinion to be rendered. He suggested I be a bit more patient, and to hang in there a little while longer. We said our goodbyes, I wished him and his family a Merry Christmas, thanked him for taking my collect call, and hung up feeling even more depressed. Who knew how much longer this would or could drag on for. It just didn't seem fair.

I went to bed early on Wednesday evening, it was the 28th of December. I all but gave up on being home for any New Year's celebration with my family, which was now only four days away.

It must've been in the wee hours of the morning, on the following day, when I broke into a cold sweat and began to shiver. I didn't know what came over me, but I could have sworn I'd just awoken from a wonderful, yet very bizarre and surreal dream. I decided to freshen up and catch an early morning breakfast, before heading to the gym for my daily workout, and then off to the inmate law library where I was reinstated as the head jailhouse law clerk once again.

It was around 11:00 a.m., when over the prison PA system came the following announcement, loud and clear: *"Inmate Steve Silva report immediately to the Administration Office."* The message was rather surprising, but I was once again stunned and very apprehensive as to what the (report immediately) message was all about. Several thoughts began rushing through my brain, as I rushed to the Administration Office. I tried to remain calm, but the sweat kept pouring from my forehead, and the first thing that came to my mind was that something bad must have happened to a family member. Both my parents were in fair to poor health and my brother as well. Could something catastrophic have happened to any of them? Could one of them have died? By the time I reached the steps of the Administration Office, and entered through the oversized, steel reinforced twin doors, another thought occurred to me. Could this be the miracle I've been praying for. Would this be the day when my nearly eight-years of confinement have finally come to an end.

When I entered the building I was greeted by the security guard on duty. He had a smile on his face and mentioned, with a whispering tone in his voice, *"This must be your lucky day, sir."* I was startled! I didn't know how to react to the guard's hush like spoken words. The next thing I remember the Warden's secretary greeted me, and asked me to have a seat in the Warden's Office. She informed me that he'd be with me momentarily.

JUDICIAL WEB

By now my adrenaline was flowing out of control. I didn't know what to expect next. Was this really happening or was this all a dream.

The Warden entered his office, greeted me with an awkward smile and handshake, and the next words he uttered were...*"I don't know how you managed to pull this off. It's rarely, if ever happened here before, but we just received official word that you are to be immediately released from this prison facility. Your family is anxiously waiting to greet you at the Visitor's Entrance, gather your belongings, and good luck to you, Silva."*

I can't express to you how I felt at that very moment, as the Warden uttered those words. I had to do everything in my power to refrain myself from screaming the words, *"Free At Last!"*

The Warden congratulated me on my newfound freedom, seems he'd been following my case ever since I first became an inmate at FCI Fort Dix. He let me know my reputation among several other Wardens, from around the country, was of the highest regard, and he seemed genuinely elated I was finally being set free.

I was instructed to pack up all my belongings as swiftly as possible, and that I'd then be escorted by two correctional officers to meet my family.

The problem for me now was I couldn't possibly pack up all my belongings, on such short notice, as instructed. I had a voluminous assortment of very important legal papers, books, plus all the things I'd accumulated over the years, which I now needed to carefully pack in boxes and take with me. I mentioned this to the Warden's secretary who fully understood my concerns. She swiftly arranged for me to have the supplies I needed to pack everything up and transported to the front gate with me.

I'd like to pause here for just a moment before I share with you how spectacular my grandiose departure was. Once the word spread throughout the entire inmate population, that I was being set free, there was an avalanche of inmates looking to congratulate me from all over the compound. They came looking for me by the hundreds, wishing me good luck. I became overwhelmed and filled with joy as tears began running down my cheeks.

I left out a very important part of my conversation with the Warden. It turned out when the Fourth Circuit Court of Appeals rendered their unanimous decision that I was improperly sentenced by Judge Moore, and the most he could have resentenced me to was fifteen years, with parole capabilities, the best part of all this excitement was the mere fact the case laws the panel used, in their unanimous written opinion, were the same cases I'd written on that toilet paper, after Judge Moore had imposed his unlawful sentence upon me, soon after I was taken back to the City Jail.

My head was spinning. I now needed to pack everything up as quickly as possible, and make a beeline for the Visitor's Entrance and greet my family. Unbeknownst to me, they were patiently waiting there since early morning. Apparently, they received the wonderful news from Mr. Rutledge the evening before, when he advised them of the Court's ruling, and to make their plans to pick me up first thing in the morning.

Imagine this scenario for a moment. I was serving my time at FCI Fort Dix, which held more federal inmates than any other federal prison or penitentiary in the Federal Bureau of Prisons. We're talking several thousand inmates who were incarcerated at this prison facility while I was doing my time there.

As I mentioned earlier, word spread like wildfire about my having won my appeal, and it was Court Ordered I be immediately released from federal prison. This had never happened before at this prison facility. At least that's what I'd been led to believe by the two correctional officers who finally escorted me safely out of FCI Fort Dix, along with my twenty-three boxes, two full duffel bags, and many other personal items I'd accumulated during the past, nearly eight years of my confinement on that extraordinary, eventful day.

As I'm being escorted by the two correctional officers, heading toward the Visitor's Entrance gate with all my belongings on a large four-wheel dolly, I noticed several hundred inmates, cheering and yelling out my name. It was as if I was some kind of hero to many of them. Most all the inmates there had come to respect me, and knew of my jailhouse lawyering skills. They knew from the conversations I shared with many of my fellow inmates, over the time I'd spent at FCI Fort Dix, how corrupt the system can be, especially in my criminal case, where the entire prosecution team was riddled with wrongdoing, some even intentional, which was eventually proven from the very start of my criminal investigation.

Most of the inmates cheering and chanting my name were sorry to see me leave. On the other hand, they were overjoyed that one of their own had beat the system, and showed them with perseverance and tenacity, coupled with patience and a good family support system, justice can, and in my case did finally prevail.

In many ways, I felt very sorry for those inmates I was leaving behind, some of whom I'd come to know quite well. Others only in passing, but they had known of my reputation, and I felt the goodwill they had toward me and for what I'd accomplished for many fellow inmates, who like me, were fighting their injustices, and for many would have a long and difficult task of seeing any favorable results anytime soon, if at all.

I said my goodbyes and waved to everyone who followed behind me. Much to my surprise, the Warden was at the Visitor's Gate, already engaged in conversation with my family. As I approached the gate area, the Warden greeted me with a firm handshake, and wished me good luck. He let me know that in all the years he'd been employed by the BOP, starting out thirty years earlier, as a correctional officer and now the Warden, with the largest inmate population in the entire BOP, he'd never seen an inmate be immediately released from custody like I was. He went on to further state that that was something that spoke volumes of my character, my ability to fight for what I believed in and to have prevailed in doing so. I felt honored by the Warden's words, and then, as the gate opened, my daughter was first to hug and kiss me, then my parents and my brother were there to greet me as well. Luckily, they'd brought two cars with them, so I could take home my 23 boxes and two duffel bags of accumulated personal items from my nearly eight years of confinement.

Being on the other side of the barbed-wire fence felt very strange for me. The inmates retreated to their normal activities; I became very emotional and broke down in front of my family members, who wound up doing the same. This lasted for about five minutes. They were all good tears being shed this time around, unlike those sad ones after my arrest, or those shed after Judge Moore sentenced me to my 35-year, non-parolable, draconian, and unlawfully imposed prison sentence nearly eight years earlier.

The next thing that transpired was my daughter presented me with a box that she insisted I open right away. Much to my surprise, it was a brand new, beautiful outfit for me to change into, which I immediately saw fit to do. A beautiful pair of jeans, a belt, pair of socks, a matching shirt, a brand new pair of sneakers, and a *New York Yankees' Baseball Cap*. Boy, did that hit the spot! I wanted to burn those prison clothes I left with, especially the orange jumpsuit I came to despise, which I finally had the pleasure of burning in the backyard of our family's home the following day.

As I finish writing my story, it's been twenty-eight years since I was released from federal prison. As a pleasant reminder, I still have the same pair of jeans, shirt, and belt my daughter presented to me when I was first released from federal custody on December 29, 1994.

JUDICIAL WEB

I had a lovely New Year's Eve celebration with my entire family, and we all had a spectacular reunion together. I made sure that I stuffed myself with food I'd yearned for and hadn't tasted in so many years.

Speaking of which, after we loaded the cars with my boxes and other personal belongings, my dad asked me where I'd like to go next. I told him I missed eating at a neighborhood diner. As fate would have it, there was one nearby, and we headed straight there. I thought how strange it would be to eat with metal and not plasticware again. Most prison facilities, at least when I was doing time, always gave us plastic utensils to eat with. This was going to be a welcome change for me to enjoy and once again get used to.

Once we entered the diner, sat down, and I glanced at the menu, I already knew exactly what I wanted. A white-albacore, tuna-salad sandwich, with all the trimmings, lettuce, tomato, mayo, muenster cheese, red onions, on whole-wheat bread, with a side of coleslaw, freshly made french-fries, and to wash it all down, I ordered a root beer float with extra root beer and vanilla ice-cream. For dessert, I ordered homemade rice pudding with cinnamon and whip cream. I remember, after polishing off the rice pudding, I also yearned for a slice of hot, apple-crunch pie, with vanilla ice-cream.

I stuffed myself while my family watched me enjoy the first solid meal I had in nearly eight years. I must admit that I broke down once we were seated and stared at the menu. I was just reminiscing why this all happened to me, and how the last eight years of my life had just flown by. I thought about how much of my life I'd missed out on, being locked up and away from my family all this time.

My mom noticed the tears running down my face and started crying, along with my dad, brother, and daughter, who began doing the same. It was like an exorcism being voluntarily conducted on all of us. Tears continued pouring out of my eyes, and all the hurt

I'd suffered so deeply from being away for all those long, painful, and arduous years, was finally being released from my mind, body, and soul.

Can you just imagine when the waitress finally came over to take our order and saw all of us crying, what she must have been thinking. She said, *"Is the menu all that bad for you guys, or is this something you all do before ordering your food?"* We all laughed, wiped our tears, and I informed the waitress of the reason for all the tear shedding. At first she didn't believe my story, but was soon convinced it must have been true. She brought us a handful of extra napkins just in case we thought about crying all over again.

After we had enjoyed our first meal together, my dad asked me what I'd like to do next. I told him I was exhausted and wanted to catch some much-needed rest on a comfortable bed, which was already waiting for me upon our arrival back at my parents' home.

The ride back home was refreshing, even though I was dozing on and off, but wishing to take in all the sites and smell the fresh outside air. It was a rather brisk and chilly day outside, but the sun was shining. It felt so great and yet so strange at the same time, riding in the car, being in traffic, watching people in passing cars, and just taking it all in. It felt so overwhelming. Just moments ago, I was locked up in a federal prison, behind barbed wire fencing, and now free as a bird driving home with my family.

I hadn't driven a vehicle in more than eight years and was wondering if I'd even remembered how. However, it wasn't long before I was driving again. Like riding a bicycle, you never forget.

Before reading the final chapter of my book, I wish to inform you how truly monumental, and against all odds, my release from federal prison, and the termination of my 35-year, non-parolable sentence really was. It's very rarely if ever accomplished on post-conviction relief. For me, I was at the end of the road, with no further

JUDICIAL WEB

judicial challenges whatsoever, regarding my unlawful drug kingpin conviction, under a Title 21, Section 848 CCE felony, which, at this time, upon conviction as a first-time offender, is punishable with a mandatory 20-year sentence, and for large scale drug offenders, life without parole, plus up to a hefty 2-million dollar fine and civil forfeiture of all of the ones illegally acquired assets, including real estate, cars, boats, planes, and money, etc.

Most often, if any relief is to be granted, it's usually done on Direct Appeal, not post-conviction relief, especially involving a reversal of a CCE, drug kingpin felony conviction. It was really nothing short of a miracle that I was able to have overturned my conviction and thirty five year prison sentence, with no possibility of parole, and equally amazing to have done it with the very last bite of the Apple of Justice, on a Post-Conviction, Rule 2255 Motion, before a very conservative senior sitting judge, who prided himself on rarely ever being overruled by any appellate court, during his thirty-five plus year tenure on the federal bench.

Judge Moore went to his final resting place, not only for being shamefully overruled for the wrongful mishandling of the resentencing phase of my criminal case, but also for the grave embarrassment he personally suffered by not heeding the Fourth Circuit Court of Appeals unanimous, 34-page published opinion, with specific instructions to resentence me properly and promptly to time served, and to order my immediate release from federal custody. Imagine how extraordinary, and truly unprecedented this accomplishment was for Mr. Rutledge and I to have achieved.

Judge Moore's lack of jurisprudence to properly sentence me in accordance with established legal precedents, otherwise etched in stone, which he prejudicially chose to ignore in the most biased and unprecedented manner, caused him grave embarrassment at the end of an otherwise exemplary career on the federal bench.

Being admonished and embarrassed from the unanimous decision rendered by the Fourth Circuit Court of Appeals, and their lengthy published opinion, was the icing on the cake for Judge Moore's demise.

This presumably, senile and insubordinate act, not only severely and permanently tarnished Judge Moore's judicial record as one of the longest-sitting federal judges in the country, but it eventually led to his demise and voluntary resignation from the federal bench. At least that's what we were led to believe, through reliable sources of information, several years after Judge Moore's passing.

AND NOW, for the final chapter of my ongoing saga!

POST RELEASE YEARS

I should have known when something is too good to be true it usually is. My immediate release from FCI Fort Dix wasn't without specific conditions.

As a pre-condition of my reinstated conspiracy conviction and subsequent resentencing, as ordered by the Fourth Circuit Court of Appeals, Judge Moore still had some leeway when finalizing my new sentence. I was to be immediately placed on Federal Probation for 3-years, which would then be followed by a consecutive 3-year period of Supervised Release. Adding these additional six years to my existing 15-year sentence, the new sentence became 21-years. I wasn't expecting those additional terms and conditions. However, this was going to be the last cheap shot Judge Moore could place as a condition of my release, and reinstated 15-year sentence, which technically I'd already fully served as stipulated in the recent Fourth Circuit Appellate Court's ruling.

Nevertheless, these additional sentencing terms could wind up negatively impacting my life, especially now that I was free and able to become a productive member of society once again. Let me explain.

Remember, I no longer had a permanent residence to call home. The government confiscated all my assets, including my personal residence and one rental property. If you recall all my assets were civilly forfeited, and otherwise used to pay my legal fees.

Since my criminal prosecution and subsequent conviction was out of the District of Maryland, the U.S. Probation Office decided that's where I was to be conveniently relocated, until such time I could re-establish myself back to my prior residence in Florida. If I didn't have an approved place to reside in Maryland, I'd be forced to enter a halfway house program, and I wasn't going to have any part of that. Luckily, my sister and daughter both resided in Maryland, but I didn't want to impose on either of them. After all, they both had their own lives to live without worrying about mine.

My daughter was living in her own apartment and involved in a serious relationship, and now that I was no longer incarcerated, she surprised me with her plans to be married in a few months. After all, she placed her life on hold, as well as her marriage plans, in hopes that I'd be released from prison and be able to walk her down the aisle, which is exactly what I wound up doing several months after my release.

My only option was to stay with my sister and her husband, who had a large home with a spare bedroom. I was certain the U.S. Probation Office would approve of my staying there until I could decide how best to eventually relocate back to Florida, which is where I had definite plans of rebuilding my life all over again.

I soon learned that being on federal probation was no fun at all. As a matter of fact it was very restrictive, and in many ways confining. I had to report for routine drug testing, unexpected visits from my Probation Officer, and tedious weekly reports to fill out detailing my whereabouts each day. I was unable to leave the state or travel outside of Maryland for the first six months after my release. I had specific call in times when I had to contact my Probation Officer, and I had routine meetings, once every month, with my entire Probation Team. Additionally, I was given a period of only thirty days from the day of my release, to find and secure a decent paying, legitimate, and approved job. To think I had to do all this for the next six years weighed heavily on my mind.

What made matters even worse was, if I violated my probation for any reason, and it could be for the most minor misconduct, I could be sent back to federal prison to complete the rest of my unfinished, 15-year sentence. This had me terribly scared half to death. What if I was set up, or worse yet, what if the government wished to get back at me for having embarrassed the entire U.S. Attorney's Office for the District of Maryland. What if the feds had a real hard-on for me, and wanted to see me back behind bars? They could easily make a few phone calls, and in no time flat it could be made to look like I was in violation of one of their rules, and back to federal prison I'd go. *WOW!* I was freaking out!

The first probation officer I was initially told to report to was very harsh, and threatened several times to hit me with a violation. In one instance it got to the point it was either going to be me going back to federal prison, or this probation officer would be reassigned or forced to resign. He falsified a report on me, made false claims that would otherwise be a cause for my receiving a violation, and he made my life miserable. In fact he finally did write me up for a violation.

To this day, I firmly believe that one of the members of my prosecution team must have gotten to him, and told him to do whatever he needed to get me issued a violation and sent back to prison. I have a pretty good idea who that culprit was, but I have no concrete proof, so it's best I don't speculate, and let it go at that.

Luckily for me, I made sure I had witnesses to prove everything I stated at my violation hearing was accurate and truthful. My witnesses backed up my story 100%. I even offered to take a polygraph test, to prove I was telling the truth, and my probation officer was lying, but the U.S. Probation Office Disciplinary Committee chose not to accept my offer to do so. After careful consideration and review of the entire record of the alleged charges lodged against me, they eventually dismissed their probation violation case, reassigned the probation officer who seemingly had a hard-on for me, and I was ultimately cleared of all charges. I later learned this probation officer, who I was initially assigned to, had several similar confrontation issues with recently released inmates, and he'd been disciplined in the past for doing so. Several months later I learned he'd resigned over an alleged sexual assault charge. So much for my close call with the U.S. Probation Office.

I wound up staying with my sister and my brother-in-law for an entire year. I earned my keep by helping them repair things around their home, babysitting for their three year old daughter every now and then, which I thoroughly enjoyed doing for them. After all, that was the least I could do. They took me in and provided me with a very comfortable room of my own, fed me, bought me clothes, provided me with a car to drive, and life was good, once again. And as an extra bonus I saw my daughter often, as she lived down the street from my sister's home.

My daughter got married in the spring, several months after my release from FCI Fort Dix, and I had the distinct honor of walking her down the aisle, as she had prayed and hoped for. She made a beautiful bride, and I'm proud to say she and her husband blessed me with two precious grandchildren, who are both grown up now. My grandson recently graduated from college, and is now gainfully employed in New York's financial sector. My granddaughter is now attending her sophomore year at a prestigious college of her choosing, and an honor roll student for her second year there.

Fast forward to December 1996, two years after my release from FCI Fort Dix, with two of the three years already behind me, that I was serving on Federal Probation, my new U.S. Probation Officer recommended to her superiors I no longer needed to be on any further probationary status, and that it would be a waste of the government's resources for me to continue doing so. She even wrote a wonderful letter of recommendation to the U.S. Probation Commissioner, on my behalf, asking that I now be allowed to relocate back to Florida where I'd be able to continue with my three years of Supervised Release, which was very similar to being on Federal Probation.

JUDICIAL WEB

Never in a million years would I have ever believed I'd be approved to relocate back to Florida, where I'd be able to once again reside in my condo, which the government had originally seized, but hadn't yet officially forfeited, more on that in a moment, but I was also informed, due to my exemplary behavior, while on Federal Probation for the past two years, coupled with the government's lack of proper funding, and looking to cut back on expenses, that my three-year Supervised Release conditions were waived and immediately terminated. I was no longer a subject of the U.S. Government, and now at last, I was free as a bird. How monumental was that!

My sister, brother-in-law, and niece, along with my daughter, who was now pregnant with her first born, soon to be son, were all sorry to see me head south, and finally back to my Florida lifestyle. They all knew this was what I'd eventually yearned for all along.

I wound up serving only two years of my otherwise six years of combined Federal Probation and Supervised Release terms. How cool was that! I can't believe I pulled that off. Just another part of my ongoing success story upon being released from federal prison.

Getting back to the Florida condo issue, and how I learned about the government not having forfeited it, even after my release from FCI Fort Dix. Through my FOIA (Freedom of Information Act) requests, while doing ongoing research for my memoir, I'd come to learn the DEA, through the undercover efforts of Special Agent Sandy Jones, you remember him, the government approved his use of not only my confiscated condo, but also my jewelry, all of which Special Agent Jones had used to entrap, set up, and eventually arrest many high-level drug dealers, while I was away serving time for the past nearly eight years. Not only that, once the Government stopped using my condo for their undercover use, they began renting it and collecting rent each month for a good many years, as well.

Since the property was never officially forfeited, and since the CCE 848 conviction was overturned and vacated, the government no longer had any legal rights using this asset of mine, and was subsequently forced to return it to me, along with the rental income they'd been collecting for many years. They were also required to return my gold jewelry and Rolex watch, which Agent Jones had been using while acting as a big-time drug dealer.

I wound up filing a multi-million-dollar lawsuit against the U.S. Attorney's Office for the District of Maryland. I sued for false imprisonment, loss of most of my assets, which would never have been confiscated if I wasn't charged with a drug kingpin felony offense, and for all my lost years of gainful employment, while having served more time than I otherwise should have served, due to Judge Moore's vindictive, and wrongfully imposed sentence, all of which cost me dearly.

The Government responded through my lawyer, and informed him if I didn't drop my lawsuit against them, they'd take me back to trial, and find a way to put me back in prison, all over again. I knew they were bluffing, since I'd already served the maximum sentence I could serve, my probation and supervised release terms were fully satisfied and terminated, and had they tried to retry my case all over again, they'd have to find a way to do so without their star witness, who was serving a thirty-five year sentence without parole, for being the real drug kingpin that he was, and then there was the issue of double jeopardy, which the government would also have to deal with.

The bigger question for me to answer was, did I wish to put myself and my family through this all over again. My mom and dad pleaded with me to drop the lawsuit. My dad, mom, and brother were not in the best of health, and my family needed me around for them. They didn't need me to risk the chance of being sent back to prison and behind bars all over again.

For me, it wasn't so much about the money, but rather the principle of it all. I fully understood my mom and dad's feelings and concerns. I made the decision to have my lawyer prepare a settlement agreement with the Government, and as it all turned out, it was probably the best advice my mom and dad could have ever given me.

Almost twelve months from the day of my release from federal prison, my dad had a debilitating stroke, which took his life, and we lost the patriarch of our family. For my dear mom, she lost her best friend, having been happily married for 55-years, and she was never the same again. Had I not heeded her sound advice, I might have regretted it for the rest of my life. Luckily, my mom had my brother still around for her. Gary was living at our family's residence, when our father died, so my mom was not alone, and Gary made sure to comfort and took good care of our mom until he passed away (11) years later.

As for me, I wound up moving back to South Florida, and into my condo, which I was successful in getting back from the Government, along with all my originally confiscated gold jewelry, plus all the back rent that I was also entitled to, which I had my lawyer successfully negotiate for me. Remember, this was all part of the deal for me to drop my pending multi-million lawsuit against the federal government, which I likely would've prevailed on.

Having no longer any travel restrictions to worry about, I was yearning to travel once again. I'd lost touch with Anthony after he was released from federal incarceration, and upon learning of my release from custody, he called me out of the blue. He wound up in Bangkok, Thailand, and was living with a middle-aged Thai woman. He'd been living there for almost ten years by the time he reached out to me. I guess you could say curiosity got the best of him, and he wanted to learn what I was up to since my release, which he'd heard about through the grapevine, as I later found out.

Anthony insisted I visit him in Bangkok, the flourishing capital city of Thailand. I didn't even know where Thailand was located, on the World map, nor had I ever heard of that country before.

Before I knew it, after doing some further research on my own, and several follow up phone conversations, I decided to take Anthony up on his offer. I'd already relocated back to South Florida, since around 1998. After just about 5-years of rebuilding my life, and doing pretty well for myself, I felt it was time to take some much needed R&R, and so off I went to explore this exotic, country, otherwise known as the *'Land of Smiles,'* on the other side of the globe.

I hooked up with Anthony and spent a marvelous time there. Originally, my plan was to stay for only four weeks. However, as fate would have it, being single for nearly 25-years, I met and fell madly in love with a lovely Thai woman, nearly 20-years my junior, and we became inseparable. I extended my stay another several weeks, which turned into several more months. In total, I spent eight months in this paradise of a country, with the new love of my life. I didn't want to leave, but I had no other choice but to do so. Things back home were getting a bit out of control with my brother's debilitating illnesses, and he was having a hard time caring for my mom. Hence, it was time for me to head home. I did so with a heavy heart, and promised my Thai sweetheart, whose nickname was Jan, that I'd be back to see her soon. I told her I loved her, and wanted to spend the rest of my life with her. She spoke little English when we first met, and I spoke not a word of Thai, but we managed to communicate, and we spent a marvelous eight months together. On my long flight back home I knew I would make Jan my bride one day soon. I wasn't getting any younger, and I didn't wish to spend the rest of my life alone, without sharing it with someone special once more.

Upon my arrival back to the states, I made a pit stop in New Jersey to visit with my mom and brother. I had a lot to sort out there, since my brother was no longer able to care for my mom, as his health continued to deteriorate. Being a heavy smoker, obese, with blood circulation issues, diabetes, and very poor eating habits, he was on a collision course with serious, life-threatening, health issues.

In the meantime, my mind was totally elsewhere. I couldn't stop thinking about Jan. I had those teenage, first love, butterflies in my stomach and the flutters in my heart. That was all the signs I needed to convince myself that I needed to get back to see Jan as soon as possible, and ask her to marry me.

I was finally able to provide my mom with some much needed professional caregiving aide, which relieved my brother from the responsibility of having to continue to care for our mom, since he was no longer able to do so. I informed both my mom and Gary of my plans to marry Jan, and while they seemed very surprised by my decision to do so, they were nevertheless very happy for me.

After flying back home to Florida and racking up huge phone bills, talking with Jan on a daily basis, I knew I had to make my way back to Thailand very soon. I made plans to fly back to see her, but this time I wanted to surprise her. She never thought she'd ever see me again. The reunion was more than I could have ever dreamed of. I invited Jan to come to the U.S. on a K1, Fiancée visa. I had no idea how difficult and long this process would take, or how much it was going to cost me to bring Jan to the U.S. to consider marrying me. I wanted Jan to see my country for herself, how and where I lived, and see if she felt comfortable here in the U.S., so very far away from her homeland. After all, my culture and traditions are a far cry from hers. It would take an awful lot of adjusting, on both our parts, to make this work, but if she was game, so was I. I was willing to roll the dice and take that leap of faith. That's exactly what we both did. I flew back to Florida, and was able to finalize the Fiancée K1 Visa process.

It was Christmas Day, Thursday, December 25, 2003, when Jan

finally arrived safely at Miami International Airport. With the K1 Visa we only had three months to make up our minds if we were going to get married, and spend the rest of our lives together. It would be a real challenge for the both of us, more so for Jan, leaving her family of five brothers, one sister, and a slew of nieces and nephews behind. I promised Jan, after we were married, I'd make certain she'd be able to visit her family at least once every few years, and speak with them whenever, and for as long as she wanted. She appreciated that gesture very much.

On March 9, 2004, just under the three-month requirement mark, Jan and I tied the knot, with a simple, Justice of the Peace, wedding ceremony. My brother, feeling a little better, managed to make the trip to be our best man, and spent a few days with us before heading back home. That was a blessing for me to have Gary there, and have him be a part of our wedding ceremony. Jan was now officially *Mrs. Jan Silva.*

Jan and I had some serious adjusting to do, in order to make our marriage work, but after some ups and downs, which were to be expected, and some deep soul searching for the two of us, we managed to get over those first few years of marriage woes and things have been pretty much smooth sailing ever since.

A number of years later another devastating blow to the family was about to happen, only this time, I was totally unprepared for the tragedy that would strike our dwindling family once again.

Jan and I decided it was time to make our way back to Thailand. I wanted to visit with Anthony again and Jan was yearning to spend time with her siblings, other family members, and her close friends, too. We made plans to do so, and off we went.

We arrived safe and sound at Bangkok's International Airport, on Wednesday, May 28, 2008. Before we made the rounds, Jan and I decided we wanted to visit Chiang Mai, in northern Thailand. Being a Thai native, but born in another remote part of her country,

JUDICIAL WEB

Jan never had the opportunity to visit Chiang Mai, the most cultural part of Thailand. She always dreamed of going there, and I wanted to fulfill her dream of doing so.

I arranged for us to stay at one of the more luxurious, Chiang Mai hotels, directly overlooking the Mekong River, renamed in the 1960's, the River Kwai. We had a spectacular view from our honeymoon suite.

We retired for the evening, and had room service deliver our dinner, watched some TV for a while, and then we both dozed off. It was 4:00 a.m. in the morning on the 29th of May in Thailand and 3:00 p.m. on the east coast of the U.S. The hotel phone rang and startled me. Jan was fast asleep. I awoke and answered the phone, thinking it must have been someone calling the wrong room. No one knew we were there, only my daughter and sister had been privy to my itinerary. Never thinking for a moment that it would've been either one of them calling me at this late hour of the night, I picked up the phone, and I heard my daughter's voice. She was hysterical and crying uncontrollably. I couldn't understand a word she was saying. The first thing that came to my mind was that something may have happened to one of my grandchildren, or maybe her husband. I didn't know what to think. Then she gained her composure, and informed me that my brother had suddenly died. I was stunned and didn't know what to say. I asked her to calm down and tell me what happened.

It turned out that my brother had gone with my mom to visit the bank to check on some precious coins he stored inside his personal vault. My mom was also there to make some deposits in the same bank. Next thing my mom witnessed was my brother had asked to sit down on the chair next to her. He said he was feeling faint. Then suddenly my brother collapsed, fell off the chair, and with his very last breath he opened his eyes, told our mom he loved her, and died right there and then in her arms. My mom became hysterical!

After hearing this tragic story, I had to gain my composure, and by this time Jan was awake and asked if I was ok. I ignored her at first, as I was still in total shock. I had just lost my only brother, and best friend in life. I was 10,000 miles away, on the other side of the world, and it was in the middle of the night in Chiang Mai. I had to think clearly, as I needed to get back to New Jersey as quickly as possible. My mom was with her two sisters at the time, and in total shock. My daughter, sister, and their families were all en route from Maryland to help my mom with the funeral arrangements, which would be held that Sunday, June 1, 2008.

Jan and I had just arrived in Bangkok, the day before, and now this tragic event not only upset our travel plans, but I had to now quickly decide how I was going to handle this sudden catastrophic news. I had to get Jan back to Bangkok to be with her family. I knew it would be unfair for her to accompany me back home, after just arriving, and I knew how much she was looking forward to spending time with her family. Jan insisted on coming back with me and paying her respects to my brother, who she was very fond of, and respected very much. After all, he was the best man at our wedding, when nobody else cared to attend. She loved Gary's humor and ability to make her laugh whenever she was around him. I had a tough decision to make, but in the end I decided to leave Jan behind, and have her spend time with her family and friends, while I made a beeline to the Bangkok International Airport, and caught a red eye flight back to Newark International Airport, the following day.

I barely made it back home in time to attend the funeral. My poor mom was a total wreck. She completely broke down when she saw me. I had to muster all my strength to remain strong for the entire family. We were down to three of us left in our immediate family. My sister, God bless her, was great, she took charge of the funeral proceedings, and all the other tasks that come with funeral protocols, from food preparations to contacting relatives, so they could attend Gary's funeral if they were able to do so. Gary was much loved by our entire extended family members.

At around 2:00 p.m., on June 1, 2008, my beloved brother Gary was laid to rest. Many family members showed up to pay their respects, and some of our relatives traveled from across the country to attend my brother's funeral. That's the kind of respect the family had for my younger brother, Gary. This loss, in our family, was especially hard to deal with. Gary was the main, emotional support system for our mom for many years, and now he was gone, and our mom was now left all alone. Meanwhile, Jan was weighing heavily on my mind. I knew I needed to see if she wanted me to come back to be with her after the funeral was over, or if she'd be able to manage flying back home on her own.

Gary's funeral proceedings were handled very respectfully, and my mom's oldest sister's son, my first cousin, Dr. Mark, offered to conduct the gravesite ceremony and eulogy, as well.

After the funeral was over; things began to settle down, and started getting back to some semblance of normalcy. However, the bigger question for my sister and I was what we were now going to do for our mom. She could no longer live alone, and we now needed immediate 24/7 caregiver assistance for her.

After a few days had passed, and having been in constant contact with Jan, we decided that I'd head back to Florida, while Gloria remained with our mom for a while longer. We desperately needed to try and find someone to help care for her. Jan and I decided she'd stay a bit more with her family before making her way back home.

A few more months passed, and Jan was finally back home with me. We had a wonderful reunion, and we were able to enjoy our lives together once more.

Fast forward to December 29, 2022. It's been exactly 28-years, to the day, since December 29, 1994, when I walked out the front gate of FCI Fort Dix a free man. A monumental day, and an incredibly vivid memory, which shall remain with me until I take my very last breath in this lifetime. I've grown wiser, learned a lot about myself and the world around me during these past 28-years I've been fortunate to still be around. I'm a survivor of two serious bouts of cancer, both required serious surgeries, and I made it through a recent life sparing surgery, for a perforated esophagus, which I barely survived from. I'm truly lucky to be alive. I still have six more cat lives, which I hope and pray I never have to use.

As strange as this may sound, I can now honestly say with conviction in my heart, I truly cherished my nearly 8-years of confinement. I gained an awful lot of knowledge and perspective about life in general, about the people I was surrounded by, from every race, color, creed, and religious background, while doing my time. For me, that experience was priceless, and self-rewarding.

I also had the ability to polish and further develop my creative talents during the time I was incarcerated, which provided me the opportunity to create and develop an intellectual property, which I eventually licensed and later sold, having allowed me to join the millionaire's club, and retire at a rather young age. Something I never would have dreamed possible, had it not been for those arduous years I spent in federal prison. I've not only learned to be humble, much more patient, understanding, and compassionate, but most of all, I've learned the value of life, and how swiftly it can be taken away from us by committing one single wrongful act, or a misjudgment of morality, which I was guilty of. However, I was most fortunate having been blessed with being granted a second lease on life. For this I shall always remain forever grateful and most humble as I continue my journey through life.

I'm still married to Jan, going on (22) years now. We've made a wonderful life together. As for me, I've been working on a very exciting children's music-animation project, which is keeping me plenty busy these days.

All in all, I can't complain. I've been most fortunate to have lived a very exciting, adventurous, productive, extraordinary and most fulfilling life thus far. Here's hoping I'm able to continue doing so for at least a little while longer.

Completing this memoir has given me a great sense of self-accomplishment and joy, while sharing it with many others has provided me with an unexplainable feeling of self-gratification, and a great deal of pride. Here's thanking each and every one of you for reading my story.

LIFE'S BEEN GREAT!

EPILOGUE

With the end of every story, especially one like mine, there is a story within the story. For me, it was nothing short of a miracle, a monumental accomplishment, and a story I needed to share and tell. A story that's taken me nearly three decades to complete. My only excuse for not having written and published it sooner, was my life was full of many complicated issues, much of which were of my own doing. I was trying to make up for the many lost years of my life, being away from my family and loved ones. I guess you could say I kinda got somewhat side-tracked, not to mention my life threatening health issues to boot.

Many times I tried to discipline myself to continue writing my unfinished work and begin to pen the remaining chapters necessary to complete the final draft. However, I found it very difficult doing so, and thus kept putting it on the back burner, or in my so-called tomorrow file. It became very emotionally draining, and brought back a lot of disturbing memories I really didn't wish to revisit, until I felt the timing was right to do so.

One day, I'm thinking it must have been mid-May or June 2018, while watching the nightly news, something I rarely found myself doing with several new projects, that always kept me plenty busy, I learned about this book, *"Fire & Fury, Inside the Trump White House,"* which was being talked about. The gist of the conversation surrounding the book's content, very much intrigued me. It was all about how corrupt our government is today, with no end in sight, under the Trump Administration era.

Many years have now passed since I was indicted, convicted, and sentenced to a draconian sentence, which I was very fortunate to have eventually been able to prove was based on gross government misconduct, corruption, treachery, cover-up, and intrigue. I was hearing words being expressed on my television screen, which were a deep part of my very own personal experiences.

A light bulb went off in my head. I thought WOW! I must now, once and for all, finish the task of completing my fictionalized memoir. This was the perfect time for me to do so. I'd already penned nearly two-hundred, type-written, riveting pages. I now only needed to discipline myself and concentrate on being able to complete the final chapters, have it professionally edited, and finally published. I firmly believed that the American public needed to read my story.

For the next several months, I'm talking for at least ten or more hours every day, seven days a week, sometimes until the wee hours of the morning, I kept typing, editing, updating, and making critical changes to my memoir, non-stop, in order to complete the most accurate, final draft I could have possibly created. I finished my extensive research, refreshed my memory after carefully reading lengthy portions of my trial transcripts, and was finally able to complete the remaining chapters to my self-satisfaction.

I finally typed the last two words of my final draft, **THE END**, on Wednesday, January 1st, at precisely 8:32 p.m., on New Year's Day, 2020. What an extraordinary feeling of accomplishment came over me at that exact moment!

I can't explain how exhilarating it was for me to have typed those final two words. I took such pride and was overcome with joy in doing so. I sat in my comfortable writing chair, stared at my computer monitor, while scrolling through the (426) typed-written pages of my now completed '*JUDICIAL WEB*' manuscript.

On that eventful evening I watched the beautiful and brightly lit full moon from my living room picture window, which overlooked the large lake in the backyard of my home, while still reclined in my comfortable ergonomic writing chair.

I hope you've enjoyed reading my book, as much as I've enjoyed writing it, and making everyone aware of how precious life is, and how easily it is to be tempted by greed, and the misjudgments of our values, which can shatter one's life in a heartbeat, and in my case nearly ruined mine forever.

Unfortunately, not everyone fighting for justice, in today's complicated, highly divisive, insensitive, and still very corrupt world, will be as fortunate and lucky as I've been.

However, if you don't fight for what you believe in, and what wrongs that may have been unjustly perpetrated against you by others, you'll never succeed in seeking justice. That's my two cents, for what it's worth, and that I wish to share with you. And yes, perseverance is an absolute must in order for you to be able to do so. Amen to all that!

It's now the end of 2022, several years since I had originally completed my final draft, however several life threatening events prevented me from having my book published until now. My mom passed away in April of 2021, two months short of celebrating her 97th birthday, which was a major setback for me and our family. As if that wasn't enough for me to deal with, I endured a life sparing surgery, lasting nearly eight hours, to repair a perforated esophagus, which nearly took my life, having choked on a 400 mg Vitamin E capsule. Let's also not forget the Covid-19 pandemic we all dealt with. All these unfortunate events precluded me from publishing my memoir any sooner. Better late than never, right!

AFTERWORD

The *Afterword* is most often penned by someone other than the author. However, in certain extraordinary circumstances, the best person to explain how and why their book was written, in my humble opinion, would be the author.

I thought long and hard as to what I was going to do with my diary notes and prison life experiences, which I accumulated during the nearly eight years of my confinement, once I was released, and finally able to tell my story. Something I desperately wanted to share with the public at large.

I was very fortunate to have gained my freedom, after my 35- year, non-parolable, sentence was vacated by the very same judge who originally imposed this draconian sentence, which I later came to learn was extremely rare to have accomplished, and thus I felt compelled to tell my story once and for all.

I needed to expose how corrupt, biased, and prejudicially motivated my entire criminal prosecution team turned out to be, and how their quest for an unjust conviction against me, for being a drug kingpin, which they knew or should have known all along, I wasn't, was a frightening task for me to think about tackling. Thus, the impetus for this story to be written and subsequently published was born.

I'd like to now provide you with a brief synopsis of how my story unfolded. My family, the media, the entire prosecution team, along with a host of locals had filled the courtroom on my Sentencing Day. It was a day well remembered by everyone in attendance on that gloomy day, especially for me and my family.

STEVE SILVA

"I hereby sentence you to thirty-five years in federal prison, without parole, and you'll now be placed in the custody of the U.S. Marshals Service for further processing and transfer purposes."

Those were the words uttered by Judge Moore, Senior District Court Federal Judge, for the District of Maryland, on Monday, April 27, 1987. Those words rang loud and clear in Courtroom 'C' on that eventful day.

For the next nearly 8-years of my life, I tried my best to muster all the energy, knowledge, willpower, and courage necessary to prove I wasn't guilty of the harshest felony offense, in the government's arsenal of criminal statutes, for which a jury of my peers subsequently found me guilty on Monday, February 2, 1987.

Taking on the United States Government was not going to be an easy task. As a matter of fact, I'd soon learn it was going to be next to impossible to accomplish.

It's still an established fact, the government's conviction rate is greater than 95% percent. Nevertheless, I was still determined to challenge our judicial system, and exercise my constitutional right to a trial, by a jury of my peers. However, I would soon learn, I was in for a rude awakening!

I was under the distinct impression that our judicial system was the greatest in the world, and that *Lady Justice* would never let me down. Surely, she'd take her blinders off, and see through all of the hood-winking I was about to suffer, and make certain that justice would prevail in my criminal case.

Since I was convicted of a Title 21, Section 848 CCE Offense, which carried a minimum mandatory ten year, up to life, without parole, sentence, in addition to a fine of up to two-million dollars, I was literally fighting, against in conceivable odds, for my life. I never imagined, in a million years, that I'd face such adversity, corruption, treachery, and betrayal by our '*Just Us*" judicial system.

JUDICIAL WEB

Before we delve any further into my criminal ordeal, let me first describe what a Title 21, Section 848 CCE Offense consists of. CCE stands for *Continuing Criminal Enterprise.*

Originally, congressional intent was to prosecute organized crime bosses, and sophisticated criminal enterprises in the enforcement of the harshest of all criminal statutes.

Word had it that Senator Robert Kennedy, who eventually became the U.S. Attorney General, under President John F. Kennedy, was responsible for getting this harsh criminal statute enacted into law. He did so, supposedly, as a retaliatory measure against the mafia, for allegedly, in part, being responsible for the assassination of his brother, President John F. Kennedy.

However, as the years unfolded, the intent of Congress had become severely compromised, and federal prosecutors began prosecuting civilians from all walks of life, even old ladies, for the CCE offense, if you can fathom that.

In order for an individual to be found guilty of a CCE offense, the following elements must be proven beyond a reasonable doubt, and a jury must be unanimous in delivering its verdict as to each of these four elements:

1). A drug felony must have been committed under Title 21, Federal Rule of Criminal Procedure,

2). such felony must be a part of a continuing series of at least three or more predicated violations, under either Title 18 and/or Title 21 of the federal criminal penal code,

3). in concert with five or more persons with respect to one such person having occupied a position of an organizer, a supervisory position, or any other position of management,

4). and from which such a person obtained substantial income or resources.

STEVE SILVA

Back in April of 1986, the Grand Jury, for the District of Maryland, unsealed its criminal indictment, originally entitled United States of America vs. Marshall L. Smith, et al., only to be later renamed, United States of America vs. Steve Silva, et al.

The reason for the change was that Marshall was no longer the target of the investigation, since he eventually became a snitch, and thus a cooperating witness for the prosecution team. The Government then decided to conveniently replace Marshall's name with mine, since I was the next man on the Government's hatchet list of co-defendants. I guess that's what you get for not becoming a stoolie or rat, as the saying goes amongst inmates throughout the federal prison system.

There I was, at the young age of thirty-nine, soon turning the big 40, with an eighteen year-old daughter about to enter her first year of college, a new-born son, and a burgeoning music career. And where was I? I was rotting away in the Baltimore City Jail, in Baltimore, Maryland, one of the worst city jails, at the time, in the nation. I was awaiting my arraignment in federal court, facing a possible life sentence without parole, being held without bail. Additionally, all my worldly possessions and assets, including my home and another rental property I'd owned at the time, had all been officially seized by the U.S. Marshals Service, pending the outcome of my criminal trial.

All these events occurred as a result of a grand jury indictment unsealed on April 21, 1986. On this bleakest day of my entire life, twenty U.S. Marshals, and Drug Enforcement Administration agents (DEA), swarmed down on my residence at precisely 7:45 a.m. They came with enough weapons and fire power to wipe out the entire neighborhood.

Talk about neighborhood excitement! Local journalists, television camera crews, and your average rubberneckers, were all over the place. My home was invaded, as though a herd of wild stallions had just run rampantly through it.

The strangest thing of all, was the chain of events that transpired shortly after my arrest. It hit me hard as nails to discover the friends I thought I once had, were mostly all gone. My one very close friend, so I thought, for the past fifteen years, turned out to be the one most responsible for my current predicament in life. His name was Jon Gerritt, a/k/a Doc by his closest friends. To think this was the same close friend whose life I'd previously saved, not once, but on two separate occasions during our long lasting friendship, was inconceivable for me to bear.

I literally wept when I later learned Doc was the one who had gone to the grand jury, in February of 1986, and through his perjured testimony, while under oath, coupled with his conniving, cunning, and deceitful manner, was the main culprit responsible for getting the grand jury to indict me.

Doc was able to bluff and deceive the federal government, and its entire prosecution team into believing I was the drug kingpin and not himself. After all, who would believe someone like Doc, a decorated law enforcement officer, for valorous duty, who claimed to be an undercover agent for the DEA, FBI, and the U.S. Customs Service, was in any way involved in the drug netherworld, especially at such a high level like Doc actually was. It just couldn't be, everyone thought at the time of his grand jury testimony. The only problem for me was, how was I now going to go about proving otherwise.

It was obvious that the government thoroughly believed Doc's story, as evidenced by granting him full immunity from any further prosecution, so long as he agreed to tell them the truth about everything he knew, and everyone he was associated with in the drug netherworld. Doc told them all he did. The only problem was that he lied! He did such a great job of lying, he was able to convince the jury in my criminal proceedings to convict me of crimes he alone was guilty of. Doc further convinced the government to ask the trial judge to sentence me to sixty years, without parole. As it later turned out, that request was denied, but the judge still handed me a draconian sentence of 35-years, without parole. A rather harsh punishment for a non-violent, first-time offender. Nevertheless, I was also subsequently stripped of all my worldly possessions and legitimately acquired assets. I was now flat broke, and faced with the possibility of having to defend myself, in such a complicated criminal matter, with a public defender representing me. Just what the government's prosecution team was hoping for.

On February 2, 1987, I was found guilty on all counts as charged, in my criminal indictment. Subsequently, on April 27, 1987, I was thereafter sentenced and on my way to USP (U.S. Penitentiary) Lewisburg, PA, a high security, federal prison, with a sixty-foot wall surrounding the entire prison compound, to begin my 35-year, non-parolable sentence.

I now had the next to impossible task of trying to overturn the travesty of justice I had just been served. Even though the odds were heavily stacked against me, as I'd soon come to learn, I was nevertheless, determined, somehow, someway, to see that justice prevailed. Armed with little more than the eager desire and wit to fight back, with little to any knowledge of the law or the inner workings of our criminal justice system, I began my quest for justice by enrolling in a paralegal curriculum afforded to me, upon starting to serve my federal sentence.

Hour upon hour, I hit the books. I studied the law and spent countless hours in the prison law libraries, while making the rounds from one federal prison to another.

Often, I would stay up until three or four in the morning, writing, researching, and reading case laws in further support of my legal issues at hand, which I needed to attack vigorously to overcome

JUDICIAL WEB

the prejudice I suffered during my unfair and highly biased criminal trial, and the railroading I received by our federal government.

I needed to somehow unveil the blindfold covering the eyes of Lady Justice, which continued to loom darkly over my criminal trial and subsequent conviction of being a drug kingpin. I became obsessed with doing so.

I began an extensive letter-writing campaign, which involved writing hundreds of letters to Department of Justice personnel, U.S. Senators, and Congressmen, numerous politicians, the governor from my home state of Florida, news journalists, and television media personnel, even the ex-United States Attorney General, the Honorable Dick Thornburgh, which were all to no avail. Not a single positive response came from any of them. How pathetic and demoralizing was that for me to endure. It was pitiful and extremely depressing, to say the least. However, perseverance and staying focused kept me on track.

It wasn't until some three and a half years into my sentence, after I had already exhausted, by now, my Direct Appeal rights and some post-conviction relief filings in the Maryland District Court, that my big break finally surfaced, and my prayers had seemingly been answered.

Apparently, one of my letters struck a nerve with a high ranking government official from the Office of Professional Responsibility (OPR), in the Drug Enforcement Administration, at their Washington, DC headquarters. His name and official title shall remain anonymous. I'll just refer to him as Agent X, from the DEA's head office.

Agent X decided, after carefully reviewing my formal letter and supporting documentation, to further investigate my allegations of government criminality, treachery, coverup, and the alleged obstruction of justice charges, as they pertained to his level of responsibility within the OPR, concerning the DEA's conduct in my criminal case.

Agent X later informed me, at first, he thought my claims seemed rather preposterous and very far-fetched. However, after several follow-up letters and phone conversations he decided to visit and interview me in early summer of 1990. It wasn't long, thereafter, that my life took a complete turnaround, which turned out to be all for the better.

By late August 1990, after a thorough investigation was conducted by the FBI, DEA and other top brass for the Department of Justice, Jon Gerritt, was finally indicted for drug felony offenses, including a Title 21, Section 848, drug kingpin charge, stemming from Gerritt's perjury, obstruction of justice, and obstructing the administration of justice, all of which Gerrit committed during my criminal investigation, including his sworn grand jury testimony, as well as his testimony during my criminal trial.

Jon Gerritt was subsequently tried, convicted, and sentenced to 35 years in federal prison without parole. He remained in federal custody for 22 plus years, while serving out his maximum sentence with good time behavior credits. Talk about *JUST DESSERTS!*

Because of this new development in my criminal case, I was eventually granted a dramatically reduced sentence, to time served, since I'd already completed nearly 8-years of my conspiracy conviction, which had a maximum sentence of 15-years. Having to only serve a maximum of one-third of that sentence, under the old sentencing guidelines, when coupled with my good-time behavior credits, I was eligible for immediate release from federal prison.

For those of you who may be wondering how and why this was possible, the answer is rather simple. Here it is in layman's terms for you to further grasp and fully comprehend.

Since the government's prosecution team finally came to learn the attorney representing me on my post-conviction relief efforts had 100% proof that the government prosecutors *knew* or at the very least, *should* have known their star witness, in my criminal prosecution, the infamous Jon Gerritt had committed perjury at the time of his grand jury and trial testimonies in my criminal proceedings, they were equally guilty of *subornation of perjury* and *obstructing the administration of justice*, both being criminal felonies, which upon conviction carry a five-year prison term on each count.

In final words, the Government's prosecution team, in my criminal proceedings, were not only very much concerned, and rightfully so, about possibly losing their prestigious careers as federal prosecutors, with potential future judgeships on the line, and other high-ranking government positions, but they must have been equally concerned about being vulnerable and possibly even prosecuted for the prejudicial and wrongful mishandling of my criminal case.

It's taken me roughly 28-years to finally complete writing this memoir. I'm proud to say, it's been well worth the effort, the journey, and the extended time it took me to do so.

My parting words are: "*I hope you enjoyed reading my story, as much as I enjoyed writing it.*"

THE END

STEVE SILVA

EXHIBIT LIST

EXHIBIT 1: Letter from Roy Black, Esq.

EXHIBIT 2: Letter from Roy L. Allen, II, Esq.

EXHIBIT 3: Letter from Roy L. Allen, II, Esq.

EXHIBIT 4: Letter of recommendation from Warden C. Burkhart, FCI Forth Worth, TX

EXHIBIT 5: Letter of recommendation from Roger Combs, Assistant Supervisor of Recreation, FCI Tallahassee, FL

EXHIBIT 6: Letter of recommendation from Michael H. Warner, Supervisor of Recreation, FCI Tallahassee, FL

EXHIBIT 7: Letter of Satisfactory Completion from President, James W. Fry, Jr., of the Blackstone School of Law

EXHIBIT 8: Blackstone's, grade, text, and complete subject report, showing satisfactory completion of their entire School of Law Curriculum

EXHIBIT 9: Blackstone School of Law, Legal Assistant/ Paralegal Certificate of Completion

* The EXHIBITS named above have been redacted where necessary, but are otherwise authentic in all other regards.

JUDICIAL WEB

LAW OFFICES
BLACK & FURCI
A PROFESSIONAL ASSOCIATION
SUITE 1300
201 SOUTH BISCAYNE BOULEVARD
MIAMI, FLORIDA 33131

ROY BLACK
FRANK C. FURCI
MARK D. SEIDEN

TELEPHONE 371-6421
AREA CODE 305

July ▓ 19▓

Steve ▓▓▓

Tallahassee, Florida 32301

Dear Steve:

It was great to hear from you. I can see that you are not only surviving, but triumphing. I expected no less. I have no doubt that your forthcoming book, "Judicial Web," will be a great read. I wish you the best of luck with it.

Needless to say, we're all happy to hear about ▓▓▓▓▓ He finally got what he deserved. The amazing thing is they don't set aside the convictions that were based on his testimony. It just shows that our government has no integrity whatsoever. They think nothing of putting perjured testimony before the jury and then not even apologizing for it.

It is truly amazing that Marshall ▓▓▓ served such a short sentence compared to everyone else.

I wish you the best of luck in forging ahead with all your lawsuits against the government. I am sure they are very concerned about your efforts. I really can't help your brother in his suit because I only handle criminal cases, and never handle any civil cases. If somebody should subpoena me to testify about a matter, I would be happy to do so. However, I don't know how my testimony would be of any great help to you. All you really need are the prosecutors and ▓▓▓▓▓ In any event, I wish you the best of luck in all of this.

Cordially yours,

Roy Black

RB/wg

[EXHIBIT 1]

STEVE SILVA

PHONE (912) 233-4914
or 233-4920
Fax 233-4960
Toll Free Inside GA. 1-800-533-0196

Reply To:
Post Office Box 9034
Savannah, Georgia 31412

ROY L. ALLEN II

Allen & Associates
Attorneys and Counselors at Law
The Nijem Building
311 East York Street
Savannah, Georgia 31401

ATLANTA: The Legislative Office Building
Suite 322
Capitol Plaza
Atlanta, GA 30334
Phone 404-656-0084

KEVIN E. PERRY
OF COUNSEL

May ## 19##

Steve ####
Fort Worth Unit
3150 Horton Road
Fort Worth, TX 76119-5996

Dear Steve:

    It was great hearing from you, and I cannot thank you enough for your prayers, support and muscle power in assisting us to get Captain Sam out. Now, please let me know what I can do to help you because you played a big part in our efforts. Please do not forget to send me the article in the Washington Post and I would love to do what I can to assist you.

    Again thank you so much.

                                      Sincerely,

                                      Allen & Associates

                                      ROY L. ALLEN, II

RLA.dl

[EXHIBIT 2]

JUDICIAL WEB

PHONE (912) 233-4914
or 233-4920
Fax 233-4960
Toll Free Inside GA. 1-800-533-0196

Reply To:
Post Office Box 9034
Savannah, Georgia 31412

ROY L. ALLEN II
C. BURCH BANKS

The Allen Firm
Attorneys and Counselors at Law
The Nijem Building
311 East York Street
Savannah, Georgia 31401

June ▇ 19▇

ATLANTA: 101 Marietta Towers
Suite 3600
Atlanta, GA 30303
PHONE 404-523-2868
FAX 404-522-1233

ADAM CERBONE
KEVIN E. PERRY
OF COUNSEL

Attn: Steve ▇
Stuyvesant Avenue
Union, New Jersey 07083

Dear Steve

Thank you so much for your letter, and yes I do remember you. How could I forget you? I am so glad that you "beat the system" and your quest for justice prevailed. I am somewhat lost trying to determine are you out of jail completely, or you will only be out after you are resentenced on ▇▇▇. Please let me know. From time to time, I do go through Tenefly, New Jersey and Union City. Is Union City and Union, New Jersey one in the same?

Yes, Leola is alive and well, and I want you to know that I spoke to her recently and she was overjoyed to hear the great news. I look forward to hearing from you again soon.

Sincerely,

THE ALLEN FIRM

By: _____
ROY L. ALLEN, II

RLA,II/d

[EXHIBIT 3]

398

STEVE SILVA

Federal Prison System

Federal Correctional Institution

3150 Horton Road
Fort Worth, TX 76119

January ██ 19██

Steve ██████
Federal Correctional Institution
3150 Horton Rd.
Ft. Worth, Texas 76119

Dear Mr. ██████

I want to take this time to let you know that the hard work you put into the preparation for the Winter Commencement activity was greatly appreciated by all in attendance. It was your special effort in joining together as a performing group less than two weeks prior to the graduation which really highlighted the activity.

Both Waylon Jennings and Jessi Colter were greatly impressed by your performance. Moreover, they were also very pleased with the style in which you presented the performance.

Again, I appreciate your having devoted your efforts toward making the 19██ Winter GED Commencement a great success.

Sincerely,

RON C. BURKHART
Warden

[EXHIBIT 4]

JUDICIAL WEB

UNITED STATE OVERNMENT

MEMORANDUM

RECREATION DEPARTMENT
F.C.I. TALLAHASSEE

DATE: March 19
REPLY TO
ATTN OF: *Roger M. Combs*
Roger Combs, Assistant Supervisor of Recreation

SUBJECT: Inmate Steve Reg. No.
Letter of Recommendation

TO: B Unit Team

___

This letter is presented on behalf of Inmate Steve Reg. No. for exemplary work in the Recreation Department. He has been a valuable asset that recognizes the needs of the Recreation Staff and works hard to satisfy those needs. Through his efforts a new filing system was incorporated into the recreation center office that allows easy access to important data. He makes a special effort to work with the inmates that come to the recreation center with problems and offers invaluable assistance to staff. Inmate brings new and innovative ideas to all areas of recreation with special consideration given to clerical concerns. He reacts without hesitation and performs much of his work with no supervision necessary.

In closing, it has been a pleasure to work with this inmate and the Recreation Department has found him to be a valuable member of the inmate detail. It is with these statements in mind, that this <u>Letter of Recommendation</u> is forwarded to his Unit Team.

[EXHIBIT 5]

STEVE SILVA

UNITED STATES. GOVERNMENT

MEMORANDUM

RECREATION DEPARTMENT
F.C.I. TALLAHASSEE

DATE: March ▇ 19▇

REPLY TO
ATTN OF: Michael H. Warner, Supervisor of Recreation

SUBJECT: Letter of Recommendation
Inmate Steve ▇

TO: B - Unit Team

This Letter of Recommendation is submitted on behalf of Inmate Steve ▇ for his exemplary work in the Recreation Department. In his capacity as clerk in the Recreation Center, he has shown to be an individual that conducts himself in a professional manner. He shows initiative and imagination and works until completion with no supervision necessary.

Inmate S. ▇ is quick to learn, eager to master any task and strives to get along with all inmates and staff. On many occasions, Inmate S. ▇ has volunteered his free time in order that he may gain the knowledge necessary to provide superior service. He drives himself exceptionally hard at all times and wastes no time in completing assigned duties.

In closing, Inmate Steve ▇ has been a valuable asset to the Recreation Department, with a excellent work record, and a likability not normally found in an institutional setting. It is with these assets, and others too numerous to mention, that this Letter of Recommendation is forwarded on behalf of Inmate S. ▇

[EXHIBIT 6]

JUDICIAL WEB

BLACKSTONE SCHOOL OF LAW
INCORPORATED

Steve ▮

NJ

Dear Mr. ▮

We wish to congratulate you upon satisfactory completion of our Legal Assistant/Paralegal Curriculum. We have enclosed your graded transcript. Your Certificate of Completion will be shipped in approximately two weeks. We hope that you will be pleased with the Certificate of Completion and that you will prize it highly. It should always remind you of a period of very earnest, conscientious effort and achievement on your part.

Your relationship with us need not end at this point. At least write us occasionally of your progress and experiences.

We consider it a privilege and honor to award you our Certificate of Completion and trust that the knowledge gained will enrich your entire life.

Sincerely,

James W. Fry, Jr.
President

P.O. Box 790906   Dallas, TX 75379-0906   (214) 418-5141

[EXHIBIT 7]

STEVE SILVA

BLACKSTONE SCHOOL OF LAW
Dallas, Texas

Student __Steve_____ Matriculation Number _____

Address _____ New Jersey _____

Matriculation Date _____ 19 _____ Completion Date _____

TEXT & SUBJECT		GRADE	TEXT & SUBJECT		GRADE
Volume 1			Volume 6		
Introduction to Law	Test 1	93	Pleadings in Civil Actions	Test 15	95
Contracts	Test 2	98	Practice in Civil Actions	Test 16	97
	Test 3	92	Criminal Procedure	Test 17	88
	Test 4	89		Test 18	92
Volume 2			Volume 7		
Law of Torts	Test 5	100	Wills & Administration	Test 19	94
	Test 6	97	Wills & Administration	Test 20	97
	Test 7	80	Guardian & Ward		
	Test 8	95	Law of Trusts	Test 21	87
Volume 3			Volume 8		
Criminal Law	Test 9	90	Law of Private Corporations	Test 22	82
	Test 10	97		Test 23	97
Volume 4			Law of Partnership	Test 24	90
Real Property	Test 11	100	Volume 9		
(Part I)	Test 12	88	Constitutional Law	Test 25	100
Volume 5				Test 26	86
Real Property	Test 13	95	Volume 10		
(Part II)	Test 14	94	Constitutional Law	Test 27	94
			Legal Research	Test 28	96

The foregoing law subjects make up the contents of the ten volume set of text-books — MODERN AMERICAN LAW. This set is published by the Blackstone School of Law and is furnished in its entirety as part of its comprehensive Legal Assistant/Paralegal course. Each volume of the set averages 200 pages and provides the major portion of the reading matter in the Blackstone course. The reading in the textbooks is implemented by lesson guides, and 27 tests, comprising 76 pages. A detailed summary of the text material given above it provides a comprehensive picture of the entire curriculum.

95-100 Excellent; 90-94 Very Good; 85-89 Good; 80-84 Fair; 77-79 Satisfactory
Below 75 Unsatisfactory

This document issued _____ 19

BLACKSTONE SCHOOL OF LAW

By _____
                Registrar

[EXHIBIT 8]

JUDICIAL WEB

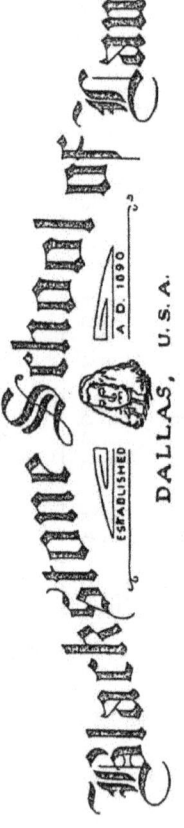

GLOSSARY TERMS & ACRONYMS

Affirm: Confirm or ratify, state a fact: to declare that a previous judgment is correct, accurate. To uphold a decision made by a lower court. To solemnly promise to tell the truth in court as in an affidavit.

Allocution: A formal statement made to the court by the defendant who has been found guilty prior to being sentenced. It is part of the criminal procedure in most jurisdiction. A defendant's right to address the court, for mitigating purposes, prior to being sentenced. It may be read or orally presented by the defendant or sometimes the defendant's counsel, at time of sentencing.

Amend: To make minor changes in a motion, brief, court order, etc., in order to make the text read fairer, more accurate, or more up to date. To modify formally, as a legal document or legislative bill. To improve, make better, put right.

Appellate Panel: A court having jurisdiction (authority) to hear appeals. A court that reviews decisions made by lower courts of administrative agencies and does not hear new cases. The authority a court has to hear an appeal against a decision made by a lower court.

Arraignment: A criminal proceeding in which the defendant, in open court, must answer criminal charges by entering a plea of guilty or not guilty. Defendant either must be represented by a lawyer or waive his/her right to legal counsel before the court. Usually, the first step in the criminal process, in which a defendant is called into court, charged with a crime, informed of his or her rights, and allowed to plead guilty, not guilty, or nolo contender.

JUDICIAL WEB

AUSA: An abbreviation, acronym for a government attorney, federal prosecutor, also known as, an Assistant United States Attorney, who reports to the United States Attorney in the designated federal district of his employment.

Bailiff: A minor court officer authorized to execute processes, protect the courtroom, oversee courtroom activities prior to, during, and after court proceedings commence. Who is also responsible for keeping order and maintaining courtroom decorum and custody of the jury.

CCE: An acronym for Continuing Criminal Enterprise. A Title 21, Section 848, criminal statue violation, mostly designated for the prosecution of alleged drug kingpins.

CI: An Acronym for a confidential informant. A person who provides privileged information about a person or organization to an agency, usually to state or federal government law enforcement agencies. The term is usually used within law enforcement circles, where the informant can often supply information without the consent of the other party or parties with the intent of malicious, personal, or financial gain. A cooperating individual for the government and often used as a government witness against others in criminal proceedings.

CID: An acronym for Criminal Investigative Division. Usually associated with the DOJ, IRS, DEA, FBI or other government investigative agencies.

DEA: An acronym for the Drug Enforcement Administration.

DEA Form 6: A Drug Enforcement Administration document, referred to as a Form 6 report, made by ta a DEA Special Agent, investigating an individual or entity, and used to chronologically log the evidence in a particular investigation. Confiscated drug inventory from an ongoing investigation for future evidence and prosecution purposes.

Debriefing: Questioning someone, about a subject or completed mission, or undertaking. A series of questions about knowledge a potential witness may have against another in a criminal case, usually by way of a formal deposition, under oath. An informal proffer session, conducted by a government agent or other law enforcement officials, of a subject in a criminal investigation, seeking knowledge from a potential witness, seeking immunity from prosecution and/or leniency at time of sentencing.

Direct Appeal: Is a formal brief, filed with a higher court, most often a federal circuit court of appeals, to seek judicial review, usually by a three-judge panel, of the legality of one's conviction or sentence. In federal courts, a direct appeal is taken to the United States Court of Appeals for the circuit that has jurisdiction over the federal district in which one was convicted.

ESQ: Is a courtesy title, usually given to and associated with lawyers. An unofficial title of respect. Abbreviation for esquire.

ET Al: Is an abbreviation for the Latin phrase et al, meaning '*and others.*' Commonly used in criminal proceedings in the shortening of a criminal case name, where there is a long list of defendants and et al is used to refer to '*others*' so named. A legal term referring to all others. Usually associated with the title to a particular case, and used as a substitute in the naming of all the other parties involved in the said litigation.

Exculpatory: To clear one of guilt or fault. To show or declare that someone is not guilty of wrongdoing. Used in legal terms to refer to evidence that is usually in favor of the defendant in a criminal proceeding to exculpate (exonerate) or clear a person of an accusation and any suspicion that goes along with it. To exculpate means to assist in finding someone not guilty of criminal charges.

FBI 302 Memo: A Federal Bureau of Investigation document, referred to as 302 report or memo. Handwritten notes by an FBI Agent of an interview or informal conversation or proffer session, that are later used to refer to and reflect exactly what transpired during the said interview or proffer session. Usually referred to as FBI's interview notes, later reduced in formal memo format. Now renamed an FD-302, is a form used by FBI Agents to report or summarize the interviews that they conduct and contains information from the notes taken during the interview by the non-primary agent. It consists of information taken from the subject, rather than the details about the subject themselves. A 302 report, now referred to as an FD-302, is a number assigned to the FBI's investigative supplemental report forms. It can be a single page or a hundred, depending upon the crime. Any action taken that is to be included in the investigation is prepared on a 302 form.

FCI: Is an acronym, abbreviation for Federal Correctional Institution. It's used in reference to a specific type of federal prison setting, within the Federal Bureau of Prisons. A federal correctional facility operated by the Federal Bureau of Prisons, which are strategically placed to house federal inmates from around the country at various security levels.

FPC: Is an acronym, abbreviation for Federal Prison Camp. A low-level prison facility, usually without restricted looking barb wire fencing, giving the outside appearance of not being an actual prison environment, where federally housed inmates are free to roam the general area and work and play outdoors most of the day. A minimum-security institution, also known as Federal Prison Camp, which has dormitory housing, a relatively low staff-to-inmate ratio, and limited or no perimeter fencing. Many other prison facilities of a higher security level have adjacent Satellite Low Security prison camps.

FRCP: An acronym for Federal Rules of Criminal Procedure. The FRCP are the procedural rules that govern how federal criminal prosecutions are conducted in the United States district courts and the general trial courts of the U.S. government. The original Federal Rules of Criminal Procedure were adopted by order of the U.S. Supreme Court on December 26, 1944, transmitted to Congress by the U.S. Attorney General on January 3, 1945, and became effective on March 21, 1946. Over the ensuing years, there have been updates, revisions, and important changes to the FRCP, to keep up with the ever-changing times in our society.

Grand Jury: Is a legal body empowered to conduct legal proceedings and investigate potential criminal conduct and determine whether criminal charges should be brought. A grand jury may subpoena physical evidence or a person to testify.

G/S: Is an acronym for Group Supervisor. One who is usually in charge of ten to fifteen men and/or women in a street drug enforcement group.

Hack: Is prison slang for a correctional officer, or prison guard. Also known as, pigs, snouts, screws, cops, bulls, etc.

Immunity: Immunity from prosecution is a legal doctrine that permits a person to avoid being prosecuted for a criminal offense. This is usually granted in exchange for something that the prosecution needs, such as information about someone else who has committed a more serious crime.

Inculpatory: Incriminating, such as in evidence. The opposite of exculpatory. Implying or imputing guilt, tending to incriminate or inculpate, such as an inculpatory, incriminating statement, act, or evidence.

Indictment: Is a legal means to bring formal accusations against another person or entity. To charge with an offense or crime, often after a grand jury convenes and finds probable cause to indict.

IRS: Internal Revenue Service. The taxing authority of the U.S. States Government. It is the revenue service of the United States

JUDICIAL WEB

Federal Government. The government agency is a bureau of the Department of the Treasury and is under the immediate direction of the Commissioner of Internal Revenue Service, who is appointed to a five-year term by the President of the United States. The IRS is responsible for collecting taxes and administrating the internal Revenue Code, the main body of the federal statutory tax law of the United States Government.

MCC: Miami Correctional Center, Miami, Florida. A Bureau of Prisons prison facility, in Dade County, Miami, Florida. It's been renamed FCI Miami and has changed dramatically since I was serving time there, upon my initial arrest, back in April 1986.

MDO: Miami District Office of the Drug Enforcement Administration.

NADDIS: National Dangerous Drug Identification System. Sometimes referred to as the Narcotics and Dangerous Drug Information System by DEA agents. A national database network, available to DEA agents, for their investigation purposes in the furtherance of seeking information in their drug related criminal cases.

NCIC: National Crime Information Center. As part of the FBI the National Crime Information Center is a national computerized repository system of criminal justice data used by local, state, and federal law enforcement agencies throughout the U.S., Canada, Puerto Rico, and the U.S. Virgin Islands. Its primary purpose is to provide criminal information and criminal history records to law enforcement personnel on individuals they are investigating and otherwise seeking criminal background records of.

Obstruction of Justice: May consist of any attempt to hinder the discovery, apprehension, conviction, or punishment of anyone who has committed a crime. The acts of which justice is obstructed may include bribery, murder, intimidation, and the use of physical force against witnesses, law enforcement officers, or court officials, etc.

Obstructing the Administration of Justice: Is referred to the act of perverting the course of justice. To try to influence the result of a court case, especially by preventing the true facts about a crime from being known.

OCDETF: Organized Crime Drug Enforcement Task Force. A multi-agency task force, established by the President's drug crime prevention counsel, dedicated to the eradication and prosecution of large scale organized criminal enterprises involving Narco trafficking, (trafficking in drugs and narcotics). Established under President Reagan's zero tolerance drug offensive, and was overseen by then, V.P. Herbert W. Bush. The program expanded over the years and is now under the direction and supervision of the Deputy Attorney General.

Oral Argument: Are spoken words to a judge or appellate court by a lawyer (or parties when representing themselves) of the legal reasons why they should prevail. Oral Argument at the appellate level accompanies written briefs, which also advance the argument of each party in the legal dispute. Most often oral arguments are rarely granted at the appellate level, from a lower court ruling brought by either the Plaintiff or the Defendant in a criminal or civil matter.

Pandora's Box: A process that generates many complicated or potentially complicated problems, or issues, as the result of unwise interference in something. If someone or something opens a Pandora's Box, they do something that causes a lot of problems to appear that did not exist or were not known about prior to doing so. Pandora's Box is an artifact, in Greek Mythology, connected with the myth of Pandora in Hesiod's Work and Days. The container mentioned in the original story was a large storage jar, but the word was later mistranslated as a '*box.*' In modern times, an idiom has evolved from its meaning of '*any source of great and unexpected troubles.*' or alternatively, '*a present which seems valuable, but which in reality, turns out to be a curse.*'

PEPI: Purchase of evidence and/or purchase of information via a special funding account used by DEA agents. Usually paid to informants, who make a living selling pertinent information to law enforcement personnel, in return for special favors, perks, assets, but mostly for financial reimbursement.

Per Curiam: In law, a per curiam decision or opinion, is a ruling issued by an appellate court of multiple judges in which the decision rendered is made by the court (or at least, a majority of the court) acting collectively (and typically, though not necessarily, unanimously). In Latin, the word per curiam means '*by the court.*'

Perjury: The offense of willfully telling an untruth in a court after having taken an oath or affirmation to tell the truth. Lying under oath, giving false evidence, testimony, making false statements, willful falsehood(s). The offense of willfully telling a lie in a court of competent jurisdiction, after taking a sworn oath or affirmation.

Plant: Another name for a government snitch, rat, informant, stoolie, or confidential informant.

Published Opinion: A selective publication, also known as a published opinion, is the legal process by which a judge or justices of a court decide whether or not a decision is to be published in a federal reporter (text), whereas '*unpublished*' federal appellate decisions are published in the Federal Appendix, and are not otherwise printed in a hardcover, textbook like format.

S/A: Special Agent. Usually a title given to DEA or FBI agents. A Special Agent, in the United States law enforcement circles is usually a title reserved for a criminal investigator or detective for a federal, state, or county government, who primarily serves in investigatory roles. In U.S. federal law enforcement, the title of special agent is used almost exclusively for federal criminal investigators, such as the DEA, and FBI.

Snitch: An informant, stool pigeon, rat, confidential informant, stoolie, plant. In the criminal sense, someone that can't be trusted and will provide damaging information to the police or feds, in order to obtain lenient treatment for themselves and provide information over an extended period of time in return for money, or for police to overlook their own criminal activities. Most snitches, also known as informants, will do so following their arrest and facing significant jail time. Snitches are most often NOT innocent and may often lie to authorities to implicate another in a crime so that they, themselves, may escape punishment.

Subornation of Perjury: The criminal act of procuring another to commit perjury, which is the crime of lying, in a material matter, while under oath. In a criminal offense, to induce someone to commit known or should have known use of perjurious statements while giving testimony, under oath, most often in a grand jury or trial-like setting.

USP: United States Penitentiary. Usually these prison facilities, operating under the direction and supervision of the Federal Bureau of Prisons, are high security prison facilities. They are used to house high level security inmates, who require strict disciplinary measures, most often twenty-three hours of lockdown and solitary confinement status, many serving a life sentence, without the benefit of parole.

WDO: Washington, D.C. District Office of the DEA. This facility handles all of the drug enforcement activities that take place in the Washington, D.C., Maryland, and Virginia state and local, government locations.